中國古代飾物展覽

華世風華

馬承源

Adornment for Eternity

Status and Rank in Chinese Ornament

Julia M. White
and
Emma C. Bunker
with contributions by Chen Peifen

Denver Art Museum

in association with
The Woods Publishing Company

This catalogue has been made possible in part by contributions from the Joseph and Loretta Law Foundation and the Woods Publishing Company.

The exhibition *Adornment for Eternity: Status and Rank in Chinese Ornament* will be on view at the Denver Art Museum from October 15, 1994, to September 3, 1995. It will be presented at Eskenazi Ltd., Oriental Art Gallery, London, from October 10 to December 16, 1995, and at the Seattle Art Museum from January 13 to July 14, 1996.

Copyright © 1994 by the Denver Art Museum
All rights reserved. No part of this publication may be reproduced or transmitted in any form or by any means, electronic or mechanical, without written permission from the Denver Art Museum.

Copublished by the Denver Art Museum in association with the Woods Publishing Company

Editor: John Stevenson
Copy editor: Jessica Altholz Eber
Photographer: Bill O'Connor
Illustrator: Anna-Maria Crum
Calligrapher: Ma Chengyuan
Map designer: Vikki Leib
Translator: Brenda Li
Designer: Ed Marquand with assistance from Tomarra LeRoy

Produced by Marquand Books, Inc., Seattle
Printed by the Woods Publishing Company, Hong Kong

Cover: Hairpin. Song dynasty, 960–1279. Gold (cat. no. 92).
Back cover: Perfume container. Song dynasty, 960–1279. Gold (cat. no. 98).
Half title: Head ornament. Yuan dynasty, 1279–1368. Gold (cat. no. 102).
Title page: Plaque. Six dynasties period, 265–589. Gold (cat. no. 47).
Page 6: Circular plaque. Eastern Zhou, Warring States period, 3rd century B.C.
    Gilded silver (cat. no. 22).
Page 79: Hairpin. Song dynasty, 960–1279. Gilded silver (cat. no. 83).
Page 80: Plaque. Western Han period, 2nd–1st century B.C. Gold (cat. no. 35).
Page 128: Pendant set (detail). Tang period or earlier, 6–7th century.
    Gold, lapis lazuli, and turquoise (cat. no. 70).
Page 172: Hairpin (one of three). Ming dynasty, 1368–1644. Gold (cat. no. 107).

Library of Congress Cataloging-in-Publication Data
White, Julia M.
  Adornment for eternity : status and rank in Chinese ornament /
Julia M. White and Emma C. Bunker, with contributions by Chen
Peifen.
    p. cm.
  Catalog of an exhibition of items from the Mengdiexuan Collection
owned by Betty Lo and Kenneth Chu.
  Includes bibliographical references (p. 206).
  1. Costume—China—Exhibitions. 2. Jewelry—China—Social
aspects—Exhibitions. 3. Lo, Betty—Art collections. 4. Chu,
Kenneth—Art collections. I. Bunker, Emma C. II. Ch'en, P'ei-fen.
III. Denver Art Museum. IV. Title.
GT1555.W49   1994
391'.7'0951—dc20   94-21037
                                              CIP

Contents

7   Director's Statement

8   Preface and Acknowledgments

10   Chronology

12   Map of China

13   Development of Objects of Personal Adornment in China
      Julia M. White

31   The Metallurgy of Personal Adornment
      Emma C. Bunker

55   Chinese translations of essays

79   Catalogue of the Exhibition
      Julia M. White, Emma C. Bunker, and Chen Peifen

   80   Early Period—Shang period through Han dynasty

   128   Middle Period—Six Dynasties period through Liao dynasty

   172   Late Period—Song dynasty through Ming dynasty

203   Glossary
      Emma C. Bunker

206   Bibliography

Director's Statement

The Denver Art Museum is proud to present the exhibition and accompanying catalogue *Adornment for Eternity: Status and Rank in Chinese Ornament*. This is the first time that material addressing the issue of personal adornment throughout Chinese history has been presented in a museum exhibition on such a broad scale. It will provide an important forum for the discussion of these art objects. The recognition of these 113 items both as beautiful works of art and as important indicators of status and rank in ancient Chinese society will hopefully lead to more study and research in the field.

The Museum is grateful to Betty Lo and Kenneth Chu, owners of the Mengdiexuan Collection, who have shown tremendous generosity in loaning the objects in this exhibition to the Denver Art Museum. Their commitment to the presentation of the material has been exemplary in that they have shared their vast knowledge of the material while at the same time encouraging the curator and consultants to pursue their own avenues of interpretation. This collaboration has resulted in a scholarly publication in a field that has heretofore been largely overlooked.

The exhibition was conceived by Associate Curator of Asian Art Julia M. White, and its execution was made possible by a close collaboration between Ms. White and Emma C. Bunker, research consultant to the Denver Art Museum. In addition to her fine essay and contributions to the object entries, Emmy is to be admired for defining many of the terms and descriptions regarding Chinese metalwork contained in the glossary. Chen Peifen, Curator and Chief, Bronze Research Department of the Shanghai Museum, contributed catalogue entries on mirrors. Many thanks also to Ma Chengyuan, Director of the Shanghai Museum, for writing the calligraphy of the Chinese title. Richard Kimball, master goldsmith, acted as a technical advisor on the project, bringing a great deal of practical expertise to the evaluation of the objects. The final product, as the reader will see, is an in-depth look at the materials, techniques, history, and social impact of a discrete collection of high-quality objects.

I would like to extend my thanks to the many people at the Museum and within the Denver community who helped bring about this landmark exhibition. To those in the Museum's Registrar's Office, Collection Management, Publications, Design, and Photography departments, I would like to thank them for all their support and efforts in bringing this collection to the Denver public. I am very grateful to Frederick and Jan Mayer for their support of this and other projects dealing with Asian collectors. Their own sensibilities in collecting have led them to a special rapport with these collectors. Celeste and John Fleming have led the way in promoting the exhibition and catalogue and have helped in many ways to secure funding for the catalogue. Many thanks to Mary Ellen and Todger Anderson, who were very supportive of the entire project. Peter Yu and Carol Werner of Richfield Hotel Management were also generous donors. A special thanks to Joseph and Loretta Law, whose invaluable contribution covered expenses associated with the preparation of the catalogue. The Woods Publishing Company also provided a substantial gift to the Museum by supporting the printing and production of the catalogue.

Lewis I. Sharp
Director

Preface and Acknowledgments

This exhibition of items of personal adornment from China was inspired by the Mengdiexuan Collection. This private collection consists primarily of metalwork from the sixth century B.C. to the Qing dynasty. In selecting the material for the exhibition and catalogue we attempted to bring together objects that had not been publicly displayed before, objects that would tell the story of the development and changes in personal adornment in China over many centuries. What we discovered about society, cultural development, and cultural attitudes, as well as cross-cultural fertilization, has been among the most rewarding aspects of the project.

It was also our intention to try to refine the terms and definitions that describe early metalwork. To this aim we have carefully examined each object under a microscope and attempted to describe our findings precisely. There is a great deal of misunderstanding regarding the correct terminology for many metalworking techniques. This catalogue attempts to address this in the object entries, essays, and in the glossary.

The variety of objects presented here required reference to many resources, from archaeological reports to historical compilations. The catalogue includes primarily objects made of metal—bronze, gold, silver, and combinations such as gilded and tinned bronzes—focusing on the materials and methods employed in their manufacture over a very long period of time. The material has been arranged chronologically in order to give the reader a sense of progression through time.

The quality of the material from which we had to select outweighed the fact that it came from a single, private collection. We feel we have benefited tremendously from the exquisite taste of two very fine connoisseurs.

This exhibition and catalogue were made possible by the generosity and support of the owners of the Mengdiexuan Collection, Betty Lo and Kenneth Chu. Not only have they shown understanding of and sensitivity to the objects they have collected, they have also rigorously studied the material with open and questioning minds. With great dedication they have assisted the authors in their pursuit of information regarding the material in this exhibition and have selflessly shared their knowledge in every area. Many thanks to them for all their generosity.

Thanks and deep appreciation also to Richard Kimball, master goldsmith, who spent many hours looking at objects and commenting on materials and techniques. We benefited immensely from the technical advice that he offered. His talents as both a goldsmith and a connoisseur of Chinese art greatly enriched the project.

Chen Peifen of the Shanghai Museum contributed most of the mirror entries for the catalogue and was a consultant on the project. We are grateful for her participation. Jenny So and W. Thomas Chase of the Freer Gallery of Art and the Arthur M. Sackler Gallery of Art, Washington, D.C., generously commented on objects and techniques and provided valuable guidance in our research. Terese Bartholomew of the Asian Art Museum in San Francisco acted as a consultant on the meaning behind rebuses. Pieter Meyers of the Los Angeles County Museum of Art assisted in assessing technical aspects of the collection. Peter Golas, Professor of Chinese History at the University of Denver, assisted in locating information concerning metal sources. We are grateful for the assistance of Professor Han Rubin of the University of Science and Technology Beijing and for that of translators Ranyin Wu, Chan Shouhua, and S. P. Kiang. Brenda Li was the translator for the essays and mirror entries, and Kenneth Chu spent many hours editing the Chinese.

Many people at the Denver Art Museum contributed to the success of this endeavor. Our Director, Lewis I. Sharp, supported the project with enthusiasm and helped to see the catalogue and exhibition to completion. Frederick Mayer, formerly Chairman of the Board of Trustees, and his wife, Jan Mayer, were very supportive of this exhibition and continue to encourage exchanges between Hong Kong collectors and the Museum.

The collection was brought safely to Denver through the efforts of the Museum Registrar's Office, for which thanks go to L. Anthony Wright and Pamela Taylor, particularly in the early stages of the exhibition. Mitchell Broadbent prepared the exhibition for travel. Debra Ashe and later Sam Plourd, John French, Pauline Edwards, Michele Assaf, and John Lupe of the Collections Department carefully stored and tracked the material while it was on loan to the Museum. Leland Murray thoughtfully designed the casework and gallery presentation, creating its dramatic setting. Patterson Williams, Dean of Education, planned the educational programs and in-gallery interpretation for the exhibition. Steve Osborne ingeniously tackled the problems of mount making for the entire exhibition. Carl Patterson of the Museum's Conservation Department took special care to ensure the stability, safety, and appearance of each object.

In the Publications Department, Marlene Chambers offered important advice and direction. Cynthia Nakamura, head of the Photography Department, organized all the photography sessions and managed the difficult task of recording and tracking photographs. Bill O'Connor did a spectacular job of photographing each object with care and concern. Anna-Maria Crum expertly tackled the illustrations for the catalogue.

The Asian Department staff, Ronald Y. Otsuka, Page Shaver, and Bj Averitt, showed tremendous support and patience throughout the preparation and execution of this project. Ronald and Page read and commented on the texts and edited many of the materials, including the bibliography, essays, and catalogue entries, and Bj organized reference and slide material. Preliminary editing on the manuscript was done by volunteer Toby Bowlby, who read and reread the essays and entries and made valuable comments on the writings. Many thanks to the department for its support.

The staff at Marquand Books, Inc., are to be commended for their efforts on this project. Ed Marquand took special care in the design of the book, with Tomarra LeRoy overseeing its layout. Marta Vinnedge handled organizational details, while Marie Weiler managed the editorial aspect, enlisting the assistance of Pamela Zytnicki, Audrey Jawando, and Tim Mundy. Very special thanks to John Stevenson, who edited the catalogue with a careful eye. Thanks also to the copy editor, Jessica Altholz Eber, who brought the whole into uniformity.

Celeste and John Fleming, and Mary Ellen and Todger Anderson, longtime friends of the Museum and its Asian Department, helped to secure funding for this publication. Peter Yu and Carol Werner of Richfield Hotel Management also gave financial assistance to the project. A contribution by Joseph and Loretta Law made the catalogue possible, and the Woods Publishing Company in Hong Kong generously donated the printing.

Julia M. White and Emma C. Bunker
April 1994

Chronology

NEOLITHIC PERIOD	ca. 6500–1500 B.C.
EARLY DYNASTIES	
Shang	ca. 1500–1050 B.C.
Zhou	ca. 1050–221 B.C.
WESTERN ZHOU	1050–771 B.C.
EASTERN ZHOU	770–221 B.C.
Spring and Autumn Period	770–475 B.C.
Warring States Period	475–221 B.C.
IMPERIAL CHINA	
Qin	221–207 B.C.
Han	206 B.C.–A.D. 220
WESTERN HAN	206 B.C.–A.D. 9
XIN	A.D. 9–25
EASTERN HAN	A.D. 25–220
Three Kingdoms Period	221–280
SHU (HAN)	221–263
WEI	220–265
WU	222–280
Southern Dynasties (Six Dynasties)	
WESTERN JIN	265–316
EASTERN JIN	317–420
LIU SONG	420–479
SOUTHERN QI	479–502
LIANG	502–557
CHEN	557–589
Northern Dynasties	
NORTHERN WEI	386–535
EASTERN WEI	534–550
WESTERN WEI	535–557
NORTHERN QI	550–577
NORTHERN ZHOU	557–581

Sui	589–618
Tang	618–906
Five Dynasties	907–960
Liao	907–1125
Song	960–1279
NORTHERN SONG	960–1126
SOUTHERN SONG	1127–1279
Jin	1115–1234
Yuan	1279–1368
Ming	1368–1644
Qing	1644–1911

Dates are in keeping with those presented in *The British Museum Book of Chinese Art*, edited by Jessica Rawson.

Julia M. White

Development of Objects of Personal Adornment in China

Introduction

For thousands of years, the objects that people have chosen to wear for their personal adornment have been culturally inspired and often laden with symbolic intent. Choice of ornament in China was from early times an affirmation of society's beliefs and a manifestation of its imagination and spirituality.[1] Ornaments selected by the living would frequently serve in the afterlife as well, accompanying the dead as adornments for eternity. The objects a man chose to wear during his lifetime helped to define the kind of person he was and what his status was in society, although his choice was often determined by laws, both written and unwritten.[2]

The Grand Historian Sima Qian states in the *Shiji* that in the sixth century B.C. China was known as "the land of caps and girdles."[3] It is clear that from early in China's history its people wore hats and belts as part of their daily dress. Personal ornaments developed from a system of dress which was eventually codified for the court. This system helped establish the recognition of rank within the imperial order.[4]

Different types of personal adornment have enjoyed varying levels of popularity over time. Hooks, both belt and garment types, were in favor from the late Warring States period through the Han, after which they began to be replaced by plaques arranged in sets to form belts. Hair ornaments, which are some of the earliest known items of personal adornment, have been found in Neolithic grave sites and have remained in vogue to the present day. Their continued popularity accounts for their extremely rich history. Earrings also maintained their popularity through time, with finds made from the Shang through the modern period.[5] Mirrors had a role in adornment as reflectors of beauty and as objects worn or carried on the person. They have been found in burial sites in far western China from as early as the late Neolithic period, and they flourished especially in the late Zhou period.[6] Each type of personal adornment has its own life span, with periods of development and decline, as is demonstrated by the numerous excavated examples from China, as well as the superb objects in the Mengdiexuan collection.

Chronological Development

Chinese personal ornaments have a history that stretches back to the Paleolithic period, with evidence of stone beads and disks that may have been worn on the person dating to the archaeological finds of Beijing man at Zhoukoudian.[7] Numerous Neolithic sites along the Yellow River have yielded items ranging from stone bracelets[8] to jade earrings and hairpins.[9] Shang- and Zhou-period tombs have also been rich resources for jewelry, both of Chinese manufacture and reflecting northern influence, with earrings, belt hooks, and hairpins among the most commonly found items.

The codification of laws and regulations begun in the late Zhou period continued with the unification of China under the first Qin emperor, Qin Shihuangdi, in the third century B.C. These laws guided the populace in the wearing of particular items that established status and rank. During the long period of the Han dynasty, from 206 B.C. to A.D. 220, additional forms of jewelry gained popularity and importance.

The expansionist nature of both the Han and Tang (618–906) periods led to interchange between China and her neighbors, both near and far. During the eleventh century, the influence of the Liao dynasty, formed by Qidan people of the north, resulted in the development of a distinctive type of jewelry that borrowed heavily from the West and China. Jewelry of the Song period (960–1279), which was frequently decorated with floral patterning, reflected a quintessentially Chinese interest in a harmonious natural world. A fascination for the antique during the Song brought many earlier forms of Chinese jewelry, such as belt hooks that resemble those of a much earlier period, back into manufacture, as symbols of the past. Ming dynasty (1368–1644) taste in jewelry reflected a similar interest in the past, emphasizing a return to traditional imagery along with what was perceived as the "Chineseness" of the objects.

Archaeological Evidence

Fortunately for us today, many of the kinds of ornaments that people wore in their lifetime were included in burials, from the Neolithic period (ca. 6500–ca. 1500 B.C.) to the Qing dynasty (1644–1911). During the last century, archaeologists have unearthed literally thousands of tombs all over China, allowing us to piece together the history of jewelry there. With the aid of archaeological reports and material evidence from these tomb sites, we can draw a coherent picture of the types of ornaments that existed and when they were popular. To some extent we can also discern how the ornaments were worn.

Neolithic Period

The Neolithic period in China covers a span that is now believed to have begun in the seventh millenium B.C. and ended with the emergence of the Bronze Age in approximately 2000 B.C. Over that extremely long period of time, numerous cultures existed all along the Yellow River Valley. The Yangshao culture of the central Yellow River Valley is now regarded as being the earliest Neolithic culture in China. Around 3000 B.C., a culture that has come to be known as Longshan developed along the eastern seaboard. Grave sites from both these dominant cultures have yielded important articles of personal adornment. Another important eastern-seaboard culture, known as Liangzhu, has recently come to light. The workmanship of many of this culture's jade ornaments far surpasses that of other Neolithic groups.[10]

Yangshao-culture jewelry is for the most part simple and undecorated.[11] Archaeologists have unearthed a number of items of jewelry at the Yangshao-culture site of Banpo, near present-day Xi'an in Shaanxi province.[12] These include stone beads that have been carefully drilled, presumably for stringing, single-tined hairpins of bone, and bracelets. Also at Banpo, jade earrings and bone beads were found in the grave sites of children.[13] The significance of these items is unknown, but the fact that they were buried with the dead indicates that they were of importance to individuals and to society in general.

The Qijia culture of western China, with a horizon date of approximately 2250 B.C., is partly indebted to the Yangshao tradition. It was at a Qijia-culture burial site in Naimatai, Qinghai province, that the earliest copper mirror was unearthed.[14] This small mirror, which has a star design on its back similar to those seen on other mirrors found in this area, is pierced with two small holes and was found on the body of the tomb's occupant. This suggests that it may have been worn on the person, either suspended around the neck or hung from an article of clothing.[15] The geographic area of the Qijia culture reached well into the area now called Ningxia and parts of Inner Mongolia, indicating that it came at least partially under northern influence.

Longshan-culture sites are found primarily in the eastern part of China. Compared to objects from the Yangshao culture, items of jewelry and personal ornament found at the Longshan-culture sites are more elaborate and show a greater attention to detail and decoration. Tombs from the Dawenkou culture, a division of the Longshan culture in Shandong and Jiangsu provinces, have yielded well-crafted ornaments of bone, ivory, and stone, including bracelets, beads, hair combs, hairpins, and pendants.[16] Perhaps one of the most remarkable items from the Dawenkou culture is an ivory hair comb with abstract designs carved into its surface (fig. 1).[17]

A jade hair ornament from the Longshan culture was recently found at Linqiu county, Shandong (fig. 2).[18] It consists of a dark green jade pin with a broad, openwork

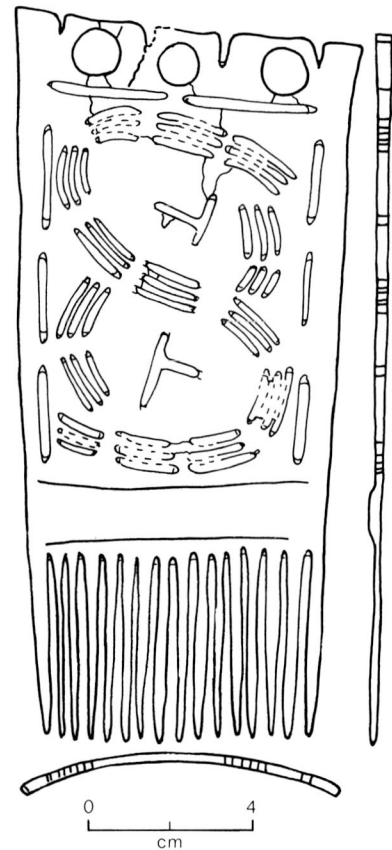

Fig. 1. Drawing of a comb from the Dawenkou culture. (Drawing after K. C. Chang, *The Archaeology of Ancient China*, p. 170, fig. 135.)

plaque of a lighter colored jade, and is inlaid with two pieces of turquoise. This exquisite ornament demonstrates an early Neolithic urge to decorate and embellish.

A number of unearthed Neolithic grave sites have shown how jewelry items were worn on the body, indicating also that the items were not strictly grave goods, placed randomly in the tomb, but were intended for the adornment of the corpse.[19] In a woman's grave from a Majiabin-culture site in Jiangsu, a hairpin of bone was found across the top of the corpse's head (fig. 3).[20] This kind of adornment reflects the long-held Chinese belief in some kind of existence after death.

Shang Period

The emergence of the Shang dynasty in the Central Plains area around 1500 B.C. brought with it a centralized form of government and an attendant social and cultural flowering.[21] The evidence for the existence of jewelry, once again coming from tomb sites, shows a burgeoning interest in items that were worn on the body. Like the Longshan Neolithic cultures of the eastern seaboard, the Shang decorated their ornaments with elaborate designs. However, in many other ways the material culture of early Shang at places like Erlitou was of a much higher quality than that of the preceding Neolithic culture. The fact that society had changed is clearly demonstrated by the kinds of tomb furnishings found from the period.

DEVELOPMENT OF OBJECTS OF PERSONAL ADORNMENT 15

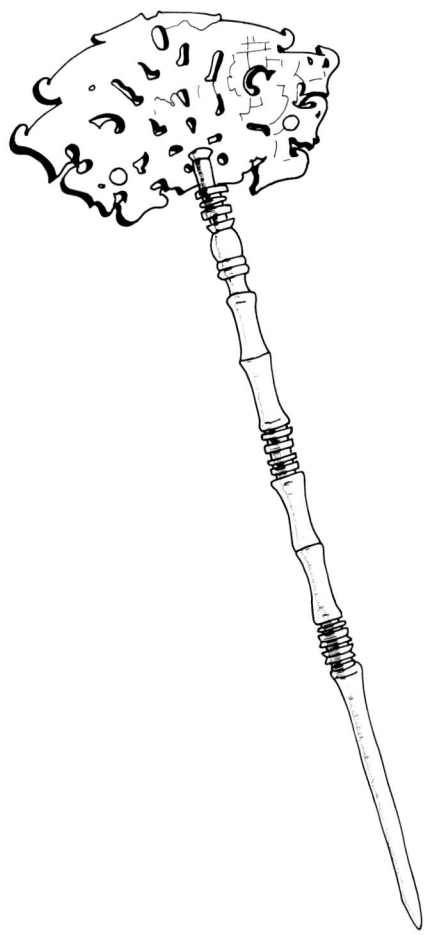

Fig. 2. Drawing of a jade hairpin from the Longshan culture excavated in 1989 in Linqiu county, Shandong province. The head of the pin is decorated with an openwork design. (Drawing after *Gems of China's Cultural Relics 1992*, p. 298, pl. 60.)

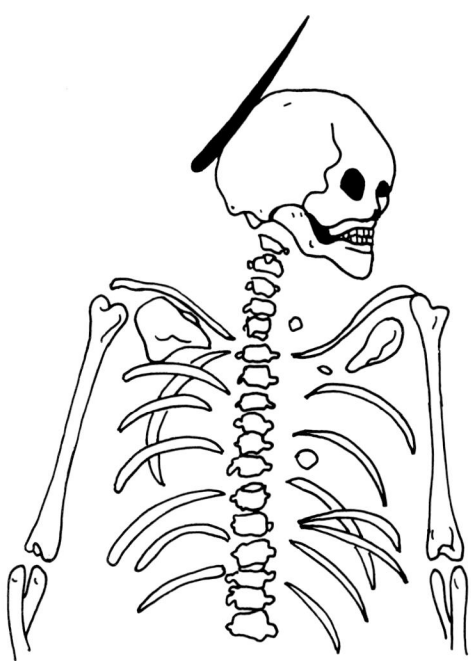

Fig. 3. A hairpin was found across the top of the corpse's head in a Neolithic-period tomb. (Drawing after Zhou Xun and Gao Chunming, *Zhongguo lidai funu jiangshi*, p. 59, pl. 54.)

According to K. C. Chang, "These new features [tombs of royal proportions . . . furnished with scarce goods, bronze ritual vessels and weapons, sets of specialized wine vessels, possible human sacrifice, and a hint of writing] point to the existence in Erh-li-t'ou society of a powerful and wealthy elite that was decidedly a level higher than the chiefly aristocracy of the Lung-shan Culture sites."[22] This "powerful and wealthy elite" supplied their deceased with elaborate ornaments of bone, jade, and other stones.

The Shang culture's sophistication in the carving and decoration of hard stone is exemplified at sites at Xiaotun and Xibeigang, where royal tombs were unearthed.[23] The Shang dynasty tomb of Fu Hao at Xiaotun, which contained jade earrings, bracelets, pendants, beads, and hairpins, is one of the richest resources for excavated Shang jade ornaments.[24] The talismanic properties associated with jade made it the most desirable material to accompany the deceased in the afterlife. Although bronze was manufactured in great quantities, it does not appear from the material evidence now available to have been used for personal ornaments in the Central Plains at this time.

Shang-period tombs that lay outside the Shang people's sphere of influence have yielded some articles of jewelry made of bronze and gold, including earrings. Gold-and-turquoise earrings from the Mengdiexuan collection (cat. no. 1) are representative of this northern tradition. Excavated examples of similar earrings from Shang-period tombs in Shanxi show the same kind of incorporation of metal and stone.[25] This evidence of gold earrings from the northern areas surrounding the central Shang state indicates that the Central Plains culture adopted the tradition of metal earrings from northern, non-Shang people.

Zhou Period

The Zhou period encompasses a very long historical time period in which different spheres of influence were in flux. The early period, beginning in the twelfth or eleventh century B.C., while the Zhou dynastic capital was at Haojing, near present-day Xi'an, is commonly known as the Western Zhou. In 770 B.C. the capital was moved to Luoyang, and the period known as the Eastern Zhou began. The latter period is in turn divided into two parts, the Spring and Autumn period (770–475 B.C.) and the Warring States period (475–221 B.C.). Some general comments relating to personal ornaments from the broad period called Zhou can be noted before we move to specific archaeological finds in the period of the Eastern Zhou.[26]

The shifts in beliefs and rituals that took place between the Shang and Zhou periods brought about a profound change in society and artifacts.[27] The transformation that was occurring in the structure of society is reflected in the arts. It has been frequently noted, for instance, that a secularization of the bronze arts occurred during the transition between the Shang and Zhou dynasties.[28] Similarly, jade carvings, which during the Shang were primarily ritualistic in nature, took on a purpose in Eastern Zhou that was more directly associated with items of luxury, particularly when these carvings were made as ornaments.[29]

The popularity of items of personal adornment appears to have increased during the Zhou period. The numbers and types of ornaments available increased as well, and now included rings, bracelets, earrings, belt hooks, hair ornaments (pins and combs), beads, buttons, and mirrors. The most important item of personal adornment to develop during the Zhou period was the belt hook; numerous examples have been found in Eastern Zhou tombs. While still found primarily in royal tombs, personal ornaments of all kinds show an improvement in quality during this period, as do the materials with which they were made. The frequency of finds in these royal tombs is evidence of the importance of personal ornament to the Zhou people.

Throughout the Zhou period, society was organized on the basis of distinctive classes dividing nobility from ordinary people. As a result, there were many layers of status and rank. Although we do not have any written documentation for the exact intention of ornament during the early Zhou, the meaning of ornament may be equated with that given to other burial goods. It is clear that the number and size of ritual vessels contained within Zhou graves reflected the status of the entombed, and it may be assumed that items of personal ornament, as they are found in tombs, also expressed status and rank.[30]

Types, colors, and materials of dress were defined for Western Zhou nobility by the state.[31] Distinctive forms of dress, such as shoes, hairpins, or caps, were often given as gifts in rituals initiating members of society into their noble classes.[32] Often mentioned along with items of dress both in historical documents and in poetry from the period, ornaments also played an important role in the ritual of the time.[33] For example, when a young man reached adolescence he was initiated into manhood with a "capping" ceremony during which he received three distinctive types of caps for different roles in society: one to mark adulthood, one to associate himself with the aristocratic obligation to the military, and one to identify him as a noble.[34] This kind of ceremony helped define a person's role in the hierarchical Zhou society, in which dress visually declared status and rank. Similarly, girls were given ornaments as a sign that they had reached adulthood. Often they received hairpins so that they could begin to arrange their hair as adult women.[35]

Eastern Zhou Period
Personal ornaments found in tombs from the Eastern Zhou period are made of a greater variety of materials. In addition to bronze, jade, and other stone, in the sixth century B.C. we begin to have concrete evidence of the use of gold in the manufacture of objects for personal adornment. The Qin state of the Warring States period is one of the richest resources for early gold objects that were functional parts of the dress of the times. The small gold hook found in the Qin-state tomb of Duke Jing, near Xi'an in Fengxiang county, may have been intended for use as a collar hook.[36] Other hooks of this type have been found across present-day Shaanxi, where the Qin rulers were entombed.[37] Three small garment hooks in the Mengdiexuan collection (cat. nos. 2, 3, and 4) are closely related to the Fengxiang county find. Those in catalogue numbers 3 and 4 employ a type of attachment device similar to those found in Fengxiang county and are cast by a piece-mold process. The hook in catalogue number 2 is quite similar to one found in Yimencun, in Baoji city, Shaanxi.[38]

Hooks become increasingly popular during the Eastern Zhou period, as indicated by the great increase in the number of belt and garment hooks found in tombs.[39] Hooks have usually been found one to a tomb, but, as Thomas Lawton has written, ". . . there were also some instances when larger quantities of hooks were amassed and buried with other funerary paraphernalia so as to enhance the prestige of the deceased."[40] The popularity of belt hooks in the Eastern Zhou period can be attributed to several factors, including the general secularization of art forms mentioned earlier, changes in dress or costume for the court, and the increased popularity of gold, silver, and bronze as indicators of status in items of personal adornment.

The intellectual climate of the Eastern Zhou encouraged the expansion of knowledge to a much broader segment of society. The period also saw a dramatic increase in contacts between the Central Plains people and their northern neighbors. This may have influenced the adoption of a new style of dress, which legend says was brought to the Central Plains Han Chinese by King Wuling of Zhao in the fourth century B.C.[41] Although this northern-plains costume may have been seen before in the Central Plains, he insisted that his men wear it, and in 307 B.C. he ordered his people to "adopt barbarian dress and to practice riding and shooting."[42]

This costume, called a *hufu*, may have been borrowed from the peoples who inhabited the state of Yan, which was well known to King Wuling.[43] This northern state was home to a large number of ethnic minorities, including the Donghu, and perhaps the Xiongnu, during the Warring States period.[44] The *hufu* consisted of a tight-fitting short jacket, long pants, and leather boots. It was a practical costume for an active people and is frequently seen on figures engaged in military or service activities. From examples of *mingqi* and figures depicted on bronzes from the Warring States period, we can see that the jacket was pulled across the chest with a belt that had a hook to hold it closed (fig. 4).[45]

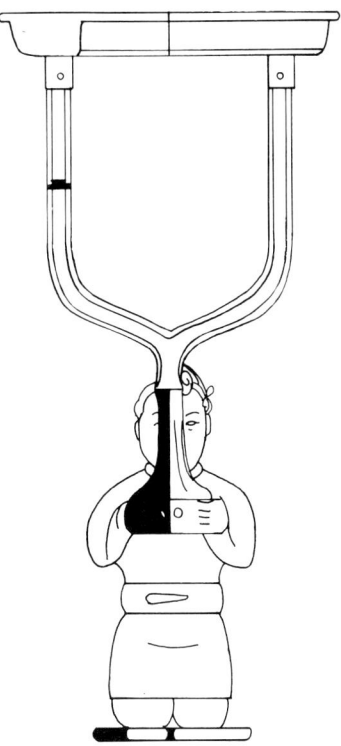

Fig. 4. Drawing of a bronze lamp from Shangcunling showing a figure wearing a *hufu* with a belt hook holding the upper garment together at the waist. (Drawing after Thomas Lawton, *Chinese Art of the Warring States Period*, p. 89.)

Fig. 5. Drawing of part of a bronze lamp from Pingshan county, Hebei province, showing a figure wearing a *shenyi* with a belt hook at the waist. (Drawing after *Gems of China's Cultural Relics 1992*, pl. 111.)

Another popular form of dress beginning in the Spring and Autumn period and extending into the Warring States period was a long, one-piece robe called a *shenyi*. The *shenyi* was tied at the waist with a girdle, which was possibly attached with a hook.[46] This type of costume is occasionally seen on bronze figures, as in the Warring States–period lamp in the form of a male figure found in Pingshan county; he is dressed in a long-sleeved robe that is closed with a belt and hook attachment (fig. 5).[47]

Eastern Zhou belt hooks from the fifth and fourth centuries B.C. have been found in archaeological sites all across northern China, including Shaanxi, Henan, and Hebei.[48] During the Warring States period, this area was the home of the independent northern states of Qin to the west, Zhao in the middle, and Yan to the east. Each of these states had considerable contact with the northern peoples mentioned above. However, hooks have also been found in Warring States–period tombs in the southern states of Zeng and Chu, as well as further south, in the royal Western Han–period tomb of the second king of Nanyue in present-day Guangzhou.[49] The exact relationship that allowed for the development of belt hooks in mainstream Han Chinese culture is still unclear, and the theory that the Chinese adopted the concept of hooks from northern peoples cannot be confirmed.[50] Many hooks have been excavated from sites in the Central Plains area; the majority of these belong to the Warring States period.[51]

Hooks of the Eastern Zhou period vary in size and decoration. The standard belt hook, however, consisted of a head—often representing a bird or dragon face—and the main body of the hook, which is frequently arched outwards. On the back of the hook, placed at its approximate middle, is a knob, sometimes referred to as a button, that served as the attachment point for the belt. A silk belt that was found in a tomb with three bronze hooks shows how the silk would have been pierced at either end to accommodate the button at one end and the hook at the other (fig. 6).[52] This is an example of the "girdle" which Sima Qian wrote about in the *Shiji*.[53]

Royal tombs tend to yield the most elaborate and finely crafted grave goods of all archaeological finds, from the Shang throughout Chinese history. From the Eastern Zhou period onward, this holds true for the royal tombs of the state of Zhou at Jincun, in present-day Henan province. Belt hooks heavily inlaid with turquoise, including two examples from the Mengdiexuan collection (cat. nos. 25 and 26), are frequently associated with Jincun.[54] However, this type of hook is not limited to Jincun, and archaeologically excavated hooks of similar design and construction have been found as widely apart as the king of Nanyue's tomb at Xianggang, in Guangzhou, and a site at Shuoxian, in Shanxi.[55] It is significant that the recorded finds of this type of hook are all from royal-lineage tombs; these hooks were intended to accompany those of high status and rank into the afterlife.

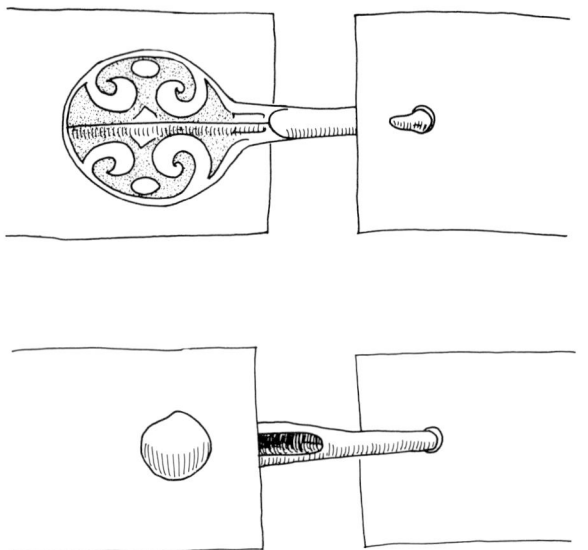

Fig. 6. Drawing to show how a bronze garment hook would have been attached to a cloth backing. (Drawing after an explanation given in Thomas Lawton, *Chinese Art of the Warring States Period*, p. 91.)

Iron was also employed in the manufacture of belt hooks from the Warring States period. Iron had been used for the manufacture of tools prior to this time, but during this period it became a material for the manufacture of luxury items.[56] In the Mengdiexuan collection, an iron belt hook decorated with a gold overlay and a silver inlay (cat. no. 20) is a particularly fine example of the use of iron at this time. Although there is considerable corrosion of the iron of this hook, it is still possible to see the intricacy of the inlay. Another archaeologically excavated iron belt hook from the Warring States period was found in the town of Zhangdaiguan, in Xinyang county, Henan province.[57] Both these examples allow us to appreciate the dramatic contrast of gold and iron.

During the Warring States period, the fascination with metals, especially bronze, gold, and silver, spread beyond hooks into other areas of personal adornment. A bronze comb from the Mengdiexuan collection (cat. no. 14) is a fine example. However, most hair combs from this early period are made of wood or bamboo, such as those found in a cosmetic set from the Western Han tomb of Mawangdui in the state of Chu.[58] The combination of bronze and gold, which was so successfully employed in the making of belt hooks, must have been impractical for hair ornaments, since bronze is heavy and difficult to shape by hammering. It appears that craftsmen moved fairly directly from bone, stone, and wood into gold as their metal of choice for hair ornaments.[59]

Northern Influence during the Late Warring States Period
Non-Han tombs from the northern tribal areas during the late Warring States period have yielded some very important ornaments made of gold and other metals. A tomb that is definitely non-Han Chinese, uncovered at Xigoupan, in Jungar banner, in the Yikezhao league of Inner Mongolia, contained many articles of personal adornment made of gold, including a necklace, plaques, and earrings.[60] On the back of one of the plaques, an inscription in archaic Chinese script defines the weight of the piece.[61] Other plaques with similar inscriptions were found at Xinzhuangtou, site of Xiadu, in Yixian, Hebei.[62] In the Mengdiexuan collection, a similar round plaque (cat. no. 22) has a "northern" design and an inscription on the back defining its weight in Chinese characters. (See fig. 7 for a drawing of the front of this plaque.) These plaques and their inscriptions have been cited as examples of the interchange between northern peoples and the central Chinese states to the south.[63]

Other examples of third-century B.C. northern personal ornaments, including belt plaques and other items, have been excavated along the northern grasslands and plains.[64] The Mengdiexuan collection contains a selection of these ornaments, including a third-century B.C. tinned bronze plaque (cat. no. 21) that closely resembles the plaques found in excavations near Yixian in Hebei. The techniques employed in the manufacture of this plaque, lost wax and lost textile, are the same as those seen at Xiadu, site of the ancient capital of the state of Yan in the third century B.C.[65] The complexity of design evident in this piece, with its interwoven pattern of animals in combat, was favored by the northern peoples.

Another significant contribution to the artistic traditions of the Central Plains was the transmission of mirrors from the north to the Yellow River basin. Western Zhou–period burials belonging to the non-Chinese, nomadic Qiang people in the northeast have yielded bronze disks and buttons, some of which appear to have originally been worn suspended from belts.[66] In addition, numerous ceramic mirror molds dating from the sixth to early fifth century B.C. were found at Houma, in Shanxi. Actual mirrors have been found in southeastern Shanxi, at noble Jin-state burial sites firmly associated with the Zhou elite.[67] The decoration on these mirrors, similar to that on a Mengdiexuan mirror (cat. no. 9), shows the influence of northern animal imagery, which is a hallmark of mirrors from this period and region.

Even after the unification of China under the brief reign of the Qin and the eventual consolidation of the empire under the Han dynasty, northerners continued to enjoy ornaments with their own distinctive style of decoration. A gilded bronze openwork plaque in the Mengdiexuan collection (cat. no. 32)—like the excavated plaques from Xichagou, Xifeng, in Liaoning province—probably belonged to the Xiongnu, a tribe that inhabited the area north of the Great Wall.[68]

Qin Dynasty, Han Dynasty, and Six Dynasties Period

We have already noted the enormous contribution of the Qin state to the Warring States period in the form of sixth- and fifth-century B.C. gold garment hooks from men. For example, a nearly life-sized clay sculpture of a "striding infantryman" wears a typical belt hook of the period.[72]

Beginning in 206 B.C. the Han dynasty settled its capital in Changan and established a unity and stability that lasted for four centuries. After a short chaotic period during the Wang Mang interregnum (when gold became nationalized as a currency and only vassal kings were allowed to possess it),[73] the capital was moved in A.D. 25 by Emperor Guang Wu, founder of the Eastern Han, to Luoyang, where it was built on the foundations of an ancient Zhou city.[74] The governmental structure of the Han dynasty, with its emphasis on imperial rule and a centralized government, created a stratified society in which rank and status were determined by association with the emperor.

Archaeological material from the Han period is richly evident in numerous royal tombs, including the southern tomb of the Western Han at Mawangdui and, in the north, the exceptionally opulent tombs of Prince Liu Sheng of Zhongshan and his wife, Dou Wan, at Mancheng, Hebei. These tombs were filled with precious objects designed to make the tomb occupant as comfortable in the afterlife as he had been during life. The emergence of Buddhism brought with it a new attitude toward the afterlife. The search for immortality that began in the Western Han was closely associated with Daoism. With the rise of Buddhism a whole new system of belief brought about changes in tomb furnishings.[75]

The luxury of the Han tombs is exemplified by the jade suits covering the bodies of the occupants in Mancheng. The suits, made of jade plaques tied together with gold thread and intended to protect the corpse from disintegration, marked the highest achievement in funerary ornament. Many other magnificent objects were found at Mancheng, including jade carvings and bronze lamps. The tombs in the south, at Mawangdui, were rich in items made of silk, lacquer, and wood, including items of personal ornament such as combs.[76] Similar in shape to the bronze comb from the Mengdiexuan collection mentioned above, these wooden combs were found in a cosmetic box along with other items for ladies' grooming, including a hairpiece. Bronze mirrors painted with lacquer designs, like the one in the Mengdiexuan collection (cat. no. 36), which has a pattern resembling textile designs, were also found among the grave goods in these southern tombs. The appearance of bronze mirrors this far south shows their rapid growth in popularity.[77] Many other items of various materials have been found in the tombs of the nobility, including lacquerware, cloth, books, and coins, as well as miniature figures, dishes, and buildings made of clay.[78]

A southern tomb of the Western Han period, located in Guangzhou and excavated in 1983, is known to be that of the second king of the Nanyue state.[79] The chief occupant of this tomb was covered in a suit of jade

Fig. 7. Photo (above) and line drawing (below) of the front surface of the plaque seen in catalogue number 22.

the area around present-day Shaanxi. The Qin state unified the whole of China in 221 B.C., and Qin Shihuangdi became the emperor of all China, finally driving the Xiongnu northward in 214 B.C. Although the *Shiji* and other contemporaneous histories indicate a great legacy left in the tombs of the Qin, the imperial tombs are largely without relics or have yet to be unearthed.[69] There is every reason to believe that the tomb of Qin Shihuangdi was filled with magnificent treasures, but it was plundered early in history, and what remains has not been excavated.[70]

Some of the attendant burial sites around the tomb itself have yielded remarkable clay and bronze sculptures, but little in the way of personal ornaments.[71] However, from clay figures found in the Qin pit at Lintong county, Shaanxi province, it is possible to discern some of the items of personal adornment that were worn by military plaques tied together with silk thread, indicating his high status. Excavations from this site have brought to light eight small gold appliqués, each decorated with images of two rams below a bearlike head (fig. 8).[80] The Mengdiexuan collection contains a similar plaque, with the same design executed in repoussé and chasing (cat. no. 35). The Guangzhou finds have been interpreted as representing the spread of Central Plains arts to the south, as well as indicating the far-reaching arm of the Han central bureaucracy.[81]

Objects made of bronze, including ritual vessels, utilitarian vessels, and ornaments, continued to be important grave goods. There is some indication that during the Han period items of personal adornment began to interest craftsmen in bronze, who employed techniques previously used for the manufacture of vessels, such as the threadlike inlay seen in some of the Mengdiexuan belt hooks from this period.[82] The elaborate skill used to create vessels with inlaid gold wire, such as the *fang jian* of the late Eastern Zhou from Henan, was adopted in the manufacture of Western Han vessels like the *hu* from Liu Sheng's tomb at Mancheng.[83] This decorative technique can be seen in personal ornament on the back and front of the bronze belt hook in catalogue number 38, which is inlaid with silver strands as well as with gemstones that are surrounded by gilded areas. The decoration on the back of this hook is typical of the delightfully lyrical quality associated with the art of the Han period.

Governmental stability during the Han period brought about a period of expansion into the areas bordering China. Chinese explorers and military detachments were sent out to the west and north, and from these borderlands new ideas and philosophies were adopted. The Silk Route west of Changan had opened trade to the West, including, by the first century B.C., the Roman Empire. Merchants along the route traded silk for numerous commodities including gold currency from the West, which undoubtedly increased the prestige of the metal.[84] Buddhism was introduced to China from India via this route during the early Eastern Han period and almost immediately began to affect the arts, from painting to jewelry. In addition, contact with China's northern neighbors, particularly the Xiongnu, continued to influence central Han China.

Archaeological finds of jewelry from along the Silk Route help to chart the influx of new ideas in Chinese decoration, construction methods, and materials. The spectacular Han-period gold belt buckle (fig. 9), excavated in 1976 from Heigeda site in Yanqi county, Xinjiang Uygur Autonomous Region, is an example of the belt buckle types that came from the West and influenced the construction of belts in China.[85] It is this type of belt buckle that began to replace the traditional Chinese belt hook during the late Han period, resulting in the production of belts made up of individual plaques attached

Fig. 8. Drawing of two of the eight plaques from a Western Han–period tomb in Guangzhou. (Drawing after *Xi Han Nanyue wangmu*/Nanyue King's tomb of the Western Han, vol. 2, pl. 18, no. 1.)

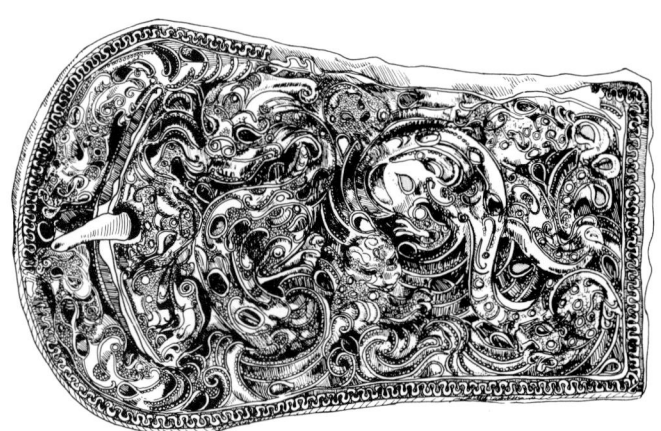

Fig. 9. Drawing of a gold belt buckle with dragon designs excavated in 1976 from Heigeda in Yanqi county, Xinjiang Uygur Autonomous Region. (Drawing after *Gems of China's Cultural Relics 1993*, p. 311, pl. 113.)

to a supporting material, usually leather.[86] The techniques and materials used in this belt buckle became very popular in the late Han and continued to influence China's jewelry manufacture for a long time thereafter. Solid gold plaques with applied wire line and granulation appealed to the Chinese nobility, and items of a similar type are found in slightly later tombs in central China. A belt buckle of similar construction from the Western Jin tomb of Liu Hong at Nanchanwang, Anxiang county, Hunan, is an example of the adoption of this kind of buckle at a slightly later period (fig. 10).[87] Another example of this type of workmanship can be seen in a similar belt buckle found in a tomb in Korea dated to the first to second century A.D.[88]

This style of workmanship in gold wire and beading continued to be important in the Six Dynasties period (A.D. 265–589), as can be seen in a gold plaque in the Mengdiexuan collection (cat. no. 47), which was probably at one time attached to a cap or cloth band. The two opposing dragons in this plaque are created with the same kind of graduated granulation seen on the belt buckles mentioned above.

A Six Dynasties–period hair comb from the Mengdiexuan collection (cat. no. 48) with gold beading around

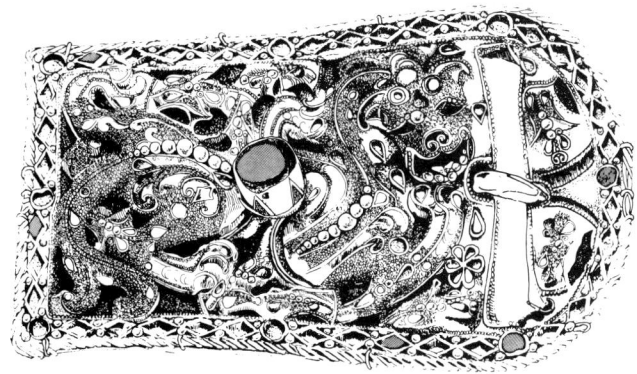

Fig. 10. Drawing of a gold belt buckle with dragon design excavated from the Western Jin tomb of Liu Hong at Nanchanwang in Anxiang county, Hunan province. (Drawing after *Gems of China's Cultural Relics 1993*, p. 311, pl. 114.)

the back, inlaid with jewels and inset with a jade plaque, shows the direction that this workmanship took. The lozenge-shaped cells around the edges of the design recall the kind of decoration seen on the belt buckle from Liu Hong's tomb at Anxiang. This comb, with its delightful combination of the best materials and craftsmanship, undoubtedly belonged to a person of considerable status. Chinese craftsmen imported this technique of beading from the West along with the practice of varying the size of the beads to help define the decoration.

Hair ornaments also enjoyed popularity in the Han period. Men wore a decorative type of hairpin known as a "white brush hairpin." This developed during the Han through the custom of taking a writing brush to the court to make notes, then placing the brush in the hair after use. Eventually the actual brush was replaced by an ornament that symbolized a brush.[89] The use of the white brush hairpin can be seen in wall paintings from Han dynasty tombs.

The cap was a very important item of headgear for men during the Han period, and the regulations governing its wear were strictly dictated, as was the status associated with different types of caps.[90] Han dynasty men still used a bar-type hairpin to wrap up their long hair, but the decorative role of hairpins for men declined significantly as the cap took over.[91] Caps are mentioned in historical documents of the period, and many wall paintings and tomb tiles show male figures wearing various kinds of caps.[92]

The fashion for Han women called for long hair, braided and tied in a bun at the top of the head. Pottery tomb figurines, wall paintings, tomb tiles, and other grave goods show the variety of hair styles popular during the Han.[93] Poetry from the Han dynasty and the periods that follow frequently evokes images of ladies in their finery. Cao Zhi, a third-century A.D. poet, in his *fu* poem "Rhyme-Prose on the Goddess of the Luo," becomes entranced by a beautiful goddess and describes her to his coachman:

> Wrapped in the soft rustle of silken garments,
> she decks herself with flowery earrings of jasper and jade,
> gold and kingfisher hairpins adorning her head,
> strings of bright pearls to make her body shine . . .[94]

The principal type of ornament for Han dynasty women's hair was the *zan*, a decorated hairpin that stuck out from the hair arrangement, which can be seen in Han dynasty wall paintings.[95] Occasionally the tops of these pins were decorated by a *buyao*, an attached ornament which was said to quiver when the wearer walked.[96] Court ladies also wore pieces of cloth called *guo* in their hair to proclaim their status.[97] Female court performers of the Han period apparently wore very elaborate headdresses, as evidenced by a pottery figurine from a Han-period tomb in Guangzhou.[98]

Stability and expansionism under the Han resulted in new forms of jewelry for an established nobility as well as for a burgeoning middle class. Ornaments, like other art forms, became more secular and less ritualized during the Han period. The many calls for austerity by the philosophers of the later Han do not appear to have stopped people from decorating themselves and their dead with beautiful objects.[99] Gold became much more popular for personal ornament. Its use as a form of currency meant that other forms of use were proscribed by the state and it was acquired through status. In general, the Han period set the stage for the development of jewelry, particularly gold jewelry, as an indicator of status and wealth in dynastic China.

Tang and Liao Periods

Tang dynasty ornaments, like those from the preceding periods, are largely functional items of dress which, because of their decoration or materials, were associated with different levels of status. From archaeological evidence we can see that, while people under the Tang continued to use and enjoy items of personal adornment that had gained popularity over a long period of time, such as hairpins and combs, they also began to use a number of new items of jewelry, including belt sets, crowns, and necklaces. Contact with foreign peoples, primarily from the West, had a great impact on the Chinese, introducing new kinds of ornaments and exerting a strong influence on the surface decoration of many traditional Chinese types.

The belt hook had evolved during the Warring States period and enjoyed popularity throughout the Western Han period, but it underwent a dramatic transition into sectioned belt plaques during the Western Jin period (265–316). The Eastern Han (A.D. 25–220) had begun the officially sanctioned decline of the belt hook when, in A.D. 59, it released an official edict in which belt hooks were not listed as appropriate dress.[100] Sectioned belt plaque sets began to take over the role of hooks, displacing them with leather belts adorned with plaques. In the

Tang dynasty there were additional changes, largely the result of influence from the north and west, including the perforation at the base of the plaque for hanging items, and the western-style belt buckle. Some of these changes were short-lived but had a period of popularity during the Tang. A brief mention of developments that occurred during the Six Dynasties helps to set the stage for the Tang innovations.

During the Western Jin, sectioned belts like those in the Mengdiexuan collection made of gilded bronze and silvered bronze (cat. no. 50) were constructed by a sandwiching of rimmed plaques that were riveted together. Excavated examples of this type of belt have been found in northern tombs.[101] The surface decoration on these and excavated examples utilizing dragons, phoenixes, and other mythological animals suggests that the decor was Chinese, though the belt type was probably from the north. This type of belt does not seem to have had great popularity in China after the Western Jin, but did appear later in Korea.[102] The idea of a sectioned belt, however, continued to be very popular in Tang China, with a number of variations, some of which will be discussed here.

In the early Tang period, belt plaque sets utilizing the Western Jin type of construction but with a very different kind of surface decoration appeared as the result of western influence. In the Mengdiexuan collection, a belt plaque set decorated with rampant lions and palmettes (cat. no. 51) shows a Chinese attempt at a decidedly foreign theme;[103] in the end this was not to be the principal direction of Chinese belts. There are several examples of similar belt sets in western collections.[104]

These Six Dynasties and early Tang belt sets point to the tremendous impact that the international expansionism of the Han and Tang periods had on items of jewelry. Tang belt plaque sets incorporated foreign influences while maintaining a Chinese quality, and the result was a distinctively Chinese style. In some instances, the foreign content came in the form of decorative motifs or a combination of foreign and Chinese motifs on an imported belt type. The Tang dynasty belt set in the Mengdiexuan collection (cat. no. 53) depicting paired ducks (a Chinese motif) combined with paired falcons (which were birds of exotic origins) demonstrates this cross-cultural borrowing. The form of the plaques, with their western-style belt buckle and small opening at the base of each plaque, was derived from a nomadic, Central Asian type developed by Turkic-speaking peoples.[105] The openings were used to hang implements necessary for the designation of status, as prescribed by the imperial court during the Tang period.[106]

Silver, previously seldom used in the manufacture of ornaments in China, suddenly became an important material during the Tang, due in large part to western influence. The Liao dynasty (907–1125) of northern China also adopted silver for ornaments, and beautiful examples of entire belt sets have been found in the tombs of the

Fig. 11. Drawing of a section of a wall painting at Dunhuang in cave 263 showing an attendant Bodhisattva. (Drawing after *Art Treasures of Dunhuang*, fig. 19.)

Qidan nobility. In the eleventh-century tomb of Princess Chenguo in Inner Mongolia, a gilt-silver belt set with gold ornaments and attached pendants was found along with many other items of gold, silver, and precious stones.[107] A gilt-silver belt set in the Mengdiexuan collection consisting of seventy-one pieces (cat. no. 77), including a pocket and a number of hanging attachments, demonstrates the high level of workmanship that fascinated the Liao people. Other examples of Liao metalwork in the Mengdiexuan collection (cat. nos. 79 and 80) show the variety of shapes in which these belt sets could be constructed in order to create slightly different visual impacts.

Two other types of ornaments that first emerged in China during the Tang period were necklaces and crowns. Both may have developed as a result of the influence of Buddhism on mainstream Chinese art. Many of the Buddhist sites from present-day Xinjiang and Gansu are decorated with Buddhist wall paintings depicting an array of figures wearing crowns. At Dunhuang, for example, such figures appear in even the earliest caves, including the Northern Wei cave 263, where an attendant Bodhisattva is adorned with a splendid crown with ring and bird design, and bold earrings (fig. 11).[108] By the Tang period, with the rise of the cult of Guanyin, practically every figure other than a monk in a section of cave 57 is depicted wearing a crown (fig. 12).[109] Secular figures shown in the Dunhuang cave wall paintings are shown in resplendent dress: the Emperor and ministers

DEVELOPMENT OF OBJECTS OF PERSONAL ADORNMENT 23

Fig. 12. Drawing of a section of a wall painting at Dunhuang in cave 57 showing Avalokitesvara, an attendant Bodhisattva, and a monk. (Drawing after *Art Treasures of Dunhuang*, fig. 58.)

Fig. 13. Drawing of a section of a wall painting at Dunhuang in cave 220 showing ministers and attendants of the emperor. (Drawing after *Art Treasures of Dunhuang*, fig. 63.)

in cave 220 give us a sense of the types of robes, head gear, and hair ornaments worn by men of the court. Standing behind these secular figures are Bodhisattvas adorned with crowns and necklaces, indicating that celestials wore crowns at this time (fig. 13).[110] From the painting in cave 158 at Dunhuang, it would appear that some foreigners also wore crowns; some of the mourners at Buddha's *parinirvana* are also depicted with hats and in some cases crowns (fig. 14).[111] Other paintings from the slightly later, Northern Song–period cave 61 show attendants of the princess of Khotan wearing both crowns and necklaces (fig. 15).[112] This kind of Buddhist imagery found its way into the central Tang capital of Changan and was dispersed to other areas of China.

Introduced to China through the religious traditions of Buddhism, both crowns and torques had been adopted for secular wear by the late Tang and Liao periods. During the late Tang it appears that crowns were associated with elaborate headdresses. Combs became larger and more elaborate, and silver and gilt-silver ornaments for the hair gained popularity.[113] Evidence for elaborate Liao-period crowns comes from the finds at Princess Chenguo's eleventh-century tomb in Inner Mongolia.[114]

Buddhist wall paintings from Dunhuang and other Buddhist sites along the ancient Silk Route also give evidence for the wearing of metal necklaces by the Chinese.[115] A painting in the Tang-period cave 329 at Dunhuang shows a secular figure wearing a necklace and a female donor wearing earrings and a necklace.[116] A gilt-silver band torque in the Mengdiexuan collection (cat. no. 69) (fig. 16) is one of the few known examples of a torque from the Tang dynasty. The silver band, with its chased bird design, is decorated in a style not unlike that found on silver vessels from Tang China that show western, especially Persian, influences.[117] A similar torque is in the collection of the Minneapolis Institute of Art.[118]

Items of jewelry and personal adornment that had traditionally been popular with the Chinese, such as hairpins, rings, bracelets, combs, earrings, and mirrors, continued to flourish in the Tang period. However, foreign impact played a significant role in altering these items also, particularly in their surface decoration.

Tang-period objects such as hairpins, combs, and mirrors tended to be significantly larger than their predecessors. Hairpins, for instance, tended to become more like crowns. Especially evident is the incorporation of Buddhist imagery into the decorative elements of these items. Hairpins of the Tang frequently depict Buddhist figures. One of a pair from the Mengdiexuan collection (cat. no. 62) depicts a small boy playing with the "wheel of life," which is symbolic of the Buddha.[119] The other pin of the pair is decorated with a lotus leaf, also a symbol of the Buddha, and an *apsaras*, or heavenly attendant, from Buddhist tradition. A silver hair comb from the Mengdiexuan collection (cat. no. 67) is also decorated with Buddhist *apsaras*. The interest in Buddhist imagery on ornament accompanied a fascination for the foreign and exotic that characterized China during the Tang.

The fish design on a Tang-period hairpin from the Mengdiexuan collection (cat. no. 63) is also an adoption of a Buddhist design. This contorted fish design is associated with the *makara*, an Indian importation, which began to appear in China on silver dishes, ceramics, and hair ornaments during the Tang period.[120] The *makara*,

24 DEVELOPMENT OF OBJECTS OF PERSONAL ADORNMENT

Fig. 14. Drawing of a section of a wall painting at Dunhuang in cave 158 showing mourners at Buddha's *parinirvana*. (Drawing after *Art Treasures of Dunhuang*, fig. 81.)

Fig. 16. Drawing of the design on the front of the torque in catalogue number 69.

Fig. 15. Drawing of a section of a wall painting at Dunhuang in cave 61 showing attendants of the Princess of Khotan. (Drawing after *Art Treasures of Dunhuang*, fig. 105.)

a "fierce water spirit widely revered in India," first appears in Buddhist caves at Ajanta in India.[121] The Chinese term for the image is *zhiwen,* or dragon-fish. During the Liao dynasty, earrings such as one in the Mengdiexuan collection (cat. no. 71) utilized the curled form of the *makara* in an effective half-circle motif. The motif underwent a revival during the Ming dynasty, as evidenced by the set of six pairs of dragon-fish earrings in the Mengdiexuan collection (cat. no. 71a).

The fascination during the Tang and later periods with Buddhist imagery probably had less to do with devotion than with fashion. However, the placing of Buddhist imagery on items of personal adornment makes it clear that the religion had permeated Chinese culture to a very basic level. An object that is not religious in nature can nevertheless represent beliefs prevalent within a society. A recent study on Buddhism in Tang and Song China notes that: "[r]eligion in its broadest sense had, of course, always played a major part in the lives of the Chinese people. From ancient times, gods, ghosts and ancestors were familiar figures in people's worlds. . . . Religious rituals, symbols, and ideas conveyed basic understandings about the nature of the cosmos and humanity's place in it."[122]

Since both Buddhist and Daoist imagery continued to be employed on hair ornaments and other items of personal adornment in the Tang and Song periods, it is worth considering what role this imagery had in defining status and rank. Buddhism had many levels of adherents, including common people, who found through their association with Buddhism opportunities that did not exist in other arenas. By associating with Buddhism they acquired a special status for themselves and their families. "Buddhism thus created its own partially independent status system. Clearly one of its appeals (stronger in the T'ang when the avenues of social mobility were more restricted than in the Sung) was that it offered the possibility of a prestigious and influential career to the talented and ambitious whose family background would have barred them from more conventional channels of success within the imperial bureaucracy."[123]

The great influx of foreign luxury goods in the Tang capital of Changan created a climate of acquisitiveness not previously experienced in China. Unlike previous periods, during which jewelry was predominantly for male use, with items like belt hooks dominating, many ornaments surviving from the Tang were made primarily for women. The significance of belt sets for men became focused on their material, usually gold or gilt silver, which was a direct reflection of the status of the wearer. However, it was women who wore the headdresses, combs, and hairpins made of precious metals, and it was they who became the subject of many poems about women's beauty and their jewelry.

Tang poets spoke frequently and passionately of the women of the court and their beauty. The descriptions of their dress and jewelry are tantalizing glimpses into the splendor of the times. Du Fu, one of the best known of the Tang poets, writes of their beauty in his "Song of the Beautiful Ladies":

> Third month, third day, in the air a breath of newness;
> by Ch'ang-an riverbanks the beautiful ladies crowd,
> warm-bodied, modest-minded, mild and pure,
> with clear sleek complexions, bone and flesh well matched,
> in figured gauze robes that shine in the late spring,
> worked with golden peacocks, silver unicorns.
> On their heads what do they wear?
> Kingfisher glinting from hairpins that dangle by sidelock borders.
> On their back what do I see?
> Pearls that weight the waistband and subtly set off the form . . . .[124]

It may also have been women who requested and enjoyed the Buddhist imagery that adorned their jewelry, as Buddhism was seen as a refuge by many Tang ladies. "Although Buddhism did not provide an equal opportunity for women to achieve positions of prominence, it did offer them a haven within which they could escape the frequently oppressive demands of marriage and family life."[125] Additionally, a lady's items of adornment may have had little interest to their wearer as indicators of official status, but the precious materials employed in their manufacture certainly enhanced the beauty of the wearer and declared the owner's high level of wealth.

A number of paintings on silk attributed to the Tang period depict women of the court adorned with hairpins and headdresses of elaborate design. "Flower-wearing ladies," a hand scroll attributed to Zhou Fang in the Provincial Museum collection in Shenyang, Liaoning, depicts ladies of the court wearing U-shaped hairpins across the back and sides of their coiffures and delicate golden ornaments on the front.[126]

Paintings and poetry attest to the popularity of mirrors and their use by ladies. In "Admonitions," the Six Dynasties silk hand scroll attributed to Gu Kaizhi, a lady is depicted with a mirror propped up on a stand as her hair is dressed by an attendant.[127] In the Tang-period poem "Feelings Wakened by a Mirror," the poet Bo Juyi expresses the yearnings associated with a mirror that had belonged to his lover:

> My beautiful one gave it to me when we parted,
> but I leave the mirror stored in its box.
> Since her flowering face left my sight,
> autumn waters have no more lotus blooms.
> For years I've never opened the box;
> red dust coats the mirror's green bronze.
> This morning I took it out and wiped it off,
> peered into it at my haggard face,
> and done peering, went on to ponder sadly
> the pair of twined dragons carved on its back.[128]

In addition to large mirrors typical of the Tang period (cat. no. 58), a very small type of mirror existed. In the Mengdiexuan collection a group of mini-mirrors (cat. no. 55) dating from the Han period through the Tang dynasty demonstrates that the decoration on mirror backs remained strong and visually appealing even in reduced size. It has been suggested that the elaborate decoration on the backs of mirrors, beginning around the latter half of the Zhou period, resulted from their acquiring "religious or spiritual purpose."[129] These mirrors are similar in size to mirrors of the Qijia culture. Like their Neolithic predecessors, they were probably carried on the person in a bag attached to a belt or cord. The ways in which these small mirrors were used have not been determined, although they were an ideal size for personal reflection or for use as signal mirrors by the military. The use of larger mirrors is similarly unclear, though many theories have been put forward.[130]

Song, Yuan, and Ming Dynasties

The jewelry of the Song dynasty (960–1279) continued to develop along the same lines as Tang and Liao jewelry, with a continuation of popular forms but some experimentation in the areas of shape and decoration. Belts, rings, bracelets, necklaces, combs, and hair ornaments all continued to be used in much the same way as they had been in preceding periods. Innovations occurred, such as a crownlike, wide diadem for women. An interest in aromatics, which had developed from the importation and wearing of scents in the Tang period, created the need for perfume containers, which were worn on the belt or attached to a shawl.[131] Belts in the form of sets of plaques attached to a leather belt continued to be used as designators of status.

The high hairstyle of the Tang remained in vogue during the Song period, and hairpins of large size and elaborate configuration helped to adorn ladies of the court. Although the Song has been recognized as a period of restraint in aesthetics, there was a continued interest in large-scale, opulent items, at least in some areas of ornament. A gilt-silver Song hairpin from the Mengdiexuan collection (cat. no. 83) exemplifies the large flat pins that came to fill the need for larger and more elaborate ornaments. The decoration, two phoenixes in flight, shows the typical pairing of these mythical birds on an elaborate floral background. This was a popular theme in metal vessels from the Liao period, one which gained popularity in both Song ornament and Yuan metal and ceramic decoration.[132]

Wide diadems, sometimes in pairs like the ones from the Mengdiexuan collection (cat. no. 87), which are similar to a group of diadems excavated from a Song dynasty tomb in Zhejiang, must have provided a spectacular adornment for ladies' hair.[133] The broad-band hair ornaments that enjoyed popularity during the Song dynasty were often gilt silver (cat. no. 86), although they were sometimes made of gold (cat. no. 90).

Surface decoration on hairpins during the Song period emphasized the natural world. Flowers frequently decorated hairpins, drawing upon the association of beautiful flowers with beautiful women. Flowers of the four seasons is a common theme in the decor of hairpins from this period. Several examples from the Mengdiexuan collection include two hairpins (cat. no. 95), both decorated with this typically Chinese motif. Excavated examples have been recovered from Southern Song tombs in the Fuzhou area.[134] These pins, with their compact shape and intricate design, are more in keeping with the reserve usually associated with the Song period.

Simple single or double hollow-tined hairpins of the Song period, like the ones mentioned above, were decorated in deep repoussé with elaborate chased detail. Occasionally the designs show western inspiration, as in a pair of hairpins (cat. no. 97) that have a honeycomb pattern across their top portions. This repeat patterning is thought to have arrived in China from the West via the Silk Route; textiles with this pattern have been found in Dunhuang.[135]

It has been noted that during the Tang period "a man or woman of the upper classes lived in clouds of incense and mists of perfume."[136] Sachet cases were part of an ancient tradition, and the Tang court raised the wearing of scents to a high art.[137] An interest in aromatics led to the development during the Song of a compact, wearable incense case like the one in the Mengdiexuan collection (cat. no. 98). This case, made of two separate sheets of gold which have been cut out and decorated with repoussé and chased designs of flowers, would have held a fragrant package of aromatics, perhaps sweet basil, a favorite scent at the Tang court.[138] Although missing from this example, a short chain and hook have been found on some excavated incense cases, indicating that they were worn hanging.[139] There is new evidence to suggest that these cases may have hung from the bottom of a shawl or cape and may have been used as weights.[140]

The relatively subdued forms of Southern Song ornaments were briefly rocked during the Yuan dynasty (1279–1368), when the decoration of ornaments once again took on the elaborate and sometimes exuberant qualities associated with the non-Chinese northerners. In hairpins, traditional Chinese themes like the paired birds seen in the Mengdiexuan collection (cat. no. 104) were executed in very deep repoussé and highlighted by detailed chasing. This beautiful rendition of a Chinese motif was executed in such an elaborate fashion as to suggest some of the overstatement typical of the Mongols of the Yuan period. The boldness in the design of this hairpin is matched by the quality of its craftsmanship, which is superb.

The return to Han Chinese rule in the Ming dynasty (1368–1644) brought another long period of stability to China. The types of ornaments that people wore changed very little, and the designs retained strong Chinese qualities. Themes that had been established during the Han and Tang periods persisted, with people during the Ming particularly interested in reaffirming those designs that had imperial and mythical meaning. Dragons, phoenixes, and assorted floral motifs, which had played an important role in defining early China as a distinct culture, were liberally applied to items of personal adornment. The court took great pains to establish hierarchy through dress with strict official dictates.[141]

The Ming's return to Chinese origins can be seen in the large jade belt set in the Mengdiexuan collection (cat. no. 113). Here is a return to the material considered by the Chinese to be the most precious of all: jade. The decoration consists of swirling dragons against a background of deeply carved clouds. At the four corners of the larger plaques are flowers traditionally associated with the four seasons. All are executed in a fine and precise manner which exploits the material through undercutting and drilling. These kinds of jade belt plaques visibly proclaimed the owner to be of imperial rank. A less elevated aristocrat would have owned the silver belt seen in catalogue number 111, with its phoenix design, or the one in catalogue number 112, with its floral motif. These are beautiful objects, but, as designated by the Ming imperial court, belt sets made with silver plaques were for those of the fifth, sixth, or seventh rank.[142]

Conclusion

From the earliest times, items of personal adornment in China defined an individual's position within society. They evolved from abstract talismanic items of personal adornment to functional items of dress. Different items matured at different times, and to some degree their evolution was never complete, for objects continued to convey meaning even when they served a functional role. Initially their appearance signified official sanction of status and rank, but over time they became as much indicators of wealth as of rank. Metal items evolved from being primarily male signifiers of rank during the Warring States period to symbols of feminine beauty during the Tang, Song, and later periods.

Archaeological data collected primarily from noble and imperial tombs help us determine what kind of people wore these items, and how ornaments were incorporated into concepts of the afterlife. Surface decoration allows us to trace influences from outside China, and confirms their importation from many cultures to the north, south, and west of China. As with so many other aspects of China's material culture, the importation of new articles of dress, styles of decoration, methods of manufacture, and uses of materials did not deter the Chinese from pursuing their own aesthetic ideals.

Notes

1. Li Zehou, *The Path of Beauty: A Study of Chinese Aesthetics*, p. 17.

2. Zhou Xun and Gao Chunming, *5000 Years of Chinese Costumes*, p. 12.

3. Burton Watson, trans., *Records of the Grand Historian*, vol. 2, p. 160.

4. Zhou Xun and Gao Chunming, *5000 Years of Chinese Costumes*, p. 12.

5. Shang-period earrings from the Central Plains were made of jade or bone. The few examples of gold or bronze earrings from the Shang period belong to non-Shang tribal people. The metal earring in China was a foreign inspiration.

6. Diane M. O'Donoghue, "Reflection and Reception: The Origins of the Mirror in Bronze Age China," *Bulletin of the Museum of Far Eastern Antiquities* 62 (1990), pp. 5–183. Mirrors have been found in Qijia-culture burial sites in Qinghai and Gansu. It is thought that these mirrors may have been worn around the neck, p. 19. See also Thomas Lawton, *Chinese Art of the Warring States Period*, pp. 81–82.

7. K. C. Chang, *The Archaeology of Ancient China*, 4th ed., pp. 22–106.

8. Bracelets made of bone and of stone were discovered at the Yangshao site of Banpo in Shaanxi province. See ibid., p. 125.

9. Earrings and hairpins of bone and jade have been found at major Neolithic sites all across Northern China. See ibid., pp. 107–233.

10. Dates for the Liangzhu culture are approximately 3300 to 2250 B.C.

11. K. C. Chang, *The Archaeology of Ancient China*, p. 125.

12. *Banpo Site: A well preserved site of a Neolithic Village*, n.p.

13. Ibid.

14. Diane M. O'Donoghue, "Reflection and Reception," p. 19. See also the first report on this find in *Qinghai ribao* (18 February 1978).

15. Diane M. O'Donoghue, "Reflection and Reception," p. 19.

16. K. C. Chang, *The Archaeology of Ancient China*, pp. 163–64, and p. 170, fig. 135.

17. Ibid., p. 170, fig. 135.

18. *Gems of China's Cultural Relics 1992*, pl. 60, p. 298.

19. Hairpins, bracelets, rings, and hair combs are frequently seen placed on the body in Neolithic burials.

20. *Kaogu xuebao*, 1958.1, pp. 72–73. For a line drawing of the same site see Zhou Xun and Gao Chunming, *Zhongguo lidai funu jiangshi*, pl. 54, p. 59.

21. K. C. Chang, *Shang Civilization*.

22. K. C. Chang, *The Archaeology of Ancient China*, p. 314.

23. Ibid., p. 331.

24. Hsia Nai, "The Classification, Nomenclature, and Usage of Shang Dynasty Jades," in K. C. Chang, ed., *Studies in Shang Archaeology*, pp. 207–36. See especially section on jade ornaments, pp. 230–36.

25. Lin Yun, "A Reexamination of the Relationship between Bronzes of the Shang Culture and of the Northern Zone," in K. C. Chang, ed., *Studies in Shang Archaeology*, pp. 237–73. See pp. 248–49 for a discussion of ornaments from the northern zone, including line drawings, p. 249, fig. 50.

26. A very succinct account of Zhou dynastic progression is given in Li Xueqin, *Eastern Zhou and Qin Civilizations*, p. 315. See also Jessica Rawson, *Western Zhou Ritual Bronzes from the Arthur M. Sackler Collections*, vol. 2a, p. 15.

27. Li Xueqin, *Eastern Zhou and Qin Civilizations*. See also K. C. Chang, *Early Chinese Civilization: Anthropological Perspectives*, pp. 174–96.

28. Cho-yun Hsu and Katheryn M. Linduff, *Western Chou Civilization*, pp. 318–37.

29. Thomas Lawton, *Chinese Art of the Warring States Period*, p. 128.

30. Cho-yun Hsu and Katheryn M. Linduff, *Western Chou Civilization*, p. 360. Evidence for this association with status comes from the *Book of Documents*, see James Legge, *The Shoo King*.

31. Cho-yun Hsu and Katheryn M. Linduff, *Western Chou Civilization*, p. 361.

32. Ibid., pp. 361, 365.

33. Ibid., p. 365.

34. Ibid., p. 374. See also the *Liji* (Book of Rites).

35. Cho-yun Hsu and Katheryn M. Linduff, *Western Chou Civilization*, p. 374.

36. *China Pictorial*, 1987.5, p. 15. The varying uses for different sizes of hooks is discussed in Thomas Lawton, *Chinese Art of the Warring States Period*, pp. 90–91.

37. *Kaogu yu wenwu*, 1991.2, p. 9, fig. 7. See catalogue numbers 2, 3, and 4 for examples from the Mengdiexuan collection. For archaeological reports for finds in Shaanxi province see *Kaogu yu wenwu*, 1991.2, *Wenwu*, 1985.2, p. 26, fig. 31, and *Wenwu* 1993.10, p. 114.

38. See entries for catalogue numbers 2, 3, and 4.

39. Wang Renxiang, "Daigou gailun" (A general survey of Chinese belt hooks), *Kaogu xuebao*, 1985.3, pp. 267–312, in Chinese with a brief English summary.

40. Thomas Lawton, *Chinese Art of the Warring States Period*, p. 91.

41. It is unlikely that the introduction of this style of dress developed in the fourth century, since there are examples of figures wearing this style in bronze vessel surface decoration from the fifth and even sixth centuries B.C. See Thomas Lawton, *Chinese Art of the Warring States Period*, no. 37, p. 80. On page 89 of the same catalogue, Lawton discusses the role King Wuling played in the development of the costume and of the belt hook. The change in costume is discussed in Zhou Xun and Gao Chunming, *5000 Years of Chinese Costumes*, p. 13.

42. Burton Watson, trans., *Records of the Grand Historian of China*, vol. 2, p. 159.

43. For a discussion of King Wuling of Zhao's association with the state of Yan see Li Xueqin, *Eastern Zhou and Qin Civilizations*, p. 100.

44. Ibid., pp. 121–22.

45. Thomas Lawton, *Chinese Art of the Warring States Period*. For other examples of this style of dress depicted on Warring States bronzes see Wen Fong, ed., *The Great Bronze Age of China*, cat. no. 91, p. 292, lower register, and p. 317, fig. 107.

46. Zhou Xun and Gao Chunming, *5000 Years of Chinese Costumes*, p. 13.

47. *Gems of China's Cultural Relics 1992*, pl. 111.

48. See catalogue numbers 6 and 15 for references to archaeologically excavated materials.

49. For an example of a Chu hook see Thomas Lawton, *Chinese Art of the Warring States Period*, p. 91, and *Xi Han Nanyue wangmu* (Nanyue king's tomb of the Western Han), vols. 1 and 2, with English abstract.

50. Wang Renxiang, "A general survey of Chinese belt hooks," pp. 267–312.

51. Ibid., pp. 267–312.

52. Thomas Lawton, *Chinese Art of the Warring States Period*, p. 91. Lawton draws from a 1954 exhibition of art from the Chu state.

53. Burton Watson, trans., *Records of the Grand Historian*, vol. 2, p. 160.

54. William Charles White, *Tombs of Old Loyang*, pls. 55:134d and 59:145 a.d.

55. *Nanyue king's tomb of the Western Han*, vol. 2, pl. 96:3. For Shanxi find see *Wenwu* 1987.6, p. 6, fig. 17:12.

56. Thomas Lawton, *Chinese Art of the Warring States Period*, pp. 101–03.

57. *Wenwu*, 1958.1, figs. 16–17.

58. *Changsha Mawangdui yihao Han mu*.

59. There are very few examples of metal hair ornaments from the Shang or Zhou periods. A bronze comb from Shaanxi was published in Zhou Xun and Gao Chunming, *Zhongguo lidai funu jiangshi*, p. 80, no. 3.

60. Li Xueqin, *Eastern Zhou and Qin Civilizations*, p. 333.

61. This inscription is in Six States script, referring to the powerful states of the Eastern Zhou period.

62. Shi Yongshi, "Yanguo de hengzhi," in *Zhongguo kaogu xuehui dierci nianhui lunwenji*, pp. 172–75. For black-and-white photos see Li Xueqin, *Eastern Zhou and Qin Civilizations*, p. 335.

63. Li Xueqin, *Eastern Zhou and Qin Civilizations*, pp. 333–36. See also Emma C. Bunker, "Ancient Ordos Bronzes," in Jessica Rawson and Emma C. Bunker, *Ancient Chinese and Ordos Bronzes*, p. 300.

64. For a detailed account of the chronology of the northern tribal people and their material goods, especially metal work, see Emma C. Bunker, "Ancient Ordos Bronzes," pp. 291–307.

65. Emma C. Bunker, "Significant changes in iconography and technology among ancient China's northwestern pastoral neighbors from the fourth to the first century B.C.," *Bulletin of the Asia Institute* 6 (1992), p. 108.

66. Diane M. O'Donoghue, "Reflection and Reception," pp. 28–29.

67. Ibid., p. 50. O'Donoghue discusses both molds and models, but does not give examples of models.

68. *Wenwu cankao ziliao*, 1957.1, p. 53.

69. The King of Han discusses the Xiongnu raids on the graves of Qin in the *Shiji*, vol. 1, p. 103. Caring for the grave of Qin Shihuangdi is discussed on p. 115.

70. Li Xueqin, *Eastern Zhou and Qin Civilizations*, p. 254.

71. Maxwell K. Hearn, "The Terracotta Army of the First Emperor of Qin (221–206 B.C.)," in Wen Fong, ed., *The Great Bronze Age of China*, pp. 353–73.

72. Ibid., p. 369, no. 98, fig. 126; this sculpture was found in trench 5, pit no. 2.

73. Michele Pirazzoli-t'Serstevens, *The Han Dynasty*, p. 143.

74. Wang Zhongshu, *Han Civilization*, p. 29.

75. Michael Loewe, *Ways to Paradise: The Chinese Quest for Immortality*, p. 16.

76. For a reference to Mawangdui tomb findings see Wang Zhongshu, *Han Civilization*, pp. 175–213.

77. Diane M. O'Donoghue, "Reflection and Reception," chaps. 5 and 6.

78. Wang Zhongshu, *Han Civilization*, pp. 206–13.

79. *Nanyue king's tomb of the Western Han*, vols. 1 and 2.

80. Ibid., vol. 2, pl. 18, no. 1.

81. Ibid., vol. 1, p. 4, English abstract.

82. Jessica Rawson noted that "[o]ver the period covered by the construction of the three tombs [Marquis Yi of Zeng, King Cuo of Zhongshan, and Liu Sheng of the Western Han], the quality of the ritual vessels and bells declined relentlessly, while other items in bronze became ever more prominent." See *Ancient Chinese and Ordos Bronzes*, p. 54.

83. Wen Fong, ed., *The Great Bronze Age of China*, p. 285, fig. 75, for the *fang jian*; p. 299, fig. 96 for the *hu*.

84. Michele Pirazzoli-t'Serstevens, *The Han Dynasty*, p. 127.

85. *Gems of China's Cultural Relics 1993*, pl. 113, p. 311.

86. *Wenwu*, 1994.1, pp. 50–64.

87. *Gems of China's Cultural Relics 1993*, pl. 114, p. 311.

88. Michele Pirazzoli-t'Serstevens dates the belt buckle from the first century B.C. or first half of the first century A.D., although that seems too early for this type of work. See *The Han Dynasty*, p. 123. This belt buckle was probably made in Han China and exported to Korea or else was made by an itinerant Chinese goldsmith. See Sun Ji, "Xian Qin Han Jin yaodai yong jinyin daigou" (The gold and silver belt buckles of the pre-Qin period, the Han dynasty and Jin dynasty), *Wenwu*, 1994.1, pp. 50–64, in Chinese.

89. Zhou Xun and Gao Chunming, *5000 Years of Chinese Costumes*, illus. no. 52, p. 36.

90. Ibid., p. 32.

91. Yoshito Harada, *Chinese Dress and Personal Ornaments in the Han and Six Dynasties*, p. 30.

92. An excellent resource for daily dress during the Han period is Lucy Lim, ed., *Stories from China's Past: Han Dynasty Pictorial Tomb Reliefs and Archaeological Objects from Sichuan Province, People's Republic of China*.

93. For an example of a seated female pottery figure with headdress see ibid., p. 138, pl. 45. Also, tiles depicting dancers and entertainers show a variety of headdresses.

94. Burton Watson, trans., *The Columbia Book of Chinese Poetry*, pp. 116–21.

95. Yoshito Harada, *Chinese Dress and Personal Ornaments*, pl. 23, and line drawing, fig. 28, p. 91.

96. Ibid., p. 25. See also Zhou Xun and Gao Chunming, *Zhongguo lidai funu jiangshi*, p. 57, illus. p. 67, no. 82, and p. 68, nos. 83 and 84, for Five Dynasties examples of *buyao*, same authors, *5000 Years of Chinese Costumes*, p. 32.

97. Yoshito Harada, *Chinese Dress and Personal Ornaments*, p. 25.

98. Zhou Xun and Gao Chunming, *5000 Years of Chinese Costumes*, p. 46, fig. 70.

99. Southern vs. northern attitudes toward displays of wealth are discussed in Lucy Lim, ed., *Stories from China's Past*, pp. 59–60. See also Michele Pirazzoli-t'Serstevens, *The Han Dynasty*, pp. 166–93, where tombs and moral issues are discussed.

100. W. Thomas Chase makes reference to this edict and states, "The belt hook was not included in this [the codification of ritual clothing], being in effect excommunicated from the repertoire of the Chinese court." See *Chinese Belt-Hooks in the Freer Gallery of Art*, p. 159.

101. *Wenwu*, 1983.4, p. 305, fig. 7, no. 6, from a tomb in Jilin. It is likely that this northern culture was influenced by tribes to the west. See also Sun Ji, "The gold and silver belt buckles of the pre-Qin period, the Han dynasty and Jin dynasty," *Wenwu*, 1994.1, pp. 50–64, in Chinese.

102. Korean examples from the 5th to 7th century have been published by Roger Goepper and Roderick Whitfield, *Treasures from Korea*.

103. Jessica Rawson, *Chinese Ornament, the Lotus and the Dragon*, pp. 110–14.

104. For reference to these belt sets see entry number 51 in this catalogue.

105. For reference to contact with Turkic-speaking tribes see entry number 54 in this catalogue.

106. This practice was temporarily revoked during the reign of Xuanzong. See Zhao Xun and Gao Chunming, *5000 Years of Chinese Costumes*, p. 93.

107. *Exhibition of Cultural Relics from the Tomb of Princess Chenguo of the State of Liao*, n.p.

108. *Art Treasures of Dunhuang*, fig. 19.

109. Ibid., fig. 58.

110. Ibid., fig. 63.

111. Ibid., fig. 81.

112. Ibid., fig. 105.

113. For Tang finds at Lantian, Shaanxi, see *Kaogu yu wenwu*, 1982.1.

114. *Exhibition of Cultural Relics from the Tomb of Princess Chenguo of the State of Liao*, n.p.

115. *Art Treasures of Dunhuang*, figs. 58, 63, 78, 79, and 83, all of which are Bodhisattva images. Necklaces of beads and stones as jewelry were known since Neolithic times, but metal necklaces seem to have appeared in the Tang, a result of western influence.

116. Ibid., fig. 56.

117. Jessica Rawson, *Chinese Ornament*, p. 77.

118. *The Arts of the T'ang Dynasty*, no. 306, p. 112.

119. C. A. S. Williams, *Outlines of Chinese Symbolism and Art Motives*, 3rd rev. ed., p. 424.

120. Jessica Rawson, *Chinese Ornament*, pp. 114–17.

121. Ibid., p. 116.

122. Patricia Buckley Ebrey and Peter N. Gregory, eds., *Religion and Society in T'ang and Sung China*, p. ix.

123. Ibid., p. 13.

124. Burton Watson, trans., *The Columbia Book of Chinese Poetry*, p. 222.

125. Patricia Buckley Ebrey and Peter N. Gregory, eds., *Religion and Society in T'ang and Sung China*, p. 13.

126. Zhang Anzhi, *A History of Chinese Painting*, p. 76, fig. 38, detail.

127. The painting is in the collection of the British Museum and is thought to be a Tang copy of an earlier work. For an illustration of this section of the hand scroll see Zhou Xun and Gao Chunming, *5000 Years of Chinese Costumes*, p. 67, fig. 109.

128. Burton Watson, trans., *The Columbia Book of Chinese Poetry*, p. 245.

129. Jessica Rawson, "Changing Values of Ancient Chinese Bronzes," in Jessica Rawson and Emma C. Bunker, *Ancient Chinese and Ordos Bronzes*, p. 55.

130. Diane M. O'Donoghue offers some theories regarding the meaning of early mirrors. See "Reflection and Reception." See also Michael Loewe, *Ways to Paradise*, and Anneliese Gutkind Bulling, *The Decoration of Mirrors of the Han Period*.

131. Sun Ji, "Xiapei zhuizi," *Wenwu tiandi*, 1994.1, pp. 22–24.

132. Jessica Rawson, *Chinese Ornament*, pp. 99–107.

133. *Wenwu*, 1984.5, p. 83, pl. 5, figs. 2, 5, and 6.

134. *Wenwu*, 1977.7, p. 10, no. 29.

135. Jessica Rawson, *Chinese Ornament*, p. 142–43.

136. Edward Schafer, *The Golden Peaches of Samarkand: A Study of T'ang Exotics*, p. 155.

137. Ibid., p. 162.

138. Ibid., p. 162.

139. Sun Ji, "Xiapei zhuizi," pp. 22–24.

140. For a Liao dynasty example see *Wenwu*, 1992.7, p. 11, nos. 19 and 20. For a Southern Song example without chain see *Wenwu*, 1977.7, pl. 3, no. 4.

141. Zhou Xun and Gao Chunming, *5000 Years of Chinese Costumes*, pp. 146–47.

142. Ibid., p. 146.

Emma C. Bunker

The Metallurgy of Personal Adornment

Introduction

Personal adornment fulfilled early man's need for a material symbol that would protect and enhance his body in this world and the next. The earliest personal ornaments in ancient China were made from natural materials such as shells, animal teeth, and claws. Little artistic attention was needed to transform these materials into auspicious objects with magical properties.[1]

After the appearance of metalworking in most ancient cultures, metal ornaments made to man's requirements began to replace natural, found objects as the chief symbols of personal prestige and protection. The graves of the elites in Bronze Age Europe and northwest Asia abound with earrings, bracelets, torques, finger rings, and hairpins made of gold, silver, or bronze, depending upon the status of the owner.[2]

In ancient China, however, this was not always the case. Metal did not immediately become the most prestigious material for personal adornment. Instead, long before the beginnings of metalworking in China, polished jade was the favorite material for the manufacture of personal ornaments.[3] Excavations at Neolithic sites such as Liangzhu have revealed that the bodies of the more fortunate were literally "shrouded in jade."[4] The quality of the jade indicated status and rank.[5]

In the Central Plains, jade continued to be the primary material for making personal ornaments throughout the Bronze Age. China's innate reverence for the past, and its historical continuity—unbroken by serious foreign intrusions until well into the first millennium A.D.—ensured that certain cultural traditions which had been formulated by the end of the Neolithic period would persist.

By contrast, among China's neighboring pastoral tribes metal was the material of preference to indicate status and rank during the Bronze Age. These non-Chinese tribes inhabited a large arc of land that extended west from Liaoning to the Ordos Desert and then south into Ningxia and Gansu. Earrings, finger rings, and hairpins made of gold, bronze, and copper began to appear in these peripheral areas early in the second millennium B.C. (cat. no. 1).[6]

Metal did not become a significant material for the creation of personal adornment in the Central Plains until the Eastern Zhou period. From that time on, it became increasingly important for this purpose, although it never completely replaced jade. A prescribed hierarchy of metals reinforced the decoration of personal ornaments to indicate the status and rank of the owner.

The purpose of this essay is to investigate the important role played by personal adornment in the history of Chinese metallurgy, a subject that has received too little scholarly attention in the past. Where, when, and why did the ancient Chinese replace stone with metal for the manufacture of personal adornment? Which metals did they choose, and where did the materials come from? Which metalworking techniques were employed, and were there regional distinctions? In other words, what do we know about the metallurgy of Chinese personal adornment?

This study will reflect primarily the metallurgy employed in the making of artifacts for the social elite, since less fortunate Chinese seldom possessed luxury items for personal adornment. It must be remembered that we are dealing here with one specific category of objects within a vast and complex cultural area. The discussion that follows is based primarily on a microscopic examination of the artifacts in the Mengdiexuan collection, the results of controlled archaeology in China, and archaeometallurgical studies both in China and abroad.[7] I was very fortunate to have the advice of Richard Kimball, a practicing goldsmith, throughout my metallurgical research for this project.

The term *Bronze Age* will be used to indicate the time period from the end of the third millennium B.C. to the early Eastern Zhou, from about the twentieth to the eighth century B.C., in place of the traditional dynastic designations which, in the light of recent archaeology, are now considered more regional than national. When possible, more specific regional reference will be supplied. *Central Plains* will be used only to refer to the region centered around the middle and lower courses of the Yellow River. The culture of the Central Plains did not always reflect the regional cultures of north and south China.

Metals, Alloys, and Other Materials

Today, the metals and gemstones used for personal adornment are chosen for subjective reasons and judged in terms of their monetary value and their appearance. In the distant past, however, metals and gemstones were imbued with symbolic meanings and valued for their amuletic properties. Early man's choice of which metal to enhance his costume or wear next to his skin was not made arbitrarily.

Archaeology has indicated that various hierarchies of metals governed the manufacture of personal adornment in China at different times during its long history. These hierarchies reflected the customs, beliefs, and metallurgy of the environment in which they were created, and frequently exhibited distinct regional traits.

One of the earliest literary references to a hierarchical system of metals occurs in the *Hou Han shu,* a history compiled in the third century A.D.: "The [jade burial] suits of the Son of Heaven are described as made with gold thread, those for kings, marquises, honorable ladies and princesses are to be made with silver thread, while those of elder honorable ladies and senior princesses are made with bronze thread."[8]

Throughout Chinese history, personal adornment was a prescribed expression of status and wealth associated with the different ranks held by the aristocracy and their officials. Under the Tang dynasty, imperial regulations governed the metal, the number of belt plaques, and the decoration of personal ornaments. A seventh-century edict "conferred girdles of gold and jade on civil and military officials above the third grades, gold girdles on those of the fourth and fifth grades, silver girdles on those of the sixth and seventh grades, brass girdles on those of the eighth and ninth grades, and assigned copper and iron girdles to the people at large."[9]

By the end of the Han period, precious metals had become a mark of beauty for women. The Han poet Cao Zhi (A.D. 192–232) describes the legendary goddess of the Luo River as wearing hairpins of gold set with kingfisher feathers.[10]

The fact that metal jewelry was not produced during the Bronze Age in nuclear China was a cultural decision, not a deficiency. Notwithstanding their innate proclivity for jade, the Chinese possessed all the necessary resources to create ornaments from the same metals and alloys that were used in many other parts of the ancient world.

The major metals and alloys used by the Chinese were copper, gold, tin, lead, bronze, iron, silver, mercury, and electrum. These will be discussed briefly in the order of their early importance in the manufacture of personal ornaments. The availability and technical advantages of each metal will be considered when known, since these features were frequently the determining factors in their choice. Secondary materials such as jade, turquoise, malachite, agate, carnelian, lapis lazuli, pearl, and glass will also be discussed in view of their use as inlays on several of the ornaments in the Mengdiexuan collection. The English names of materials are followed by their Chinese names in parentheses.

Copper (tong)

Copper is a soft, reddish metal and probably the first metal worked in the ancient Chinese world. Early copper was available as native metal, but mining was practiced in northern Jiangxi province at Ruichang as early as the fourteenth century B.C.[11] The primary locations of copper ore deposits in ancient China were in the northeast, the Central Plains, and the south, with smaller deposits occurring in Xinjiang.[12] In more recent times, the richest copper-producing areas recorded are in Yunnan and Hubei.[13]

Pure copper is difficult to cast and tarnishes quickly. It was rarely used for making personal ornaments after the appearance of gold and the discovery of bronze. Its importance lay rather in its use as the major metallic component of bronze, an alloy consisting of copper and tin. Chinese bronzes usually also contain lead.

Recent archaeology has revealed evidence of a few personal ornaments made of copper among the pastoral peoples inhabiting north China during the late Neolithic period.[14] A crudely made copper-and-stone earring was excavated from a man's burial at the famous Hongshan Neolithic site of Niuheliang, Lingyuan, Liaoning province.[15] Copper penannular-shaped earrings with one flaring terminate have been found at early Bronze Age sites in Liaoning and Hebei,[16] and a copper finger ring was discovered at Zhukaigou, in Yijinhuoluo, in the Ordos Desert of northwest China.[17] Surprisingly, no early copper ornaments have yet been recorded from southern China, where the greatest concentrations of copper ores were found.

Gold (jin)

In spite of many scholarly statements to the contrary, gold was not rare in ancient China.[18] A search for early literary references to gold is hampered by the fact that the character *jin,* which means gold today, is the "metal" radical, and referred to copper in ancient literature.[19] In the *Erya,* a third-century B.C. dictionary, gold is described specifically as *huangjin,* yellow metal.[20]

Gold is a brilliant yellow and is found in a metallic state in vein (*maijinguang*) and placer (*shajinguang*) deposits throughout the Chinese world.[21] Gold was readily available in ancient China. Eastern Zhou texts list numerous sources throughout China.[22] The major source of gold in antiquity appears to have been alluvial gold, which comes from placer deposits that have been washed down the mountains and deposited in streams, where they are easily collected. There is little physical evidence for gold mining before the Tang period, but a statement in the *Yantielun,* Discourses on salt and iron, that "they bore into the rocks to get gold and silver" certainly suggests that some form of gold mining was practiced as early as the Western Han period, when this text was written.[23]

By the tenth century A.D. China had become a major producer of gold. The Mongols who ruled China during the Yuan dynasty (1279–1368) were great gold consumers. One of their largest mines was located in Shandong. They also encouraged gold mining in the newly acquired territories of Yunnan province which, by the Ming period, had become the primary source of placer gold in China.[24]

Gold is easily workable and always naturally alloyed with silver. An increase in the amount of silver will tend to whiten the alloy (cat. no. 96), while the addition of copper will redden it (cat. no. 107). For example, note the varied tints of gold on two Song ornaments in the Mengdiexuan collection (cat. nos. 87 and 90).

Gold appears to have been one of the earliest metals worked by the pastoral tribes in the northwest areas peripheral to the Central Plains. Qijia-culture burials dating to the early second millennium B.C. at Huoshaogou, near Yumen in northwest Gansu province, have yielded gold as well as bronze earrings.[25] The Huoshaogou earrings are penannular in shape with a single flaring terminate, similar to Bronze Age copper and bronze examples found in Liaoning and Hebei and in the Ordos Desert.[26]

Hammered-gold hair ornaments and earrings similar to a pair in the Mengdiexuan collection (cat. no. 1) were found at a Bronze Age site on the periphery of Shang China at Shilou, in Shanxi province.[27] A gold hairpin, gold earrings, and a gold bracelet were found at another Bronze Age site in Liujiahe, Pinggu, Beijing district, Hebei province, that was contemporary with the late Shang period at Anyang.[28] The people buried at these northern peripheral sites were not Shang, but their grave goods indicate that they were probably economically involved with the Shang. The Liujiahe earring is a more sophisticated version of the Huoshaogou gold earrings, penannular in shape with a single trumpet-shaped terminate. This type of earring is a diagnostic artifact universally associated with Andronovo sites in Siberia and the foothills of the Urals.[29] The presence of such items close to nuclear China provides evidence for early long-range contact with tribal groups farther west in Central Asia and beyond.

Gold was also used in the Central Plains during the Bronze Age, but not for personal adornment. Instead, it was used decoratively to enhance bronze items, such as the harness buttons covered with gold foil found at Anyang, a late Shang site in Henan province.[30]

A serious interest in gold for personal ornaments did not occur in the Central Plains until the early Eastern Zhou period. Among the earliest known examples are the gold belt plaques recovered from an early Eastern Zhou–period royal grave in the Guo state cemetery at Shangcunling, outside Sanmenxia, in Henan province.[31] Numerous small gold garment hooks similar to three Mengdiexuan examples (cat. nos. 2, 3, and 4) are frequently found in Eastern Zhou–period burials associated with the Qin state in Shaanxi province.[32] The use of gold for personal adornment also penetrated the south during the Warring States period. Several gold garment hooks were found among the grave goods in the fifth-century B.C. tomb of the Marquis Yi of Zeng in Suixian, Hubei province.[33] Gold was also used to embellish the surfaces of many cast-bronze garment hooks with an overlay of gold, an inlay of gold, or mercury-amalgam gilding (cat. nos. 17, 20, 29, and 37).

A proliferation of gold artifacts occurs among the grave goods associated with the nomadic herding tribes living along China's northern borders in the Ordos region of western Inner Mongolia during the Eastern Zhou period.[34] Several items in the Mengdiexuan collection illustrate the nomads' love of gold and gilded surfaces (cat. nos. 16 and 32). Personal ornaments among these herding peoples were not just for display. The designs on their belt plaques gave visual form to the supernatural world that governed their lives, and the metal from which these were cast—whether gold, silver, or bronze (often tinned or gilded)—indicated the owner's individual rank and status. Gold earrings were exceedingly ornate, with dangling elements that relate them to styles found farther west in Central Asia (cat. no. 16). Toward the end of the Eastern Zhou period, much of the nomads' gold and gilded finery appears to have been made in China, such as the gilded silver roundel in the Mengdiexuan collection that carries an inscription in Chinese characters on its reverse side (cat. no. 22).

Gold became extremely valuable during the late Eastern Zhou period, after the Chu adopted it for coinage. The *Hanfeizi* records the pronouncement of a death penalty for the illegal extraction of gold from sand beds controlled by the state of Chu.[35]

By the Han period, gold had joined jade as a symbol of immortality, inspired by the Daoist search for longevity and the "elixir of life." This emphasis on immortality manifested itself in great scientific advances in alchemy, which had inspired the development of mercury-amalgam gilding during the late Eastern Zhou period.[36]

During the first and second millennia A.D., gold became increasingly popular for personal ornaments in China due to the infiltration of non-Chinese peoples who revered gold, and the arrival of Buddhism, with its gold and gilded statues and ritual paraphernalia.[37] By the Tang period, gold had become a major choice for personal ornaments, a preference that continued in the Song and Ming and was exploited during the rule of the foreign Liao, Jin, Yuan, and Qing dynasties.

Tin (xi)

Tin is a shiny white metal that is found in abundance in south China today.[38] In ancient times many tin sources, now depleted, are said to have existed within a 300-kilometer radius of the metalworking centers of the Shang in Henan province, but these have not yet been satisfactorily confirmed by archaeology.[39]

Tin added to copper forms bronze, the most important copper alloy in ancient China. Tin ingots were found along with lumps of copper at the Shang foundry site of Anyang.[40] The fact that tin ingots and not tin ore were found at Anyang suggests that the tin was imported in a refined form from some distance and not mined locally.[41]

Tin was one of the "three auspicious metals" which, along with copper and lead, combined to form the special alloy used to cast early mirrors.[42] Tin was also used to produce shiny white-colored surfaces on certain early bronze artifacts.[43] Deliberately tinned surfaces have been identified on numerous Eastern Zhou–period belt hooks associated with the Qin state located in Shaanxi province (cat. no. 8) and on belt plaques worn by the nomadic pastoral tribes inhabiting ancient China's northwestern frontiers (cat. no. 21). The decorated surfaces of two early Warring States–period bronze mirrors (cat. nos. 9 and 11) and a Tang-period bronze comb (cat. no. 68) appear also to have been deliberately tinned.[44]

Lead (qian)

Lead is a heavy, soft, gray metal with a brilliant luster which dulls rapidly on exposure to air and moisture. Lead appears to have been plentiful in ancient China, but was almost never used for making personal ornaments.[45]

The importance of lead was as an additive to early bronze. Bronze vessels cast by the Shang and Western Zhou tend to have much smaller amounts of lead than those cast during the Eastern Zhou period.[46]

Lead is an extremely ductile and malleable metal. When added to bronze it lowers the melting point and increases fluidity during the casting process. The increased fluidity makes casting easier and enables the craftsman to achieve sharper details in the finished product.

Lead mixed with tin makes soft solder, an alloy used for joining non-precious metals. Lead is also one of the "three auspicious metals" recorded in Han inscriptions as a component of the alloy used to produce mirrors.[47]

Iron (tie)

Iron is a shiny, white, ductile metal which is very malleable and takes a high polish. Iron was first known in meteoric form as early as the Shang period and was probably viewed with some awe due to its supposedly celestial origins.[48] Meteoric iron was worked by forging, not by casting in a foundry.[49] Iron was readily available in ancient China, but serious iron mining, smelting, and casting did not develop until the Eastern Zhou period.[50] The *Zuozhuan* notes the casting of iron cauldrons in 513 B.C.[51]

One of the contributions to personal ornament made by iron was the manufacture of iron tools which allowed craftsmen to engrave other metals. The inlay channels on some Western Han belt hooks appear to have been carved manually rather than cast (cat. nos. 27, 29, and 30).

Iron was used to cast belt hooks during the latter half of the Eastern Zhou period (cat. no. 20). It was probably a novelty, cheaper than bronze, with a shiny white appearance when polished. Numerous cast-iron belt hooks, some plain and some overlaid and inlaid with precious metals and jade, have been excavated at sites in Henan, Hubei, Shanxi, and Shaanxi provinces.[52] Iron bracelets dating to the sixth to fifth century B.C. have been excavated at sites on the Pamir plateau in Xinjiang, but the owners were local pastoral groups, not Chinese.[53]

During the Han period, cast iron was also used to make mirrors. Excavations at Shaogou, near Luoyang in Henan, yielded eight badly corroded iron mirrors.[54]

Silver (yin)

Silver is a brilliant white metal which is malleable and extremely ductile. Like gold, silver is very soft and usually alloyed with other metals to increase its durability. The addition of other metals can vary the color of silver.

Silver does not occur in alluvial placer deposits and is not as easy to obtain as gold. It does occur in veins that can be mined in mountainous regions, but only in very small amounts in China.[55] Silver is more commonly obtained by extraction from other silver-bearing ores through the cupellation process.[56] Ancient literature indicates silver sources in northwest and southwest China, but the metal was never plentiful and was frequently imported.[57]

Silver did not play an important role in ancient Chinese metallurgy before the late Western Han period. The earliest literary reference to silver occurs in the *Erya*, a third-century B.C. dictionary, where it is described as *baijin*, white metal, in contrast to gold, which is referred to as *huangjin*, yellow metal.

The earliest known silver artifact in the Chinese world is a nose ring discovered at Huoshaogou, a Qijia-culture site in Gansu province dated to the early Bronze Age.[58] Silver seems to have been conspicuously lacking at other Bronze Age sites and does not appear to have been considered desirable in Bronze Age China.

Silver was not used in nuclear China until the middle of the Eastern Zhou period. Strand silver was not used to inlay an inscription on a bronze sword made for King Gou Jian (reigned 496–465 B.C.), as reported when it was first excavated from a Chu tomb in Wangshan, Jiangling, Hubei province.[59] By the mid–Warring States period the ductility of silver had made it popular for inlaying bronze vessels, chariot fittings, and belt hooks (cat. nos. 27, 29, and 30). The choice of silver appears to have been based partly on its shiny white color, which provided a striking contrast with the yellowish red of bronze and gold. Occasionally, belt hooks themselves were made of silver.[60]

The earliest date for silver coinage is not clear. Hollow-headed silver *bu* coins have been excavated at Guchengcun, Fugou county, in Henan province, but whether or not they were real coins and where they were minted have not yet been determined.[61]

Silver ornaments did not occur among the pastoral tribes who inhabited western Inner Mongolia until the fourth to the third century B.C.[62] Most interesting are several silver bridle ornaments found at Xigoupan, Jungar banner.[63] These carry inscriptions in Chinese characters on their reverse sides referring to the weight of the silver, suggesting that such pieces were made at some late Eastern Zhou metalworking center expressly for a Sino-nomadic joint venture, such as trading Chinese luxury goods for nomadic horses and furs. A gilded-silver roundel in the Mengdiexuan collection fits into this category (cat. no. 22).

Unlike gold, silver was not associated with the "elixir of life." Daoist adepts did not search for it or ingest it in hopes of achieving immortality. It is interesting to note that silver appears also to have been rather rare in ancient Korea and Japan in comparison to gold.

Silver did not really become a desirable metal for personal adornment until the Six Dynasties, Tang, and Song periods, after China was exposed to foreign contact through the medium of the trans-Asian Silk Route. Even then, beautifully fashioned silver hair ornaments were frequently highlighted with gilding (cat. nos. 61, 63, 64, and 65).

Silver ornaments made for the Tang court often reflected styles practiced as far away as the Sasanian and Byzantine worlds of northwest Asia. Metalsmithing replaced casting for most of the silverwork, and chasing replaced inlay for surface decoration other than gilding (cat. nos. 63, 66, and 67). Tang bronze mirrors were occasionally overlaid with a decorated silver or gold sheet that had been worked in repoussé with chased details; this was an added embellishment which had nothing to do with optics (cat. no. 55).

During the late Six Dynasties period, silver was mined in the vicinity of Changan, present-day Xi'an, in Shaanxi province.[64] By the Tang period, mines were operating in Fujian and Zhejiang provinces,[65] but Lingnan and Annam to the south of China had also become important sources.[66] The first serious literary descriptions of cupellation date to the Tang and Song periods.[67]

In spite of literary references to silver sources, there is sufficient evidence to suggest that silver was imported into China more often than has been acknowledged. During the reign of the Yongle emperor (1403–24), the silver supply was augmented by imports from the silver-lead mines at Bawdin in Burma.[68] In the late Ming period, the financial burden of supporting troops to quell the menacing tribes on the northern borders and the pirates along China's southern coasts resulted in massive shipments of silver from Japan and the New World brought in by Portuguese traders.[69] Whether any of this imported bullion was used for personal finery is unclear.

Bronze (qingtong)

Bronze is a synthetic alloy of copper and tin with good casting properties. The alloy frequently contains small amounts of other metals, such as lead. Its color ranges from a reddish yellow to a more golden yellow or white, depending upon the proportions of the metals in the alloy.

Ancient Chinese bronze is generally a leaded tin bronze, yellow in color.[70] The addition of lead lowers the melting point of the alloy and makes casting easier, allowing for sharper details in finished products like the magnificently cast bronze vessels of the Shang.

Bronze was used for small personal ornaments in the peripheral areas of northern and western China but never in the Central Plains or the south during the Bronze Age.[71] Cast-bronze penannular-shaped earrings were found in Bronze Age sites at both Huoshaogou, in Yumen, Gansu province, and at Zhukaigou, Yijinhuolou, in the Ordos Desert.[72] In the Central Plains, bronze was reserved for the manufacture of ritual vessels and weapons used to support the political legitimacy of the local aristocracy during the Shang and Western Zhou periods. It was seldom used for personal adornment until the Eastern Zhou period.

During the Eastern Zhou, the lavish secular tastes that developed among fiercely competitive regional states, and their contact through trade and marriage with their northern nomadic neighbors, resulted in the production of sumptuous metal personal ornaments not seen earlier in the Central Plains. Bronze belt hooks, both plain and embellished with precious metals and gemstones, abound among the grave goods from this period.

Among the 113 bronze belt hooks in the Freer Gallery of Art in Washington, D.C., thirty-five have a copper content of above 95 percent and eighteen have a copper content above 97 percent. In both cases, the bronze is rather reddish in color where the patina has worn off.[73] Copper hardens in relation to an increase in the amount of tin added to the alloy.[74] Bronze was the major metal used for casting belt ornaments throughout Chinese history, but it is often unrecognizable because of the many ingenious surface enrichments developed by Chinese craftsmen by the end of the first millennium B.C. and used to this day.

Mercury (gong)

Mercury, popularly known as quicksilver, is a shiny white metal which is liquid at room temperatures. Mercury is most commonly obtained by sublimation from the ore known as cinnabar. Ancient texts have recorded sources of mercury in Shanxi, Sichuan, and Gansu, and in the Hubei-Jiangxi area.[75]

The importance of mercury in the manufacture of personal ornaments lay in its ability to dissolve other metals such as gold, silver, and tin, and to unite with them to form alloys known as amalgams. These intermetallic amalgams were occasionally used during the fourth century B.C. to inlay bronze. By the third century B.C. mercury-amalgam gilding and silvering were employed to transform the surfaces of bronze and silver artifacts.[76]

The fascination with mercury in the production of man-made gold was due to a preoccupation with aurifiction and aurifaction that began during the last few centuries of the Eastern Zhou period with the rise of Chinese alchemy.[77] The founder of Chinese alchemy may have been Zou Yan, a Daoist contemporary of Mencius (fourth century B.C.), but, as many scholars have pointed out, the search for an elixir of eternal life derives ultimately from an ancient universal primitive ideology, which was later adopted by the Daoists.[78] The Daoist goal was perfection, which for man was longevity and for metals was gold. One of the major Western Han texts concerning the transformation of metals is the *Huainanzi,* written during the second century B.C.[79]

Electrum (huangyin *or* jinyinshi)

Electrum is a naturally occurring alloy of gold and silver that contains 20 percent or more silver and ranges in color between shiny white and yellow. Electrum can also be produced synthetically. Microscopic examination of several ornaments in the Mengdiexuan collection suggests that craftsmen understood electrum and used varying shades of gold and silver to enhance the appearance of their products (cat. no. 87).

Electrum seems not to have been an important alloy during the Eastern Zhou, Qin, and Han periods. Silver itself received little notice before the later Eastern Zhou period, and never enjoyed the popularity of gold. The first use of electrum in China may have been accidental, associated with the manipulation of a range of gold colors for decorative purposes.

Though electrum is seldom mentioned in Chinese literature or in connection with the manufacture of Chinese artifacts, the alloy appears to have been understood by the Tang period. Ninth-century A.D. records mention an electrum mine in northern Shandong province that had been in operation since the late sixth century A.D. under the Sui.[80] Whether electrum was used as a source of gold and silver or used in the natural alloy state to produce artifacts is not indicated.

Craftsmen could have used a man-made electrum alloy to their advantage in making jewelry. The addition of silver to gold increases its durability and decreases its price, while maintaining the desirable yellow tint of gold without the danger of tarnishing associated with silver.

Gemstones, Pearls, and Glass

Small gemstones, glass, and other colored materials were frequently inlaid in bronze, gold, or silver to enliven the surfaces of personal ornaments during the late Eastern Zhou, Qin, and Han periods. Examples in the Mengdiexuan collection are the belt hooks of catalogue numbers 23, 24, 26, and 38. Stone cutting for the fashioning of amulets and other ritual paraphernalia had already been mastered during the Neolithic period.

Jade, *yu,* was the supreme symbol of excellence in ancient China and, in many ways, remains so today. Its early importance and superior qualities are well known, and only a few points need be made here.

Jade is a hard stone which is difficult to work. It must be abraded, rather than carved, and then carefully polished to achieve a smooth lustrous surface. Sources of jade inside early China have recently been identified in the Lake Tai district around Shanghai and the northeast provinces from Liaoning to Shandong, but it was also imported in large quantities at various times from outside China.[81] Jade was used to inlay only the rarest artifacts, such as the gold Mengdiexuan comb (cat. no. 48).

There is strong literary evidence that jade was obtained from farther west during the Tang period. In A.D. 632, during the reign of Taizong (627–649), it is recorded that the king of Khotan offered a jade girdle as tribute. The fascination with exotica that characterized the Tang court may have resulted in the imitation of such belts.[82] The presence of a belt designed in Khotan may explain the design similarities that exist between belts belonging to the Turkic-speaking peoples of Central Asia and belts manufactured in China during the late Tang, Liao, Song, and Ming periods, which consist of an ordered rotation of rectangular, square, semilunar, and pear-shaped plaques (cat. nos. 53, 79, 111, and 113).[83]

Turquoise, *lüsongshi,* was probably the earliest and most frequently used gemstone in ancient China apart from jade. Turquoise is a hard stone which takes a good polish and has a glorious color that ranges from pale blue to a bluish green.

Turquoise was used to make pendants in ancient China as early as the Neolithic period, and it is found at Hongshan-culture sites in northeast China.[84] Its use for inlay can be traced back to the turquoise-inlaid bone items found in the Dawenkou-culture burials of the third millennium B.C. and the inlaid bronze artifacts from Erlitou. During the Shang period, turquoise was inlaid into the surfaces of a variety of bronze artifacts, but there is little evidence for its use during the Western Zhou period.

Turquoise became extremely popular during the Eastern Zhou period for decorating garment hooks and other luxury items. It was inlaid in the form of cut stone as well as paste (cat. nos. 23 and 26). Whether the turquoise used in ancient China was imported into the Central Plains regions from Xinjiang or Russia, or obtained from deposits in Anhui and Hubei provinces, is unclear.[85] Sources of turquoise are not discussed in ancient Chinese literature. The Xiangyang region of Hubei province has been suggested as a source for the turquoise found at Erlitou.[86] The brilliant clarity of the turquoise inlay on the two ornate late Warring States belt hooks in the Mengdiexuan collection suggests that their inlay also came from Hubei province (cat. nos. 25 and 26). During the Yuan period, rich deposits were known to have existed at Zhu, Yunxi, and Yunxian in Hubei province.[87]

Malachite, *kongqueshi,* was also popular for inlay during the Eastern Zhou period. Its color is emerald green with a banded, fibrous structure in which the bands display different shades of green, as they do on the two Mengdiexuan Western Han belt ornaments from Yunnan (cat. no. 34).

Malachite can be carved like a stone or ground up to make a paste or pigment. Malachite is a carbonate mineral which can take a high polish, but it is soft compared with turquoise. Malachite is also a primary source for copper and was probably mined quite early. During the Tang period it was mined in Daizhou in northern Shanxi province; by the eleventh century A.D. it was found in Xinzhou in eastern Jiangxi province. Xuanzhou in southern Anhui is also recorded as a source of malachite.[88]

Agate, *manao,* in a wide range of colors—amber, green, red, and a bluish-gray or white banded stone— was known and used in ancient China.[89] It was often used to adorn belt hooks, such as the ornate Western Han example in the Mengdiexuan collection (cat. no. 38), and to make ceremonial items, such as the Liao hawking accessory (cat. no. 81).

Carnelian, *hong yusui,* is a translucent, flesh-red stone. It was often used as an inlay on Dian bronzes found at Shizhaishan near Kunming, Yunnan, which are similar to the circular bronze plaque with agate inlay in the Mengdiexuan collection (cat. no. 33). Carnelian is extremely durable. It owes its reddish color to the presence of iron oxide. During the Tang period, some carnelian was imported from the West, particularly Samarkand.[90]

Lapis lazuli, *qingjinshi,* is a royal blue gemstone containing various minerals, including bits of golden-yellow iron pyrites. It is a hard stone which takes a lustrous polish. The great source in antiquity was the famous lapis lazuli mines of Badakhshan in what is now Afghanistan.[91] Today, sources are also known in Siberia and Burma.

Lapis lazuli was a popular material for ornaments in the ancient world from the third millennium B.C. onward. It occurs in abundance among the grave goods of ancient Iraq and Egypt. Its appearance at these sites far from its source is ample evidence for the extensive trade in luxury material that flourished during antiquity.

The identification of lapis lazuli must be approached with caution. Several less important blue gemstones, such as sodalite and lazulite, have often been mistaken for lapis lazuli.[92]

The first appearance of lapis lazuli in ancient China is unclear, but one late Warring States Mengdiexuan belt hook has lapis lazuli inlaid on the neck of the hook as a contrast to the turquoise (cat. no. 25). To date, its early Chinese name has not been identified with certainty, but it may have been *sese.*[93] In the Song period, lapis lazuli was referred to as *jinxingshi,* gold star stone.

By the Six Dynasties and Tang periods lapis lazuli had become a popular gemstone in the embellishment of personal ornaments, such as the Mengdiexuan pendants (cat. no. 70). A Tang belt decorated with lapis lazuli is listed among the eighth-century treasures housed in the Shosoin in Kyoto, Japan.[94] According to Tang records, lapis was considered a Persian gem, which could be purchased at the gem markets in Khotan, a major trading center on the Silk Route.[95]

Pearls, *zhenzhu,* have been identified in the decoration of belt hooks as early as the Han period. Pearls have always had an aura of power and wonder for the Chinese, who frequently associated them with the hoard of a dragon. Ultimately, with the introduction of Buddhism, pearls also became a symbol of the Buddha and his law. During the Han period, pearls were obtained from beds off the coast of southwest Guangdong, but the most prized were brought by merchants from the South Seas.[96] Some freshwater pearls were also obtained from western Sichuan province.[97] Pearls are very beautiful and need no cutting or polishing, but they tend to decay. The remains of two pearls can still be seen on an early Six Dynasties–period gold comb in the present exhibition (cat. no. 48).

Glass, *boli,* was first introduced into China during the Eastern Zhou period.[98] Early glass eyebeads were brought from the West and then adopted by Chinese craftsmen. Chinese glass often has a considerable amount of barium in it, and so can be identified scientifically. Most glass inlays in late Eastern Zhou and Han belt hooks are imitations of jade and other gems. Presumably a colorful effect was the primary goal, such as that achieved by a superb Western Han inlaid hook in the Mengdiexuan collection (cat. no. 38).

Metallurgical Techniques

A microscopic examination of the artifacts in the Mengdiexuan collection revealed technical features that have often gone unnoticed in examinations of Chinese metallurgy. The purpose here is to identify the techniques that produced these artifacts and to establish a working metallurgical chronology into which they can be placed. This chronology uses recent archaeological discoveries, but it should be remembered that archaeological reports do not always describe the production methods employed.

A brief history and description of the technical methods identified should help viewers understand how the objects were made and supplement the archaeological records in authenticating and dating artifacts that were not scientifically excavated. An attempt has been made to use technical terminology that is universally understandable and to provide an equivalent Chinese term.[99]

Two distinct and contrasting metalworking trends were popular in the ancient Chinese world: foundry work and metalsmithing. The Chinese possessed knowledge of both from the beginning of the Bronze Age and chose the most suitable techniques available for their immediate purposes.

Throughout Chinese history, these two trends dominated the metalworking industry alternately, depending upon the needs of consumers. An emphasis on foundry techniques distinguishes Chinese metalworking during the Bronze Age. What little jewelry has been recovered from that period was produced by craftsmen working in peripheral areas for a non-Chinese clientele.[100] Most of the pieces appear to have been cast in bivalve molds, but a few ornaments were shaped by hammering, such as the Mengdiexuan Bronze Age gold earrings (cat. no. 1).

Dramatic changes in metalwork occurred in dynastic China during the Eastern Zhou, Qin, and Han periods. Bronze was employed to cast personal ornaments. Marvelous secular objects such as garment hooks and mirrors were produced, first at foundries in north China during the Spring and Autumn period, and then introduced into the south during the Warring States period.[101] The earliest hooks are rather simple in design, and their subsequent development may well have been stimulated by contact with non-Chinese peoples with whom the northern Chinese states were economically involved (fig. 1).[102]

During the early Warring States period, the elite of the northern states had adopted the wearing of garment hooks. These became increasingly important items of personal paraphernalia in dynastic China. Rampant experimentation characterizes the metallurgy of the second half of the first millennium B.C. This resulted in a great number of ingenious metallurgical techniques for the embellishment of metal surfaces, as demonstrated by the spectacular group of late Eastern Zhou and Western Han belt hooks in the Mengdiexuan collection.

Overlay and inlay of both stone and metal have transformed the surfaces of these hooks into jewel-like fields of color which must have glittered impressively at the waists of their aristocratic owners. The introduction of mercury into the gilding process during the late fourth and third centuries B.C. reflects the increasing preoccupation with aurifiction that prevailed among the Daoists, who preyed upon the frailties of the court elite in their search for immortality during the waning days of Eastern Zhou and early days of Han.

Casting in piece-molds continued to be the major foundry technique during the Eastern Zhou period, but, by the sixth century B.C., the so-called lost-wax process was also practiced in China.[103] This newly acquired casting process did not replace piece-mold casting in China. Instead, both methods were used contemporaneously, occasionally even used together on the same object. The superb Mengdiexuan gold garment hooks were cast in piece-molds (cat. nos. 2, 3, and 4), while the bronze belt hook in the shape of a displayed bird was cast by the lost-wax process (cat. no. 5).

Fig. 1. Bronze figure from Yixian, Hebei. (Drawing after *Wenwu*, 1965.2, p. 43.)

During the Han period, the many regional techniques that had developed during the Eastern Zhou period were assimilated and perfected by craftsmen in the service of the newly formed empire and its elite. Granulation, which originated in the West, had been adopted by goldsmiths in China from the mounted warrior-herdsmen who arrived in the Ordos area during the latter half of the fourth century B.C. as a reaction to Alexander the Great's Central Asian campaigns.[104] During the Han period, the use of gold for personal adornment began to take on an importance not seen earlier, as gold challenged jade as the major symbol of excellence.

By the end of the Six Dynasties period, personal adornment had been transformed from the minor art of bronze casters into the major art of gold- and silversmiths. The influx of non-Chinese peoples, who were distinguished culturally by their metal accessories, and the introduction of Buddhism, inspired an increasing preference for the use of precious metals in personal adornment during the first millennium A.D., including an appreciation of silver not found earlier in China. This preference was further stimulated by international trade along the Silk Route, which brought foreign merchants, metalwork, and other exotica from Sogdiana, in Central Asia, as well as from Sasanian and Byzantine centers in northwest Asia for the pleasure of the Six Dynasties, Sui, and Tang elites.[105]

Personal ornaments from the Tang period exude a certain solidity and robustness. Belts made of various grades of metal and jade identified the rank and wealth of the people who owned them. The belts, with their prescribed number of cast or hammered multishaped plaques, governed by a strict hierarchy of metals, imitated the belts of the northwest Turkic-speaking Uygur tribesmen, with whom the Tang had diplomatic relations (cat. no. 54). A combination of foundry and metalsmithing techniques was used to produce these belt plaques, which were far superior in quality to anything produced on the Eurasian steppes, as shown by the superb example in the Mengdiexuan collection (cat. no. 53). By contrast, the women's ornaments (primarily for the hair) were masterpieces of metalsmithing and became increasingly thin and light for both aesthetic and economic reasons. Hammered and pierced designs of precious metals, accented with minute chased details, glistened amidst the heavy black hair of the women who graced the court (cat. nos. 61, 63, 66, and 67).

The Song period produced personal ornaments that were even more light and decorative. Precious metals and gilded imitations were transformed into objects of great beauty and delicacy. Life at court was less robust than during the Tang period, and women had become almost immobilized on bound feet. Polo was seldom played, and the hunt was no longer of prime importance. The opening up of the southern sea routes to compensate for the decline of the old trans-Asian Silk Route after the advance of Islam continued to fuel the market for precious gems and exotica, but the most popular acquisitions were not falcons. This gentler world is superbly expressed by the gold earrings depicting two birds and a butterfly (cat. no. 99).

A conscious archaism on the part of the Song court, which hoped to gain access to the virtues of the past, produced jade and bronze belt hooks based on ancient prototypes. A wonderful hook in the Mengdiexuan collection stands as a high-water mark of archaistic metalworking (cat. no. 101). The piece is superb, its archaism betrayed by its combination of diverse styles. The hook itself is triplanar in cross section, a shape popular during the late Warring States period. By contrast, the style of the dragon head that adorns the base of the hook belongs to the Spring and Autumn period; similar dragon heads can be seen on numerous plaques of this period carved in jade.

The personal ornaments of the northern alien rulers, such as the Qidan (Liao dynasty, 907–1125), the Jurchen (Jin dynasty, 1115–1234), and the Mongols (Yuan dynasty, 1279–1368), continued to favor the robustness of the Tang period. Gold and silver crowns, frequently sparkling with dangling elements, and ornate belts hung with straps for the attachment of portable paraphernalia distinguished Liao dress (cat. nos. 77 and 78).

Often an artifact's place of manufacture is difficult to determine. In some cases the objects may have been produced by gold- and silversmiths in the service of alien rulers, but in many cases they were Chinese-made as diplomatic gifts to northern neighbors. Gifts of golden crowns and belts were an early form of export ware and are specifically referred to as Song gifts to the Liao court in Song literary sources.[106]

The passion for exotica and precious metals in personal adornment continued throughout the second millennium A.D., culminating in some of the ornate concoctions worn as headdresses during the Ming and Qing periods. The major change was in technology. Metalsmiths who worked predominantly with thin sheets began to use wire filigree and mesh, as seen on several pairs of Ming earrings in the Mengdiexuan collection (cat. no. 109).

Foundry Technology

Foundry work in ancient China was a labor-intensive production system in which a sequence of technical steps in an assembly line was performed by different craftsmen or groups of craftsmen. The remains of foundry sites and workshops discovered since 1949 reveal the advantages and complexities of ancient Chinese foundry practices. An almost complete division of labor between the various steps characterized this process and left little room for artistic recognition.[107]

Piece-Mold Casting

The piece-mold technique was the major technique used by the ancient Chinese to cast ritual vessels, weapons, and other paraphernalia from the Bronze Age through the Han dynasty.[108] Thousands of mold fragments and pattern blocks, which have been recovered from the ancient Jin-state foundries located at present-day Houma in southern Shanxi, have greatly increased our understanding of the piece-mold process during the early Eastern Zhou.[109] Huge casting complexes like Houma were necessary to produce the vast numbers of metal objects required in China during this period. A reference in the *Chuci,* an anthology of poetry that originated in the state of Chu, describes "buckles of Jin workmanship [that] glitter like bright suns," suggesting that the Jin served an extensive market.[110]

In the piece-mold process, a section-mold can be formed in one of two ways.[111] In the first method, a clay mold is formed around a model of the object to be cast and then removed in sections (fig. 2). In the second method, no model is necessary. Instead, a piece-mold is created within a container that has been lined with clay and then stamped with the required surface decoration. In both methods, the mold sections are fired and then reassembled. A casting of clay is then made, and the sections are removed. The resulting clay casting, which looks like the finished object, is allowed to dry and then filed down to form a core. This establishes the casting space, which determines the thickness of the finished product. The sections are then reassembled around the core, and the piece is cast. The clay mold is then broken, and the finished casting is removed and polished with abrasives to achieve a shiny surface. The number of sections into which a mold is cut depends entirely upon the shape and design of the object to be cast.

Several garment hooks in the Mengdiexuan collection reveal evidence of piece-mold casting. Mold-joint seams are visible under the microscope on six hooks, indicating the construction of their casting molds. Some of these hooks were cast in simple, two-piece molds (cat. no. 8) (fig. 3),[112] while others required more complex,

40 THE METALLURGY OF PERSONAL ADORNMENT

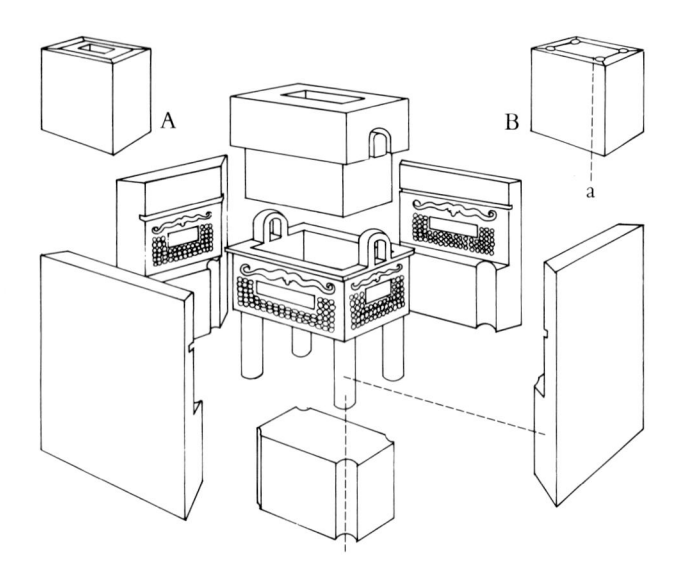

Fig. 2. Mold assembly for casting the *Zuo ce fang ding*. The four outer mold pieces surround the model, shown with the inner core above and the interleg core piece below. The outer mold pieces with the decoration in reverse could have been pulled from the model; or they could simply have been made and decorated without the help of a model. Details in the outer mold pieces would be touched up and refined before firing. The inner core could have been made by shaving down the model; but in this case, it is more likely that the inner core piece was made by inserting a fairly coarse clay mixture into the fired and reassembled mold sections. When the mold sections are removed, the core is shaved down to make the casting space. The process would be repeated with the interleg core piece. The reassembled molds are shown in the inset (A). When the molten metal is ready to pour, this assembly is inverted, with legs up, as illustrated in inset (B). (From W. Thomas Chase, *Ancient Chinese Bronze Art: Casting the Sacral Vessel*, p. 24, fig. 1, courtesy of the China Institute of America.)

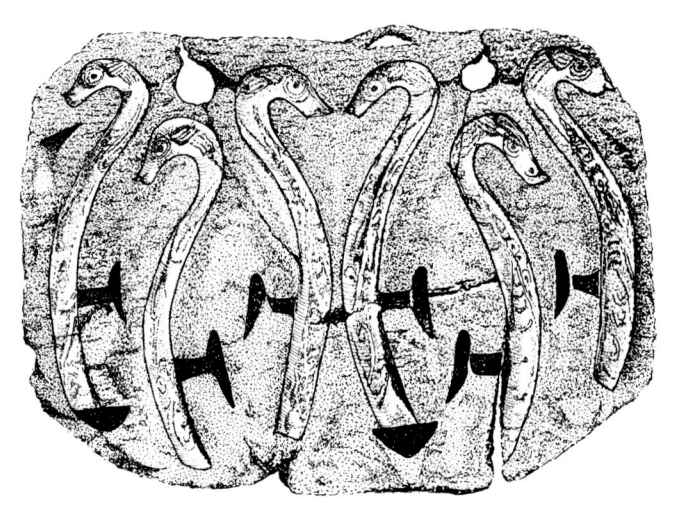

Fig. 3. Fragment from a two-piece clay mold for casting bronze belt hooks. (Drawing after Nils Palmgren, ed., *Selected Chinese Antiquities from the Collection of Gustaf Adolf, Crown Prince of Sweden*, p. 51, fig. 149.)

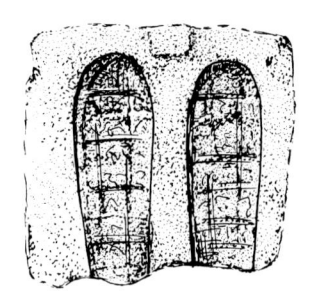

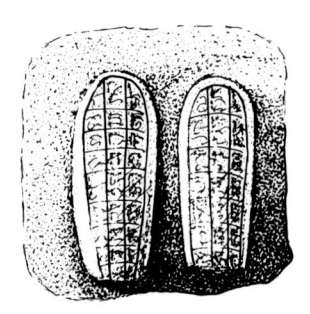

Fig. 4. Fragments from two clay section-molds excavated from the Jin foundry site at Houma, Shanxi. (Drawing after *Kaogu*, 1959.5, pp. 222–28, and pl. 4.)

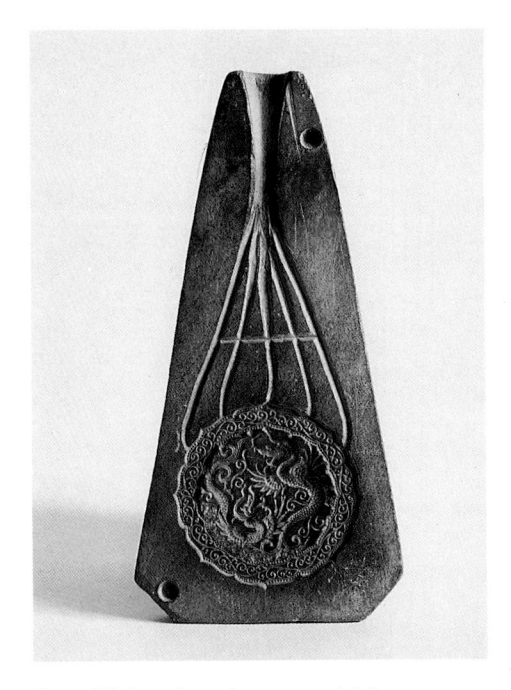

Fig. 5. Wedge-shaped stone mold for casting a circular dragon medallion, Ming dynasty, Chenghua period (1465–87). Gray stone. L. 15.2 cm, W. 7.3 cm, diam. of medallion 5.2 cm. The Harvard University Art Museums, acc. no. 1948.6. Gift of Mrs. Edward Norris.

multisection molds (cat. nos. 2, 3, 4, 7, and 17) (fig. 4).[113] Each Eastern Zhou–period foundry apparently had its own piece-mold construction system.

Stone molds dating to the Bronze Age have been found in areas to the north of the Shang and Zhou, but do not appear to have been used in dynastic China until the Han period, when they were adopted for casting mirrors.[114] Much later, during the Ming period, stone molds were apparently used for casting small ornaments, as is demonstrated by a stone mold in the collection of the Harvard University Art Museums (fig. 5).

Casting-On

Casting-on was the foundry technique used in ancient China to attach precast handles and other small fittings to larger bronze objects.[115] This technique was already in use during the early Bronze Age, appearing first in the south and then in the Shang nuclear area of the Central Plains.[116]

The importance of casting-on in the manufacture of personal ornament was its use in manufacturing linked bronze chains. The two Mengdiexuan carnivore-shaped plaques that together constitute a complete belt buckle were originally connected by two such linked chains (cat. no. 7). The chains consisted of bone-shaped links cast onto circular rings.[117]

This type of chain was cast in several stages. The smaller, bone-shaped links were each cast first in a two-piece mold. The circular elements were each cast in a penannular shape, with an opening through which the bone-shaped elements could be threaded. The chain was then placed in a mold, and the precast link openings were closed by a second pouring of bronze.

Lost Wax

The earliest archaeological evidence for lost-wax casting in China was discovered at the sixth-century B.C. Chu-state cemetery in Xiasi, Xichuan, in Henan province.[118] A bronze *jin* cast by the traditional piece-mold technique was further embellished by the addition of precast ornate openwork handles, which were produced by the lost-wax process and then attached.[119] Lost wax was introduced into China ultimately from much farther west in the ancient Near East, where the process had an early and long history, but exactly when and how the process was introduced is unclear.[120]

The lost-wax process is more practical than the piece-mold process for casting ornaments with deeply undercut and openwork designs, which complicate the removal of the mold sections from the model. A modern goldsmith would certainly have employed the indirect lost-wax process to cast the three gold Mengdiexuan garment hooks (cat. nos. 2, 3, and 4). Nevertheless, a microscopic examination of these three hooks reveals that they were actually cast in multisection piece-molds designed to overcome the problems of removing the sections from a model with undercutting.

Though never used for making large vessels, lost-wax casting became increasingly popular during the late Eastern Zhou, Qin, and Han periods for casting small fittings and belt hooks, such as the bronze example with a complex openwork design in the Mengdiexuan collection (cat. no. 5). The lost-wax process was more economical than the piece-mold process because the amount of metal used could be more easily controlled.

The object to be cast is first modelled in wax. The wax model is then invested with clay to form a mold. Often the first coat of clay is carefully brushed on to prevent the entrapment of bubbles; subsequent coats can be coarser. The invested wax model is then burnt out under high heat, hence the term *lost wax,* though founders usually salvage all the wax they can in a pan under the mold. Molten metal is then poured into the mold and takes the place of the burnt-out wax model. After the metal has cooled, the model is broken open to reveal the finished object. The resulting cast object is a metal copy of the original wax model.[121]

A variation on this method is the indirect lost-wax process. In this process, the wax model of the object to be cast is not carved freehand but formed in a "mother mold." The mother mold itself is created by pressing a carved model of the object to be cast into a piece of clay. Wax is then poured into the negative space of the mother mold and allowed to cool. The result is a wax model which is then cast in metal by the traditional lost-wax method. The advantage of the indirect method is that it allows for multiple castings and does not destroy the original model.[122] Many belt plaques made by the Chinese for nomadic consumption appear to have been mass produced by the indirect lost-wax process (cat. nos. 28 and 32).

Lost Wax and Lost Textile

The lost-wax-and-lost-textile process was used during the late Eastern Zhou and Han periods primarily to cast belt plaques, made of precious metals or bronze, that were to be tinned, overlaid with silver, or gilded.[123] The technique is easily identified by the woven pattern that occurs on the back of plaques cast by this method. This woven pattern duplicates the piece of fabric that supported the wax model during the casting process. The available archaeological evidence suggests that this technique was developed by Chinese craftsmen under the influence of contemporary lacquer practices, in which the shapes of certain pieces were reinforced with lacquer-impregnated fabric.[124]

This particular casting technique is a variation of the indirect lost-wax method.[125] An open-section mold was formed by pressing a model of the plaque to be produced into a piece of clay. After the clay dried, wax was poured into the open-section mold and a piece of textile, probably woven hemp, was pressed onto the wax. After the textile-backed wax model hardened, it was removed. It was then packed in clay to make a mold, which was baked at a high temperature. Both the wax and the textile reinforcement were burned out of the mold and replaced by molten metal, which was poured into the mold during the casting process. The great advantage of this casting process was that it allowed the craftsman to produce a very thin wax model, supported by textile, that would reduce the amount of metal expended and diminish the weight of the finished plaque. This technique also allowed for multiple castings decorated with the same design.

Evidence for the use of this technique has been found at Xinzhuangtou, near Yixian, in Hebei province.[126] This was the location of foundries belonging to the state of Yan from 311 to 222 B.C. Two thin gold belt plaques with a woven pattern on their reverse sides have been excavated at this site. The design on each plaque is similar to that depicted on a tinned-bronze plaque in the exhibition (cat. no. 21), which also carries a woven pattern on its back. These similarities suggest that catalogue number 21 may also have been cast at the Yan site at Xinzhuangtou expressly for nomadic consumption.

Inlay Techniques

Two of the most important forms of decoration used to embellish garment hooks during the Eastern Zhou, Qin, and Han periods were stone and metallic inlay. Stone inlay was a revival of an earlier technique used in north China during the Bronze Age, but metallic inlay did not develop until the sixth century B.C., during the Eastern Zhou period, when it was first used to adorn weapons and ritual vessels.[127]

Stone inlay was first used to decorate garment hooks during the late sixth century B.C. On most hooks cast during the Warring States period, the inlay grooves and cells were integrally cast with the hook, and the stones were pre-cut to fit, as they are on catalogue numbers 3 and 23. By contrast, microscopic examination reveals that the inlay cells on two other Warring States–period Mengdiexuan hooks were produced by soldering on a series of gold strips fixed on edge that then formed a network of cloisonlike cells (cat. nos. 25 and 26). Such cloisonné work was well known in the ancient Mediterranean world, but was not known in ancient China before the third century B.C.[128]

Metallic-strand inlay was the standard form of inlay from the sixth century to the first century B.C.[129] It was first used to decorate belt hooks during the middle of the Warring States period. In this process, the inlay is accomplished by working many thin strands of gold or silver placed side by side into channels in the bronze, and not just hammering them into the channels.[130] According to the *Hanshu,* special tools were developed that would have been used to inlay, file, secure, and burnish.[131] A late third-century B.C. silver-inlaid bronze hook in the Mengdiexuan collection is a classic example of metallic-strand inlay (cat. no. 30). The *Shuowen* dictionary, written in the second century A.D., implies the use of a whetstone for grinding down the surface of a bronze object after it had been inlaid in order to achieve a smooth, polished surface.[132]

Metallic-band inlay was also used to embellish belt hooks during the late Eastern Zhou, Qin, and early Han periods.[133] The metal, either gold or silver, was cut into thin, narrow bands and inlaid in channels cut into the bronze surface of a belt hook. The channels had deep edges that lay below the channel floor. The borders of the gold or silver inlay bands were worked into these boundary grooves in order to anchor them. A third-century B.C. gold inlaid hook in the Mengdiexuan collection (cat. no. 31) is an excellent example of this technique, which is typical of artifacts found at Jincun in Henan.

Stone-paste inlay appears to have originated during the fifth to fourth century B.C., during the Eastern Zhou period, to enrich the surfaces of bronze vessels.[134] By the third century B.C. the technique was used in combination with other inlay processes to adorn belt hooks such as catalogue number 26.[135] The tiny wild boars on the sides of this piece are depicted with ground turquoise paste inlaid within a gold outline, and their pelts and manes are highlighted with gold.

Mirror Metallurgy

Mirrors first developed during the Bronze Age on the northern periphery of ancient China, but were not manufactured in dynastic China until the Eastern Zhou period. Contrary to popular opinion, mirrors did not become popular in south China until the late Eastern Zhou period, when they were vigorously adopted by Daoism.[136]

Much has been written about the functions, symbolism, and decoration of mirrors.[137] They served as firemakers and demonifuge armor, and ultimately under Daoism and Buddhism their reflective qualities became imbued with philosophical meaning, ritual, and magic.[138] Some mirrors were associated with beauty and its reflection, as portrayed in a famous scene from Gu Kaizhi's "Admonitions" scroll in the British Museum.[139]

The methods of casting Chinese mirrors have received very little attention, in contrast to the many studies devoted to their iconography and symbolism.[140] A detailed discussion of the subject is beyond the scope of this essay, but it is hoped that the following brief remarks will give readers a better understanding of the Mengdiexuan mirrors.

The earliest mirrors found in the northwest border areas of China were flat disks decorated with radiating linear patterns, such as the Qijia-culture copper mirror excavated in Qinghai province.[141] Bronze mirrors also occur in the Central Plains among the grave goods of Fu Hao, consort of the Shang king Wu Ding, at Xiaotun, Anyang, in Henan province, but these mirrors are not Shang products.[142] Instead, they represent exotic items obtained by the Shang through trade or warfare from their northern herding neighbors.

Mirrors were first cast in dynastic China during the Eastern Zhou period. These mirrors were made with a special alloy. According to the *Zhouli,* metal mirrors were composed of 50 percent copper and 50 percent tin, but such proportions are not confirmed by modern analyses.[143] Instead, the most common mirror alloy is basically a leaded high-tin bronze which reflects well and contains about 71 percent copper, 26 percent tin, and 3 percent lead.[144] Numerous inscriptions on later Han mirrors refer to these metals as the "three auspicious metals."[145] Iron was also used, though rarely, to cast mirrors such as the eight examples excavated at a Han site in Shaogou in Henan province.[146]

Ancient Chinese mirrors were cast in piece-molds, one piece for the reflecting surface and another for the decorated back.[147] The designs on the backs were stamped or carved into the mold; after casting, the reflecting surfaces were finished by grinding and polishing.

A mold section discovered at the sixth-century B.C. foundry site at Houma in Shanxi province suggests that the state of Jin may have been one of the first states to cast mirrors.[148] An early Warring States–period mirror in the Mengdiexuan collection appears to have been cast at Houma (cat. no. 9). The two concentric bands of mythical beasts crunching zoomorphic victims that decorate the back are related to a similar band of predatory beasts found on the famous Liyu *hu* in the Shanghai Museum, which was cast at Houma early in the Warring States period.[149] The decorated back of the Mengdiexuan mirror appears to have been intentionally tinned, a surface enrichment described in the section on metal plating in this essay. The reflecting side is slightly convex. Convex reflecting surfaces have traditionally been considered to be a late Warring States or Han phenomenon, but this small Jin mirror proves otherwise.

Another Warring States–period mirror in the Mengdiexuan collection (cat. no. 11) is decorated with six full- and two partial-profile zoomorph heads delineated in relief by curls and striations within a frame of two concentric circles. The decorated area is divided by crisscrossed hairline ridges into small, equal-sized rectangular units, which reflect the stamps used to create the pattern in the mold, a typical Warring States foundry practice that allowed for the mass production of mirrors.[150] The use of pattern blocks for decorating mirror backs was not a Jin foundry practice, but mirrors with a similar overall field of ornament achieved with pattern blocks have been found at sites in Henan province and farther south in Chu territory.[151] Under the microscope, the decorated area appears to have been intentionally tinned, but not the rim. The reflecting side of this mirror is flat.

Several early Mengdiexuan mirrors have slightly convex surfaces (cat. nos. 9, 43, 44, 45, 46, and 55k), but others are absolutely flat (cat. nos. 11, 12, and 13). Only two of the later mirrors in the collection have curved reflecting surfaces (cat. nos. 55h and 57). Whether or not the shapes and curvatures were dictated by their functions is unclear.

The methods used to produce the curved reflective surfaces on the mirrors are not yet completely understood. Research in optics was stimulated by Daoism from the fourth century B.C. onward, but none of the literature deals with the optical features in mirror manufacture.[152] The mirror-mold fragments recovered so far are all for decorated mirror backs, not for the reflecting surfaces. Presumably the slight curvature was produced on the model and then cast by the traditional piece-mold process. The mold halves for the reflecting surfaces would have been uninteresting, slightly curved, clay bits, which during excavations would have easily gone unrecognized by archaeologists and grave robbers alike. Hence, no mold fragments for the reflecting surfaces have yet been identified.

fig. 6. Fragment from the bottom of a mold for casting a bronze mirror with four T-shapes, 4th–3rd century B.C. Reddish-buff earthenware. H. 6.9 cm, W. 12.1 cm. The Harvard University Art Museums, acc. no. 1948.3. Gift of Mrs. Edward Norris.

Eight late Eastern Zhou mirror-mold fragments were discovered in China on the eve of World War II, but have since disappeared. They were said to have been found at the village of Tanghu, Yixian, in Hebei province, near the ancient site of Xiadu, the southern capital of the state of Yan from 311 to 222 B.C.[153] The molds were not all identical but carried designs that would have produced several different kinds of mirrors, suggesting that local centers existed for mirror manufacture. Recent excavations have confirmed that Xiadu served as a prominent manufacturing center catering to a diverse market, both Chinese and nomadic, during the late Eastern Zhou period.[154] A clay mold fragment for a mirror back in the collection of the Harvard University Art Museums is very similar to those found at Yixian, and may well have originally come from the Yan foundries at Xiadu (fig. 6).[155]

Stone appears to have replaced clay for making mirror molds by the late Han period. Another mold fragment in the Harvard collection is probably made of soapstone (fig. 7).[156] It has three ducts: the center channel for the sprue and the other two for the risers. The mold also displays square holes for the pegs that locked into the other side of the mold, which may have been made of clay rather than stone.[157]

The casting of mirrors appears to have become a major industry by the Eastern Han period. Inscriptions on mirrors cast during the first and second centuries A.D. abound and contain all sorts of useful information.[158] Large, government-sponsored workshops were set up for the production of mirrors at various centers throughout China. Many of the inscriptions on mirrors indicate the locations of these workshops, besides listing the sources from which the "three auspicious metals" were obtained. Sometimes even the craftsmen were named, a rare occurrence within the prescriptive metallurgical practices of ancient China.

44 THE METALLURGY OF PERSONAL ADORNMENT

Fig. 7. Mold for casting a bronze mirror with animals, 1st–2nd century A.D. Three ducts, the center one for the sprue and the other two for the risers. Stone. D. 19.9 cm. The Harvard University Art Museums, acc. no. 1951.109. Gift of Philip Hofer in honor of Langdon Warner.

The surface treatment of mirrors has long been the subject of debate. Some mirrors were intentionally tinned, while others display shiny, silver-colored surfaces which are the result of an inverse segregation of the tin-rich phase of the low-tin bronze.[159] A high-tin bronze was not normally tinned because it became silver in color naturally when polished (cat. no. 13). Debate over the identification of the process that produced the so-called black mirrors (cat. nos. 43 and 46) still rages. In the past, the beautiful, dark, lustrous surfaces of certain black mirrors have been attributed to an applied layer of some as yet unidentified substance. More recently, such black surfaces have been attributed to a natural patina resulting from burial conditions, including contact with humus in the soil.[160]

A few Warring States and Han mirror backs have decoration that is painted rather than cast. This suggests a relationship between metalwork and painting. Such a relationship is illustrated by the cast decoration of curvilinear birds on catalogue number 13, which reflects similar creatures more often found painted on southern lacquers of the period. A bronze mirror with painted lacquer decoration in the Mengdiexuan collection represents a type of mirror produced in the south under the influence of Chu taste during the late Eastern Zhou and Han periods.[161]

Mirrors continued to play an important role during the Six Dynasties period. By the fourth century A.D. the Daoists even had a patron saint of mirror polishers, and they enthusiastically pursued their optical investigations into the eleventh century A.D. According to Daoist literature, square mirrors were used to collect dew from the moon, a belief that may have inspired the shape of a small, square, slightly convex Tang mirror in the Mengdiexuan collection (cat. no. 55h).[162]

The Tang period was one of the great high-water marks of Chinese mirror production, with an explosion of new shapes and robust, ornate decoration. Mirrors were richly embellished with hammered sheets of gold and silver with repoussé designs refined by chasing, the ultimate marriage of foundry and metalsmithing work on the same object (cat. no. 55g). The repoussé work was not accomplished by hammering the silver over a cast design underneath but was probably worked from behind freehand.

Mirrors have been very important items throughout Chinese history. Far too little scientific research has been devoted to them. Serious metallographic studies should be performed on as many datable mirrors as possible. The data gathered may assist research into the mirrors' alloys and production methods. Although attempts have been made in the past,[163] without such data the problem of authenticity can hardly be addressed.

Metalsmithing Techniques

The art of the metalsmith lends itself far more easily to the creation of personal ornaments than does that of the foundryman. An ornament shaped by hammering can be more delicate and generally uses less metal than an ornament formed by casting. Ideally, to produce an object, a single metalsmith selects the appropriate metal and then works it directly in several interrelated steps. Such a procedure is more spontaneous than the labor-intensive sequence of isolated technical steps followed in casting, which is a "secondary" technique.

It is not known if metalsmithing techniques in China were all performed by single craftsmen or by an assembly line of artisans. Even though individual goldsmiths may have had name recognition, they generally worked in concert with an entire workshop that was set up under the auspices of a single name.

Continued statements that metalsmithing techniques were unknown in Bronze Age China ignore the results of recent archaeology.[164] Bronze horse harness ornaments covered with hammered gold foil were excavated at Central Plains sites such as Xiaotun in Henan province, but no evidence has come to light to support the use of gold foil for the adornment of humans at that time.[165]

By contrast, Bronze Age sites belonging to the northern pastoral tribes on the periphery of the Central Plains have yielded numerous ornaments made by metalsmiths for human use.[166] A pair of gold earrings in the Mengdiexuan collection formed by hammering are almost identical to excavated examples from Shilou in Shanxi province (cat. no. 1).

By the middle of the Eastern Zhou period, many metalsmithing techniques were employed in north China and the Central Plains as surface embellishment for cast-bronze garment hooks (cat. no. 15). During the Qin and Han periods which followed, metalsmiths mastered and refined all the major metalsmithing techniques needed to create the splendid jewelry produced during the first and second millennia A.D.

No written records remain that describe how Chinese metalsmiths worked, so we must learn about their techniques from the objects themselves. The primary materials used by Chinese metalsmiths in making jewelry were gold, silver, and occasionally copper. The metal was first made into ingots. It was then shaped by hammering and chisel-cutting, and decorated with impressed designs achieved by repoussé, chasing, and stamping. Further embellishment was accomplished by granulation and by the application of wire articulated to produce spiral ornaments, linked chains, beading, cloisons, and filigree work.

Hammering

Hammering is the metalsmith's first step in the production of a work of art after the metal has been selected, occasionally refined, and then poured into an ingot mold. Beating first with rounded hammers and then with flat-faced ones produces metal in sheet form. The optimal thickness of a hammered sheet depends upon its future function. To form extremely thin sheets, the metal is usually placed between layers of leather or a similar material. Metal hardens when hammered, but malleability can be regained by heating it and then quenching it in liquid (annealing). Precious metals were usually obtained in small convenient masses, such as nuggets or ingots. Two Mengdiexuan ornaments show evidence of having been hammered from a cast ingot or slug (cat. no. 103).

Chisel-cut Shapes and Pierced Work

A chisel (rather than shears or scissors) was used for cut and pierced work after the overall shape had been achieved by hammering. The superb Liao flower hairpins (cat. no. 76), for example, were shaped by chisel-cutting, not scissors. If faint marks left by two opposed cutting edges are found on a piece dated earlier than the Song period, its authenticity may be in question.

The intricate openwork designs that characterize many of the Tang (cat. nos. 61 and 63) and Song (cat. no. 83) hairpins are also the result of chisel-cutting. Upon close examination, some chisel-cut designs may have slightly jagged edges, which can look a little ragged under a microscope, as they do on a set of Song hairpins (cat. no. 85).

Cloisons

The thin gold strips that form the cloisons on two Mengdiexuan late Warring States belt hooks (cat. nos. 25 and 26) were chisel-cut from hammered sheets and then soldered on edge to the hooks' surfaces. The small cloisons that decorate the top of an early Six Dynasties gold comb (cat. no. 48) were also formed in this way. Cloisons were produced in a similar way in the ancient Near East and Egypt, suggesting that this early Chinese cloisonné technique probably originated somewhere in the West.[167]

Repoussé

Designs in repoussé are produced by working a piece of metal from the back. The metal is displaced, either by pushing it into a die (cat. nos. 54 and 86) or by working it with a rounded tool from the back while the front of the metal is supported on some type of soft material. The resulting design appears in relief on the front of the piece. Sometimes repoussé designs are further refined by chasing, as in the feather patterns on a Tang ornament (cat. no. 64) and on two superb Song gilded-silver examples (cat. no. 84).

Some hollow objects were made in two halves that were each formed by repoussé and then soldered together (cat. no. 75). In some cases the metal has been decorated by repoussé and then curved around a wooden core (cat. no. 96).

Chasing

Chasing is performed by working the metal from the front, so that the marks that create the design are indented into the front of the piece. Traces of a raised pattern on the back often result, as on a pair of Tang silver hairpins that display classic chased decoration (cat. no. 62). Chasing tools, known as punches, come in a variety of shapes with slightly rounded ends which will displace the metal but not cut it. Such tools can be made of metal, bone, wood, or stone. A punch is moved along with the tap of a hammer. Under a microscope, the marks frequently appear as a continuous series of overlapping lines or tiny shapes, such as dots, crescents, or circles. Chased lines have the appearance of snowplow tracks, with the displaced metal pushed up along the edges but not removed.

Chasing is often used to define and sharpen details of designs that have been shaped by casting or repoussé. Many Tang and Song hair ornaments were created with a whole range of metalsmithing techniques, including chisel-cutting, repoussé, and chasing (cat. no. 64).

Matting is a form of chasing produced by repeatedly tapping a punch with a patterned end into a gold or silver sheet. Patterned punches were frequently used to produce repeated designs such as the semicircular scales of the dragons that curl around two Yuan hairpins (cat. no. 105). A punch can also be used to create texture, such as the myriad circles that make up the background on the cast Tang belt plaques (cat. no. 52). A punch with a convex end was a labor-saving device used to imitate granulation during the Song period (cat. no. 97), when true granulation appears to have gone out of favor.

Engraving

Engraving uses a hand-held sharp tool to cut away or remove surface metal. This technique was seldom used on repoussé work because the sheet metal was too thin to cut away. By contrast, engraving worked well on cast objects. The Chinese characters that occur on the back of the Mengdiexuan cast-silver roundel (cat. no. 22) were produced by engraving. An engraved line can often be identified by its tapered beginning, where the graver dug gradually into the metal, and its abrupt end, where the graver stopped.

Crimping

Crimping is a mechanical join between two pieces of metal, in which the edges of one are deformed to shape an overlap on the other. Crimping was used to attach the repoussé tops of several Song hairpins (cat. nos. 95, 96, and 97) and was often combined with various binding methods. For example, the individual rounded shapes of several Song hair ornaments were each formed with several elements that were assembled by crimping and soldering (cat. no. 88).

Granulation

True granulation is a technique whereby small gold spheres are attached singly or in a pattern to a gold background by diffusion bonding without the use of solder. The technique has a long history in the ancient Near East, dating back to the third millennium B.C.[168]

Granulation first appeared in the ancient Chinese world on gold artifacts associated with the nomadic tribes in the Ordos region at the end of the fourth century B.C. and had been adopted by Chinese goldsmiths by the Western Han period.[169]

A gold headdress ornament in the Mengdiexuan collection (cat. no. 47) is a masterpiece of granulation work. The tiny granules are applied in graduated sizes, in a manner similar to the granulation work that distinguishes the superb Western Jin gold buckle found in Anxiang county in Hunan.[170]

The Chinese often used pseudo-granulation, employing solder to adhere the beads to a background. This method produced the look of true granulation, but upon microscopic examination the granules appear indistinct, the spaces between them filled with solder (cat. no. 48). Granulation was extremely popular during the Six Dynasties period. It continued to be a popular technique for the enhancement of ornaments during the Tang (cat. no. 70) and early Song periods (cat. no. 91), but had been replaced by ring-matting designs and filigree work by the Ming period.

Beading

Beading is the name given to a border consisting of gold granules arranged in sequence to form a line. Beading occurs on a gold headdress ornament in the Mengdiexuan collection (cat. no. 47).

Wire

Gold and silver wire found many uses in the manufacture of personal ornament, from chains to applied decoration to filigree. The earliest use of gold wire occurs on pieces discovered in tombs associated with hunting and herding groups on ancient China's northern fringes, such as the two gold spiral bracelets that were excavated at Zhongtoncun in Xinle in Hebei.[171]

In ancient times, wire was made by strip-twisting, which is achieved by taking a thin sheet of hammered metal and slowly twisting it tighter and tighter (fig. 8). Today most wire is drawn, made by pulling a cast or hammered rod through a tapered hole in a draw-plate. The two processes can be distinguished under a microscope. Strip-twisted wire displays spiral seam lines. Spiral seam lines are visible on the coiled wire that forms the three cones that decorate the Ordos gold earring in the Mengdiexuan collection (cat. no. 16). By contrast, the wire used on two Song hairpins (cat. nos. 83 and 92) appears to have been drawn and is marked by longitudinal indentations.

When wire was first drawn is the subject of some debate. Western scholars claim that wire was strip-twisted and not drawn until sometime in the first millennium A.D.[172] Indian scholars claim that drawn wire was used as early as the third millennium B.C. in the Indus Valley civilization.[173]

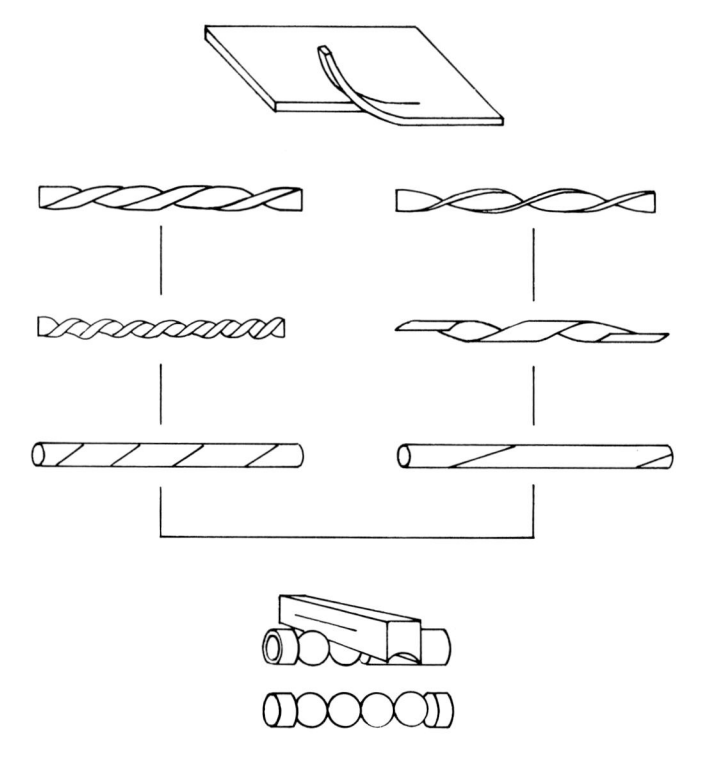

Fig. 8. Diagram of twisted-wire and beaded-wire production methods. (Drawing after Jack Ogden, *Ancient Jewellery*, p. 46, fig. 30:a–h.)

Applied Wire
Wire was also applied to the surface of gold and silver objects to add details. Wire ending in double spirals describes the nostrils of the dragons on the gold Western Jin headdress ornament (cat. no. 47).

Beaded Wire
Beaded wire is produced by indenting a strip-twisted wire in such a way as to make it resemble actual beading (cat. no. 73).

Linked Chains
The typical linked chain used by gold- and silversmiths in ancient China was known as loop-in-loop. Such chains were constructed with previously prepared loops linked together in a complex way (fig. 9).

Loop-in-loop chains, which date back to the mid-third millennium B.C. in Sumeria and Egypt, became increasingly popular among Greek goldsmiths during the Hellenistic period, fourth to third century B.C. Such chains were also prized by the pastoral peoples of the Eurasian steppes.[174] A very handsome example was discovered in a nomadic tomb at Aluchaideng in Hangjin banner in the Ordos Desert region of western Inner Mongolia.[175] Whether this chain was made locally or was imported from farther west has not yet been determined.

Loop-in-loop chains were first introduced into China during the late Eastern Zhou period, and their use continued throughout the first millennium A.D.[176] The tiny attachment loops on a Six Dynasties–period Mengdiexuan earring appear to be loop-in-loop variations (cat. no. 49). Such links and chains were the metalsmith's counterpart to the foundry-produced bronze chains formed by casting and casting on.

Fig. 9. Stages in the "loop-in-loop" chain construction: a. single; b. double; c. simple loop-in-loop; d. figure eight loop-in-loop. (Drawing after Emma C. Bunker, "Gold in the Ancient Chinese World: A Cultural Puzzle," p. 42, fig. 23:1–4.)

Filigree
Filigree refers to decorative openwork patterns made of wire. This type of work did not become popular in China until the Ming and Qing periods, but had a far earlier history in the West. Several Ming earrings in the Mengdiexuan collection display filigree work (cat. no. 109).

Metal Plating
Deliberately applied layers of gold, tin, and silver enhance the surfaces of numerous metal ornaments in the Mengdiexuan collection. Plating the surface of one metal with a thin layer of another had symbolic and aesthetic as well as practical benefits in the creation of jewelry. The study of metal plating in China is still in its infancy, but the following descriptions of the most important developments and their advantages may help to explain how and why such metal plating was accomplished before electroplating was invented.

Gilding
Ancient Chinese metalworkers practiced two distinct methods of gilding. The earliest method, *baojin,* was employed as early as the Shang period by overlaying an object with a thin hammered sheet of gold foil. The more important gilding technique, mercury-amalgam gilding, *gongji liujin,* did not develop until much later, during the Warring States period. In archaeological literature today, this process is more commonly described as *liujin.*

Foil gilding during the Shang period appears to have been used chiefly to adorn harness ornaments rather than ornaments for humans.[177] The use of gold-foil overlay in the manufacture of personal adornment did not occur until the Eastern Zhou period, when metal itself began to be popular for making ornaments for humans.[178] Several bronze belt hooks in the Mengdiexuan collection are enhanced with applied gold foil (cat. nos. 15 and 17). Gold foil was mechanically attached by roughening the bronze surface with a chisel to produce tiny raised burrs that would grab, close, and secure the foil when it was pressed over them.[179]

Mercury-amalgam gilding did not develop until the late Eastern Zhou period, when a Daoist preoccupation with immortality and scientific advances in alchemy stimulated a search for man-made gold.[180] Mercury-amalgam gilding is technically unrelated to the mechanical *baojin* process. Instead, mercury-amalgam gilding is a chemical process, achieved by dissolving gold in mercury to make a paste that is applied to the object to be gilded. The object is then heated, the mercury is burned off, and the resulting gilded surface is finished by burnishing.[181] By the beginning of the Western Han period mercury-amalgam gilding had begun to replace foil gilding as a technique for surface enrichment on bronze. Numerous bronze garment hooks and nomadic belt plaques in the Mengdiexuan collection are enhanced by mercury-amalgam gilding (cat. nos. 28, 32, 39, and 42).

Since both gilding methods, *baojin* and *liujin*, produce a thin layer of gold on the surface of a metal object, it is sometimes difficult to distinguish which technique has been used. Under microscopic examination, surfaces that have been overlaid with foil tend to display areas where tiny pieces of foil have broken off, revealing the bare bronze beneath (cat. no. 15). By contrast, a mercury-amalgam gilded layer tends to be thinner but more tightly bonded to the metal surface. Mercury-amalgam gilding may also reveal telltale areas where the gilding has been worn away or penetrated by tiny corrosion eruptions from the bronze surface beneath. Microscopically, a mercury-amalgam gilded surface may also show a grainy texture in the recessed areas.

The reasons for gilding the surface of another metal in the ancient Chinese world were somewhat complex. Gold foil may have been used first as a color contrast to the reddish tint of bronze or to give a bronze artifact the illusion of being made of a yellowish rather than a reddish metal. There is no indication that gold had any monetary value or significant associations with immortality in ancient China before the latter half of the Eastern Zhou period. Instead, early literary sources describe gold as *huangjin*, yellow metal, and silver as *baijin*, white metal, suggesting that color was an important defining feature.[182]

By contrast, mercury-amalgam gilding appears to have been Daoist inspired. By the late Warring States and Western Han periods gold had begun to rival jade in its associations with immortality.[183] Gold was also highly valued among the frontier pastoral tribes. Many bronze belt plaques made by the Han Chinese for their northern neighbors were mercury-amalgam gilded (cat. nos. 28 and 32) to indicate the superior status of the owner compared to that of an owner of a plain bronze plaque.[184]

The mercury-amalgam gilding process is often so sophisticated that it is hard to detect. At first glance, the Mengdiexuan Liao earrings (cat. no. 73) appear to be made of pure gold. A microscopic examination reveals that they are actually made of mercury-amalgam gilded bronze. Gilded bronze gives the illusion of gold without the expense, as demonstrated by the existence of many gilded-bronze hair ornaments produced during the Tang and Song periods (cat. nos. 88 and 89).

Gilding was sometimes used for purely aesthetic reasons as a selective decorative feature. The gilded areas that accent certain anatomical details on the animals depicted on a late Warring States silver roundel in the Mengdiexuan collection (cat. no. 22) were created for aesthetic rather than symbolic reasons. A fashion for gilding certain areas on silver artifacts continued during the first millennium A.D., particularly on silver hair ornaments made during the Tang and Song periods (cat. nos. 64 and 83). Metal surfaces with selectively gilded areas are sometimes described as parcel-gilt, a misleading term which is not universally understood.

Mercury-amalgam gilding, sometimes called fire-gilding, was replaced with electroplating during the latter half of the nineteenth century. The new technique avoids the health hazard of working with poisonous mercury fumes. Early twentieth-century forgeries are easily unmasked when electroplating is detected. Today, the mercury-amalgam gilding technique is again alive and well in China and Hong Kong, where metalsmiths create forgeries for the burgeoning art market.[185]

Tinning

Tinning is another metal-plating technique that developed in China during the early Eastern Zhou period. The earliest method was achieved by applying hot molten tin to a low-tin bronze object without the aid of mercury, either by wiping or dipping.[186] A belt hook in the Mengdiexuan collection was tinned on both sides by being dipped in a molten tin bath (cat. no. 8). By contrast, only the decorated side of one Mengdiexuan belt plaque (cat. no. 21) is tinned, suggesting that it was wiped with molten tin.

A high-tin bronze was not normally tinned because it became silver in color naturally when polished, as demonstrated by the polished surfaces of several high-tin bronze mirrors in the Mengdiexuan collection (cat. no. 58).[187] In the past, such tin-rich surfaces were erroneously attributed either to mercury-amalgam tinning or to inverse segregation of the tin-rich phase on a high-tin bronze during cooling, commonly described as tin sweat. Recent scientific research has demonstrated that such high-tin bronze mirrors have not been mercury-amalgam tinned, and that tin sweat does not occur on a high-tin bronze, but only on a low-tin bronze.[188]

Mercury-amalgam tinning, *gongji liuxi*, has been detected on the surfaces of several Warring States–period weapons, but, to date, the technique has not been identified in the manufacture of personal ornaments.[189] The technique used to enhance the reflective powers of bronze mirrors was not mercury-amalgam tinning but a process in which a mirror surface was polished with a mercury-tin compound without the use of heat.[190]

Tinning was employed for several different reasons. It could give a bronze object a handsome, shiny white surface which was extremely durable and resistant to corrosion. The shiny white metal surfaces achieved by tinning were probably first created primarily for the way their color contrasted with those of other metals, such as red copper and yellow gold, and not as an imitation of silver. Deliberately tinned bronze predates a serious interest in silver in ancient China, again suggesting that color and decorative effect may have been a factor in early metal-plating decisions.[191]

Tinning also predates mercury-amalgam gilding as a status indicator in the manufacture of belt ornaments made for the northwestern pastoral tribes.[192] Numerous tinned-bronze belt plaques dating to as early as the sixth to the third century B.C. have been identified among both excavated and collected examples, including one plaque in the Mengdiexuan collection (cat. no. 21).

The use of tinning in the enhancement of personal adornment declined sharply after the Han period but was apparently not abandoned. A handsome Tang comb in the Mengdiexuan collection is made of a copper alloy that has been tinned and then highlighted by gilding (cat. no. 68).

Silvering

Silvering another metal was not practiced until late in the Eastern Zhou period, and then only rarely. The earliest method was silver-foil overlay, *baoyin*, which was used to embellish the front surface of one Mengdiexuan belt hook (cat. no. 24) and the back of another (cat. no. 15).

Mercury-amalgam silvering, *gongji liuyin*, developed during the Western Han period but appears to have been used primarily to produce silver surfaces on vessels and horse fittings, which were then adorned with selectively gilded accents.[193] To date, mercury-amalgam silvering does not appear to have been used extensively in the manufacture of personal ornaments, although a few examples do exist, such as the Western Jin belt mounts in the Mengdiexuan collection (cat. no. 50b).

Silver did not play an important role in Chinese metallurgy at all, and never acquired the same associations with immortality as did gold. In many cultures silver was considered a symbol of purity and was associated with the moon, but not in China. A passage in the *Shiji* which reads, "The Shang dynasty ruled by metal, and silver flowed out of the mountains," may be a product of Han interpretation by the historian Sima Qian.[194] The passage was apparently taken from a section of the Qin dynasty text titled *Lushi chunqiu*, The spring and autumn of Mr. Lu, where a subsection titled *Yingtong*, Responding to what is the same, in chapter 13 says, "the Shang dynasty ruled by the power of metal and honored the color white," but does not mention silver specifically.[195]

Conclusion

Chinese personal ornaments made of precious metals and gemstones have not until now been the focus of any major art collection. In China, metal personal adornment was an integral part of the overall costume that a person of rank was required to wear, but not something to be collected. For the elite and the literati, collecting "did not have aesthetic goals but was stimulated by a wish to gain access to the past."[196] Jewelry made of gold and silver did not fulfill this goal, which was chiefly concerned with ancient ritual objects made of jade and bronze that had conferred moral authority and virtue in the past.

The current exhibition from the Mengdiexuan collection gives us a rare opportunity to investigate and appreciate the importance of personal adornment in the history of Chinese metallurgy. Technical advances often appear first in the manufacture of small objects such as jewelry.[197] The results of researching and examining the objects in the Mengdiexuan collection will challenge many long-held assumptions about the development of certain Chinese metallurgical techniques. Granulation, cloisonné, and several other major metalsmithing techniques once thought not to have been introduced into China until the first millennium A.D. can now be shown to have been practiced as early as the first millennium B.C. Although the initial inspiration to wear metal next to the skin was probably introduced into nuclear China from outside—through contact with the non-Chinese pastoral tribes with which China interacted—metal personal adornment was soon sinicized and became a major indicator of status and rank.

Notes

1. *China Pictorial*, 1992.9, pp. 30–31. Excavations on the southern slope of Longgu Mountain, Zhoukoudian, in the southwestern suburb of Beijing, have revealed clamshells, fish bones, pebbles, animal teeth, and claws with holes worn by northeast-Asian peoples more than 100,000 years ago.

2. Grahame Clark, *Symbols of Excellence*, pp. 50–57.

3. *Archaeology* (July/August 1993), p. 22. Discoveries at Xinglongwa in Inner Mongolia yielded jade ornaments dating to the sixth millennium B.C.

4. David N. Keightley, "Early Civilization in China: Reflections on How It Became Chinese," in Paul S. Ropp, ed., *Heritage of China*, pp. 22–28.

5. The most important graves contained items made mostly of true jade (nephrite), while the lesser graves contained items carved of pseudo-jade and other hard stones. Wen Guang, "A Geoarchaeological Study of Ancient Chinese Jade." See also *Kaogu*, 1993.7, pp. 627–44.

6. For a brilliant discussion of these early pastoral tribes see Katheryn Linduff, "Here Today and Gone Tomorrow: The Emergence and Demise of Bronze Producing Cultures Outside the Central Plains," *Bulletin of the Institute of History and Philology* (forthcoming).

7. Each artifact in the Mengdiexuan collection was carefully examined under a Swift Stereo Binocular Microscope, working at ten times one magnification, which could be increased to twenty times one magnification—ECB.

8. Quoted by Robert Thorp, "Mountain Tombs and Jade Burial Suits: Preparations for Eternity in the Western Han," in George Kuwayama, ed., *Ancient Mortuary Traditions of China*, p. 36.

9. Berthold Laufer, *Jade: A Study in Chinese Archaeology and Religion*, pp. 286–87.

10. Burton Watson, trans., *The Columbia Book of Chinese Poetry,* p. 118.

11. Robert Bagley, "An Early Bronze Age Tomb in Jiangxi Province," *Orientations* 24, no. 7, p. 36; Lu Shizong, Lu Benshan, Hua Jueming, and Zhou Weijian, "Antiker Kupfererzbergbau von Tongling bei Ruichang (Provinz Jiangxi)," *Der Anschnitt* 45, H.2-3, pp. 50–62; and Zhou Baoquan, Hu Youyan, and Lu Benshan, "Ancient Copper Mining and Smelting at Tonglushan Daye," in Robert Maddin, ed., *The Beginning of the Use of Metals and Alloys,* pp. 125–29.

12. Noel Barnard and Sato Tamotsu, *Metallurgical Remains of Ancient China,* fig. 11. See also Ping-ti Ho, *The Cradle of the East,* p. 184, table 7.

13. Ernest Watson, *The Principal Articles of Chinese Commerce,* p. 234.

14. For a survey of early copper metallurgy in the ancient Chinese world see Noel Barnard, "Thoughts on the Emergence of Metallurgy in Pre-Shang and Early Shang China, and a Technical Appraisal of Relevant Bronze Artifacts of the Time," *Bulletin of the Metals Museum* 19, pp. 3–48.

15. Han Rubin, "Recent Archaeometallurgical Achievements at the University of Science and Technology Beijing." The earring consists of a cast-copper penannular ring and a tiny polished stone found near the head of a deceased male. The copper is 99 percent pure. The stone is referred to as jade but is not nephrite.

16. For these early Bronze Age sites in Liaoning see *Kaogu,* 1992.5, p. 403, fig. 8:5, and *Kaogu xuebao,* 1992.4, p. 452, fig. 14:19. For Hebei see *Kaogu,* 1976.1, p. 60, fig. 4:2. The earrings are described as copper in the excavation reports.

17. *Kaogu xuebao,* 1988.3, p. 321, fig. 24:4.

18. Emma C. Bunker, "Gold in the Ancient Chinese World: A Cultural Puzzle," *Artibus Asiae* 53, pp. 27–50.

19. Joseph Needham, *Science and Civilisation in China,* vol. 2, pp. 51–54. See also Herrlee G. Creel, *The Origins of Statecraft in China,* pp. 140–41, n. 29.

20. Robert Dale Jacobsen, *Inlaid Bronzes of Pre-Imperial China: A Classic Tradition and Its Later Revivals,* pp. 23 and 39, n. 36.

21. Peter J. Golas, "History of Mining Technology in China," working draft for Joseph Needham, *Science and Civilisation in China* (forthcoming).

22. Shanxi, Zhejiang, Henan, Hebei, Anhui, Sichuan, Shandong, Hubei, Hunan, and Yunnan. The texts referred to are the *Zhanguo ce, Shanhaijing, Yugong, Guanzi,* and *Hanfeizi,* dating from the late Eastern Zhou period. See Lu Shizong, Lu Benshan, Hua Jueming, and Zhou Weijian, "Antiker Kupfererzbergbau."

23. Quoted by Peter J. Golas, "History of Mining Technology in China." For the *Yantielun* see Esson M. Gale, *Discourses on Salt and Iron,* p. 21.

24. Peter J. Golas, "History of Mining Technoloy in China." See also Rose Kerr, *Later Chinese Bronzes,* pp. 59–60.

25. Emma C. Bunker, "Gold in the Ancient Chinese World," p. 31, and Noel Barnard, "Thoughts on the Emergence of Metallurgy," pp. 11–13. The burials at Huoshaogou have been roughly dated by carbon-14 to 1600 B.C. The earrings contain 93 percent gold and 7 percent silver, according to Han Rubin, "Recent Archaeometallurgical Achievements."

26. See notes 16 and 71.

27. *Wenwu,* 1962.4-5, pp. 33–34, fig. 10. See also Lin Yun, "A Re-examination of the Relationship between Bronzes of the Shang Culture and of the Northern Zone," in K. C. Chang, ed., *Studies in Shang Archaeology,* pp. 248–49, fig. 50:2–5.

28. *Wenwu,* 1977.11, p. 6, fig. 17. See also Lin Yun, "Bronzes of the Shang and of the Northern Zone," fig. 50:7–9.

29. Marija Gimbutas, *Bronze Age Cultures in Central and Eastern Europe,* p. 101, fig. 61:14. See also Karl Jettmar, "The Altai Before the Turks," *Bulletin of the Museum of Far Eastern Antiquities* (hereafter *BMFEA*) 23, pp. 135–223, pl. I:B:10.

30. Noel Barnard and Sato Tamotsu, *Metallurgical Remains of Ancient China,* p. 69, n. 83.

31. Wen Tianshen, "Buried Treasures from the Ancient State of Guo," *China Today* 41, no. 5, pp. 44–45. See also Wang Min, "Ancient Tomb Discoveries Harvest China's Buried Treasures," *China Pictorial,* 1991.5, pp. 34–37. The state of Guo had been located farther west, but moved eastward to Henan in concert with the Zhou court in 771 B.C. These belt ornaments may well have been made earlier, during the waning years of the Western Zhou period, but not buried until the early Eastern Zhou period, after the state of Guo had moved. A recently published Jin-state tomb, I11M8, excavated at Beizhao in Tianma-Qucun site, Shanxi, and dated to the late Western Zhou period contained the remains of a belt adorned with gold rings and a plaque. *Wenwu,* 1994.1, p. 16, fig. 18:163–77, and p. 17, fig. 20.

32. *Kaogu yu wenwu,* 1981.1, p. 30, fig. 19:15. See also *Wenwu,* 1993.10, p. 3, fig. 3, and p. 5, fig. 9:1, 2, and 6.

33. *Zeng Hou yi mu wenwu yishu / Artistic Style of Cultural Relics from the Tomb of Zenghouyi,* pl. 235, p. 210. The highest gold content among the artifacts is 93 percent.

34. Jessica Rawson and Emma C. Bunker, *Ancient Chinese and Ordos Bronzes,* pp. 298–300.

35. Robert Dale Jacobsen, *Inlaid Bronzes of Pre-Imperial China,* p. 31.

36. See sections on mercury and metal plating in this catalogue, pp. 35–36, 47–49.

37. Victor Cunrui Xiong and Ellen Johnston Laing, "Foreign Jewelry in Ancient China," *Bulletin of the Asia Institute* 5, pp. 163–73.

38. Ernest Watson, *The Principal Articles of Chinese Commerce,* pp. 282–86.

39. For tin sources near Central Plains Shang sites see Noel Barnard and Sato Tamotsu, *Metallurgical Remains of Ancient China,* p. 25, and Ping-ti Ho, *The Cradle of the East,* p. 185, table 8. There is no clear proof that these sites were mined during the Bronze Age. See Tong Enzheng, "Zhongguo gudai qingtongqi zhong xi yuan liao de laiyuan," *Zhongguo xinan mingzu kaogu lunwenji,* pp. 224–39. Tin sources in Jiangsu, Gansu, and Linxi county, Inner Mongolia, may have played an important role in ancient times. See Zhu Shoukang, "Ancient Metallurgy of Non-Ferrous Metals in China," *Bulletin of the Metals Museum* 11 (October 1986), pp. 1–13.

40. Noel Barnard and Sato Tamotsu, *Metallurgical Remains of Ancient China,* p. 26.

41. Tong Enzheng, "Zhongguo gudai," pp. 224–39.

42. See the section on mirror metallurgy in this catalogue, pp. 42–44.

43. Emma C. Bunker, "Ancient Ordos Bronzes with Tin-Enriched Surfaces," *Orientations* 21, no. 1, pp. 78–80. See also Han Rubin and Emma C. Bunker, "Biaomian fuxi de Eerduosi qingtong shipin de yanjiu" (The study of ancient Ordos bronzes with tin-enriched surfaces in China), *Wenwu,* 1993.9, pp. 80–96.

44. See the section on metal plating in this catalogue, pp. 47–49.

45. The specific sources of lead in ancient China are not totally agreed upon today. For further information see Ernest Watson, *The Principal Articles of Chinese Commerce,* pp. 262–63. See also *Communist China* (map folio, United States Central Intelligence Agency), minerals and metals map; Noel Barnard and Sato Tamotsu, *Metallurgical Remains of Ancient China,* pp. 18–22, and 70; and Lu Shizong, Lu Benshan, Hua Jueming, and Zhou Weijian, "Antiker Kupfererzbergbau."

46. Noel Barnard and Sato Tamotsu, *Metallurgical Remains of Ancient China*, p. 70.

47. See mirror metallurgy section in this catalogue, pp. 42–44. According to Noel Barnard and Sato Tamotsu, p. 128, lead was also used to cast mirrors.

48. Mircea Eliade, *The Forge and the Crucible: The Origins and Structures of Alchemy*, pp. 19–26.

49. Donald B. Wagner, *Iron and Steel in Ancient China*, pp. 94–95.

50. Ibid., pp. 60–66, and 407. See also Lu Shizong, Lu Benshan, Hua Jueming, and Zhou Weijian, "Antiker Kupfererzbergbau," for a list of sources in Shandong, Shanxi, Hebei, Henan, Hubei, Hunan, and Sichuan-Yunnan in antiquity.

51. Robert Dale Jacobsen, *Inlaid Bronzes of Imperial China*, pp. 21–22.

52. For a discussion of iron belt hooks see Donald B. Wagner, *Iron and Steel in Ancient China*, pp. 165–70. For Henan, *Hui Xian fajue baogao*, p. 132; for Hubei, *Wenwu*, 1966.5, p. 48, fig. 2:top; for Shanxi, *Wenwu*, 1972.1, pp. 63–67, fig. 6; and for Shaanxi, Wagner, pp. 161–65.

53. *Kaogu xuebao*, 1981.2, p. 216.

54. Michael Loewe, *Ways to Paradise, The Chinese Quest for Immortality*, p. 213.

55. Peter J. Golas, "History of Mining Technology in China," section on silver.

56. For a description of the cupellation process see R. F. Tylecote, *A History of Metallurgy*, pp. 45, 157–58. Cupellation appears to have been practiced far earlier in India than it was in China, where silver was of little interest until the first millennium A.D. See B. Prakash, "Metallurgy in India through the Ages," *Bulletin of the Metals Museum* 8, p. 24. For a seventeenth-century Chinese reference see Sung Ying-hsing in *T'ien-Kung K'ai-Wu*, pp. 238–42, fig. 14-3.

57. Lu Shizong, Lu Benshan, Hua Jueming, and Zhou Weijian, "Antiker Kupfererzbergbau." The sources listed were in Shanxi, Ningxia, Gansu, Jiangxi, and the Liang mountain range in Sichuan and Yunnan. According to contemporary reports, the silver mines found in Henan province may not have been active in antiquity. See Li Jinghua, "Metallurgical Archaeology Over the Past Forty Years in Henan Province, China," *Bulletin of the Metals Museum* 20, pp. 21–22.

58. The silver ornament recently recovered from a man's burial in Huoshaogou, near Yumen in Gansu, dated to 1600 B.C. by carbon-14, may not belong to the ancient Chinese metallurgical horizon but to an extension of the metallurgical traditions prevalent at that time in northwest Asia and Central Asia. See W. Thomas Chase, "Bronze Casting in China: A Short Technical History," in George Kuwayama, ed., *The Great Bronze Age of China*, pp. 106–07. Excavations at Huoshaogou also yielded a bronze standard or pole ornament adorned with four projecting rams' heads which was published in a drawing by Noel Barnard, "Thoughts on the Emergence of Metallurgy," p. 12, fig. 4. Although the object was cast by the piece-mold process, it clearly derives ultimately from cultural traditions in Central Asia and northwest Asia. For an object with similar projecting caprid heads see the arsenical copper "standard" from Nahal Mishmar in Israel, in L. B. Hunt, "The Long History of Lost Wax Casting over Five Thousand Years of Art and Craftsmanship," *Gold Bulletin* 13, no. 2, p. 64.

59. Robert Dale Jacobsen, *Inlaid Bronzes of Imperial China*, p. 23, p. 39, n. 36, and p. 51, figs. 61–62; the inlay referenced by Jacobsen as a *terminus-post-qiem* has been shown not to be silver.

60. *Kaogu*, 1959.12, pl. 1:7. See also Giuseppe Eskenazi, *Inlaid bronze and related material from pre-Tang China*, no. 47.

61. Li Xueqin, *Eastern Zhou and Qin Civilizations*, K. C. Chang, trans., pp. 378–79.

62. Jessica Rawson and Emma C. Bunker, *Ancient Chinese and Ordos Bronzes*, pp. 299–300. See also *Nei Menggu wenwu kaogu*, 1992.6–7, p. 92, fig. 1:5.

63. *Wenwu*, 1980.7, p. 2, fig. 2.

64. Peter J. Golas, "History of Mining Technology in China."

65. Ibid.

66. Edward H. Schafer, *The Golden Peaches of Samarkand: A Study of T'ang Exotics*, p. 255, and p. 339, n. 61.

67. Peter J. Golas, "History of Mining Technology in China," and personal communication from Hua Jueming, February 1994.

68. Rose Kerr, *Later Chinese Bronzes*, pp. 59–60.

69. Ibid., p. 60.

70. For an excellent introduction to Chinese bronze see W. Thomas Chase, "Bronze Casting in China," pp. 100–23. See also Noel Barnard, *Bronze Casting and Bronze Alloys in Ancient China*, and Noel Barnard and Sato Tamotsu, *Metallurgical Remains of Ancient China*, pp. 1–75.

71. Noel Barnard, "Thoughts on the Emergence of Metallurgy," pp. 3–48.

72. For Huoshaogou see note 25. The bronze earring from Zhukaigou has not been published but was observed by Katheryn Linduff among the material from Level 3 during the summer of 1993.

73. W. Thomas Chase, "Bronze Casting in China," draft form (May 1981), p. 4.

74. Ibid.

75. Lu Shizong, Lu Benshan, Hua Jueming, and Zhou Weijian, "Antiker Kupfererzbergbau," p. 61. See also Ernest Watson, *The Principal Articles of Chinese Commerce*, pp. 268–71, and CIA map.

76. Joseph Needham, *Science and Civilisation in China*, vol. 3, pp. 1–19, 33. See also Robert Dale Jacobsen, *Inlaid Bronzes of Pre-Imperial China*, pp. 30–31, and 95, and inlay and metal plating sections in this catalogue, pp. 42, 47–49.

77. Aurifiction is "the conscious imitation of gold (and by extension . . . silver and other precious substances), often with the intent to deceive—whether by 'diluting' gold with other metals . . . or by surface enrichment . . . by amalgamation gilding." Aurifaction "was the conviction of philosophers rather than artisans." For further definition see Joseph Needham, *Science and Civilisation in China*, vol. 2, pp. 10–11.

78. Mircea Eliade, *The Forge and the Crucible*, pp. 109–26. See also Nathan Sivin, "Research on the History of Chinese Alchemy," in Z. R. W. M. von Martels, *Proceedings of the International Conference on the History of Alchemy at the University of Groningen*, pp. 3–20.

79. John S. Major, *Heaven and Earth in Early Han Thought: Chapters Three, Four and Five of the Huainanzi*, pp. 212–16.

80. Peter J. Golas, "History of Mining Technology in China," section on gold mining.

81. For information on the sources of jade and the intricacies of working it see Joan Hartman-Goldsmith, *Chinese Jade*; Roger Keverne, ed., *Jade*, pp. 53–55, and 112; and Jenny So, *Chinese Neolithic Jades*.

82. Berthold Laufer, *Jade: A Study in Chinese Archaeology and Religion*, pp. 291–92.

83. Ibid., p. 292, and for belts associated with the Turkic-speaking tribes see S. A. Pietneva, ed., *Arkheologiya SSSR*, pp. 29, 100, and 127–28.

84. *The Valuable Cultural and Historic Sites of Liaoning Province*, no. 16, p. 41.

85. Robert Thorp, "Erlitou and the Search for Xia," *Early China* 16, p. 29.

86. Luan Bing'ao, *Zenyang jianding gu yuqi*, pp. 16–23.

52 THE METALLURGY OF PERSONAL ADORNMENT

87. *Catalogue of the Exhibition of Qing Dynasty Costume Accessories,* pp. 36–37.

88. Edward H. Schafer, *The Golden Peaches of Samarkand,* pp. 230–31.

89. Ibid., p. 228. See also Sung Ying-hsing, *T'ien Kung K'ai Wu,* pp. 304–08.

90. Edward H. Schafer, *The Golden Peaches of Samarkand,* pp. 228–29.

91. Jack Ogden, *Jewellery of the Ancient World,* p. 101. To date, the identification of other ancient Asian sources has not been satisfactorily confirmed.

92. Ibid., pp. 100–01.

93. Edward H. Schafer, *The Golden Peaches of Samarkand,* pp. 230–34, 333–34, nn. 86–92.

94. Ibid., p. 232.

95. Ibid., pp. 231–34. There was no local source for lapis, but in Persia it enjoyed a special symbolism associated with the sky.

96. Ibid., pp. 242–45.

97. Ibid., p. 245.

98. C. G. Seligman, "Far Eastern Glass: Some Western Origins," *BMFEA* 10, pp. 1–64, pls. 1–16. See also Joseph Needham, *Science and Civilisation in China,* 4:1, pp. 101–11. For a discussion of eyebeads from the West see Maria Luisa Uberti, "Glass," in *The Phoenicians,* pp. 474–90. The most recent glass studies suggest that an early phase of glass making existed in China before the Warring States period, but this has yet to be identified and studied, see Robert H. Brill and John H. Martin, *Scientific Research in Early Glass.*

99. A glossary is provided at the end of the catalogue for the convenience of the reader. Certain terms, such as *incised, etched, embossed, bezel,* and *parcel gilding,* will be avoided because they are imprecise. I am enormously grateful to Professor Han Rubin and her associates at the University of Science and Technology Beijing for helping me with the Chinese names for the technical terms—ECB.

100. Emma C. Bunker, "Gold in the Ancient Chinese World," pp. 30–31, and figs. 1–4. See also sections on copper, gold, and bronze in this catalogue, pp. 32–33, 35.

101. For the early history of Chinese mirrors see Diane M. O'Donoghue, "Reflection and Reception: The Origins of the Mirror in Bronze Age China," *BMFEA* 62, pp. 5–183. For the early history of the Chinese garment hook see W. Thomas Chase, *Chinese Belt-Hooks in the Freer Gallery of Art.*

102. *Wenwu,* 1965.2, p. 43. A late Warring States bronze figure of a man wearing a belt hook was excavated at Yixian, Hebei, near the location of Xiadu, the ancient capital of the state of Yan. The figure is clearly not Chinese and probably represents a member of one of the northern herding tribes with whom the Yan had commercial relations. For the relations of Yan and the nomads see entries for catalogue numbers 21 and 22.

103. See section on lost-wax casting in this catalogue, p. 41.

104. See section on granulation under metalsmithing techniques in this catalogue, p. 46.

105. Victor Cunrui Xiong and Ellen Johnston Laing, "Foreign Jewelry in Ancient China," pp. 163–73. For Byzantine and Sasanian coins found in China see Jan Fontein and Tung Wu, *Unearthing China's Past,* pp. 183–85.

106. Jan Fontein and Tung Wu, *Unearthing China's Past,* pp. 185–87.

107. Inscriptions on the bellies of two spectacular silver-inlaid bronze animals from the Zhongshan royal tombs (late fourth century B.C.) do not name an artist but rather the foundry supervisor and craftsman in charge of the animals' production, see Robert L. Thorp, *Son of Heaven: Imperial Arts of China,* pp. 132–34.

108. For a history and discussion of the piece-mold technique see Robert Bagley, *Shang Ritual Bronzes in the Arthur M. Sackler Collections,* pp. 16–18. See also Robert Bagley, "Shang Ritual Bronzes: Casting Technique and Vessel Design," *Archives of Asian Art* 43, pp. 6–20.

109. *Kaogu,* 1962.2, pp. 55–62, pls. 1–5. The Eastern Zhou–period state of Jin should not be confused with the Jin dynasty, which ruled northern China from 1115 to 1234.

110. David Hawkes, *Ch'u Tz'u, The Songs of the South,* p. 108. This reference was also noted in W. Thomas Chase, *Chinese Belt-Hooks in the Freer Gallery of Art.*

111. The description of the two variations of the piece-mold process is based on conversations with W. Thomas Chase. For a detailed discussion of the piece-mold process see W. Thomas Chase, *Ancient Chinese Bronze Art: Casting the Precious Sacral Vessel,* pp. 23–29, fig. 1.

112. Half of a two-piece mold for casting belt hooks can be seen in an example said to come from Shouzhou, Anhui, in Nils Palmgren, ed., *Selected Chinese Antiquities from the Collection of Gustaf Adolf, Crown Prince of Sweden,* p. 51, fig. 149.

113. *Kaogu,* 1959.5, pp. 222–28, and pl. 4.

114. Donald B. Wagner, *Iron and Steel in Ancient China,* p. 20, n. 50.

115. Noel Barnard, *"Casting-On"—A Characteristic Method of Joining Employed in Ancient China.* See also Noel Barnard and Sato Tamotsu, *Metallurgical Remains of Ancient China,* p. 74.

116. Donald B. Wagner, *Iron and Steel in Ancient China,* pp. 19–20.

117. An excavated plaque recently found in northern Shaanxi still retains its chains but is missing the matching second plaque, see *Gems of China's Cultural Relics 1992,* no. 112.

118. Li Xueqin, "Chu Bronzes and Chu Culture," in Thomas Lawton, ed., *New Perspectives on Chu Culture During the Eastern Zhou Period,* pp. 1–22.

119. Ibid., fig. 16. See also *Xiasi Xichuan Chun Qiu Chumu* (Chu tombs of the Spring-Autumn Period at Xiasi, Xichuan), pl. 49.

120. The question of when lost wax was first known in ancient China has been debated for years. The possibility that it was practiced by the herding tribes on China's northern borders as early as the second millennium B.C. should be considered, see Maxwell K. Hearn, *Ancient Chinese Art: The Ernest Erickson Collection,* no. 67. As Robert Bagley has suggested, "Chinese metalworkers may well have known of the technique long before they chose to make use of it." See *Shang Ritual Bronzes in the Arthur M. Sackler Collections,* p. 44.

121. I am indebted to W. Thomas Chase for help in clearly describing this technique—ECB.

122. Ruth Whitehouse, *The Macmillan Dictionary of Archaeology,* p. 112. The indirect lost-wax process was used as early as the seventh century B.C. in ancient Greece.

123. Emma C. Bunker, "Lost Wax and Lost Textile," in Robert Maddin, ed., *The Beginning of the Use of Metals and Alloys,* pp. 222–27. See also James J. Lally, *Chinese Archaic Bronzes, Sculpture and Works of Art,* no. 39.

124. Emma C. Bunker, "Sino-Nomadic Art: Eastern Zhou, Qin and Han Artifacts Made for Nomadic Taste," part 2, pp. 578–79.

125. This technique has been successfully duplicated by Richard Kimball, a master goldsmith working in Denver, Colorado. I am most grateful to him for all his help and advice to me in researching this technique—ECB.

126. For a discussion of the Xinzhuangtou plaques see Emma C. Bunker, "Significant changes in iconography and technology among ancient China's northwestern pastoral neighbors from the fourth to the first century B.C.," *Bulletin of the Asia Institute* 6, pp. 99–115, and fig. 19. Xinzhuangtou is located at the site of Xiadu, the southern capital of the state of Yan from 311–222 B.C., when it was overrun by the state of Qin.

127. Robert Dale Jacobsen, *Inlaid Bronzes of Pre-Imperial China.* See also Jessica Rawson, *The Bella and P. P. Chiu Collection of Ancient Chinese Bronzes,* pp. 17–18. Inlay techniques not represented in the Mengdiexuan collection will not be discussed here.

128. Mahmoud M. Farag, "Metallurgy in Ancient Egypt," *Bulletin of the Metals Museum* 6, pp. 26–27.

129. Jessica Rawson, *The Bella and P. P. Chiu Collection,* p. 18. Bronze was first inlaid with gold in the form of gold script on bronze weapons, such as those excavated from the sixth-century B.C. Chu tombs at Xichuan, Xiasi, in Henan.

130. Robert Dale Jacobsen, *Inlaid Bronzes of Pre-Imperial China,* pp. 78–87.

131. Ibid., p. 81.

132. Ibid., pp. 68–69.

133. Band inlay is a term coined by W. Thomas Chase.

134. For a technical analysis of this technique see Giuseppe Eskenazi, *Early Chinese Art from Temples and Tombs,* pp. 22–27. Stone-paste inlay may have been a further development of the non-metallic, pseudo-copper, red-pigmented paste inlay on certain pictorial bronze vessels of the late Spring and Autumn period. It has been researched by Noel Barnard, *Bronze Vessels with Copper Inlaid Decor and Pseudo-Copper Inlay of Ch'un-Ch'iu and Chang-Kuo Times.* For a recent study of non-metallic paste inlay see Keith Wilson, "A Recently Acquired Archaic Sculptural Bronze," *Oriental Art* 38, no. 4, pp. 222–30. The blue and green on Cleveland's bird *bian* (CMA 91.8) are azurite and malachite paste.

135. Keith Wilson, "A Recently Acquired Sculptural Bronze," p. 228, fig. 8. A late Spring and Autumn–period bronze belt hook also in Cleveland (CMA 92.49) is embellished with blue and red non-metallic paste inlay, which has yet to be scientifically identified.

136. Bernhard Karlgren, "Huai and Han," *BMFEA* 13, pp. 1–25. See also Diane M. O'Donoghue, "Reflection and Reception."

137. Anneliese Gutkind Bulling, *The Decoration of Mirrors of the Han Period.* See also Michael Loewe, *Ways to Paradise,* pp. 60–85.

138. Joseph Needham, *Science and Civilisation in China,* vol. 4:1, pp. 87–97. See also Diane M. O'Donoghue, "Reflection and Reception," pp. 80–82.

139. Peter Swann, *Art of China, Korea and Japan,* pp. 74–75.

140. Some very helpful technical information has been included in Anneliese Gutkind Bulling, "The Dating of Chinese Bronze Mirrors," *Archives of Asian Art* 25, pp. 36–57.

141. Diane M. O'Donoghue, "Reflection and Reception," figs. 1–2.

142. Ibid., figs. 5–6.

143. Joseph Needham, *Science and Civilisation in China,* vol. 4:1, p. 89. See also William Watson, "Technique in Bronze and Precious Metals," in Giuseppe Eskenazi, *Chinese and Korean Art from the Collections of Dr. Franco Vannotti, Hans Popper and others,* p. 14.

144. Noel Barnard, *Bronze Casting and Bronze Alloys in Ancient China,* p. 192, table 9. See also Suzanne Cahill, *Chinese Bronze Mirrors.*

145. Bernhard Karlgren, "Early Chinese Mirror Inscriptions," *BMFEA* 6, pp. 9–79.

146. Michael Loewe, *Ways to Paradise,* p. 213, n. 14. Lead was also apparently used to cast mirrors, see Noel Barnard and Sato Tamotsu, *Metallurgical Remains of Ancient China,* p. 128.

147. Suzanne Cahill, *Chinese Bronze Mirrors.*

148. Diane M. O'Donoghue, "Reflection and Reception," fig. 24. See also *Kaogu,* 1962.2, pl. 4:9.

149. Wen Fong, ed., *The Great Bronze Age of China,* no. 69, pp. 277–79, and pp. 267–68.

150. Barbara W. Keyser, "Decor Replication in Two Late Chou Bronze *Chien,*" *Ars Orientalis* 11, pp. 127–62.

151. For a mirror with a similar curl and striation pattern divided into discrete units by the use of a pattern block see *Zhengzhou Erligang,* p. 71, fig. 27; for a mirror back with a similar relief pattern including zoomorph-profile heads see *Luoyang Zhongzhoulu,* p. 91, fig. 60:12; and for a discussion of mirrors with this type of curl and striation decoration see Diane M. O'Donoghue, "Reflection and Reception," pp. 83–98. The decorated background of interlocking T-shapes on another Mengdiexuan mirror (cat. no. 13) was also achieved by pattern blocks. Similar mirrors were probably cast in the vicinity of Luoyang in Henan. See James J. Lally, *Chinese Archaic Bronzes, Sculpture and Works of Art,* no. 32. For suggestions on how pattern blocks were used see Orvar Karlbeck, "Notes on the Fabrication of Some Early Chinese Mirror Molds," *Archives of Asian Art* 18, pp. 48–54.

152. Joseph Needham, *Science and Civilisation in China,* vol. 4:1, p. 93.

153. Liang Shangchun, *Yanku cangjing* 4, suppl.

154. Emma C. Bunker, "The Chinese Artifacts Among the Pazyryk Finds," *Source: Notes in the History of Art* 10, no. 4, pp. 20–24.

155. I am most grateful to Robert Mowry for bringing these objects to my attention—ECB.

156. A very similar mold fragment in the Seattle Art Museum was published in W. Thomas Chase, *Ancient Chinese Bronze Art: Casting the Precious Sacral Vessel,* p. 79, no. 45.

157. Ibid., p. 79, no. 45.

158. Bernhard Karlgren, "Early Chinese Mirror Inscriptions." See also William Watson, "Technique in Bronze and Precious Metals."

159. Without a metal analysis by X-ray fluorescence spectrometry or scanning electron microscopy (SEM), the means of achieving such surfaces are difficult to determine. W. Thomas Chase and Ursula Martius Franklin, "Early Chinese Black Mirrors and Pattern-Etched Weapons," *Ars Orientalis* 22, pp. 215–58. See also Nigel Meeks, "Patination phenomena on Roman and Chinese high-tin bronze mirrors and other artifacts," and "Surface characterization of tinned bronze, high-tin bronze, tinned iron and arsenical bronze"; in Susan La Niece and Paul Craddock, eds., *Metal Plating and Patination: Cultural, Technical and Historical Developments,* pp. 63–84, and pp. 248–75. How and when mercury was used in the tinning process is unclear and can only be determined by a scientific laboratory examination of each mirror under discussion. Analysis rarely confirms mercury on the reflecting surfaces of mirrors. Instead, mercury may have been used with tin and other materials as a polishing compound referred to as *xuan xi,* which was applied cold to the mirror surface, without heat, leaving no detectable mercury; see Meeks, pp. 80–81 and pp. 264–65. Such treatment after casting is mentioned in the *xiuwu* chapter of the early Han text of the *Huainanzi:* "When it is powdered with dark tin (*xuan xi*) and rubbed with white felt, the fine hair of the temples and eyebrows can be examined." See William Watson, "Technique in Bronze and Precious Metals," p. 14. See also notes 187 and 188.

160. Nigel Meeks, "Patination Phenomena," pp. 81–82. See also Sun Shuyun, Ma Zhaogeng, Jin Lianji, Han Rubin, and T. Ko, "The Formation of Black Patina on Bronze Mirrors."

161. For cast-bronze mirrors decorated with painted lacquer designs see the Jingman-Shashi Railway Archaeological Team, Hubei Province, *Baoshan Chumu* (Chu Cemetery at Baoshan), color pl. II:4–5.

162. Joseph Needham, *Science and Civilisation in China,* vol. 4:1, pp. 90–91.

163. Anneliese Gutkind Bulling makes some excellent observations concerning the questions of authenticity and date. See "The Dating of Chinese Bronze Mirrors."

164. Three bronze weapons, a *ge,* a knife, and dagger, excavated at Zhukaigou in western Inner Mongolia, are found to have been worked after they were cast by hammering and annealing. See Han Rubin, "Recent Archaeometallurgical Achievements." Two meteoric iron *yue* axe blades at Taixicun, Gaocheng, near Shijiazhuang, in Hebei, suggest that metalsmithing techniques were practiced close to the heartland of the Central Plains during the early Bronze Age. *Kaogu,* 1973.5, pp. 266–75, pl. 1. See also Robert Bagley, *Shang Ritual Bronzes in the Arthur M. Sackler Collections,* fig. 17.

165. Noel Barnard and Sato Tamotsu, *Metallurgical Remains of Ancient China,* p. 69, n. 83.

166. Lin Yun, "Bronzes of the Shang and of the Northern Zone," pp. 237–73, fig. 50:2. See also Katheryn Linduff, "Here Today and Gone Tomorrow."

167. Mahmoud M. Farag, "Metallurgy in Ancient Egypt," pp. 26–27. See also Karl Jettmar, *The Art of the Steppes,* p. 225, pl. 49. For an excellent example of cloisonné associated with the neighboring pastoral tribes who may have helped introduce this technique into China see the gold earrings from Tomb 4 at Xigoupan, Jungar banner, Inner Mongolia, in Adam Kessler, *Empires Beyond the Great Wall: The Heritage of Genghis Khan,* p. 62, fig. 35.

168. Jack Ogden, *Ancient Jewellery,* p. 51.

169. The presence of granulation on a gold crown and a pair of gold earrings excavated at Aluchaideng, Hangjin banner, in western Inner Mongolia, suggests the route by which this technique was introduced into northwest China. See Tian Guangjin and Guo Suxin, eds., *E'erduosi shi qingtongqi,* pls. 48 and 50:1.

170. *Wenwu,* 1993.11, color pl. 1. For two similar versions see Youngsook Pak, "The Origins of Silla Metalwork," *Orientations* 19, no. 9, pp. 44–53, figs. 16 and 17; and *Wenwu,* 1994.1, p. 55, fig. 6.

171. *Wenwu,* 1985.6, pp. 16–21, fig. 17.

172. Jack M. Ogden, "Classical Gold Wire: Some Aspects of its Manufacture and Use," *Jewellery Studies* 5, pp. 95–105.

173. Rai Govind Chandra, *Indo-Greek Jewellery,* p. 100. It has recently been suggested that two gold hairpins excavated from a Western Han tomb at Shizhaishan, Kunming, Yunnan, were made of rods that had been drawn. See Noel Barnard, *The Entry of Cire-Perdue Investment Casting, and Certain other Metallurgical Techniques (Mainly Metalworking) into South China and Their Progress Northwards,* p. 73.

174. Emma C. Bunker, "Gold in the Ancient Chinese World," p. 45.

175. *Kaogu,* 1980.4, p. 12.

176. Emma C. Bunker, "Gold in the Ancient Chinese World," p. 45. See also *Wenwu,* 1992.7, p. 11.

177. Gilding with gold foil goes back at least five thousand years in the ancient Near East, see Andrew Oddy, "Gilding Through the Ages," *Gold Bulletin* 14.2, pp. 75–79. For its earliest beginnings in China see Emma C. Bunker, "Gold in the Ancient Chinese World," p. 29; and Noel Barnard and Sato Tamotsu, *Metallurgical Remains of Ancient China,* p. 69, n. 83.

178. Emma C. Bunker, "Gold in the Ancient Chinese World," p. 35.

179. Technical information supplied by goldsmith Richard Kimball. Whether or not fusion by heating or an adhesive was used in the *baojin* process has not yet been investigated scientifically.

180. Mircea Eliade, *The Forge and the Crucible,* pp. 109–26. See also P. A. Lins and W. A. Oddy, "The Origins of Mercury Gilding," *Journal of Archaeological Science* 2, pp. 365–73. The authors note the fact that the earliest evidence of mercury-amalgam gilding appears to be Chinese. See p. 371. For an in-depth discussion of Chinese alchemy see Nathan Sivin, *Chinese Alchemy: Preliminary Studies.*

181. P. A. Lins and W. A. Oddy discuss the variations of this technique in "The Origins of Mercury Gilding." The suggestion that the presence of large amounts of lead in a bronze interferes with the process of mercury-amalgam gilding (W. A. Oddy, "Gilding Through the Ages," p. 78) has recently been contradicted convincingly by Paul Jett, "A Study of the Gilding of Chinese Buddhist Bronzes," in Susan La Niece and Paul Craddock, eds., *Metal Plating and Patination,* p. 197.

182. Emma C. Bunker, "Gold in the Ancient Chinese World," p. 29. See also Sarah Allan, *The Shape of the Turtle: Myth, Art, and Cosmos in Early China,* pp. 29–30, 65–66. There are early indications that certain colors had symbolic and auspicious meanings. This subject needs more investigation.

183. See mercury section in this catalogue, pp. 35–36. See also Mircea Eliade, *The Forge and the Crucible,* pp. 109–26.

184. Jessica Rawson and Emma C. Bunker, *Ancient Chinese and Ordos Bronzes,* p. 302.

185. Emma C. Bunker, "A New Dilemma: Recent Technical Studies and Related Forgeries," *Orientations* 25 (March 1994), p. 90.

186. Nigel Meeks, "Surface characterization." See also Han Rubin and Emma C. Bunker, "The study of ancient Ordos bronzes with tin-enriched surfaces in China," pp. 80–96.

187. Nigel Meeks, "Surface characterization," p. 255.

188. Ibid., p. 262. A low-tin bronze contains up to 14 percent tin, and a high-tin bronze contains 19–27 percent tin. See ibid., p. 247.

189. Scientific testing performed by John Twilley and Alexander Kossolapov of the Los Angeles County Museum of Art on a Warring States bronze blade with mottled patches of another metal now determined to be the result of mercury-amalgam tinning. The results to be published.

190. See note 159.

191. Recent research suggests that horse harness fittings described as *wu* in the first and second chapters of the *Xiao Rong* of the *Odes of Qin* in the *Shijing* (James Legge, *The Chinese Classics,* vol. IV, *The She King* [The Book of Poetry], part I, Book XI, Ode III, pp. 193–94), were probably "tinned" and not "gilded" (James Legge, ibid.), or "silvered" (Bernhard Karlgren, "Glosses on the Kuo Feng Odes," *BMFEA* 14, pp. 211–12). For further discussion, see Joseph Needham, *Science and Civilisation in China,* vol. 2, pp. 232–33.

192. Emma C. Bunker, "Ancient Ordos Bronzes with Tin-Enriched Surfaces," pp. 78–80. See also Jessica Rawson and Emma C. Bunker, *Ancient Chinese and Ordos Bronzes,* pp. 295–96; and Han Rubin and Emma C. Bunker, "The study of ancient Ordos bronzes with tin-enriched surfaces in China."

193. Research performed by Alexander Kossolapov and John Twilley of the Los Angeles County Museum of Art on a small Han mercury-amalgam gilded bronze ornament suggests that some silvery-colored areas accompanying some gilded areas are the result of two-tone gilding rather than actual mercury-amalgam silvering and gilding. For a recent history of silvering see Susan La Niece, "Silvering," in Susan La Niece and Paul Craddock, eds., *Metal Plating and Patination.*

194. Burton Watson, trans. *Records of the Grand Historian of China.* 1961, p. 22.

195. Quoted from a much-appreciated personal letter dated March 26, 1993, from Burton Watson, who is currently living in Niigata City, Japan.

196. Jessica Rawson, *The British Museum Book of Chinese Art,* p. 75.

197. Cyril Stanley Smith, "Art, Technology and Science: Notes on Their Historical Interaction," *Technology and Culture* 11.4, p. 494.

白珠麗

中國飾物藝術的歷史和發展

前言

自古以來，人們佩戴的飾物都跟其民族文化有莫大關連，且大多賦有象徵意義。中國古代的各種飾物正好反映出當時的社會信仰，人們的想像力及其心靈所寄。由於相信人死後能在另一個世界得到永生，以死者生前心愛飾物隨葬的風氣相當盛行。雖然飾物類型和規格往往受明文或不明文規定而有特定的形式限制，但大多足以界定其主人的身份和社會地位。

《史記》以春秋之世的中國為「冠帶之邦」，可知早至約公元前六世紀人們已普遍頂冠束帶。而經過多個世紀以來的發展，服飾制度已日臻完善，成為統治階層「定名份、辨等威」的工具。

飾物的類型與款式往往隨時代而變易，流行程度亦不盡相同。帶鉤盛行於戰國末至漢，其後逐漸為一組可裝在腰帶上的飾牌及帶扣所取代。髮飾則是歷史最悠久的飾物之一，一些新石器時期的隨葬髮飾，造型跟千百年來以至現今流行的髮飾竟無大差別，且因髮飾的盛行程度從未間斷，其發展過程亦豐富多姿。耳飾亦是另一項歷久不衰的飾物，自商至近代都有不少實例(自黃河流域一帶出土的商代耳飾多以玉或骨製成，少數的金或銅耳飾則源自其他族裔)。銅鏡除了鑑容整妝外，還可以繫於身上或懸於衾前作裝飾用，盛行於周末，然西陲青海甘肅一帶新石器時代晚期墓葬亦有發現。所有這些飾物都有不同的發展與盛衰軌蹟，無數的出土文物及夢蝶軒的珍貴藏品彌足佐證。

中國飾物藝術的沿革

憑周口店的北京人化石及有可能是佩戴用的石珠和圓形石片推斷，中國飾藝的盟芽最早可追溯至舊石器時代。近百年來，黃河流域一帶無數的新石器時代遺址均有發現玉或石製的原始飾物，如陝西半坡仰韶文化遺址的石鐲及其他遺址出土的玉耳飾和玉簪等。商周墓葬中飾物數量亦甚豐，最常見的為耳環、帶鉤和髮簪等，有純中原風格，亦有帶北方遊牧民族色彩的例子。

公元前三世紀，秦始皇併吞六國而統一天下，結束了春秋戰國以來多個世紀的紛亂局面，東周以來確立的服飾制度至此更趨嚴格。漢代(公元前206年－公元220年)國祚綿長，其間飾物造型及工藝不斷創新，一些嶄新的飾物漸見盛行，並地位日重。

漢、唐(618-906)兩朝在中國歷史上均以武功聞名，疆土的擴大與國威的顯赫使中外文化及飾物藝術得到空前交流。十一世紀之際，遼人創造了一種非常獨特，集中原與西域特色於一體的飾物風格。宋代(960-1279)製品多飾以各種花卉圖案，反映出宋人嚮往自然，追求天人合一的思想；由於崇古觀念使然及人們對古物的鍾愛，仿古飾物如帶鉤等乘時而興。明代(1368-1644)飾物風格亦受復古風氣影響，飾物造型和紋飾以傳統和古意盎然為尚，並著意標榜「華夏正統」之特質。

從考古證據看中國飾物的發展

要尋找中國古代，尤其是遠古時期的飾物實例，殊非易事。可幸自新石器時期(約公元前6500-1500年)至清代(1644-1911)，人們都有用飾物隨葬的風俗，為現今學者提供了不少方便。近百年來，考古學者在中國各地發掘了數以千計的古代墓葬，考古報告與出土實物零星地提供了有關中國飾物藝術發展的寶貴資料。經過細心整理及分析後，不難歸結出各類飾物的精神面貌，瞭解其佩戴方法及找出其盛衰的軌蹟。

新石器時期

中國的新石器時期約肇始於公元前七千年，結束於約公元前二千年，與青銅文化的冒起年代相接。在這極其漫長的五千年，黃河流域產生了無數的文化體系，而大部份考古學家都認為發祥於中游的仰韶文化是最早的新石器時期文化。約五千年前，龍山文化崛起於中國東部臨海地區。這兩個新石器文化的墓葬遺址都埋有珍貴的原始飾物。近年發現的另一臨海文化─「良渚文化」(約公元前3300-2250年)的出土玉器，造型與製作更冠於其他新石器時期文化的出土物。

大部份仰韶文化的飾物都是結構簡單和缺乏紋飾。陝西半坡仰韶文化遺址出土的飾物中有經仔細鑽孔的石珠，估計是作繫繩用的，此外又有單股骨簪及鐲等。半坡的小孩墓葬亦發現玉耳飾及骨珠等。雖然用這些飾物陪葬的實際意義仍然有待研究，但既作為陪葬用，很可能是死者生前常用或有特殊價值之物。

在公元前2250年左右崛起於中國西陲的齊家文化部分是發展自仰韶文化。1978年，青海鼎馬台齊家文化遺址發現了年代最早的銅鏡。此鏡體積不大，鏡背圖紋呈星形，跟這一帶出土的其他銅鏡紋飾大致相同。由於銅鏡是在墓主人身上發現，且邊緣鑽有兩孔，很可能是懸於胸前或繫於衣帶之用。鑑於齊家文化分佈於今寧夏及內蒙以南一帶，故或多或少會受到北方文化的影響。

龍山文化主要分佈於中國東部，出土飾物無論造型設計或製作工藝都比仰韶文化的飾物精細和講究。從龍山文化發展起來的大汶口文化則分佈於山東與江蘇一帶，其墓葬遺存中有造工精細的各類骨、石和象牙製飾物如鐲、珠、梳、簪及佩飾等，其中最具特色的要算一只刻有抽象紋飾的象牙小梳(見圖一)。

山東臨朐縣龍山文化遺址所出的一件玉髮簪，簪尖玉色呈墨綠，簪頭部份玉色較淡，並鑲有兩片綠松石(見圖二)，異常別緻，可見早在新石器時代，人們已對裝飾藝術有相當認識與研究。

發掘新石器時代墓葬時，常會在死者身上發現鐲、梳、髮簪和指環等物。從出土位置看來，這些飾物顯然並非隨意擺放在墓裡純粹作陪葬之用，而是經過刻意挑選，配戴在死者身上特定地方以取其裝飾效果。1957年，江蘇一座馬家濱文化墓葬發現一女性骸骨，頭頂上橫置一骨製髮簪(見圖三)。這種為死者美容整妝的做法，顯示古以來中國已普遍存在人死後生命會以另一方式延續的觀念。

商代

約公元前十六世紀左右，商民族在中原冒起，繼而建立商朝。在其中央集權式的統治下，黃河流域一帶的經濟文化得以蓬勃發展。從殷商墓葬遺存可看到飾物日益受重視。商代飾物設計精巧繁複，基本上可算是新石器時期龍山文化裝飾風格的延續，但質料取材更廣更精，河南二里頭遺址的商代早期遺存便是其中一例。隨著時代的進化，隨葬品的選擇亦越來越講究，張光直在其《中國古代考古學》(The Archaeology of Ancient China)一書中指出：「這些新特色(墓穴規模媲美皇族陵寢....擺放著各種珍品、青銅禮器與兵器、配套的酒器，甚至有人殉的痕蹟及類似文字的圖形)標示著二里頭曾居住著地位極為顯赫的家族，比諸龍山文化一些主要為貴族的墓葬主還要尊貴。」此等顯赫家族自然能為死者提供各式用骨及珠寶玉石製成的飾物。

商代墓葬的隨葬飾物有各款耳飾、釧鐲、佩飾、珠子和簪釵等。河南安陽小屯與西北崗商代皇族墓葬出土的飾物，更反映出商代玉雕工藝與裝飾工藝的高水平，其中以婦好墓的玉飾數量最為豐富。玉器向被視為具有驅邪擋煞的神祕力量，自然是陪伴死者前赴幽冥的最佳隨身飾物。雖然此時青銅製品數量甚豐，但並無實例顯示中原人士有佩戴青銅飾物的習慣。

離開了中原的商民族活動範圍，商文化影響漸弱。從一些中原以外的墓葬可發現青銅及黃金製的飾物如耳飾等。夢蝶軒藏品中有一對飾松石金耳墜(目錄編號1)正代表著當時北方一些部族的飾物風格。山西的商墓亦發現造型相似而又同樣結合了金石工藝的耳飾，在一定程度上證明了佩戴金耳飾的風氣並非中原的商民族所創，而是來自北方的其他族裔。

周代

周朝國祚極長，前後幾近八個世紀，其間多個地域與性質各異的文化得以融匯交流。由大約公元前十二至十一世紀建國開始直至公元前770年周室東遷洛邑之前為止，因以鎬京(今西安附近)為都，後世稱為西周，遷都後迄於周亡則稱為東周。東周又再分為春秋與戰國兩個時期，前者由公元前770-475年，後者由公元前475-221年。在深入研究個別東周墓葬的飾物遺存前，本文會先從整體上簡略探討一下周代的製飾工藝。

在不同的信仰與禮制觀念影響下，商周兩代的社會文化及工藝製品大異其趣。隨著社會結構的遞變，藝術風格亦產生了變化，例如兩朝交替之際的青銅器造型漸趨通俗；商代的玉器主要是作為禮器，但東周時已漸成為奢侈品，其中以玉飾尤然。

就墓葬遺存作比較，周代飾物無論在數量、類型及普及程度方面都較商代優勝。周代製品花樣豐富，有指環、手鐲、耳飾、帶鈎、髮飾(簪和梳)、珠子、鈕扣及銅鏡等，其中以帶鈎的發展最受注目，自東周墓葬出土的帶鈎多不勝數。基本上，兩朝的飾物遺存都是來自皇族墓葬，然周代製品在選材與工藝水平方面皆比前朝進步，且由於出土飾物數量極豐，證明早在周代人們已對各類首飾製品需求甚殷。

周代社會階級劃分嚴格而繁複，各階級間的尊卑貴賤壁壘分明。雖然周代早期的飾物到底有何實質意義已無從稽考，但既然墓葬品中禮器的數目與規格都得依循一定法則，視墓主人身份地位而有所變易，可以推想到憑墓葬中的飾物亦可界定墓主人之階級等第。

西周貴族服飾有定制，加官晉爵時獲賜的衣履冠飾等往往有一定的形式，周代的文獻與詩歌亦有關於冠服與飾物的描述，顯然這等衣飾跟當時的禮制有很密切的關係。舉例來說，據《禮記》所載，男子二十行冠禮，冠而後成人，「始加緇布冠，再加皮弁服，三加爵弁服」，一件比一件尊貴，代表著成年、從戎與晉身貴族三個階段。此等禮儀的目的是讓貴族子弟清楚意識到自己在整個階級架構擔當的角色，而相應的飾物則用以標示其身份地位。女子十五則行笄禮，笄是一種成年女子安髮用的頭飾。

東周時期

東周墓葬所出的飾物質料取材較廣，有青銅、玉及其他寶石等。更有證據顯示從公元前六世紀開始，人們已用黃金製造各種飾物。戰國時期秦國生產了大量具實際用途的黃金衣飾，西安附近鳳翔縣秦景公墓出土的小型金鈎很可能是扣攏衣領用的，而現今陝西一帶的秦墓亦有同類型的小鈎出土。

夢蝶軒藏品中有三件小型帶鉤(展品目錄編號2、3及4)，與鳳翔縣出土的金鉤有著很密切的關係。其中編號3及4的帶鉤有相同的扣繫設計，且同是以範鑄法製成；編號2則跟陝西寶雞益門村出土的一件小鉤相若。

由於東周墓葬所出的帶鉤數量霍然大增，可知其盛行程度亦高於西周時期。普遍來說，每個墓葬只發現一件帶鉤，但當然亦有例外，正如學者羅覃(Thomas Lawton)在其著作《戰國時代的中國藝術》(Chinese Art of the Warring States Period)中提及：「根據現有考古資料顯示，似乎每個墓葬只放一件帶鉤是中國一貫的慣例，但亦有個別例子顯示帶鉤數目不止此數，相信是用來壯大隨葬品的陣容以強調墓主人之顯赫地位。」帶鉤之所以在東周變得更普及，大概與工藝美術品的漸趨通俗化(見前文)、朝服形式的改變、和各種用以表現身份的貴重飾物原料如金、銀及青銅的產量日增有關。

東周之世，是中國思想文化史上一個鼎盛時期；百家爭鳴，學術較前普及，庶民受教育的機會亦相應增加。此外，特殊的政治與經濟環境亦導致中原漢族與北方部落的頻密接觸，促使了「胡服」的盛行。相傳首先推行者為趙武靈王，《史記》記載他於公元前307年下令國人「胡服騎射」以適應戰爭需要，使趙國能日趨強盛。但以趙武靈王為始作俑者的說法顯然不可信，因為一些公元前五及六世紀的銅器已有胡服模樣的人像紋飾。

所謂「胡服」，大抵是北方燕國流行的服式。戰國時期，燕與趙同居七雄之列，齊起爭霸。燕據有今東北之地，聚居了多個不同的少數民族，有東胡、或甚至匈奴等非華夏族裔。一般胡服為緊窄短衣、長褲與革靴，便於馳騁格鬥，跟常見的戎服有很多共通點。從一些戰國墓俑及銅器紋飾都可看到這種裝束的上衣前衿作橫掩式，勒有帶，以帶鉤扣攏(見圖四)。

春秋戰國之際還出現了一種叫「深衣」的服式，並無上衣與下裳之分，而是上下連成一體的長袍，腰間繫帶，可能以帶鉤扣攏。這個時期的青銅器亦間中有這種服式的紋樣。河北平山縣出土的戰國舉燈銅人即為一例，該男性銅人身上所穿的長袖袍服正是深衣，腰間束帶，用帶鉤扣攏(見圖五)。

陝西、河南及河北等地出土的帶鉤中，很多都是公元前五至四世紀東周時代遺物。這一帶地區正是戰國時期燕、趙、秦的疆土所在，分別據峙於其東部、中部及西部，與北方部族都有或多或少的接觸。然而，一些較南面的戰國墓如楚墓、曾墓，甚至遠至位於現今廣州的西漢南越王墓亦有帶鉤的發現。有關帶鉤是如何在漢族衣飾中佔一席位這問題至今尚未明朗，且亦難以確定漢人是受北方民族影響才採用帶鉤。黃河流域出土的帶鉤數量很多，大部份是戰國時期文物。

東周時期的帶鉤大小不一，造型與紋飾亦豐富多姿。基本上帶鉤的結構可分鉤首與鉤體兩部份；首為鉤狀，多作鳥首或龍頭形，體則呈拱狀，背後約中間位置為一凸起鈕形，用作扣繫衣帶用。一處戰國楚墓曾發現一根絲織腰帶及三件帶鉤，腰帶兩端穿有小孔，一端用於嵌進帶鉤背後的凸鈕而另一端則讓鉤首扣著(見圖六)。如此式樣的腰帶，《史記》中亦有記載。

考古發掘已證實自商代開始，歷來皇室陵寢的遺存物在質與量方面都是其他墓葬所不及，河南金村東周時期周室墓葬是其中一例。有一種鑲滿綠松石而甚具特色的帶鉤，部份即來自金村遺址。夢蝶軒藏品中有兩件帶鉤跟這些金村遺物亦十分相似(目錄編號25及26)。然而，這類帶鉤卻並非金村獨有，在多個不同的地域如山西朔縣，甚至遠至廣州象崗南越王二世墓也曾發現造型與結構相若的例子。這些墓葬都有一個重要的共通點，就是全屬皇族墓葬。以這種帶鉤作陪葬物，目的是要令墓主人的顯赫身份和地位在幽冥世界也得到認同。

戰國時期亦有鐵造的帶鉤，夢蝶軒藏品中有一件錯金銀鐵帶鉤可算是其中表表者(目錄編號20)。雖然帶鉤因年代久遠而多所磨損，但仍可看錯金銀紋飾是如何精細別緻。在戰國之前，鐵主要是用來製作各種生產工具，但戰國之時，漸流行鐵製的飾物和奢侈品。河南信陽縣長台關亦有一件戰國的鐵帶鉤出土。這兩件飾物讓我們看到黃金與鐵兩種金屬的強烈對比。

除帶鉤外，戰國時期還流行以青銅、金、銀及其他金屬製造各種飾物。夢蝶軒藏有一只銅梳，是當時銅製飾物的典型例子(目錄編號14)。中國早期的梳子普遍是用竹或木製成，河南長沙馬王堆西漢墓所出的一套妝奩用具便是例證。雖然青銅與金兩種金屬的結合在製造帶鉤方面產生了很好的效果，但對髮飾而言則似乎不太實際，因為青銅除了太笨重外，其柔軟度與韌性亦不夠，很難製出細緻的式樣。考古報告亦顯示商周墓葬鮮有發現金屬製髮飾。照現有資料看來，似乎古代的髮飾是相當直接地由骨、木及石等材料發展至用黃金這種貴重金屬。

戰國晚期北方文化藝術對飾物的影響

部份戰國晚期北方部族的墓葬曾發現一些很有價值的金飾及用其他金屬製成的飾物。內蒙伊克昭盟準格爾旗西溝畔發掘得的墓葬肯定並非漢裔所有。其中一男性墓葬埋有大量金飾，包括有項飾、飾牌及耳飾等。其中一件飾牌背面刻有銘文及重量。河北易縣辛莊頭燕下都遺址出土的飾牌亦有類似銘文。夢蝶軒藏品中有一件圓形飾牌亦屬北方風格，背後亦刻有重量(目錄編號22，飾牌正面紋樣見圖七)。這些飾牌是當時中原民族與北方諸部族文化交往的明證。

內蒙一帶亦發掘到不少公元前三世紀的帶飾牌和其他飾物，都標示著當時北方的飾物風格。夢蝶軒有一組藏品，正代表著其時北方流行的飾物；除了包括前述的圓形飾牌外，尚有編號21的鍍錫青銅飾牌，屬公元前三世紀文物，跟河北易縣燕下都一帶出土的同年代飾牌除造型極為相似外，更同是用失蠟失織法鑄成；紋飾構圖複雜，動物作咬鬥狀，正是當時北方盛行的裝飾風格。

中原文物受北方文化藝術影響的另一重要例子是銅鏡的南傳。東北地區出土的一些西周時代圓形銅片和銅鈕，應爲當時東北遊牧民族繫於腰間的飾物。山西侯馬發現的大量陶製鏡範，全屬公元前六至五世紀的產物。山西東南部戰國時代晉國貴族墓葬所出的銅鏡，跟夢蝶軒藏品中一面銅鏡十分相似(目錄編號9)，同樣反映出這個時期中原一帶的銅鏡紋飾是以動物圖案爲主流。

北方民族的獨特裝飾風格，並未因秦漢以後天下歸於一統而受到同化。夢蝶軒所藏的鎏金透雕青銅帶飾牌(目錄編號32)正代表著這種北方獨有裝飾風格的延續。這飾牌應與遼寧西豐西岔溝發現的飾牌一樣，可能屬於聚居長城以北的匈奴遺物。

秦、漢與六朝

前文已述及陝西一帶的戰國秦墓有大量的公元前六至五世紀的金製帶鉤出土。秦始皇於公元前221年統一天下，繼而在公元前214年將匈奴遠逐北方。雖然《史記》及其他同期的文獻都曾提及秦室陵墓藏有極豐的文物，但據目前發掘所得，大部份秦墓都無甚遺存，或有可能已盡爲前人盜掘。始皇陵寢原本藏有大量珍寶這說法極爲可信，可惜歷來盜墓者眾，而倖存的又或未被發現。

陝西臨潼縣秦始皇陵東端出土的兵馬俑陣容雖然空前地龐大，但飾物遺存卻少之又少。幸而從這些近乎眞人大小的陶俑身上可看到當時戎服的式樣，例如5號溝2號坑的武士俑身上所塑的帶鉤，便是當時盛行的款式。

公元前206年，劉邦即帝位，以長安爲都，奠定了漢皇朝的基業。在以後差不多四個世紀，除了王莽篡位自立的十五年外(王莽的新朝將黃金列爲貨幣的一種，但只限於貴族使用)，天下歸於一統，政治局面亦相當穩定。公元25年，光武帝遷都洛陽，即周室舊都，史稱東漢，而之前則稱西漢。漢代實行中央集權制統治，嚴謹的宗法與政治制度使全國由上至下階級分明，皇公貴胄按與皇帝的親疏來定等第，文武百官則依官位高低而尊卑有序。

漢代皇族墓葬的出土物異常豐富，湖南長沙的西漢馬王堆墓及河北滿城的中山靖王劉勝墓與夫人竇綰墓爲典型例子。墓中陳設華麗，遍佈珍寶，目的是要讓墓主人能繼續有豐富的物質享受。西漢時道敎思想大行其道，神仙與鍊丹致長生之說深入民心，加上佛敎思想的傳入，人們對生命的看法有很大的改變，繼而影響到墓葬品的內容與墓中的陳設。

漢代墓葬的奢華程度，從中山靖王與其妻的殮服可窺一二。二人所穿的金鏤玉衣是以金絲、玉片精工編綴而成，據云可令屍身不腐，是殮服中之極品。墓中尚有大量珍貴文物與飾物，包括有玉刻和燈飾。馬王堆漢墓則存有大量絲織品、漆器和木器，其中包括個人飾物如梳子等。存放在妝奩盒內之木梳造型跟夢蝶軒藏品中那只銅梳相近。盒內尚有其他婦女梳妝用品，且有假髮一具。此外亦發現漆繪織錦紋銅鏡，與夢蝶軒藏品目錄編號36的漆繪幾何紋銅鏡相類似。長江流域也有銅鏡出土，證明銅鏡發展迅速，流播日廣。大體來說，皇族墓葬的出土物種類豐富，有漆器、紡織物、書籍、錢幣、陶碟、小型陶俑及陶屋等。

1983年，廣州發現了西漢時期南越王二世趙胡的陵墓。墓主身穿絲鏤玉衣，以標示其尊貴身份。玉衣面罩上蓋一絲絹面幕，面幕綴有八片飾有對稱羊頭及熊首紋的薄金片(見圖八)。夢蝶軒藏品中有一件飾牌(目錄編號35)，與之紋飾相若，紋樣是以錘沖和鏤刻技法造出。此墓的隨葬物反映出中原文化藝術的南傳，及漢室聲威的無遠弗介。

至於青銅器，包括各式禮器、日用器及飾物，仍然在漢代墓葬品中佔一重要席位。有蹟像顯示漢代青銅飾物的紋飾與技法是取材自各種青銅容器，夢蝶軒所藏的幾件漢代錯銀絲青銅帶鉤即爲一例。河南出土的東周末方鑑所用的錯金絲技法，精巧而複雜，西漢時的青銅器亦有沿用，劉勝墓所出的一件銅壺便是明證。這些技法亦有用於漢代飾物工藝，夢蝶軒所藏一件正面與背面皆錯有銀絲，並鑲有寶石的鎏金帶鉤(目錄編號38)；帶鉤背面的紋飾流暢婉約，正是漢代的典型風格。

經過整個世紀的休養生息後，國內政安人和，漢室便興起外揚國威、大拓疆土之念。除了用武力臣服四夷外，又遣使通好，使中原禮敎得以傳至西域及北面各部族，造成空前的文化大交流。公元前一世紀，中國商旅的足蹟已沿著橫貫中亞細亞的絲路遠及歐洲。影響所及，連當時羅馬帝國的商人亦加入與中國貿易的行列。各國商旅在絲路上絡驛不絕，用各式貨品或甚至西方用以作貨幣的黃金來交換漢人的絲綢，使黃金越加得到時人的重視。東漢初期，佛敎亦經絲路傳入中國，很快地便給中國文化藝術如繪畫及飾物設計等帶來很大的沖擊。至於來自北方部族，尤其是匈奴的影響，則從未間斷。

絲路沿線的漢代遺址所出的飾物，無論結構、紋飾與質料都反映著中原與西域文化藝術融合的成果。1976年，新疆維吾爾自治區焉耆縣黑格達遺址發現一件別具特色的漢代龍紋金帶扣(見圖九)。這種形式和質料的帶扣源於西域，應用時是將一連串帶飾牌裝於多爲皮革造的腰帶上，漢末時開始在中原取代傳統勻形帶鉤的地位，隨後多個世紀依然盛行不衰，其他飾物工藝亦受其影響。以金絲盤出精細紋飾及用金珠點綴的裝飾法使飾牌看來玲瓏浮凸，富麗華美，故極受貴族階級的喜愛。湖南安鄉黃山頭西晉劉弘墓亦有形式相若的龍紋帶扣出土(見圖十)，顯示其在漢以後的流行情況。朝鮮平壤石岩里一處公元一至二世紀的墓葬亦發現一件以同樣形式工藝製作的帶扣。

六朝時候(265-589)，這種金絲和金珠工藝在飾物製作中仍然佔著重要的地位。夢蝶軒藏品中的龍紋金飾牌(目錄編號47)應屬冠飾類，正是這類裝飾工藝的典範之作。龍紋成對稱狀，在蜿蜒曲折的龍軀上滿綴大小漸進的金珠，技法跟前述的帶扣並無異致。

另一例子是夢蝶軒藏品中的六朝金梳(目錄編號48)，梳背滿綴金珠，並鑲有寶石和玉牌，顯示出當時這種工藝技術的取向。菱形的邊緣紋飾與安陽劉弘墓所出帶扣的裝飾風格非常相似。從金梳的貴重質料與精湛工藝推斷，物主一定非富則貴。這種金珠工藝本源自西域，藉顆粒大小不一的金珠來表現紋飾的細節，極具裝飾效果。

漢代亦流行各種髮飾。文士頭上所插的「白筆簪」實演變自當時文臣攜筆上朝而用後插於耳邊髮際的習俗，漸而筆尖不醮墨而純粹用作裝飾，從一些漢墓壁畫亦可看到這類髮飾。

冠服是漢人最重要的服飾之一，是身份等第的標識，有明文嚴格規定何種等級的人應戴何種冠服。漢代男子一般將長髮在頭頂束成髮髻，用簪固定。隨著冠帽的日益講究，髮簪的裝飾作用便漸為人忽視。各種冠帽的形式與用途可見於文獻，而很多漢壁畫及畫像磚也有描繪戴著各式冠帽的男子像。

漢代婦女以長髮為美，編成辮子後挽起在頭頂結成髮髻。從漢代的女墓俑、壁畫、畫像磚及其他墓葬物都可看到當時婦女流行的各種髮式。漢代樂府詩賦中詠及士女皎麗容妝的例子甚多。三國時期魏詩人曹植受洛水之神傳說所感而作《洛神賦》，其中描述洛神宓妃的服飾更是妙蔓多姿，閃爍生輝：「披羅衣之璀燦兮，珥瑤之華琚，戴金翠之首飾，綴明珠以耀軀」。

漢代婦女的髮飾主要為簪，插在髮髻上除了綰住頭髮外，更有裝飾效果，漢壁畫中常有描繪。很多時，簪頭上懸垂著嵌有各式珠寶的金鏈索，隨著人的步伐搖動，煞是好看，故有「步搖」之稱。宮中貴婦戴在頭上用以標示身份的「幗」是一種帽圈，式樣繁多，其上再可插各種髮飾。至於宮中舞樂藝伎的髮式與頭飾則異常繁縟，廣州漢墓所出的一具頭梳盛髻的女舞俑是為明證。

漢代大拓疆土，聲威震懾四夷，締造了中外文化藝術的大交流。由於國內政治穩定，社會經濟得以日趨發達，飾物工藝亦多所創新，以滿足當時貴族與新興中產階級的需求，飾物亦漸脫離禮器的行列而趨向於通俗。雖然漢末衛道之士對當時社會上奢華的服飾及隨葬品風氣大事評擊，但都改變不了人們對美的追求及以服飾和隨葬品展示財富的心態。此時金飾越加流行，且鑒於黃金已成為貨幣的一種，歸嚴格管制之列，一般人無從擁有，故此金飾便成為身份的象徵。大體來說，漢代的飾物，尤其是金飾，主要是統治階層與富商巨賈的專利品，是衡量身份財富的標準。

唐代與遼代

唐代飾物的作用跟前朝沒有甚麼分別，主要是作為衣飾之用，造型紋飾和質料則視物主身份地位而定。據考古資料顯示，當時除了傳統的簪釵和梳篦等飾物仍繼續流行外，還創製出很多新穎的種類與造型，如組帶具、花冠及項飾等。由於與外族尤其是西域地區的交往頻密，使飾物花樣不斷豐富，紋飾方面亦受到極其深遠的影響。

自戰國以至漢末，帶鉤一直盛行不衰。西晉(265-316)是帶鉤形式轉變的過渡期，其間傳統的形式漸趨式微，代之而興的是「蹀躞帶」上配套式的帶飾牌。究其原委，是因為公元59年時漢室頒下一道詔書，將帶鉤剔除於禮服的必然飾件之外。自此帶鉤日漸衰微，演變為長腰帶上配置多個帶飾牌。至唐代，由於受北方與西域帶具風格的影響，帶飾牌造型又再創新。除了在飾牌下端穿孔以懸掛飾物和引進西域形式的帶扣外，尚有很多其他異於傳統的特色。部份設計雖然未能在唐以後繼續流行，但在當時的確是大受歡迎。為了要瞭解唐代帶飾牌的發展背景，本文先約略窺探一下其在六朝的發展狀況。

西晉時期的青銅帶飾牌，有鎏金或鎏銀，如夢蝶軒藏品中多件鎏金或鎏銀青銅帶飾牌(目錄編號50)顯示，是由兩塊四周有突棱的金屬片相夾而成，用鉚釘釘牢，前後並非緊貼而是留有空間。吉林省和龍縣北大渤海墓葬亦有同類型製品發現。這些飾牌上的龍鳳及神獸紋雖為中國傳統紋飾，然腰帶形式則顯然來自北方，西晉以後亦鮮見流行於中土，但卻在稍後期的一些朝鮮墓葬出現。至唐代時，這類形式的腰帶繼續流行，然細節則有些變化。

唐初帶飾牌在結構上跟西晉製品分別不大，但紋飾卻因受西域裝飾風格影響而迥異。夢蝶軒藏有一組狻猊紋帶飾牌(目錄編號51)，張牙舞爪的狻猊和棕櫚紋顯然是取材自西域紋飾。誠然，中國帶飾的發展過程並非以此為終結，但事實上中國亦未有發現這類型的配套帶飾牌，現有實例全屬西方藏品。

從這些六朝與唐初配套帶飾牌，可以清楚看到漢、唐兩代大拓疆土對飾物藝術造成的巨大影響。唐代帶飾牌在傳統的基礎上融進西方藝術菁華，繼而創出別樹一幟的風格，顯示了中國文化對外來文化兼收並蓄的特性。來自西域的帶具，紋飾有時候是典型的西方風格，但亦有揉合了中西特色的創新題材。夢蝶軒藏品中有一組唐代帶飾牌，除了傳統的雙鴨紋外，還有帶西域色彩的雙鷹圖案(目錄編號53)，反映出當時中西裝飾藝術交流的實況。其西土風格的帶扣和飾牌下端穿孔的設計均來自居於中亞的突蹶系遊牧民族。除了玄宗之世，「蹀躞帶」於唐代是文武官員必佩之物，飾牌穿孔是便於懸掛標識身份用的飾件。

銀製飾物在唐以前並不多見，但在唐代卻大盛，主要是受西域藝術風格影響。北方的遼國(907-1125)亦對銀飾同樣喜愛，一些契丹貴族墓葬曾發現整副的銀帶具，質料與製作都極其精麗。十一世紀內蒙遼代陳國公主墓發現大批金、銀器和寶石製品，其中有一副鎏金銀帶具，飾有金質飾件及掛飾。夢蝶軒藏有一組鎏金銀帶具，包括掛袋與各種掛飾，全數達七十一件之多(目錄編號77)，製工極精，顯示出遼人高超的工藝水平。至於另外兩套帶飾牌(目錄編號79及80)，則形狀各異，藉此營造較為多樣化的視覺效果。

除了傳統的飾物種類外，唐代還創製了一些新穎的項飾和花冠，為前朝所無，靈感大抵來自當時盛行於中國的佛教藝術。新疆和甘肅一帶佛教遺址的壁畫常畫有一列戴著花冠的菩薩像。就敦煌而言，年代最早的石窟壁畫都有這類花冠的描繪。以263窟北魏「說法圖」壁畫為例，其中一菩薩頭上的髮冠綴滿環形和鳥形紋飾，極其華美，所戴耳飾亦誇張奪目(見圖十一)。唐末時，觀音成為最普遍的崇拜對象。從57窟壁畫所見，除了比丘外，觀音和其他的供養菩薩像均戴著各式花冠(見圖十二)。至於畫中所繪的俗世人物造像，則衣裝華麗，如220窟所繪的帝皇和群臣像，清楚反映出當時朝中人士的衣冠和髮飾式樣。站在這些人物身後的菩薩頭戴花冠，頸纏項鏈，顯示出當時的佛教造像大多戴著這種花冠(見圖十三)。胡人中亦有戴花冠者，如158窟「涅盤變」壁畫所繪的胡人模樣的信眾中，有戴帽形冠，亦有戴這種花冠(見圖十四)。此外，61窟的北宋時期「于闐公主圖」壁畫，畫中的公主亦頭戴花冠，頸纏項鏈(見圖十五)。這些源於佛教藝術的瑰麗飾物，先在唐都長安興盛起來，繼而流傳至全國各地。

唐末及遼代時，本是佛教造像裝飾物的花冠和金屬項圈逐漸在民間流行開來。自唐末開始，其他髮飾的造型和紋飾亦受絢麗的花冠所感染而變得繁複起來，例如梳子比前大和設計較複雜，銀質與鎏金銀髮飾比前普遍。內蒙十一世紀遼代陳國公主墓所出的華麗花冠正代表著此時流行的頭飾。

至於金屬項圈，與花冠沿起相若，同樣可以從敦煌壁畫與絲路沿線各佛教遺址的壁畫看到例證。敦煌329窟唐代壁畫中之女供養人像戴有耳環及項圈，顯示這種項圈已不單是佛像身上的裝飾品。夢蝶軒藏有一件鏤刻有鳥紋的鎏金銀項圈(目錄編號69)(見圖十六)，風格與唐代一些帶西方色彩，尤其是受波斯工藝影響的銀器頗為相似。美國明尼亞波利斯美術學院亦藏有一件類似的項圈。

其他傳統飾物類型如簪釵、指環、釧鐲、梳子、耳飾和銅鏡等在唐代繼續盛行，但都受到外來藝術風格的影響而有不同的面目，其中以紋飾方面尤然。簪釵、梳子和銅鏡等的體積變得較大。以髮簪為例，一般較漢代製品為大，甚至有直追花冠的趨勢；鑑於佛教題材紋飾的興起，綴以佛像的簪釵比比皆是。夢蝶軒藏品中有一對髮簪，其中一件刻有小男孩在玩「法輪」，另一件則刻有蓮花紋及「飛天」，同樣是佛教意味極重的紋飾(目錄編號62)。另外一只銀梳亦是以「飛天」作裝飾(目錄編號67)。唐代時外來文化藝術在中國如百花盛放，促使了以佛教為題材的飾物的發展。

夢蝶軒藏品中一件唐代髮簪(目錄編號63)，其上的扭曲魚紋是根源自佛教紋飾中的「摩竭羅魚紋」，是印度所創，唐代時中土的銀碟、瓷器及髮飾等都有採用。據說摩竭羅魚是一種兇悍的水中精靈，在印度很受尊崇，首先見於阿建塔地區的佛教石窟，傳入中國後稱作「龍魚」。遼代的耳飾(如目錄編號71)亦有這種龍魚紋飾，以扭曲的魚巧妙地設計出半圓形的圖案。這種龍魚紋在明代復興，可從夢蝶軒所藏的六對紋飾相若的明代耳環反映出來(目錄編號71a)。

唐人及後世人們之所以對佛教題材的紋飾趨之若鶩，似乎是潮流使然多於宗教因素。由於飾物亦用上這類題材的紋飾，可見佛教已深入民心。有時侯，某些題材本身並無宗教意義，但卻反映了其時社會的普遍信仰。學者帕特麗夏·阿布利(Patricia Ebrey)和彼德·格力哥利(Peter Gregory)在《中國唐宋兩朝的宗教和社會》(Religion and Society in T'ang and Sung China)中曾指出:「廣義而言，宗教當然在中國人生活中佔著很重要的地位。自古以來，中國人對各種神祇、鬼魅和祖先的形像都十分熟識...他們通過各種宗教儀式、徵象與意念探索宇宙的本質及人類在宇宙中的地位。」

鑑於唐宋兩朝的髮飾和其他飾物都受佛教及道教藝術影響甚深，我們有必要研究一下宗教紋飾究竟在標示身份地位方面起著甚麼作用。佛教將信眾分為很多階層，他們在皈依佛教後會從中得到一些別處沒有的機會，使個人與家庭的地位得到提升，一般庶民亦不例外。前述著作中有如下一段：「於是佛教建立了一套它自有的半獨立的地位標識制度。很明顯地，佛教其中一項吸引力是為有才學的普羅士子提供了向上爬的階梯，使其不致因出身寒微而未能晉身仕途。(此情況以唐代尤然，因為晉身仕途的渠道比宋代多限制)。」

由於大量奢侈品由國外湧入唐都城長安，使人人崇尚奢華，程度之烈為前朝所未見。婦女用的飾物大行其道，一反向來以男子飾物如帶鉤等為主導的傳統風尚。當時各種男用帶具的價值均以質料為著眼點，多為金及銀這兩種常用來標示身份的名貴金屬，質料越珍貴則表示物主地位越高。然而，以金銀珠翠點綴頭飾、簪釵和梳子等卻是女性的專利，唐代詩歌以此為題材的非常多。

唐代騷人墨客對宮中美女的嫋娜丰姿和動人裝扮有無窮的讚美。從他們的作品可以看見當時貴婦衣裝的一鱗半爪。膾炙人口的杜甫《麗人行》有如下佳句：

> 三月三日天氣新，長安水邊多麗人。
> 態濃意原淑且真，肌理細膩骨肉勻。
> 繡羅衣裳照暮春，蹙金孔雀銀麒麟。
> 頭上何所有？翠微㔼葉垂鬢唇。
> 背後何所見？珠壓腰衱穩稱身。...

由於很多唐代婦女都視佛門為遁世之所，故此特別喜愛並要求訂製佛教紋樣的珠寶首飾。前述著作有此見解：「雖然婦女未能像男性一樣，藉著佛教令一己的社會地位得到提升，但佛門往往成為她們逃避不如意婚姻和家庭生活的安身之所。」縱使這些飾物在標識身份方面起不了多大作用，但其華貴資料卻能增添美態和顯示配戴者的財富。

許多唐代的絹畫都有描繪宮中盛裝貴婦的華麗頭飾。瀋陽遼寧省博物館藏有唐代周昉的《簪花仕女圖》，畫中貴婦梳起高高的髮髻，前端飾有精巧別緻的金飾，後面及兩側則插著馬蹄形的髮簪。

銅鏡的使用和流行狀況，亦可從繪畫與詩詞中看到端倪。相傳為晉代畫家顧愷之所繪的《女史箴圖卷》，描畫了貴婦對鏡梳妝的情形。貴婦前置一架子，上繫銅鏡，身後則站著替她梳理頭髮的侍女。此外，唐代詩人白居易的《感鏡》，充滿了對鏡傷別離的哀愁：

美人與我別，留鏡在匣中。自從花顏去，秋水無芙蓉。經年不開匣，紅埃覆青銅。今朝一拂拭，自照憔悴容。照罷重惆悵，背有雙蟠龍。

唐代銅鏡一般體積較大，夢蝶軒藏品目錄編號58便是典型的唐式銅鏡。此外，亦有一種體積非常小的鏡子，如編號55的一組銅鏡便是。此組鏡屬漢至唐代製品，雖然小巧，但鏡背紋飾依然雄渾有力，優美動人。自周中期以來，銅鏡紋飾豐富多姿，據說是為了切合當時宗教或人們精神上的需要。這組小型銅鏡體積跟前文提到的齊家文化銅鏡不相上下，應同屬隨身攜帶用，可置於小袋中，然後懸於腰帶或掛於身上。從其輕巧體型看來，這類佩鏡最適合作為隨身的個人修飾用品或軍事上發訊號之用，然而其實際作用則尚未有定論。同樣而言，大型銅鏡的確實用途亦是眾說紛芸，莫衷一是。

宋、元、明三朝的飾物

宋代(960-1279)飾物工藝基本上是沿著唐代與遼代飾物工藝的發展軌蹟前進，一些在唐及遼代已經盛行的飾物仍然在宋代廣受歡迎，只是造型和紋飾略有改變。腰帶、指環、手鐲、梳子及各種髮飾的使用情況與前朝無大分別。有一種婦女配戴的闊身冠型頭飾則屬於創新設計。又由於唐代以來不斷由外地輸入香料，薰香已成為一種習俗，拴在腰帶上或綴於婦女用的霞帔底部的香囊應運而生。至於嵌滿飾牌的蹀躞帶，仍然是身份地位的標識。

唐代婦女盛行梳高髻，宋代亦然。宮庭貴婦頭上的簪釵造型大而結構複雜。雖然宋代的首飾設計已較前代含蓄簡樸，但部份飾物仍然繁縟而璀燦。夢蝶軒藏有一只宋代鳳紋鎏金銀髮簪(目錄編號83)，體積較大而作扁平形，正是為了切合當時潮流而設計。紋飾為一雙鳳凰作飛翔狀，襯以精細的花卉圖案，為典型的鳳紋式樣，是遼代金屬器皿的常用紋樣，宋代飾物及元代金屬器具與瓷器均沿用。

宋代還流行一種造型頗別緻的簪釵，很多時是成雙成對的，由釵杆和橫枝組成，橫枝上綴有各樣花紋。浙江永嘉宋代窖藏銀器中便有一批例子，夢蝶軒藏品目錄編號87亦屬此類。質料方面，有鎏金銀質如目錄編號86及金質如編號90。

宋代簪釵紋飾多取材自各種自然界景物，常見的有花卉圖案或將花卉與美人結成優美的組合。四時花卉亦是常見的題材。夢蝶軒藏品中有多只髮簪，都是用這些傳統的圖案作裝飾(目錄編號95)。福州市北郊南宋墓出土的銀釵亦提供了實物的例證。這類髮飾造型結實、紋飾玲瓏綺麗，與宋代大部份飾物的風格吻合。

上述宋代簪釵造型簡單，杆作中空單股或雙股狀，頂端錘沖和鏤刻成高度立體而精緻的紋樣。有時候，紋飾題材會散發著西方色彩，夢蝶軒藏品中有一對髮簪上端的蜂巢紋便是其中一例(目錄編號97)。這種由無數六角形組成的紋樣相信是經由絲路自西方傳入中國，敦煌發現的絲織品亦見有這類圖案。

唐代上流社會燃香的風氣極盛，除了薰爐飄出裊裊香煙外，各人身上亦散發著陣陣香氣。香囊本是古已有之物，至唐代隨著薰香風氣大盛而得以發揚光大。宋代的香囊設計精巧，可隨身攜帶，夢蝶軒亦藏有一件典型實例(目錄編號98)。此香囊由兩塊金片合成，其上錘沖及鏤刻花卉紋，中間可放置一小包香料，可能是紫花羅勒，是一種唐代宮廷愛用的香料。據一些出土實物顯示，這種香囊應連有鏈索和鉤，便於懸掛，但相信這件藏品的鏈索和鉤經已脫落和遺失。而據最新研究所得，這些香囊亦有可能是用作霞帔墜子，既可使婦女的霞帔平展地下垂，又可盛載香料及作衣飾用。

飾物藝術發展至元代(1279-1368)，又擺脫了南宋以來崇尚含蓄的風格而趨向豪華絢麗，紋飾帶著濃烈的北方遊牧民族色彩。以夢蝶軒藏品中一對髮簪為例(目錄編號104)，雖然雙鳥紋為中國固有的紋飾題材，但以錘沖法打出高度立體和鏤刻出極精細的紋樣後，裝飾風格便充滿異族情調。傳統的題材經過誇張的技法演繹後，散發著特殊的美態，反映了元代蒙古民族的裝飾風格。生動有力的紋樣設計與精湛洗鍊的鍛金工藝結合得天衣無縫，使飾物更為珍貴。

元朝滅亡後，明室(1368-1644)取而代之，天下再歸漢人統治，此後數百年，堪稱國泰民安。明代飾物範圍無大轉變，但設計卻極富傳統漢族藝術氣息。漢唐以來慣用的紋飾題材依然流行，其中帶皇權與神話色彩的紋飾尤其深得人心。一直以來都在傳統紋飾中佔著重要地位的龍鳳紋和各種花卉紋廣泛地出現在明代的首飾上。明朝建國之初，廢除元朝服飾制度，之後花了二十多年的時間才令新的制度得到確立。

夢蝶軒藏品中有一組玉帶具(目錄編號113)可以印證明代首飾工藝回歸傳統的說法。單從質料選材方面已顯示出明人的崇古意識，玉片上刻有蟠龍及高浮雕雲紋，較大的玉片則四角刻有四季花紋；雕工精湛，割切及鑽鑿手法俐落。毋庸置疑，能擁有如此珍貴的玉帶具，地位一定極為尊貴，且極有可能是皇室中人。據知，地位稍次的貴族只可佩戴銀製帶具，如夢蝶軒藏品中的鳳紋帶飾牌(目錄編號111)和花卉紋帶飾牌(目錄編號112)便屬此列。這些飾物都是極為精美的製品，而根據明制，只有五品、六品和七品的官員才用銀製帶飾牌。

結語

自古以來，個人飾物在中國都是人們界定身份地位的標誌。飾物的作用，由最早期的闢邪護身、個人裝飾，逐漸演變成實用的衣冠飾件。不同類型的飾物都有不同的發展歷程，在不同時期達到其發展高峰，之後型態面貌與意義仍然不斷隨時代而變化，多彩多姿。早期的飾物主要是用作標示尊卑貴賤，但漸而變成炫耀財富之物。戰國時代的金屬飾物主要是男性地位的標識，但在唐、宋及後世則成為女性增添美態和魅力的道具。

從古代墓葬中，尤其是貴族及皇室墓葬，我們可得到大量有關古代飾物的實物資料，瞭解到不同身份地位的人所佩戴的飾物有何差異，及飾物在人死後生命仍會以另一方式得到延續這觀念上所佔的意義。此外，飾物上的紋樣亦讓我們得悉來自西、南、北面的外族文化對中國文化有何影響。跟很多其他中國的物質文化發展一樣，中國人對美自有一套標準，不曾因外來輸入的各種服式、紋樣設計和工藝技術而有所改變。

* 所有圖片參見英文版

圖一	大汶口文化遺址出土象牙小梳圖樣。
圖二	1989年山東臨朐龍山文化遺址出土玉髮簪圖樣，簪頭部份作透雕。
圖三	江蘇馬家濱文化墓葬髮現的女性骸骨，頭頂上橫置一骨製髮簪。
圖四	上村嶺出土戰國銅人圖樣，銅人身穿胡服，上衣勒有帶，以帶鉤扣攏。
圖五	河北平山縣戰國舉燈銅人圖樣，銅人穿深衣，腰間束帶，以帶鉤扣攏。
圖六	帶鉤扣繫設計示意圖。
圖七	展品目錄編號22之鎏金獸紋銀飾牌圖樣。
圖八	廣州西漢南越王墓出土八片金飾其中兩片之紋樣。
圖九	1976年新疆維吾爾自治區焉耆縣黑格達出土龍紋金帶扣紋樣。
圖十	湖南安鄉黃山頭西晉劉弘墓出土龍紋金帶扣紋樣。
圖十一	敦煌263窟「說法圖」壁畫上之菩薩像圖樣。
圖十二	敦煌57窟壁畫上之觀音、菩薩及比丘像圖樣。
圖十三	敦煌220窟壁畫上之皇帝及群臣像圖樣。
圖十四	敦煌158窟「涅盤變」壁畫上之信眾圖樣。
圖十五	敦煌61窟「于闐公主圖」壁畫上之于闐公主及侍女圖樣。
圖十六	展品目錄編號69之銀項飾造型及紋樣。

埃瑪・邦克

飾 物 冶 煉 學

前言

早在原始時代，飾物除了是人們美化自己和驅邪擋煞的工具外，還用作隨葬品以使死者能在另一個世界 得享同樣的裝飾和保護。就北京周口店舊石器時代文化遺址發現所得，中國最早期的飾物都是用貝殼、魚骨、獸齒和獸爪等自然物質所製，並無刻意修飾以祈達致趨吉避凶的效果。

一般而言，隨著各種冶煉技術的發明，石器文化便會為銅器及鐵器等文化取代，世界各地多個上古文化都是循著這軌蹟前進。飾物不再只是簡單的原始質料所造，金屬製品地位日隆；除了作為裝飾和護身外，還成為身份的標識。歐洲和亞洲西北部一些銅器時代貴族墓葬都曾發現各式耳飾、釧鐲、項圈、指環及髮簪等飾物。質料有金、銀或青銅，視墓主人身份的顯赫程度而定。

然而，中國古代的飾物工藝卻並未緊隨這軌蹟發展。在進入青銅時代以後，金屬並沒有即時成為最貴重飾物的原料，歷史源遠流長的玉器仍然是人們心目中的至愛。從良渚等地的新石器文化墓葬出土物看來，一些顯然屬富貴中人的死者全身上下都飾有無數玉器，玉質高下則視死者身份地位的尊卑而有別。

在整個青銅文化的發展過程中，玉器自始至終都在黃河中下游的飾物工藝 享有最崇高的地位，除了是基於中國人的崇古本質外，還可歸究於中國文化的穩定性。因為直至進入公元之前，中國文化都未嘗經歷重大的衝擊，使一些萌生於新石器時期的文化能夠在這個時期結束後仍然歷久不衰。

相對而言，在整個青銅時代 ，中原比鄰的遊牧民族卻對金屬飾物有特殊偏 好，以之為身份的象徵。這些被視作外族的部落，聚居地分佈極廣，東起遼寧，西至河套，南達今日寧夏及甘肅境內。約公元前二千年時，這一帶地區已出現各種用金、銅及青銅製成的指環、髮簪和耳飾(目錄編號1)。

直至東周之世，金屬飾物才在中原地區抬頭，且因日益受珍視而地位日隆。 玉器的發展雖然受到影響，但卻並未因此而衰微。周代的階級及服飾制度均十分嚴格，金屬飾物的規格和紋樣要配合佩戴者的身份，絕對不能僭越混淆。

歷來學者都極少從冶煉學的角度去研究中國古代飾物的發展，而本文正打算在這方面進行探討，希望得知各種金屬在古代飾物工藝中所佔的地位，找出古人以金屬飾物代替玉石製品的種種原因、時代背景和地域分佈。除此之外，還希望瞭解金屬的來源和選擇標準，工藝技術的取向和其地區性特色等等相關問題。

由於佩戴金屬飾物只是古代皇室貴冑和豪門大戶的專利，一般庶民鮮能擁有貴重的飾物，故此本文將會集中探討與這少數階層所用的飾物有關的冶煉工藝。 中國文化浩如煙海，我們所涉獵的只是其中一個專題，資料來源主要是有賴夢蝶軒藏品的顯微觀察、中國各地的考古發掘報告，和中外現有的冶金考古學研究。 在這個金屬冶煉研究項目中，更多蒙從事金飾工藝的李祭・金伯(Richard Kimball)不吝賜教，提供寶貴的技術資料。

文中談及的中國「青銅時代」是指約由公元前二千至八百年(中國歷史上的 東周初期)的一段時間。由於近世考古研究著重地域性多於民族性，故此將不會以相對的中國朝代名稱和階段套入此時代。文中亦盡量多舉有關的地域性資料，以供參考。至於「中原」一詞，則純指黃河中下游一帶地區。要知道，很多時中原文化並不能反映北方與南方其他地域的文化。

金屬、合金和其他質料

現代人選用金屬及寶石以製作飾物的理由通常是很主觀的，選擇標準則多著眼於這些物料的幣值和外觀。然而，這等物料對上古人們來說卻有很強烈的象徵意義和闢邪擋煞的作用。故此，無論是貼身佩戴的或加諸衣冠上的金屬飾物，所選金屬都有一定的用意，並非出於偶然。

據考古資料顯示，金屬飾物在中國有很悠久的歷史。不同時代有不同的服飾制度，通常憑著金屬飾物的質料便可界定佩戴者的身份地位。這套制度能反映出當時的習俗、信仰和冶煉工藝的發展背景，而且往往帶有鮮明的地域特色。

有關中國古代金屬飾物的等級定制，很早便有文獻記錄。公元三世紀的《後漢書・禮儀志》記載了殮服的不同規格：天子用金縷玉衣；諸侯王、列侯、始封貴人、公主等用銀縷玉衣；其他大貴人、長公主等則用銅縷玉衣。

一直以來，個人飾物在中國都是貴族官宦身份和財富的標識，飾物的式樣和紋飾更依等第尊卑而各有定制。唐代亦明文規定帶飾牌的數目和所用的金屬，及飾物的紋樣。十七世紀時清室曾頒下詔書明示三品以上文武官員束金玉腰帶，四品及五品束金腰帶，六品及七品束銀腰帶，八品及九品束黃銅腰帶，庶民則只可用紅銅或鐵腰帶。

漢末的時後，各種用名貴金屬製造的飾物已成為婦女增添美態的必然工具。曹植(192-232)在其《洛神賦》中對洛水女神宓妃的服飾有如下描寫：「披羅衣之璀粲兮，珥瑤碧之華琚，戴金翠之首飾，綴明珠以耀軀」。

中原地區在青銅時代之所以沒有生產青銅首飾，完全是文化取向的問題，非關任何缺憾。儘管中國人對玉器有一種與生俱來的深厚感情，但卻沒有因此影響其他金屬飾物的發展。世界上很多其他古老民族懂得利用的金屬和合金，他們都有足夠的資源去開發和用來發展各種飾物工藝。

中國工匠常用的金屬和合金有銅、黃金、錫、鉛、青銅、鐵、白銀、汞和金銀石等，此文會依其在古代飾物工藝中所佔地位的輕重順序探討。又由於金屬的供應情況與其製作技巧上的優點往往直接影響製品的普遍程度，故此本文亦會盡量列舉資料，以供參考。至於其他物料如玉、綠松石、孔雀石、瑪瑙、紅玉髓、青金石、珍珠和玻璃等，文中亦會以夢蝶軒一些藏品為例，談及其作為鑲嵌材料的特色。

銅（紅銅）

銅質軟而色帶紅，故又叫紅銅，早期的銅是以純銅形態出現，可能是中國古代最先應用的金屬。據考古資料顯示，早至公元前十四世紀江西北部的瑞昌縣已有銅礦的開採。中國古代銅礦主要是分佈於東北部、黃河中下游及南部一些地區，而新疆亦有少量礦藏。近世則以雲南和湖北產量最豐。

由於純銅不但熔鑄困難，而且很快便暗啞失色，故此在黃金和青銅出現後人們便很少用純銅來製造飾物，其重要性是在於它是青銅合金的主要成分。中國古代的青銅除了含有銅和錫外，還大多含有鉛。

近年考古學者從遼寧凌源縣牛河梁的著名新石器時代晚期紅山文化遺址發掘得數件銅製飾物，屬東北遊牧民族遺物。其中一件用銅和玉石製成的耳飾，造工粗糙，出土自一男性墓葬。凌源及河北的青銅時代早期遺址亦發現銅製玦形耳環，一端扁寬呈喇叭狀。鄂爾多斯高原內蒙伊金霍洛旗朱開溝更發現有銅指環。然而令人奇怪的是中國南部銅礦產量豐富，但至今竟仍未有銅製飾物出土。

黃金

雖然許多學者都認為黃金在中國古代是一種稀有金屬，但實情卻並非如此。由於中國文字中很多與金屬有關的字都是以「金」為部首，而此字在古時原意是指銅而非今日我們所指的金，故此欲想從古代文獻中尋找資料便會遇到相當困難。據《爾雅》記載，金在古時是稱作「黃金」。

顧名思義，黃金色澤鮮黃。礦藏分「脈礦」和「砂礦」，分佈於中國各地，發現時已呈金屬狀態。古時黃金並非稀有產物，東周文獻如《戰國策》、《山海經》和《禹貢》等都記錄了無數產金地點，遍佈全國各地。當時所採的大多是砂金，經溪水自山的砂金礦沖下來，沉澱在河溪下游，淘採容易。雖然並無實例證明唐代以前中國已有脈金礦的開採，但由於西漢文獻《鹽鐵論》曾提及掘石採金銀之事，故此可推斷西漢時期已有某種形式的金礦開採。

公元十世紀時，中國已是世界上主要的產金國。蒙古民族對黃金尤其酷愛，黃金製品在元代(1279-1368)需求甚殷。當時最大的金礦之一位於山東，而朝廷又極力鼓勵在新歸入版圖的雲南地區進行開採活動。至明代時，雲南已成為砂金的主要產地。

黃金鑄造性能好，加工容易，亦常與白銀調成合金。白銀成分越高則合金色越白(目錄編號96)，加銅則色呈紅(目錄編號107)。以夢蝶軒藏品為例，該兩件編號87和90的宋代金飾便呈現著不同的色澤。

對西北部的遊牧民族來說，黃金極有可能就是他們最早應用的金屬。1976年，考古學者在甘肅西北部玉門火燒溝發現了約屬公元前十六世紀的齊家文化墓葬，出土物包括有金質及青銅質耳環(金耳環的成分為黃金93%，白銀7%)。所有耳環都是玦形，一端扁平呈喇叭狀，造型與遼寧、河北和鄂爾多斯地區青銅時代遺址所出的青銅和紅銅耳環相近。

山西石樓縣青銅時代遺址，即商民族活動區域的邊緣，發現了以鍛造法製成的金質髮飾及耳飾，耳飾的造型與夢蝶軒藏品中一對耳墜很相似(目錄編號1)。河北平谷縣劉家河的青銅時代遺址亦掘得金製髮簪、耳飾及手鐲，與安陽遺址所出同屬商末文物。此等墓葬均非商民族所有，但從墓葬品的內容看來，這些人與當時位於中原的商民族應有經濟上的交往。劉家河所出的耳環，造型基本上跟火燒溝的玦形金耳環一致，但整體上卻較為細緻和考究。實則上，這類耳環的造型已被公認為西伯利亞安德羅諾沃(Andronovo)及烏拉爾山脈的上古文物特徵，而在中國北陲之地能看到同樣造型的器物，證明很久以前這些地區已經與中亞或甚至更西的部落有交往。

黃河流域中下游在青銅時代也有應用黃金，但金製飾物則未見出現。然而，青銅器卻常用黃金作裝飾，以添華麗氣派，河南安陽商末遺址所出的包金箔青銅馬具泡飾是其中一例。

金製飾物要晚至東周初期才在中原地區大行其道。河南三門峽上村嶺東周初期虢國皇族墓地所出的金質帶飾牌是其中最早的實例。此外，陝西的東周秦墓又有大量小型金質帶鉤出土，造型跟夢蝶軒藏品中的三件帶鉤相若(目錄編號2、3及4)。戰國時，佩戴金飾的風氣已傳至南方，湖北隨縣的公元前五世紀曾侯乙墓所出的數件金帶鉤可茲證明。此外，各種飾以錯金、包金或汞齊鎏金的青銅帶鉤亦在這個時期相當流行(目錄編號17、20、29、及37)。

內蒙西部鄂爾多斯地區的東周墓葬埋有大量金器，反映出當時北方遊牧民族對黃金及鎏金飾物，尤其是黃金製品的酷愛程度，夢蝶軒藏品中亦不乏例證(目錄編號16及32)。對遊牧民族而言，飾物除了起著誇耀作用外，也是他們的護身法寶和地位標識。以帶飾牌為例，其紋樣正代表著某種神祕力量的形象化，而選用的金屬如黃金、白銀或青銅(通常鎏金或鍍錫)等，則標示著物主的不同身份和等級。金耳墜的設計尤其華麗，懸有垂飾的造型更使人聯想到中亞以西的飾物風格(目錄編號16)。至東周末期，這些北方民族的金飾或鎏金飾物似乎都是產自中原地區，其中一例為夢蝶軒所藏的一件背後刻有漢文字的圓形鎏金銀飾牌(目錄編號22)。

鑒於戰國時楚國以黃金為貨幣，使這種金屬更形珍貴。據《韓非子》記載，擅自淘採楚國轄下金砂者罪當處死。

漢代時，神仙學說和煉丹致長生等道家思想深入人心，金與玉成為永壽的象徵。自東周末開始，由於煉丹術大行其道，道士方士們不斷研究各種金屬和玉石的化學配方，間接促成了汞齊鎏金技術的發展。

在過去二千年來，金製個人飾物在中國的受歡迎程度不斷提升，一方面是由於與外族文化融匯的過程中一併吸收了他們對黃金的崇拜意識，而另一方面則要歸究於佛教的傳入。燦爛奪目的黃金及鎏金佛像，和絢麗無比的佛教裝飾藝術都讓人們對黃金產生一種特別的敬意。自唐代開始，金製飾物的地位已淩駕其他飾物之上，明代及宋代亦以金飾為貴。至於遼、金、元、清等外族統治者，更視黃金珍如拱璧。

錫

錫色白而亮，今日中國南部的錫礦蘊含量極豐。商朝時候，大部份錫礦場均位於河南的冶金中心方圓三百公里範圍內，現都已枯竭，但這論點仍有待滿意的考古證據支持。

錫與銅調合則成青銅，是中國古代最重要的合成金屬。安陽殷墟一處鑄造作坊遺址發現有錫錠及銅塊，由於發現的是錫錠而非錫礦石，可推想是產自外地，經加工後才運至此處。

錫與銅及鉛在古時被認為是性質祥瑞的金屬，早期的銅鏡即以此配成合金而鑄造。部份青銅器表面呈銀白色，就是鍍錫的結果。無數陝西的東周秦墓都有發現鍍錫的帶鉤(目錄編號8)，而西北的遊牧民族遺址亦有鍍錫的帶飾牌(目錄編號21)。另夢蝶軒藏品中有兩件戰國早期的銅鏡(目錄編號9及11)和一只唐代銅梳(目錄編號68)，相信都經鍍錫處理。

鉛

鉛身重，質軟，色灰，打磨後發出耀目光澤，但接觸空氣與濕氣後便迅速變得暗啞。中國古代鉛礦產量豐富，但用來造飾物者絕無僅有。

鉛的重要性在於它是早期青銅合金的附加劑。商代及西周青銅器的含鉛量比東周時期的製品低得多。

鉛的可塑性和可鍛性均極高，除了能降低青銅合金的熔點，並可提高其在鑄造過程中的液化程度，使鑄造更容易，器具細節及紋飾更清晰。

鉛錫結合則成一種軟焊藥，可用來焊接一般金屬。據漢代銘文記載，鑄銅鏡所用的三種金屬中，其一即為鉛。

鐵

鐵色白而亮，性韌，可鍛性高及須高度打磨。早在商代時已有隕石形式的鐵礦石出現，因為是從天而降，故古人對之敬畏有加。其時鐵製品的生產方法並非是鑄造法，而是鍛冶法。雖然中國很早以前已經有鐵礦的開採，但要待東周時才有具規模的採鐵、熔鐵和鑄鐵活動出現。據《左傳》記載，公元前513年時已有鐵鑊的鑄造。

鐵對飾物工藝的其中一項貢獻是提供鐵製工具予工匠們從事各種雕刻細工。從一些西周帶鉤上之嵌飾槽的造工看來，似乎是經人手刻出而非原身鑄成(目錄編號27，29及30)。

東周中期以後出現了鐵鑄的帶鉤(目錄編號20)，比青銅製品成本低，打磨後又發出耀目銀光，故成為一時珍奇。河南、湖北、山西及陝西等地發現的鐵鑄帶鉤不勝枚舉，有素身無紋的，亦有鑲綴貴金屬及玉石的。新疆帕米爾高原則發現公元前六至五世紀的鐵鐲，是當地遊牧民族而非漢族的遺物。

漢代更有鐵鑄的鏡子。河南洛陽燒溝便發現有八面蝕不堪的鐵鑄鏡。

白銀

白銀色白而生輝，可鍛性高，且韌性極佳，與黃金一樣同是十分柔軟的金屬，故常與其他金屬結合以增加堅實程度，色澤則隨著附加金屬的種類和成分而相異。

白銀比黃金難採，不像後者可以從河溪中的沉澱淘得。白銀礦脈只存於山區，但全中國蘊藏量不豐。一般的白銀都是通過灰吹法從別的含銀礦石提煉出來。據古文獻記載，中國西北部的山西、寧夏、甘肅和江西，與西南部的四川涼山和雲南都有白銀礦藏，但產量不多，歷代都有從外國輸入白銀以補不足。

西漢末之前，白銀在中國飾物工藝中所佔地位並不高。有關白銀的最早記載見於《爾雅》，稱為「白金」，以別於「黃金」。

最早的中國銀器是一枚鼻環，出土自甘肅玉門火燒溝一處青銅時代早期的齊家文化遺址，經碳十四測定為公元前十六世紀文物。其他青銅時代遺址發現的銀器則絕無僅有，故此可以推斷這個時期的中國並不流行用銀器。

至東周中期，中原地區才有白銀的應用。著名的青銅劍「越王勾踐劍」於湖北江陵望山楚墓遺址出土初期，一般都認為其上的鳥篆銘文是用錯銀造出，但近年已証實所用金屬並非白銀。戰國中期，由於白銀韌性極佳，各種青銅器皿、馬具飾件和帶鉤(目錄編號27、29及30)頗多是用銀絲錯嵌造成，加上其色白而亮，與青銅和黃金的黃赤色形成強烈的對比，產生奪目的視覺效果。有時候，亦有用白銀製成帶鉤。

以白銀為貨幣的最早年代仍然存疑。河南扶溝古城村發現有銀製的「布幣」,但至於是否真的流通貨幣,及在何處鑄造等則至今仍未有確實答案。

至公元前四至三世紀,中原北陲即今內蒙以西的遊牧民族才開始用白銀製飾物。其中最具特色的要算準格爾旗西溝畔所出的數件銀製馬具飾件,飾件背面用漢字刻上白銀重量。由於當時漢人與其他部族常進行物換物的交易,例如以漢人的奢侈品換取對方的馬匹和獸皮,看來這些飾物是東周末的金工作坊為此而特製的。夢蝶軒藏品中有一枚圓形鎏金銀飾牌(目錄編號22)亦屬此類文物。

白銀並沒有像黃金一樣跟煉丹扯上關係,沒有人會吞服白銀以祈求長生不老。值得注意的是,在古代的朝鮮和日本,銀器的數量亦顯然比金器少得多。

事實上,白銀飾物要晚至六朝、唐和宋代才普遍受人重視。主因是絲路的暢通導致西土文化不斷東傳,連帶銀器地位亦得到提升。然而,很多造型別緻的銀製髮飾仍會鎏金以求更華麗璀璨(目錄編號61,63,64及65)。

唐代的銀製飾物往往能反映出亞洲西北地區薩珊皇朝和拜占廷帝國的藝術風格。冶煉工藝方面,鍛造法在很大程度上取代了鑄造法;裝飾細工方面,鎏金仍然盛行,但鏤刻法卻替代了鑲嵌法(目錄編號63,66及67)。唐代的銅鏡常在鏡背包有用錘沖和鏤刻法造出紋飾的金或銀殼,令銅鏡更添華麗(目錄編號55)。

六朝之際,陝西長安附近有銀礦的開採。至唐代時,福建與浙江亦有採銀礦活動,而嶺南和安南也成為重要的產銀地。有關灰吹法冶銀術的具體記載,最早見於唐宋文獻。

雖然歷代文獻中都不乏有關開採銀礦的資料,但亦有相當證據顯示從外地輸入的白銀為數不少,且很多都沒有記錄在案。明朝永樂帝在位期間(1403-24),來自緬甸之產銀和產鉛地巴凜的白銀使國內白銀供應量大增。明代由於需要龐大軍費以抵禦北方外族的入侵和剿滅南面沿海倭寇,除了要從日本輸入白銀外,還經葡國商人購買新大陸的白銀。究竟其中有否拿來製造飾物則不得而知。

青銅

青銅是一種由銅和錫調成的合金,往往亦滲有少量如鉛等的其他金屬,鑄造性能非常好,色澤由赤黃至金黃或甚至白色不等,視各種金屬的成分而定。

中國古代的青銅多含鉛及錫,色黃。加入鉛可降低合金熔點,使鑄造較容易,製品輪廓細節更清晰。鑄工極精美的商代青銅器便是最佳例子。

青銅時代之際,小件的青銅個人飾物只流行於中原以北和以西的遊牧地區,黃河流域中下游和黃河以南則沒發現此類製品。甘肅火燒溝和鄂爾多斯高原伊金霍洛旗朱開溝的青銅時代遺址均有發現青銅鑄成的耳飾。商代和西周時候,中原地區的青銅是用來製造禮器和兵器,作為皇室和貴族用來統治天下的工具,直至東周時才開始用來製造飾物。

東周之世列國爭雄,競尚豪奢,加上與北方部落因通商和通婚而造成文化藝術的相互借鑑與融合,促使中原飾物工藝發展空前蓬勃,無數極為精美絢麗的飾物相繼出現。這個時期的墓葬有大量素身無紋或滿綴貴金屬及寶石的青銅帶鉤出土。

美國華盛頓佛利爾美術館藏有113件帶鉤,其中35件的銅成分為95%,18件為97%,沒有被銅掩蓋的部分同樣顯出色澤帶紅。青銅合金中錫的成分越高則合金越硬。自古以來,大多數帶鉤都是用青銅鑄造,但鑒於由公元前一世紀開始工匠們流行給青銅帶鉤加上其他金屬造的外衣以添姿彩,而且這種裝飾手法一直盛行不衰,故此很容易被錯認為別的金屬製品。

汞

汞俗稱水銀,色白而亮,在室溫下呈液體狀,多自硃砂的純化過程提煉而得。據古文獻記載,產汞的地區有山西、四川、甘肅、湖北和江西。

汞對飾物工藝的貢獻在於它能熔化其他金屬,例如將金、銀及錫融合而成汞齊。這種金屬化合劑在公元前三世紀時施用於青銅器的鑲嵌工藝,至公元前三世紀時汞齊鎏金和汞齊鎏銀已被應用於改變青銅器和銀器表面的色澤。

自戰國時期開始,人們漸漸迷信服食黃金玉石提煉的丹藥可致長生,因此黃金的價值大升,其作用亦渲染上神祕色彩,使人趨之若鶩,促使了汞齊鎏金技術的蓬勃發展。煉丹術的始作俑者相信是與孟子(公元前四世紀)同期的道家騶衍,但正如很多學者都曾指出,煉丹術是源自一種世界通有的古老觀念,只是道士們將之發揚光大。道家提倡的是消極的避世思想,主張順應自然,達致人生最高境界,後來演變至為了達到永恆而求長生,而眾多金屬中又以黃金為永恆的象徵。西漢時期有很多關於製煉金屬的著作,成於公元前二世紀的《淮南子》是其一。

金銀石(黃銀)

金銀石是一種天然的金銀合金,銀的成分佔20%或以上,顏色由白至黃不等,閃閃生輝。運用人工技術亦可製造出金銀石。通過夢蝶軒好幾件髮飾(目錄編號87)的顯微觀察,得知古代工匠對金銀石的成分掌握得很好,能充分利用不同深淺的金色和銀色造出美妙的裝飾效果。

金銀石在東周、秦及兩漢時似乎沒有多大地位。實則上,在東周中葉以前白銀根本不受重視,而後來雖然漸受歡迎,但始終未能跟黃金相提並論。初時金銀石的應用可能只是出於偶然,原意是以不同深淺的金色造出特別的裝飾效果。

雖然中國古代文獻甚少有關金銀石及其在工藝製作方面應用情況的記載,但唐代工匠對這種金屬似乎並不陌生。唐末文獻曾提到山東北部的金銀石礦自隋朝(公元六世紀末)已開始投產,但卻無說明其礦產是作合金之用抑或進一步提煉出黃金和白銀兩種元素。

人工技術製造出的金銀合金對飾物的製作頗為有利。黃金加入白銀後，堅實度增加而價錢則降低，色澤保持金黃，無銀器會日久變晦暗之弊。

寶石、珍珠和玻璃

東周末、秦和兩漢的時候，青銅及金銀飾物往往綴有各色珠寶玉石及顏色物料，使飾物看來璀璨奪目。夢蝶軒藏品中亦有很不少珍貴例子(目錄編號23、24、26及38)。而早在新石器時代，人們已懂得將石塊割切及打磨成各種護身飾物及與祭祀有關的器物，並充分掌握此種技術。

玉在中國古代是至善至美的象徵，而這種觀念至今日仍大致不變。玉器在古代社會的超然地位和古玉器的精湛工藝已是眾所週之，無須贅述，以下談到的是另外幾點。

玉石硬度非常高，所以加工困難，不易雕琢，要用研磨法造出細節，然後再經磨光，表面才會顯得光滑潤澤。據近年學者研究所得，中國古代的玉材主要是採自太湖地區和東北的遼寧至山東一帶。然而，歷代從外地輸入的玉材亦不在少數。由於玉的地位崇高，故此只有最珍貴的工藝品才會用玉石鑲嵌，夢蝶軒藏品中的一只金梳便是實例(目錄編號48)。

據唐代文獻記載，當時中國有部分玉器是源自西域。據云，公元632年，即唐太宗在位時(627-649)，于闐國王獻上玉腰帶。由於唐室對西域文化藝術甚為欣賞，故此亦有可能下令工匠仿製這些腰帶的式樣，解釋了為何中亞地區突蹶系民族的文物中會有些腰帶跟唐末、遼、宋和明代的製品有相似的紋樣，都是有一列順序循環的長方、正方、半月形和梨形的帶飾牌(目錄編號53，79，111及113)。

除了玉以外，綠松石是中國古代最早和最普遍採用的寶石。綠松石硬度高，須高度打磨，色澤艷麗，顏色由淺藍至藍綠不等。

早在新石器時期，中國已有綠松石製的佩飾，東北部遼寧地區紅山文化遺址亦有發現。至於作為鑲嵌材料的使用，則可見於公元前三千年大汶口文化遺址所出的鑲綠松石骨器和二里頭遺址的鑲綠松石青銅器。多類商代青銅製品都鑲有綠松石，但西周時期的實例則極少。

東周時期非常流行以綠松石鑲嵌帶鉤和其他奢侈製品，所用綠松石有切成石片狀，亦有磨成軟泥狀(目錄編號23及26)。至於中國古代綠松石的來源，古文獻無記載，有可能是採自安徽及湖北地區，或自新疆及中亞一帶輸入，但實情仍然有待研究。有說二里頭遺物中的綠松石是來自湖北的襄陽。夢蝶軒藏品中有兩件戰國末帶鉤(目錄編號25及26)，所鑲綠松石晶瑩亮麗，亦有可能是源自湖北。元代時，湖北的竹山、鄖西縣和鄖縣有很豐富的綠松石礦藏。

孔雀石亦是東周時期流行的鑲嵌材料，顏色翠綠，紋理斑駁，形成深淺相間的綠色條紋。夢蝶軒藏有兩件出自雲南的西漢帶飾(目錄編號34)，是為實例。

孔雀石是一種碳化礦石，須高度打磨，硬度比綠松石低，除了可以雕成飾物外，還可磨成粉末作鑲填或顏料用。孔雀石亦是銅的主要來源，相信開採的年代相當早。唐代時，位於山西北部的代州有產孔雀石。十一世紀時，江西東部的信州和安徽南部的宣州都是此礦石的產地。

據《天工開物》記載，中國古代已有白、綠、紅、藍灰及琥珀等不同顏色而帶斑紋的瑪瑙石。除了用來鑲嵌帶鉤以添裝飾效果外，還可以用來製造禮器，夢蝶軒藏有一件西漢帶鉤(目錄編號38)及遼人放鷹用的腕飾(目錄編號81)，都是例子。

紅玉髓石呈半透明肉紅色，質地極堅實，以氧化鐵為呈色劑。雲南昆明石寨山所出的滇式青銅器中，很多都鑲有紅玉髓。這些青銅製品的造型跟夢蝶軒藏品中一枚圓形銅飾牌(目錄編號33)很相似。唐代的時候，部分紅玉髓來自西域，其中以索馬爾罕輸入最多。

青金石為品藍色，質硬，磨光後閃爍生輝，含有多種礦物質，其中有少量黃鐵礦。古代最著名的青金石產地是今阿富汗境內的八達山，現時西伯利亞和緬甸亦有青金石的開採。

距今五千年前，青金石已是製造飾物的常用材料，伊拉克和埃及的古代墓葬都有大量的青金石飾物作隨葬品。由於出土地點與青金石產地相去甚遠，可知當時奢侈品物料的貿易一定發展得相當蓬勃而廣泛。

鑑定青金石要非常小心，因為很容易會把方鈉石和天藍石這些較次等的寶石誤認作青金石。

青金石在中國應用的最早年代仍然是一個謎。夢蝶軒藏品中有一件戰國時期的帶鉤(目錄編號25)，鉤頸所鑲的青金石，與綠松石互相輝映。青金石在古時另有叫法，有可能是「瑟瑟」，但確實名稱還未肯定。宋代之金星石亦即現時的青金石。

六朝和唐代很流行用青金石點綴飾物，例子可見於夢蝶軒藏品中的佩飾(目錄編號70)。日本京都正倉院所藏八世紀文物中有一條唐代的鑲青金石腰帶。據唐代文獻所載，青金石是一種波斯寶石，從絲路的主要貿易集中地于闐可以購得。

漢朝帶鉤上的綴飾中，已發現有珍珠的存在。在中國人心目中，珍珠具有特殊的靈氣和法力，是與龍關係密切的珍寶。佛教傳入以後，珍珠又成為佛陀與佛法的象徵。漢代時，廣東西南沿海的海床可以採得珍珠，但最珍貴的要算是商旅自南海地區帶回來的品種。珍珠晶瑩亮麗，無須割切或打磨，但缺點在於容易腐朽。是次展品中的六朝早期金梳(目錄編號48)，仍留有兩顆珍珠的遺蹟。

玻璃不是中國創製，而是東周晚期以玻璃珠的形式從西方傳入，用於工藝製品上。中國製玻璃通常含有少量的鋇，可通過科學方法作出甄別。在東周及西漢帶鉤上鑲上玻璃，用意大多是模仿珠寶玉石等物料，並造出繽紛的色彩效果。夢蝶軒藏品中有一件西漢帶鉤(目錄編號38)，造工精湛而色彩斑爛，是其中代表作。

冶煉技術

通過夢蝶軒藏品的顯微觀察，發現了一些歷來研究中國冶煉技術俱忽略的要點。下文將識別出與這些飾物製作有關的冶煉技術，按發展先後一一探討，藉此反映其進化軌蹟。此外，文中亦會盡量引用考古資料印證這些技術的發展年代。遺憾的是，有時候考古發掘報告也未必會提供有關技術的詳盡資料。

為了能瞭解各種飾物的製作方法，及鑒於部分文物的發掘過程並不科學化，發掘報告對文物的真偽和所屬年代無從肯定，故此有必要先從冶煉技術的內容和歷史入手，進行探索。

中國古代的冶金工藝分鑄造與鍛造兩大流派，各有鮮明特色，大異其趣。自青銅時代開始，中國工匠已掌握了這兩種技術的操作，根據各自所需而作出適當決擇。

一直以來，這兩種冶煉技術隨著人們需求的轉變而輪流在中國冶金史上佔著優勢。青銅時代採用的是鑄造法，青銅首飾出土數量極少，都是當時中原以西和以北的外族文物，大部分用兩片範模鑄成，亦有些是錘打成型，夢蝶軒藏品有一只青銅時代的金耳環(目錄編號1)便是其中例子。

東周、秦及兩漢之際，金屬工藝起了重大的變化。春秋時期，中原的鑄造作坊開始用青銅鑄造日用飾物，所製帶鉤及銅鏡奇麗無比，戰國時南方亦爭相仿效。最早期的帶鉤設計簡單，其後造型和紋飾漸趨複雜華麗，相信是因為當時北方諸國與外族頻密通商，受其影響所致(見圖一)。

戰國初期，帶鉤已是北方諸國貴族們所不可缺的衣飾，而且地位日趨重要。此時期的冶煉業空前蓬勃，經過大膽的嘗試和創新，發明了不少窮工極巧的技術，使金屬表面看來更美侖美奐。夢蝶軒所藏之一批東周末和西漢帶鉤正是其中代表作。

為了使帶鉤看來更華貴，其上還綴滿彩色繽紛的珠寶玉石，佩戴在腰間時閃爍生輝，倍顯不同凡響。東周至漢初的幾百年間，戰亂頻仍，人心不安，道士們乃利用皇室中人和貴族極需精神寄托的心理而大事鼓吹服食丹藥可致長生。汞齊鎏金技術出現於公元前四世紀末至三世紀，此後日趨流行，反映出當時人們深受道家煉丹風氣影響而對黃金有超乎尋常的崇拜。

公元前六世紀的東周，除了一貫慣用的範鑄法外，還發明了叫「失蠟法」的熔鑄術。從此兩種技術並駕齊驅，相輔相承。夢蝶軒藏有數件極為優美的金帶鉤(目錄編號2、3及4)，正是前者的典範，而另一件青銅鳥形帶鉤(目錄編號5)則以「失蠟法」鑄造。

漢繼秦之後統一天下，不同地域的冶煉技術和金屬工藝得以共冶一爐，捨短取長，精益求精，為漢室和貴族們竭誠服務。金珠工藝原是西方發明的技術，公元前四世紀後期因亞歷山大帝發動東征，讓其騎兵深入中亞而東抵河套，使這種工藝得以傳入中國。漢代的時候，黃金地位直逼玉石，金製飾物亦受到前所未有的重視。

六朝末年，飾物製作已不再是鑄銅作坊的次要任務，而是金銀匠們的主要營生。自公元一至十世紀，外來文化不斷傳入中國，人們亦由此感染了外族人士酷愛佩戴金屬飾物的風氣，加上佛教的傳入，使金飾地位不斷提升，銀器亦日受重視。此外，自六朝以至唐代，經絲路來中國的西方商旅不絕於途，給中國皇室及貴族帶來了不少中亞索格底亞那地區、薩珊皇朝及拜占庭帝國的金屬製品和其他奇珍異寶。

唐代流行堅碩而氣派不凡的飾物。憑腰間蹀躞帶的金屬質料和玉石綴飾便可識別佩戴者的身分等第。這種腰帶本是西北地區突厥系部族的飾物，因與唐代通好而傳入中國。腰帶上嵌有多種形狀帶飾牌，有的是鑄成，有的則是錘打成形，數目及所選金屬均有嚴格限制(見目錄編號54)。唐代的帶飾牌，可謂集澆鑄與鍛冶兩種工藝精華於一身，比之任何中亞地區的製品都優勝得多，其巧奪天工，有夢蝶軒藏品為証(目錄編號53)。相對來說，以髮飾為主的婦女飾物則崇尚纖細輕巧，全是精湛鍛冶技術的結晶品，除了是迎合時人的審美觀念外，更能切合經濟原則。唐代宮廷貴婦們所戴花冠和簪釵皆用名貴金屬鍛打及透雕成各種玲瓏浮凸的形狀，繼而鏤刻出極精細的紋樣，在如雲秀髮上閃耀著眩目光芒，更顯女性嫵媚(目錄編號61、63、66及67)。

宋代飾物更形纖巧綺麗，名貴金屬及鎏金製品妍秀別緻，美不勝收。宋代宮廷貴婦不似唐代般豪情奔放，而是以嫻靜為貴，且因纏足而極少走動。此外，馬球及狩獵等活動亦漸受冷落。雖然橫跨歐亞的絲路因伊斯蘭人勢力的擴張而日趨末落，但中西交往並未因此中斷，南海航線的發展使各色寶石和珍品不虞或缺。但由於社會風氣已不復尚武，獵鷹等物已不再是人們競逐的目標，代之而興的是妍巧婉約的飾物，夢蝶軒藏有一對鳥蝶形金耳環，是這類風格的代表作(目錄編號99)。

宋室的崇古觀念特別重，對古聖賢及制度推崇備至，器物型制亦以古為貴，由是出現了仿古的青銅和玉帶鉤。夢蝶軒藏有一件錯金銀青銅帶鉤，能反映出當時仿古金屬工藝的高水平(目錄編號101)。這件帶鉤雖然在型制上是因襲古物，但因集合了不同時期的藝術特色，故露出了仿製品的破綻。帶鉤的橫切面呈三葉形，是戰國末年流行的設計，但鉤底龍首的造型卻是春秋時期的風格。無數春秋時期的玉飾牌都有類似的龍首紋飾。

與中原的宋朝相反，北方的外族統治者如遼(907-1125)的契丹、金(1115-1234)的女真和元(1279-1368)的蒙古部族都承襲了唐代飾物堅碩奔放的風格。契丹婦女喜愛頭戴金或銀花冠，並多綴有閃爍璀璨的垂飾，搖曳生姿；遼人的蹀躞帶則飾以吊帶，可供懸掛各種飾物及工具，皆極具特色(目錄編號77及78)。

要辨別這些飾物的原產地殊非易事，有時候它們是來自異族統治下的金銀作坊，但更有可能是宋室賜贈之物。據宋代文獻記載，早期外銷物中及宋室致遼人的禮品中都有金製花冠及腰帶。

元明以後，人們對舶來品和珍貴金屬熱愛依然。明清時代，婦女頭飾尤其複雜華麗。其間，製造技術有很大的轉變，金銀絲裝飾工藝和網絡細工漸漸代替了錘鍱工藝成為最受歡迎的裝飾手法。夢蝶軒藏品中有幾對明代耳環便屬此例(目錄編號109)。

鑄造術

中國古代的鑄造業需要極密集的人手，生產過程中分工仔細，工序井然。1949年以來，發現了不少鑄造業遺址，揭露了古代鑄冶技術的繁複和優點。由於分工極細，每個工序都由不同的工匠負責，故此難以識別個別工匠的藝術才華。

範模鑄造法

自青銅時期以至兩漢，大部分的禮器、兵器和裝飾品都是用範模法鑄成。山西南部侯馬東周時期晉國冶鑄遺址埋有數以千計的範塊和紋飾印模碎片，提供了有關範模鑄造法的寶貴資料。東周時期上層社會對金屬製品需求極殷，冶鑄作坊的規模和爐具便得與侯馬所發現的不相上下，才能應付龐大的生產量。《楚辭·招魂》有云：「晉製犀比，費白日些」，意為晉國造的帶鉤閃耀似日光，可見當時晉國製品的精美。

製陶範方法有二，其一是用泥片附捺在預先製成的母模表面，用力緊壓使模上花紋反印在泥片內，半乾時用刀將泥片依器形分成不同部分，以榫卯相接，待乾透後剝下便成(見圖二)。另一方法是無須預製模型，只要在容器內鋪上一層泥片，用印模將紋飾戳在泥片上作為範。陶範陰乾後還要用火焙烘，便成外範。將兩片或幾片外範合在一起，澆注泥漿，乾後拆開，內的泥蕊便是內範，須將表面挫低以使內外範之間存有虛位，虛位之寬狹則決定日後鑄成器壁的厚薄。泥範準備就緒，便合攏在一起，榫眼互扣，跟著灌注金屬熔液，待凝固後便揭破陶範，繼而將棱角搓杈的鑄成品砥礪打磨，使之光彩煥發。陶範塊數，全視器物形狀而定。

經過顯微觀察後，發現好些夢蝶軒所藏的帶鉤都是用範鑄法製成，因其中六件帶鉤顯示出合範造成的接縫痕蹟。有些只用兩面範(見目錄編號8及圖三)，但有些卻出自比較複雜的複合範(見目錄編號2、3、4、7、17及圖四)。看來東周時期不同的鑄造坊有不同的範鑄方式。

石範的應用可遠溯至青銅時代，一些商周時期的北方遺址曾有石範的發現，但中原地區則直至漢代才採用石範鑄造銅鏡，明代亦有用石範鑄造小型飾物。美國哈佛大學美術館藏有一件明代的小型石範(見圖五)。

鑄接法

中國古代的鑄接法是先鑄附件，再在澆注器身時鑄接成一體。其起源可上溯至青銅時代早期，在商民族活動地區以南首先應用，跟著才向中原推廣。

對個人飾物工藝而言，鑄接法的重要性在於其解決了製造青銅鏈索的技術問題。夢蝶軒藏有一對獸形帶飾牌，原本以兩根鏈索相連(目錄編號7)，鏈索是利用鑄接法將骨形鏈節扣進鏈環而成。

鑄接這類鏈索有幾個步驟：先用簡單的合範法分別鑄出骨形鏈節，再鑄塊形鏈環，將鏈節從缺口處扣入，連成一串鏈索，最後以範鑄法將缺口補上。

失蠟鑄造法

有關失蠟法的最早考古證據來自河南淅川下寺公元前六世紀楚墓。出土物中有一件銅禁，器身用傳統的範模法鑄造，透雕紋手把則用失蠟法鑄造，再用鑄接法與器身連合。失蠟法並非中國所創而是小亞細亞地區早已沿用的鑄造技術，但至於是何時及通過何種渠道傳入中國則不得而知。

以失蠟法鑄造玲瓏浮凸及透雕的飾物，效果會比用範鑄法好，因為後者在脫範時會有困難，可能傷及鑄成品。夢蝶軒有三件金帶鉤(目錄編號2、3及4)，若交諸現今之金銀匠鑄製，一定會採用間接失蠟法。但據顯微觀察所得，這些帶鉤實際上是範鑄法的產品，範模由多塊合成，以求脫範容易。

雖然失蠟法並不適用於鑄造大型器物，但在東周末、秦和兩漢的受歡迎程度卻有增無減，成為製造小型鑄件和帶鉤的常用方法。夢蝶軒藏有一件紋飾精細複雜的透雕帶鉤(目錄編號5)，便是其中代表作。此外，失蠟法亦比範鑄法合符經濟原則，因為金屬熔液分量較易掌握，減少損耗。

首先，用蠟刻出製成品的模型，用澄泥漿多次塗抹及澆淋造成鑄型。首次塗抹時一定要小心進行，避免氣泡內閉，其後則可較為粗略。跟著以用高溫烘燒，使蠟溶掉，「失蠟」之名即由此來。但很多時，工匠們會將容器置於鑄型底下，盛載滴下的蠟液，以便再用。出蠟後鑄型面便形成一個空間，跟著便是將金屬熔液注入，待冷卻後揭破鑄形便成，鑄成品跟當初的蠟模是一式一樣的。

除此之外，還有所謂間接失蠟法，無須用人手雕製蠟模，而是先以一器物原型翻出陶範，謂之「母範」，將蠟液注入，冷卻後便成蠟模，其後的鑄造程序則跟前述失蠟法無異。此法的優點是可鑄造大量相同的器物而無須損毀原模。很多漢人製來供應給遊牧民族的帶飾牌都是用此方法大批生產(目錄編號28及32)。

失蠟失織鑄造法

失蠟失織鑄造法在東周末年和兩漢時期主要是用於製造帶飾牌，這些飾牌的質料多為名貴金屬或鍍錫、鎏銀、鎏金的青銅。憑飾牌背後的織紋，可斷定是用這種方法鑄造。織紋來自蠟模外層的紡織物，熔鑄時印附在鑄件上。據考古資料顯示，此法是中國工匠所創，靈感來自當時漆器的夾紵工藝。

失蠟失織實則上是演變自間接失蠟法。首先是以帶飾牌原型翻出單面陶範，待乾後澆注蠟液，其上敷以麻布，蠟液凝固後連麻布整塊揭起，以澄泥漿多次塗抹及澆注造成鑄型，以高溫火烘燒讓蠟與織物一起溶掉，再灌注金屬熔液造出鑄件。以布敷蠟最大優點是蠟層可以很薄，能減低金屬熔料的耗用量及令製成品更輕更薄。此法亦適用於生產紋飾相同的帶飾牌。

從河北易縣辛莊頭燕下都冶鑄遺址(公元前311-222年期間此地為燕國屬土)可找到古代失蠟失織法的例證。遺址發現兩件薄身的金飾牌，背後有織紋，飾牌紋樣跟是次展出的一件背面亦有織紋的鍍錫青銅飾牌很是相似(目錄編號21)，反映出這件展品亦可能是出自同一作坊，是遊牧民族之遺物。

鑲嵌工藝

東周、秦和兩漢時期帶鉤的裝飾法主要有兩種：寶石鑲嵌及金銀錯。寶石鑲嵌工藝其實是中國北方古工藝的復興，起源可上溯至青銅時期，而金銀錯則創於公元前六世紀的東周時代，最初是用來裝飾禮器及兵器。

寶石鑲嵌工藝最早應用於公元前六世紀末的帶鉤。大多數戰國時期鑄造的帶鉤上供鑲嵌用的凹條和凹坑都是原身鑄出，寶石則裁成所需大小，然後嵌上。展品目錄編號3及23所示的帶鉤便是這種裝飾手法的典型例子。然而，另外兩件戰國帶鉤所用的手法則大相逕庭。通過顯微觀察，可看到鉤面焊有金絲盤成的小框框，內鑲寶石(目錄編號25及26)。這種掐絲法是古代地中海地區流行的裝飾法，至公元前三世紀才傳入中國。

公元前六至一世紀，金屬編絲鑲嵌是中國最典型的器物鑲嵌手法，在戰國中期開始流行，最初是用於帶鉤的裝飾。此法是將多根金絲或銀絲並排嵌進青銅器表面預留的凹槽，而並非用錘將之錘入。據《漢書》記載，各個鑲嵌、挫磨、固牢和抛光的程序都有特定的工具。夢蝶軒藏有一件公元前三世紀末的錯銀絲青銅帶鉤，正是這種裝飾技術的代表作(目錄編號30)。東漢的《說文解字》亦提到青銅製品經鑲嵌後要以礪石打磨，盡去槎枒才可令器面平滑。

金銀片鑲嵌法主要見於東周末期、秦及兩漢的帶鉤，是將扁帶狀的金或銀片鑲進青銅表面的凹槽，槽邊刻有深坑，讓金銀片邊緣嵌入，使其更牢靠。夢蝶軒藏有一件公元前三世紀的錯金帶鉤(目錄編號31)，是這類精湛工藝的最佳典範，亦是河南金村出土物中的典型例子。

寶石軟泥鑲嵌法大概是創於公元前五至四世紀的東周時代，初期是用作青銅器上的裝飾，公元前三世紀時與其他裝飾法結合而成為帶鉤的裝飾手法之一。目錄編號26的一件帶鉤便是此工藝的代表作，兩側的小野豬是用金絲勾勒出線條，然後填以綠松石磨成的軟泥，毛皮及鬃毛則用描金點綴。

銅鏡鑄造術

銅鏡肇始於青銅時代，是北方遊牧民族所創，直至東周之世黃河中下游才有銅鏡的生產。與一般說法剛好相反，南方地區在東周末之前極少銅鏡的出現，後來是受道家思想影響才變得大為流行。

有關銅鏡的各種用途、象徵意義和紋飾的論說已非常豐富。除了用於鑑形容外，銅鏡還是生火的工具及驅邪擋煞的靈物。在道教及佛教思想影響下，銅鏡更漸與人生哲理、靈異之說及神器扯上關係。此外，銅鏡又與美人及其倩影結下不解緣，大英博物館所藏的顧愷之《女史箴圖卷》，便是與銅鏡有關的經典之作。

雖然有關銅鏡紋飾及其象徵意義的研究異常豐富，但涉及銅鏡製造方法的卻少之又少。本文無意探討其詳細鑄造過程，只希望能點出一些值得注意的地方，使讀者對夢蝶軒所藏銅鏡有更深入的認識。

最早的銅鏡只是簡單的圓形金屬片，來自中國西北的邊陲地區，如青海齊家文化遺址發現的紅銅鏡便是。河南安陽小屯商王配偶婦好墓的隨葬物中亦有銅鏡，但卻非中原所製，而是因通商或戰爭而得自從北方的遊牧民族。

中原地區在東周時期才開始鑄造銅鏡，所用的青銅其實是一種合金。據《周禮》記載，銅鏡中銅與錫的成分各佔一半，但現代科學分析未能確定此說法的可靠性。而據大部分實物顯示，青銅的合金成分是銅佔71%，錫佔26%而鉛佔3%。無數漢末的鏡銘都有提及這三種「瑞金」。雖然鐵鏡極為罕有，但漢代亦有製造，河南燒溝漢遺址便有六面鐵鏡出土。

中國古代銅鏡的範模是由兩片範塊合成，一作鏡面而另一作鏡背，作鏡背的一塊印或雕有紋飾。鑄成脫範後鏡面須經打磨及拋光才能鑑照形容。

山西侯馬公元前六世紀鑄冶遺址有鏡範的發現，反映出當時的晉國有可能是最早的鑄鏡國之一。夢蝶軒有一面戰國初期的銅鏡(目錄編號9)，相信亦是出自侯馬，因為鏡背有兩圈神獸噬動物紋帶，跟著名的戰國早期侯馬鑄造的「李峪壺」(現藏上海博物館)上的動物紋帶很是相似。鏡背似經鍍錫處理(鍍錫技術會於稍後論及)，鏡面則略呈拱狀。通常而言，拱狀鏡面是戰國末及漢鏡的特色，但此面晉鏡是一個例外。

夢蝶軒藏品中另一面戰國銅鏡(目錄編號11)亦飾有一圈龍紋帶，上面以起棱直線及弧線刻畫出六隻正面及兩隻側面的動物頭部。此動物紋帶以幼如髮絲的十字形棱線分隔成多個面積相等的小長方框，顯示出戳印紋飾的痕蹟。用戳印法可省卻個別雕刻的麻煩，戰國時期的鑄造坊經常採用此法大量生產銅鏡。晉國鑄銅坊並無採用此法，但用戳印法造出類似紋飾的銅鏡卻在河南及更南面的楚遺址有發現。通過顯微觀察，可看到此鏡(目錄編號11)背面除邊沿外皆鍍有錫。鏡面則平而不凸。

夢蝶軒所藏的早期銅鏡中，有些鏡面稍凸(目錄編號9、43、44、45、46及55k)，而其餘則完全是平的(目錄編號11,12及13)。較後期的藏品中只有兩面凸面鏡(目錄編號55h及57)。暫時還未知鏡的形狀和鏡面的拱度是否與鏡的用途有密切關連。

至於鏡面的拱狀是如何形成，則答案還不肯定。自公元前四世紀開始，人們受道家思想影響而對光學發生興趣，但當時文獻卻對鑄造銅鏡所涉及的光學根據極少述及。一直以來，出土的鏡範都只見鏡背部分，鑄造鏡面的範塊始終未有發現。不妨作一假設，用作翻泥範的銅鏡鏡面已作拱形，泥範是簡單的合範，鑄造鏡面的一塊因為光滑無紋，難於辨認，故往往為考古學者或盜墓者忽略，致使缺乏實物例證。

中國在第二次世界大戰前夕發現了八塊東周末的鏡範，但之後便不知所蹤。據說出土地點是河北易縣西南的塘湖村，鄰近燕下都(公元前311-222年燕國以此為下都)。範塊並非完全相同，而是屬於不同款式的銅鏡，反映出當地有銅鏡的鑄造作坊。據近年考古資料顯示，燕下都是東周時期一個重要的器物製作中心，所製器物除了供應本地市場外，還供其他遊牧民族使用。美國哈佛大學美術館藏有一塊鏡背陶範，跟易縣發現的非常相似，有可能亦是來自燕下都的鑄銅作坊(見圖六)。

漢末時，石範鑄鏡取代了陶範。哈佛大學美術館另有一塊用皂石造的鏡範(見圖七)，有三條凹槽，居中的作澆口用，其餘的是冒口，以免空氣內閉。範塊側有方形榫眼，以便與另一邊可能是陶造的範塊扣接。

東漢之世，鑄鏡業似乎已成為一種舉足輕重的工業，官營鑄鏡作坊遍佈全國。公元二世紀出產的銅鏡銘文豐富，內容包羅萬有。除了列有「瑞金」的出處外，很多銘文還記載了官營作坊的所在地。有時候甚至刻上工匠名字，在當時的冶煉業中是極罕有之舉。

長久以來，學者對鏡面的處理方法都有不同的論點。有些鏡面是特意鍍上一層錫，而另一些則因青銅的錫含量高而逆凝成銀白色的表面。一般而言，含錫量高的青銅在打磨後自然會發出銀白亮光，無須再鍍錫(目錄編號13)。然而未經X射線熒光光譜或掃描電子顯微術分析，很難確定鏡面的銀白亮光是如何形成。據科學分析，很少在鏡面發現汞的存在，但古代研磨鏡面用的物料則可能有汞的成分。《淮南子‧修務訓》云：「明鏡之始，下型矇然，未見形容，及其粉以玄錫，摩以白旃，鬢眉微毫可得而察。」由於無須加熱，故表面不會留下汞的痕蹟。有關「黑漆古」鏡(目錄編號43及46)的製造過程，爭拗甚烈。這些優美古鏡的鏡面黑而亮，以前多歸究於鏡面上一層不知名物質所致，但近年卻認為是銅鏡長埋地下與泥土的腐殖質接觸，致產生異樣的銅。

有些戰國及漢代銅鏡的紋飾並非鑄成而是描繪成，反映出金屬工藝與繪畫的關係。夢蝶軒藏品中有一面銅鏡(目錄編號13)，背面所鑄的曲體鳥紋，跟同期南方漆器上常見的紋飾很相近。至於藏品中另一面漆繪銅鏡，則是東周末期及兩漢時南方楚地的典型器物。

六朝之際，銅鏡業依然十分興盛。公元四世紀時，道教甚至為磨鏡匠編造了一位守護神，而在跟著的六個世紀，道士們仍不斷對光學作出種種的探索。道教典籍尚提到一種可以採集月露的方形鏡子，夢蝶軒藏品中的一面唐代小型凸面方鏡(目錄編號55h)可能與此有關。

唐代銅鏡製作水平非常高，形狀多彩多姿，紋飾絢麗生動，為歷代銅鏡的典範。為了使銅鏡更華美璀璨，銅鏡常包有金殼或銀殼，其上以錘沖法或鏤刻法造出極其綺麗的紋飾，將鑄造與鍛造兩種工藝共冶一爐，達到巔峰造極的境界，夢蝶軒藏品中亦不乏此類實例(目錄編號55g)。銀殼上的紋樣並非是以錘子在其上按凸模打成，而是在銀片背面隨手錘沖而成。

銅鏡在中國歷史上有非常重大的意義，但有關銅鏡的科學研究卻少之又少。如要深入探討這方面的資料，必要從金相顯微學入手，盡量搜集有年代可考的實例進行研究，所得數據可能對瞭解銅鏡所用的合金及其生產技術有幫助。雖然已有前人就這方向作過努力，但鑒於數據的缺乏，結論的準確性頗成疑問。

金屬鍛造術

與鑄造工匠比較，飾物鍛造匠的工作似乎輕鬆得多。以冷鍛法錘打而成的飾物通常比熔鑄的更為纖巧，金屬耗用量亦較少。製造飾物的最理想程序是由鍛造匠選好材料，然後一氣呵成地親手完成各個製造工序，直接了當，比起熔鑄法的密集人手和仔細分工簡單得多。故此，在飾物製作而言，熔鑄技術漸退居次要的地位。

究竟古代的鍛製飾物是全歸一個工匠負責抑或由一組工匠合作完成則至今還未有定論。雖然個別金銀匠可能相當有名，但一般來說，他們都是受聘於作坊，製品亦以作坊寶號為記。

雖然歷來很多學者都認為中原地區在青銅時期根本未有鍛造法的出現，但據近年考古資料顯示，實情並非如此。黃河中下游一帶的考古遺址如河南小屯等都發現包金箔的青銅馬具飾件，但卻未有實例證明金箔亦應用於製作個人飾物。

相對來說，北方的遊牧民族卻在青銅時期已經充分利用鍛造法生產出無數飾物。夢蝶軒藏有一對鍛打成形的金耳環(目錄編號1)，造型跟山西石樓的出土物幾乎一樣。

至東周中期，中原及其以北地區已普遍利用鍛造法在鑄冶成的帶鉤上裝飾加工(目錄編號15)。秦及兩漢時期，工匠們已掌握了各種鍛造技法，造出工藝精湛而紋飾綺麗的飾物，後世亦一直沿用。

由於缺乏記錄各種鍛製技法的文獻，我們只好從實物入手進行探索。古代鍛造匠最常用的金屬是金和銀，間中亦有用銅。鍛製法的過程是首先將鑄成錠狀的金屬以冷鍛法錘打成所需厚薄，鑴刻成形，然後以錘沖法、鏤刻法或戳印法造出玲瓏浮凸的紋樣，或更進一步以金珠及金銀絲在飾物表面堆砌出各種螺旋紋、連鎖紋、連珠紋、掐絲紋及絲花細工。

錘打法（冷鍛法）

工匠在選好金屬材料後，先是用圓頭錘，然後用平頭錘將鑄煉成錠形的金屬按所需厚薄鍛打成片狀。若要打出極薄的片塊，則要用皮革或相類物質將金屬片夾著鍛打。金屬經冷鍛後會變得更堅硬，但若用熱淬法，即燒熱後迅速放入水中冷卻，便會回復其延展性。為方便加工，名貴金屬原料多鑄成小塊或錠狀。夢蝶軒藏品中有兩件飾物看來是直接從金塊或金條鍛製成形(目錄編號103)。

鑴刻及透雕

用冷鍛法打出大致外形後，便可進一步鑴刻或透雕出造型細節，所用工具並非切刀或剪刀，而是鑿子。舉例來說，夢蝶軒藏品中有一件遼代花形髮簪(目錄編號76)便是用鑿子鑴刻成形。在鑑定宋代以前的飾物真偽時，若發現金屬邊緣有利刃相交造成的痕蹟，則該飾物有可能是後世仿製品。

透雕是唐(目錄編號61及63)宋(目錄編號83)髮簪常用的裝飾手法，所用工具亦是鑿子。若以顯微鏡觀察，不難發現鑿子在金屬邊緣留下鋸齒狀痕蹟。夢蝶軒藏品中有一組宋代髮簪(目錄編號85)便有此現象。

掐絲工藝

夢蝶軒藏有兩件戰國晚期掐絲帶鉤(目錄編號25及26)，金絲是從鍛打成的金片鑿出，然後焊到帶鉤上去。展品中一只六朝金梳(目錄編號48)上方的掐絲紋飾亦用此法製成。古代近東地區和埃及所用的掐絲技法亦大同小異，反映出此種工藝可能是源自西方。

錘沖凸紋工藝

製造錘沖凸紋飾的方法有二：一是將金屬片置於模上錘沖成形(目錄編號54及86)，一是將金屬片反轉過來以軟物墊好，然後在其背面以圓頭工具錘出紋樣。製成後金屬的正面便出現浮凸的圖案。有時候工匠會在其上再作鏤刻，使紋樣看來更精細。夢蝶軒藏品中有一件唐代髮飾(目錄編號64)和兩件精美異常的宋代鎏金銀髮簪(目錄編號84)，其上的羽紋即用此法製成。

有些中空的飾物是由兩半錘沖成形的金屬片焊合而成(目錄編號75)。亦有在木蕊外包裹錘沖出紋樣的金屬殼(目錄編號96)。

鏤刻法（鈒鏤法）

此法是以名為沖頭的鏤刻工具在金屬片正面施工，刻出凹陷的花紋。從背面看紋樣往往呈浮凸狀。夢蝶軒藏品中有一對唐代銀簪(目錄編號62)，是此裝飾法的典型例子。沖頭有多種形狀，末端略圓，能使金屬片變形就位而不開裂；質料有金屬、骨、木及石，應用時以錘子在其上敲打。從顯微鏡觀察，鈒鏤痕蹟看上去像一連串重疊的短線或圓點、半月形、圓圈等。由於沖頭的作用只是將金屬向兩旁擠壓而不是將之刮去，故此鈒鏤線條就像雪犁經過留下的軌蹟一樣，兩邊起棱。

飾物經熔鑄或錘沖成形後，往往再以鏤刻法加工使紋飾線條更精細俐落。不少唐宋髮簪在製造過程中都全面用上錘打、鑴刻、錘沖及鈒鏤等鍛造技術(目錄編號64)。

用末端裝上圖模的沖頭在金片或銀片表面反覆扣打，除了能造出悶光效果外，還可以刻出重覆的圖案。夢蝶軒藏品中有兩件元代龍紋髮簪(目錄編號105)，龍身上的半圓形鱗紋便是用此法造成。此法又可令金屬表面產生不同的質感。藏品中有一組唐代鑄造的帶飾牌(目錄編號52)，無數小圓圈構成的地紋，亦用此法製成。宋代時，有末端作凸面形的沖頭，可仿製出金珠紋效果，省卻不少麻煩(目錄編號97)，正統的金珠工藝反而不甚流行。

雕刻法

此法是以一鋒利的刻刀將金屬切去或撤去，很少跟錘沖法一起應用，因為錘沖法用的金屬片太薄，無從切割，但施用在熔鑄品上則效果非常好。夢蝶軒藏有一件鑄成的圓形銀飾牌(目錄編號22)，背面的銘文就是用此法刻成。線條若是以雕刻法造出，開端部分一定較尖，因為刻刀是逐步嵌進金屬，結尾則因刻刀停頓抽離而顯得有猝然而止的感覺。

咬合法

此法是將兩片金屬相疊，以器械將其中一片的邊緣摺起覆在另一片的邊緣上咬合。夢蝶軒藏有數件宋代髮簪，錘沖凸紋的金屬殼與底下的金屬便是以此法咬緊(目錄編號95、96及97)。有時候咬合法亦會與其他技法結合使用。例子是夢蝶軒所藏的數件宋代髮釵(目錄編號88)，構成髮釵的圓型飾件是由多個不同部分以咬合法及焊接法結合而成。

金珠工藝

正統的金珠工藝是將小滴金珠以擴散接合法固定在金器表面成獨立或輔助紋飾，無須焊錫。此技法是近東地區所創，歷史悠久，其起源可追溯至公元前三千年。

金珠技法在中國出現的最早年代是公元前四世紀末，首先採用的是當時鄂爾多斯地區的遊牧民族，中原金銀工匠要到西漢時期才運用此法。

夢蝶軒藏有一件金製冠飾，是金珠工藝的傑出例子(目錄編號47)。金珠按大小順序排列，造成極佳的裝飾效果，媲美湖南安鄉西晉墓所出的精美金帶扣。

很多時，工匠以焊接法將金珠固定在金器表面，模擬正統的金珠技法，肉眼看來無大分別，但通過顯微鏡便會發現金珠顆粒不夠明顯，顆粒之間充滿焊錫(目錄編號48)。金珠裝飾法在六朝風靡一時，唐代時仍然是飾物上常用的裝飾技法(目錄編號70)，宋早期亦然(目錄編號91)。明代時漸式微，代之而興的是圓圈紋悶光技法及金銀絲裝飾工藝。

串珠狀緣飾

此裝飾法是在器物或紋飾的邊緣滴上或焊上一連串的金珠。夢蝶軒藏有一件金製冠飾，是這種技法的實物例證(目錄編號47)。

金銀絲工藝

在製作飾物的過程中，金銀絲的用處很多，可以造鏈索、堆飾或金銀絲花裝飾。金絲的最早應用，與北方的遊獵民族關係密切。河北新樂縣中同村發現的兩件螺旋紋金手鐲即為早期例子。

　　古代的金銀絲是用絞絲法製成，將錘打得極薄的金屬片慢慢扭絞成長絲(見圖八)。現代多用拔絲法，將鑄造或鍛造成棒狀的金屬擠壓進拔絲板中央的錐型細孔，然後從另一端的小孔將細絲抽出。在顯微鏡下，這兩種技法很易分辨。前者的螺旋痕蹟顯而易見，如夢蝶軒所藏的鄂爾多斯地區金耳墜上的三個錐狀飾件便是由此法製造的金絲盤成(目錄編號16)；後者則有縱向的凹紋，如另外兩件宋代髮簪便是例子(目錄編號83及92)。

　　有關拔絲法的創製年代，眾說紛紜。西方學者認為是公元一至十世紀之間所創，但印度學者卻認為早在公元前三世紀印度河流域已有拔絲工藝的存在。

金銀絲堆飾

金銀絲可在器物表面堆出精細的紋飾。夢蝶軒藏有一件西晉龍紋金製冠飾，龍的鼻孔就是用金絲盤成的螺旋形代表(目錄編號47)。

串珠狀金屬絲

在絞絲法製成的金屬絲上刻出一連串凹紋，使之看來像串珠狀邊緣紋飾(目錄編號73)。

鏈索

中國古代金銀工藝最典型的鏈索是「連環套」，先造好個別鏈環，再用很複雜的方法將之連起來(見圖九)。

　　連環套鏈的創製可追溯至約公元前二千五百年的索瑪利亞和埃及。公元前四至三世紀，古希臘的金銀工藝亦漸流行製造這類鏈索，中亞草原的遊牧民族對之亦非常珍視。鄂爾多斯高原內蒙西部杭錦旗阿魯柴登的匈奴墓發現了一件非常精美的實例，至於是本土製造抑或來自西域則尚未有定論。

　　連環套鏈的製作技法在東周末傳入中國，之後歷十多個世紀盛行不衰。夢蝶軒藏有一只六朝的耳墜，其上的細鏈索似是連環套的變體(目錄編號49)。這種用鍛造法製成的鏈索，與鑄造及鑄接法製成的青銅鏈索可謂各有千秋。

金銀絲裝飾工藝

此法是以金銀絲製成極精細而玲瓏剔透的網狀紋飾，在西方有頗悠久的歷史，但在中國則是明清兩代才見流行。夢蝶軒藏品中有些明代的耳環便是以此法裝飾(目錄編號109)。

鎏金、鍍錫及鎏銀等技法

夢蝶軒藏品中有很多飾物的表面都是刻意鍍上一層金、銀或錫，使飾物看來更華貴耀目。除了美觀和實用外，在金屬飾物表面附加另一種金屬這個做法還有其象徵意義。有關中國這種工藝的研究還在起步階段，下文將會探討最重要的幾種技法及其優點，藉此瞭解在電鍍術發明之前古人為何及如何運用這些技法。

鎏金

中國古代的鎏金分包金和汞齊鎏金。包金是以錘打成薄片的金箔加諸器物表面，商代時已有應用。汞齊鎏金，現代考古學亦簡稱鎏金，是戰國時才興起的技法，但卻後來居上，重要性超越包金。這兩種技法各有特色，同是中國古代金屬工藝常用的裝飾法。

　　商代的包金技法主要是用於美化馬具飾件，而非用於個人飾物。東周時期人們開始流行佩戴金屬飾物，包金工藝才應用於飾物製作。夢蝶軒所藏的帶鉤中亦不乏包金的例子(目錄編號15及17)。鋪上金箔前先要用鑿子將青銅表面刮得粗糙，然後將金箔鋪在其上，反覆推磨，使金箔能嵌進刮痕，緊貼青銅，無須借助任何黏貼劑也不會脫落。

　　東周末期汞齊鎏金技術的出現可謂非常偶然，起因是道士們煉丹藥求長生時意外地發現了人造金的化學程式。故此汞齊鎏金並非發展自包金，二者在技法上根本毫不相干。前者是一種化學加工，是將黃金熔於汞，然後塗在器物表面，再加以烘燒。汞在加熱過程中消失，器面須經打磨才發出燦爛金光。西漢時，汞齊鎏金開始替代包金成為青銅器上的裝飾。夢蝶軒藏有多件青銅帶鉤和遊牧風格的帶飾牌，都屬汞齊鎏金製品(目錄編號28、32、39及42)。

　　由於兩種鎏金製品外觀相似，憑肉眼實難定斷，唯有用顯微鏡觀察才能發覺包金表面會有剝落現象，露出底下的青銅(目錄編號15)，而汞齊鎏金雖較薄但卻較緊密，但若遭磨損或受底下銅侵蝕而剝落，亦有可能令玄機外露。此外，在顯微鏡下亦可看到凹陷處的汞齊鎏金表面會呈穀紋狀。

　　在中國古代，鎏金的目的可謂十分複雜。初時可能只是作為襯色用，讓赤黃色的青銅器看來近黃色多於近紅色。在東周中期以前，並無文獻提及黃金有何金融價值或與煉丹致長生有何關係，只是以顏色區分金和銀這兩種金屬，前者叫黃金，後者叫白金。

汞齊鎏金則很明顯與道教關係密切。戰國末及西漢時期，黃金在煉丹致長生中的重要性直逼玉石。此外，北方及西方的部族對黃金亦極為珍視，向漢人買來很多汞齊鎏金的帶飾牌(目錄編號28及32)，以顯示物主的地位高於佩戴純青銅帶飾牌者。

很多時候，因為所用的鎏金技術實在太高超，簡直令人難分真假。夢蝶軒藏有一對遼代耳環(目錄編號73)，驟眼看來似用純金製成，但經過顯微觀察後發覺實際上是汞齊鎏金青銅。鎏金可令青銅看來像黃金，但成本卻比黃金低，所以唐宋時期有大量的髮飾都是鎏金青銅製品，夢蝶軒亦有不少這類藏品(目錄編號88及89)。

除了經濟因素外，鎏金還有美化金屬表面的作用，讓飾物看來金光燦爛。夢蝶軒藏有一件戰國末的圓形銀飾牌(目錄編號22)，動物身上有些細部鎏成金色，似乎是裝飾作用大於象徵意義。秦漢以後，鎏金銀器繼續成為風尚，唐宋兩朝的鎏金銀髮飾尤其普遍(目錄編號64及83)。除了將整件飾物鎏金外，亦有局部鎏金的作法。

十九世紀中葉以後，電鍍法漸取代汞齊鎏金法。電鍍法除了較先進外，製造時亦不用擔心受汞氣荼毒。有些製於本世紀初的贗品，便因採用電鍍法而遭識破。近年由於古玩市場異常蓬勃，汞齊鎏金技術在中國大陸及香港又再興起，令贗品的像真程度大大提高。

鍍錫

中國的鍍錫技術創始於東周早期，最初是用塗抹法或浸漬法使錫熔液附在含錫量高的青銅表面，無須用汞。夢蝶軒藏有一件前後都鍍錫的帶鈎(目錄編號8)，用的就是浸漬法，而另一件帶飾牌則只有正面鍍錫(目錄編號21)，用的應是塗抹法。

含錫量高的青銅在研磨後自然會發出銀光，所以大多無須鍍錫，夢蝶軒藏品中有些含錫量高的銅鏡便是例子(目錄編號58)。前人常把這種自然的銀光誤會為錫汞齊的效果或青銅含錫過豐導致冷卻時產生錫逆凝或「錫汗」現象。據近年科學分析所得，這類含錫量高的青銅鏡並無經錫汞齊處理，而「錫汗」現象只出現於含錫量低而非高的青銅。

一些戰國時期的兵器曾發現汞齊鎏錫的痕蹟，但卻未有實例顯示此法在當時有應用於個人飾物製作。實際上，要令銅鏡光可鑑人，只要用一種含錫和汞的研料磨礪便可(見前文引《淮南子》)，無須加熱，亦不一定要經汞齊鎏錫處理。

古代鍍錫的目的有多個：鍍錫後的銅鏡不但銀光閃耀，還對鏡面起著保護作用，防止蝕而令其更為耐用；早期的鍍錫並非要模仿白銀，而是銀白色的錫跟其他金屬如赤銅及黃金的顏色對比強烈而具美感；隨著銀器之漸受歡迎，便有利用鍍錫刻意模仿白銀。這些因素頗能反映出古代鍍金工藝的取向與其時流行的色澤和裝飾潮流有莫大關連。

古代西北遊牧民族以帶飾為身份地位的標識，鍍錫帶飾的應用比鎏金帶飾早。考古掘得的實物及傳世品中都有大量公元前六至三世紀的鍍錫青銅帶飾牌，夢蝶軒藏品中亦有一件(目錄編號21)。

鍍錫首飾在漢以後突然不再流行，只有少量實例。夢蝶軒藏有一件非常精美的唐代鍍錫銅合金梳子，部分紋飾且以鎏金點綴(目錄編號68)。

鎏銀

鎏銀技術是東周末年才發展起來的，而且並不普遍。最早期的鎏銀法叫「包銀」，是將銀箔嵌於器物表面。夢蝶軒有一件帶鈎的正面(目錄編號24)及另一件的背面(目錄編號15)便是用此法造出紋飾。

汞齊鎏銀技術創始於西漢時期，主要用於容器及馬具，使其表面成銀色，並間中以鎏金紋飾點綴。汞齊鎏銀技術很少用於製作個人飾物，故實例不多，夢蝶軒藏品中有一組西晉帶飾(目錄編號50b)，是很罕有的例子。

事實上，白銀在中國的冶煉工藝中的地位並不重要，亦沒有像黃金一樣與煉丹求長生扯上關係。世界上很多民族都以白銀為純潔的象徵，將之與月亮聯系，但中華民族卻例外。《史記》有云：「殷得金德，銀自山溢」，此說前半部應本源自《呂氏春秋‧應同》：「凡帝王之將興也，天必先見祥乎下民....及湯(商)之時，天先見金刃生於水，湯曰"金氣勝"，故其色尚白，其事則金。」但後半部有關白銀的說法則不知是何出處。

結語

一直以來，以中國金銀玉石製作的個人飾物為主題的藏品並不多見。歷來中國的金屬首飾都是貴族或官宦人士用以標識身份等第的必然佩件，不入於收藏文物之列。對他們而言，蒐集文物並非是基於對美的追求，而是希望藉此探討過去。由於金銀飾物歷史地位不高，不及古代的青銅及玉製禮器莊重和有意義，故此始終未能成為蒐集對象。

是次夢蝶軒藏品展覽為我們提供了極其珍貴的機會以欣賞及探討中國古代飾物冶煉工藝的精萃。科學技術的進步，通常最早體現於小型器物如個人飾物等之製作。通過夢蝶軒藏品的研究及觀察，發覺一些有關中國冶煉技術的舊有假定似乎有修改的必要。例如，以前總認為金珠、掐絲及另外一些鍛造技法是公元後才傳入中國，但據最新研究所得，早在公元前多個世紀中國已有此等技法的應用。此外，雖然貼身佩戴金屬飾物的重要的習慣是感染自遊牧民族，但傳入中土後不久便漸受同化，終成為身份與等第重要的標識。

＊所有圖片參見英文版

圖一　　河北易縣燕下都遺址出土的銅人圖像。

圖二　　鑄方鼎合範示意圖：四邊為外範，上為泥蕊，下為四足間之內範。外範內壁的反向紋飾可借助母模完成或直接雕出與截出，焙烘前須將細節修整。將母模表面挫低，便成內範，但就此方鼎來說，似乎做法是將外範合在一起，澆注泥漿，乾後拆開，再將泥蕊表面挫低而成，四足之間的內範亦用此法造出。插圖A顯示合範後外貌，插圖B顯示澆注熔液前要將整個範模倒轉，四足向上。

圖三　　鑄帶鉤用範塊，以兩面範方式製作。

圖四　　山西侯馬出土之範塊，屬複合範類。

圖五　　明成化楔形石範，鑄龍紋圓飾牌用。

圖六　　屬鏡範底部之範塊，鑄四山鏡用，公元前四至三世紀，紅黃陶土。

圖七　　鑄獸紋鏡用之石範，公元一至二世紀，有三條凹槽，居中的作澆口，其餘為冒口。

圖八　　絞絲法步驟及串珠狀金屬絲製法。

圖九　　製「連環套」步驟，a.單連環，b.雙連環，c.基本式連環套，d.8字式連環套。

Catalogue of the Exhibition

Early Period

Shang period through Han period,
13th century B.C.–3rd century A.D.

1 Pair of Earrings 商飾綠松石金耳墜一對

Shang period, 13th century B.C.
Gold and turquoise
L: 5.4 cm
GI-112

These earrings each have a flat, curved shape that terminates at one end in a spiral and at the other with the shank. These graceful curvilinear shapes were created by metalsmithing techniques. Each earring was made from a single piece of gold that was hammered and chisel-cut. Microscopic examination reveals the hammer marks. The addition of a small turquoise bead to the shaft of each earring lends a pleasing color-contrast to the gold.

Metal earrings are rare in the ancient Chinese world and, to date, have only been found along the northern borders. The distinctive shape of the Mengdiexuan earrings associates them with one specific area: almost identical gold-and-turquoise earrings have been excavated from sites in Shilou county, in Shanxi province.[1] Such sites are contemporary with the Anyang period of the Shang dynasty in the Central Plains, but the people buried in Shanxi were not Shang. Instead, the Shilou sites belonged to pastoral tribes living along the northern frontier with whom the Shang often interacted through trade and warfare.[2] Evidence for relationships between these tribes and the Shang is provided by the presence of Shang bronzes at some of their sites.[3] Northern Shanxi has traditionally been a source of horses for the Central Plains throughout Chinese history, and may well have been so during the Shang period. —ECB

82 EARLY PERIOD

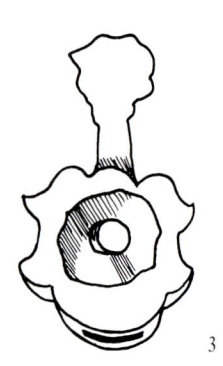

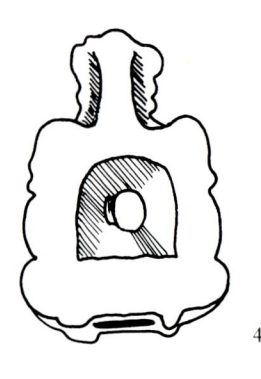

2 Garment Hook   東周獸紋金帶鉤

Eastern Zhou period, 6th–5th century B.C.
Gold
L: 2.2 cm W: 2.2 cm D: 1.6 cm
H-061

This cast-gold garment hook is decorated with zoomorphic motifs. The hook is formed by a fantastic bird head with a short, flaring, flat beak. The body of the hook, front and back, is covered with a pattern of zoomorph heads, with ears and eyes indicated by raised outlines on a pseudo-granulation-patterned ground. Such patterns are typical of the late sixth- to fifth-century B.C. designs seen on bronzes found at Liyu, in northern Shanxi.[4] The underside of the hook is hollow, with a vertical post for attachment purposes (see drawing).

The piece was probably cast by the piece-mold process. A faint mark on the side of the head represents a joint seam between two mold sections. Clay fragments of piece-molds used for casting objects decorated with similar designs have been found among the foundry remains at Houma, in southern Shanxi.[5] This was a famous metalworking center belonging to the Jin state during the Spring and Autumn and early Warring States periods.

A cast-gold garment hook with a similar shape and attachment device was excavated from the late sixth-century B.C. Qin tomb of Duke Jing at Yimencun, in Baoji city, near Xi'an, in Fengxiang county, Shaanxi.[6] Duke Jing of Qin is mentioned several times in the *Shiji*, the early history of China written by Sima Qian.[7] Duke Jing lived from 577 to 537 B.C. and is recorded to have successfully attacked the neighboring state of Jin. Another Qin tomb in Fengxiang county contained a similar hook.[8] Another similar small bronze hook, from a Qin tomb at Gaozhuang, Fengxiang county, is described as a collar hook, suggesting a possible function for such tiny hooks.[9]   —ECB

3 Garment Hook   東周鳥紋金帶鉤

Eastern Zhou period, 6th–5th century B.C.
Gold
L: 3.2 cm W: 2.9 cm D: 1.3 cm
H-062

This gold garment hook was cast in the shape of a bird-like creature with outspread wings and tail. Empty cells suggest that it was originally inlaid with small pieces of some material that marked certain body parts. The reverse reveals an attachment device consisting of a hollow circular space with a central vertical post (see drawing). Tiny brownish stains may be iron oxide deposited on the surface. This piece presumably was cast in the same way as was the hook in catalogue number 2.

A bronze garment hook with a similar shape was found in a late Spring and Autumn–period Qin burial, tomb 2 at Yimencun, in Baoji city, Shaanxi.[10]   —ECB

4 Garment Hook   東周鳥獸紋嵌飾金帶鉤

Eastern Zhou period, 5th century B.C.
Gold with modern inlay
L: 2.9 cm W: 2.2 cm D: 1.6 cm
H-043

The body of this small gold hook is decorated in raised relief with intertwined zoomorphs inlaid with blue accents. Four raptor heads in profile occur at each corner, and there are two feline masks in the center of the hook. The head of the hook is formed by a fantastic animal head with asymmetrical pointed ears, outlined by a raised line with its ends curled inward, and a flaring, flat beak. The reverse side is hollow and has a vertical post for attachment purposes (see drawing).

This piece presumably was cast in the same way as were the two gold hooks discussed in catalogue numbers 2 and 3. Microscopic examination of this piece reveals a faint longitudinal line around the side of the body that represents a joint seam between two mold sections. The granular surface and small indentations on the gold indicate that the investment material used for casting was a very granular clay. The ears and certain other areas are inlaid with some modern blue substance probably intended to imitate turquoise.[11]

Two bronze hooks very similar to this gold example were excavated from a Qin tomb at Gaozhuang, Fengxiang county, Shaanxi, and date to the early Warring States period.[12]   —ECB

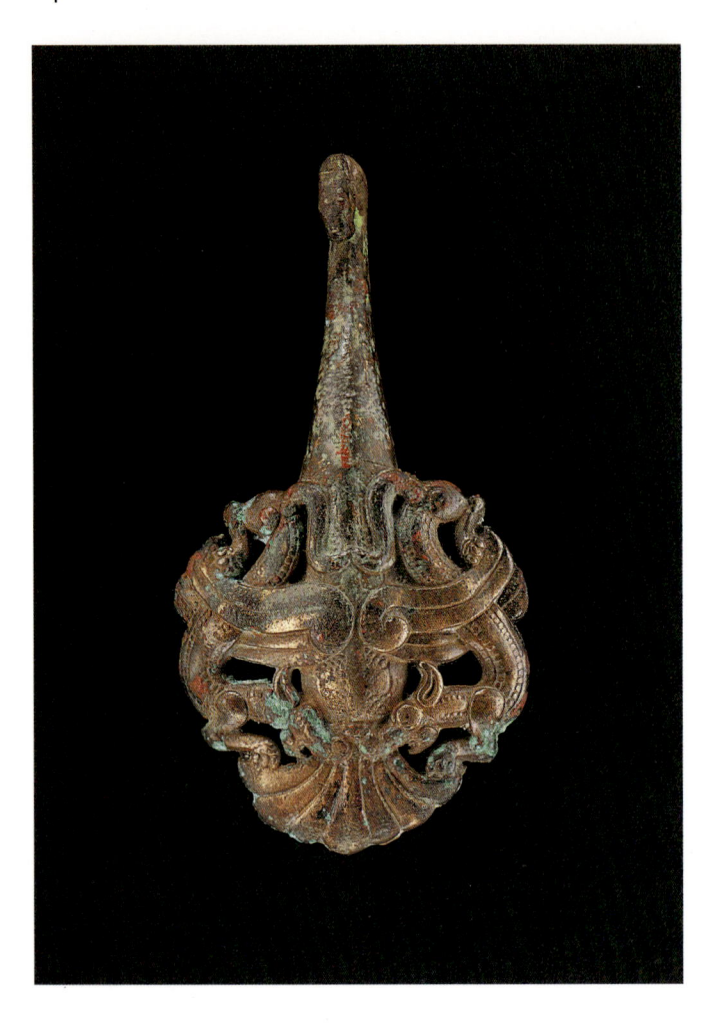

5 Belt Hook 東周/戰國鳥獸紋青銅帶鉤

Eastern Zhou, Warring States period, 5th century B.C.
Bronze
L: 9.5 cm W: 5.1 cm D: 6.7 cm
H-049

This belt hook was cast in the shape of a large bird with outspread wings and tail. In its wings and biting its tail are two inverted wolf-headed carnivores shown in profile. The head of the bird forms the hook. The carnivores have three claws on each paw; stylized, round, bulging eyes; curled-up snouts; and comma-shaped ears within a raised outline. The bird's body is distinguished by small, crisscrossed rectangles. The carnivores each have two parallel longitudinal lines of pseudo-beading marking their body contours. The back of the belt hook is concave and displays a round button in the middle of the bird's body. The surface of the bronze has been overcleaned to reveal bright, golden-looking areas, but faint silk pseudomorphs still remain on the back.

This hook was cast by the lost-wax process. A microscopic examination reveals no piece-mold marks; instead, there is evidence on the back of the piece that a knife was used to trim off the excess wax from the model after it was removed from the mother mold in which it had been formed.

This hook is similar in concept to a large bronze hook, formerly in the David-Weill collection, that shows a large bird with four carnivores superimposed on its body.[13] These hooks belong to a small group of early Warring States objects that bear some distant relationship to compositions and iconography associated with cultures farther west, in the ancient Near East. For example, compare the bronze ornament depicting a displayed bird with two winged, nude figures held in its wings, which was excavated at Zhongzhoulu, near Luoyang, in Henan.[14] 　　　　　—ECB

6 Garment Hook 東周/戰國鳥獸紋金帶鉤

Eastern Zhou, Warring States period, 5th century B.C.
Gold and bronze
L: 7.0 cm W: 3.5 cm D: 1.3 cm
H-035

The head of this piece, forming the hook, is that of a bird with round eyes, each indicated by a dot within three concentric circles. The bird has two small spiral-shaped wings and feathers described by intaglio U-shaped marks. Superimposed on its body is a formalized design of two intertwined zoomorphs, which it grasps in its claws. Each of the two zoomorphs is represented with different anatomical features. One has ears indicated by raised circular sockets; the other has ears formed by raised spirals. The body of one is marked by diagonal striations in a herringbone pattern accented by a raised longitudinal ridge; that of the other is distinguished by a pseudo-granulation pattern produced by crosshatching. Both zoomorphs have curled-up snouts; round, bulging eyes; and two paws, each with three claws.

The back of the garment hook is heavily encrusted with corrosion, which may have resulted from extreme dampness. Pseudomorphs in the corrosion on the back are the remains of the cloth in which the garment hook was wrapped when buried. The button has been broken off, but it originally occupied the middle of the back. The head of the hook was broken off and reattached. A band of gold foil around the neck of the hook disguises the mend.

The casting method for creating this garment hook is quite unusual. The gold shell, with its raised zoomorphic decoration, was crisply cast in a clay mold over a precast bronze core. Microscopic examination reveals that some details of the decoration were further defined by chasing after this piece was cast.

Similar zoomorph heads with round, socketlike eyes occur on the decoration of a belt hook in the Freer Gallery of Art, in Washington, D.C.[15] Such belt hooks have been excavated from early Warring States tombs at Xinyang, in Henan.[16]

—ECB

7 Buckle　東周雙獸紋青銅飾牌帶扣

Eastern Zhou period, 5th century B.C.
Bronze
Right: H: 4.8 cm W: 6.8 cm
Left: H: 4.6 cm W: 8.5 cm
H-053

This buckle consists of two plaques, each in the shape of a caninelike carnivore. The tail of one carnivore is transformed into a hook, which fits into a loop formed by the tail of the carnivore on the opposing plaque. The reverse of each plaque displays a round button for attachment purposes. Traces of iron rust occur on the surface.

The two carnivores are each shown in profile, half-crouching on a ground line which has a snake head on either end. Their heads are turned backward and their pointed ears are each indicated by a raised line whose ends are curled inward. Their snouts are curled upward like that of a wolf. Their jaws are slightly open, and each is described by a pseudo-granulation-patterned band. Their shoulders and haunches are accented by comma-shaped enclosures filled with spirals and angles. Their paws each have two prominent claws which hold worn, empty rings. The two bands around each neck suggest collars, and thus domestication. References abound in both art and literature to trained falcons, dogs, leopards, and cheetahs used in hunting.[17]

The reverse of each plaque displays a round button centered within two raised crescent-shaped marks. Such marks are also seen on the reverse of the hook in catalogue number 17. These are mold marks, and they indicate that the pieces were cast in multisection molds like those found at Houma, the Jin foundry site in southern Shanxi. The rings below the paws once held linked chains, such as those suspended from several similar buckles in Stockholm.[18] Such chains also were cast in section molds and then cast onto the plaques.

Similar plaques with pendant chains were recently discovered in Yanchuan, Yan'an, in northeast Shaanxi.[19] Another plaque with one chain was unearthed in 1983 at Ansai county, Shaanxi.[20] The fact that this plaque represents only half a belt buckle is not indicated in the Chinese description.

Stylistically, many of these beasts appear to relate to those of the Jin state, which flourished during the sixth to fifth centuries B.C. in what is now southern Shanxi. The Mengdiexuan carnivores have paws with two claws, a typical feature also found on felines that adorn the fifth-century B.C. Jin bell in the British Museum.[21] The half-crouching position, bands of pseudo-granulation that outline the jaws, and decorative shoulder and haunch marks are all typical of the Jin style, as seen in artifacts excavated at Fenshuiling, Changzhi, in Shanxi.[22] Further study shows that the carnivores' ears are almost identical in shape to those of the tiny carnivores on the Liyu-style mirror in the Mengdiexuan collection (cat. no. 9). It is not unreasonable to suggest that the Jin foundries at Houma may have served a far wider market than has hitherto been realized.　—ECB

8 Belt Hook   東周/戰國鍍錫鳥紋青銅帶鉤

Eastern Zhou, Warring States period, 5th–4th century B.C.
Tinned bronze
L: 8.3 cm W: 3.5 cm D: 1.9 cm
H-044

This bronze belt hook was cast in the shape of a stylized bird with a round body and a long neck. The bird's head forms the hook. The body is decorated with symmetrical intaglio spiral designs that suggest wings. Tiny, random, intaglio dots give a textured appearance to the surface. The surface is worn in places, but the remains of an intentional layer of tin are still visible.

On the back of the hook is a round button supported on a short column. A mold-joint seam is visible across the top of the button, indicating that the hook was cast in a two-piece mold. Slanting file marks along the sides, under the tinning, reveal post-cast filing. The tinning was probably achieved by dipping the piece in liquid tin, since both the front and reverse sides reveal traces of tinning.

A belt hook with the same shape and design was excavated from tomb M46 at Huangjiagou, near Xianyang, in Shaanxi province, a pre-dynastic Qin site dating to the mid-Warring States period.[23] Whether or not the excavated hook was tinned is unclear, because the excavation report does not discuss the surface appearance. An earlier belt hook associated with the Jin state has the same shape and spiral designs as the Mengdiexuan garment hook.[24]

Qin, located in present-day Shaanxi, was one of the most powerful independent states of the Eastern Zhou period before the Qin dynasty was founded in 221 B.C. The tinning of belt ornaments appears to have been a pre-dynastic Qin specialty. Several Qin belt hooks that are formed by an S-shaped ribbon of bronze were tinned, as were many of the plaques cast in zoomorphic shapes by Qin craftsmen for neighboring pastoral tribes.[25]

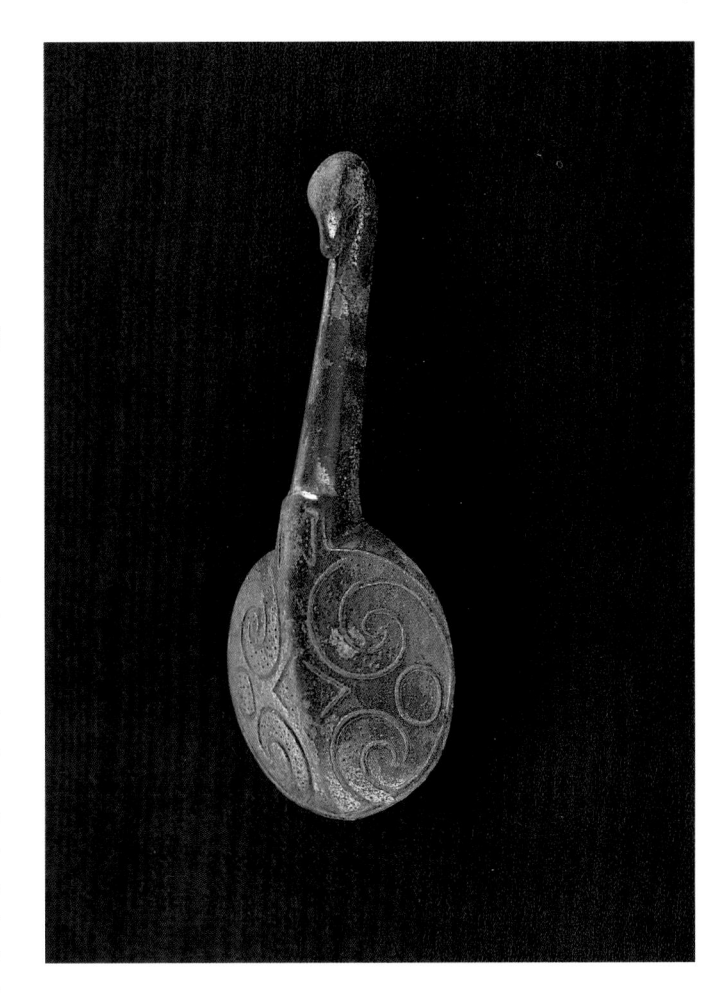

—ECB

88 EARLY PERIOD

9 Mirror 東周/戰國鍍錫龍紋青銅鏡

Eastern Zhou, Warring States period, 475–221 B.C.
Bronze
D: 7.6 cm
M-113

A knob in the form of a crouching hare on a round base is surrounded by a circle of four mythical animals in strong, rounded relief. A circle of eight similar animals surrounds the inner circle. The S-shaped animals follow each other in a counterclockwise direction, head to tail. In their jaws each holds a zoomorphic victim, either a bird or a snake. The twelve animals are shown from above, with all four legs visible and each head and tail clearly defined.

In the outer band two styles of animals alternate. One has a pointed ear, the other a rounded ear. The style with a pointed ear is scaly and longer than the other style, which has markings indicating fur. The animals in the outer ring all appear clawed, while those in the center are hoofed.

Filling the limited space between the animals are triangular spirals. The mirror's border is rather narrow.

Mythical beasts are very popular Eastern Zhou motifs. Those on mirrors unearthed from the Chu area of the south are generally more abstract in form and spontaneous in outline. The decoration of this mirror is rare, and its high relief suggests an origin in northern China. A mirror with similar animal designs can be found in the collection of the King of Sweden.[26]

Though heavily covered with patina, this mirror with its very rare motif remains an object of immense artistic value. The decorated back has been tinned, while the reflective surface is heavily encrusted with malachite and shows evidence of a textile imprint. —CPF

10 Mirror 東周/春秋晚期虎紋青銅鏡

Eastern Zhou, late Spring and Autumn period,
6th–5th century B.C.
Bronze
D: 11.0 cm
M-122

This mirror has a bridge-shaped knob set upon a round base. The inner zone is decorated with four crouching tigers, in high relief, facing in the same counterclockwise direction. They are each shown full face with their bodies in profile. Their pelts are marked by crosshatching to produce raised dots which indicate their fur. These felines appear in two slightly different styles alternating with each other. Framing the inner circle is a broad band of tiny dots with four pointed cloud heads projecting from its inner edge and eight projecting from its outer edge. An outer circle contains eight tigers similar to the four inner animals in form and arrangement.

The broad and slightly raised border of the mirror contains a ring of rope pattern. Compared to most mirrors of the Warring States period, this piece has a thicker and heavier body. The dot motif on the tigers is similar to that used as the ground decor on a bronze *pou,* or jar, unearthed from Houma, Shanxi, and they were probably made by the same technique. Since this dot motif is seldom found on other early bronzes, we believe that this mirror belongs to a period close to that of the Houma bronze *pou.* Mirrors with twelve tigers are rare.

A mirror decorated with a single band containing four similar felines is in the Ostasiatiska Museet in Stockholm and dated by Bernhard Karlgren to the late Spring and Autumn period.[27]

The decoration is similar but not identical to the decoration of a late Spring and Autumn–period mirror excavated in Shaanxi.[28]   —CPF

11 Mirror 東周/戰國鍍錫交龍紋青銅鏡

Eastern Zhou, Warring States period, 475–221 B.C.
Bronze
D: 9.5 cm
M-109

A double-fluted knob rests on a round base framed by a broad band with scooped surface, while the border of the mirror rises to a slightly higher rim. Within the rim is a narrow ridge dividing the rim somewhat unevenly from the interior patterning. The flat area of the field is covered by a *jiaolong,* or interlocking dragon, motif. This highly stylized motif is formed by the entwining of two sturdy dragons with spirals on their bodies and is repeated three times across the surface of the back for a total of six complete dragon heads. Two vertical pattern-mold edges can be discerned from right to left. The central panel appears to contain the complete width of the design, measuring four centimeters across, while the two panels on either side are partial elements of the same design. These designs, created with pattern stamps, have been turned 180 degrees on either side of the central panel, which is made of two stamps.

A similar bronze mirror on which the design was also achieved by pattern stamps was found among the grave goods in a Warring States tomb at Mashan in Jiangling, Hubei.[29]

The term *jiaolong* was derived from the statement "The emperor erected the Royal Banner;[30] the feudal lords erected their own banners,"[31] contained in the ancient classic *Zhouli,* Rituals of Zhou.[32] This was annotated by Zheng Xuan as follows: "The feudal lords' banners were decorated with *jiaolong,* one in ascending and the other in descending motion, to denote respectively the opening and closing of the court." This motif was often used on Warring States bronzes but seldom on mirrors.

This mirror is rather thin. It is well preserved, and the exquisite motifs show clearly. The silvery color on its surface is a result of tinning.   —CPF

12 Mirror 東周/戰國菱形羽地紋青銅鏡

Eastern Zhou, Warring States period, 475–221 B.C.
Bronze
D: 11.2 cm
M-108

The triple-fluted knob rests on a square base set within a scooped rectangular band. On each side is a lozenge made of two chevrons. These are linked to each other by another right-angled chevron; all have a scooped surface. Each portion of the lozenge shapes is outlined by a thin border line. The background is composed of a stylized feather pattern.

Geometrical patterns flourished during the Warring States period, and the motifs of this mirror are typical of those prevailing in its later stage. They are prepared in the same way as mirrors with T-shaped motifs, and the scooped surfaces have been highly polished to give an extremely smooth surface. The silvery appearance of this mirror may be due to the high tin content of the bronze.
—CPF

13 Mirror 東周/戰國連弧鳳紋青銅鏡

Eastern Zhou, Warring States period, 475–221 B.C.
Bronze
D: 15.4 cm
M-084

The double-fluted knob set on a small round base is enclosed by a ring in the form of a quatrefoil. Rising from the field are three stylized phoenixes, with heads turned and necks curling toward their backs. Their long tails adorned with leaf designs scroll gracefully to give each bird an S-profile. From each of their heads rises a double crest. Each body balances on a strong, clawed foot.

The background is filled with a network of interlocking lozenges inscribed with spirals and alternate triangles, set off by tiny dots, four in a row. This motif continues into the quatrefoil around the knob. The flat border is taken up by sixteen arcs with a scalloped inner edge.

Other mirrors of very similar design may be found in a number of private and public collections. The design is found on mirrors from the Warring States period, and examples have been found in Henan province.[33]

—CPF

14 Comb　東周/戰國翼獸紋青銅梳

Eastern Zhou, Warring States period, 3rd century B.C.
Bronze
H: 8.3 cm　W: 6.0 cm
HP-025

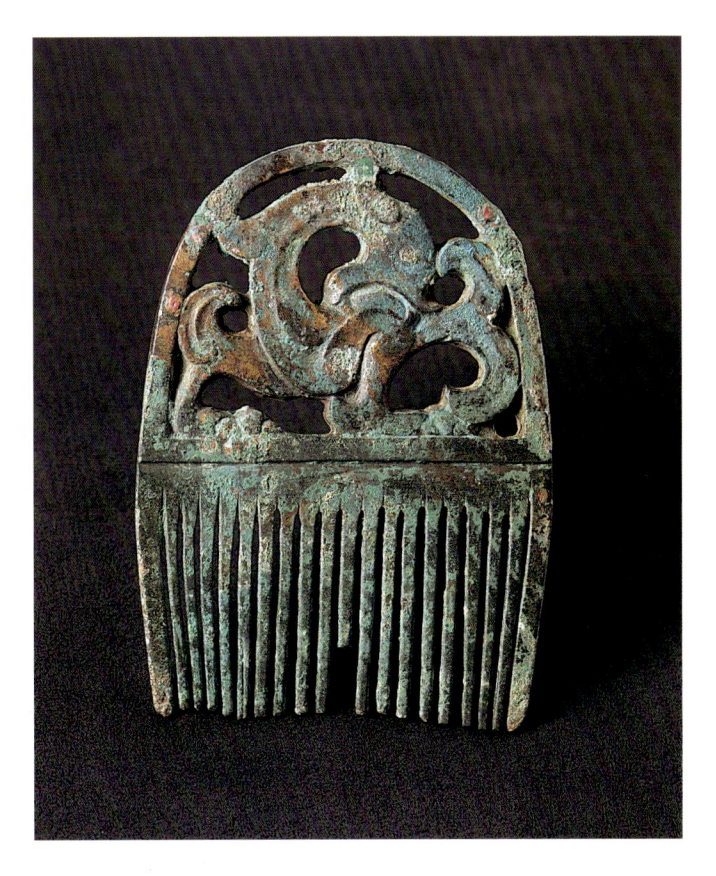

This bronze horseshoe-shaped hair comb was cast to depict a winged mythical animal wrapped around and biting its own body. The upper portion of the comb surrounds this intertwined design. The casting is slightly raised on the body of the beast and articulates the body and the winglike protrusions that meet the rim. The pierced bronze is well finished and shows no casting marks. The teeth of the comb formed part of the original cast; one side is more finely finished than the other. There is a greenish patina overall, with heavy encrustations on the top portion.

Only a few early metal combs are known, with this late Warring States–period piece complementing other such combs from the Shang and Western Zhou periods.[34] This comb is particularly heavy; it would probably not have been worn in the hair but could have been used for combing the hair, or it may have been made expressly for burial.

In later periods, combs were more commonly made from bone and wood, as in catalogue numbers 14a and 14b, from the Song period, and 14c, from the Liao period. The shapes of metal and bone combs differ, with bone combs tending to be broader and have more teeth.[35] Traces of pigment on catalogue number 14c indicate that it was probably painted and perhaps gilded. These combs are of a weight and type that could have been worn in the hair. In tomb finds, combs appear as sets with other combs, as in catalogue number 14a, and in cosmetic sets with mirrors and other ladies' accoutrements.[36]

—JMW

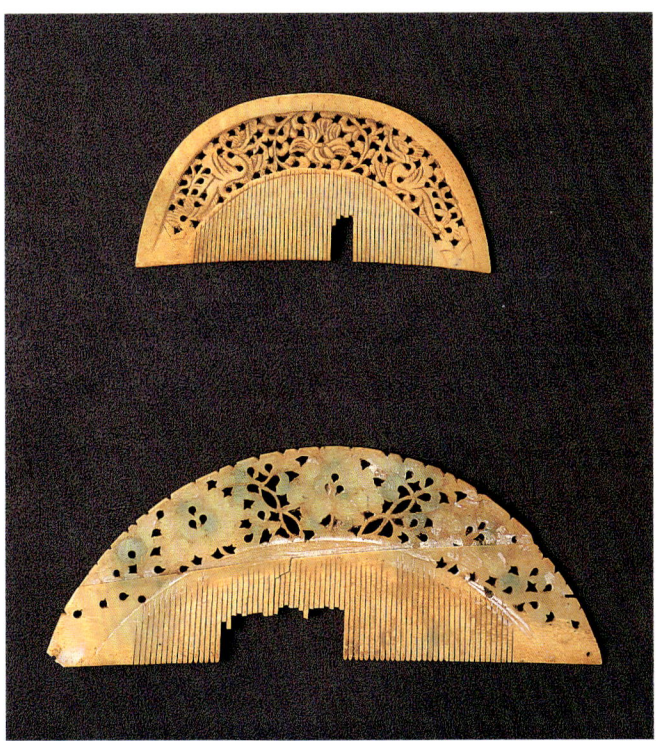

14b,c. Bone combs (HP-023, above; HP-014, below).
宋及遼骨梳各一件

14a. Wood combs (HP-013).
宋木梳三件

15 Belt Hook
東周/戰國包金交纏獸紋青銅帶鉤

Eastern Zhou, Warring States period, 4th century B.C.
Bronze with gold foil overlay
L: 21.3 cm W: 3.2 cm D: 5.1 cm
Published: Jessica Rawson and Emma C. Bunker,
Ancient Chinese and Ordos Bronzes, no. 128
H-002

The body of this gilded-bronze belt hook is a long convex rectangle that narrows to a rounded neck terminating in a well-sculpted animal head. Two chunky horned dragons, opposed and interlaced, appear to undulate over the rounded surface of the body of the hook. Both dragons are presented as if seen from above, each with wolf-like head and four legs which appear here and there in the composition. One dragon faces toward the narrow end of the hook and appears to clamp the hook in his jaws. The other dragon faces the opposite end of the hook and appears to be consuming some creature represented only by the back half of its body and two legs with claws desperately grasping at the dragon's horns.

The gilding was achieved by the application of thin gold foil to the raised decorated surface of the cast-bronze hook. The zoomorphic decoration was chased after the gilding process to sharpen the details. The back of the hook is concave and was silvered by the application of thin silver foil. The flat button is damaged, but it too appears to have been silvered.

This splendid hook appears to be of a special type made in north China during the latter part of the Eastern Zhou period. A very similar belt hook was excavated in 1956 at Pingshan county in Hebei province,[37] and an almost identical example in Stockholm is said to have come from Huixian, in northern Henan.[38] —ECB

16 Earring with Three Gold Cones
戰國帶錐飾金耳墜

Eastern Zhou, Warring States period, 4th–3rd century B.C.
Gold
L: 12.2 cm
GI-073

This earring consists of three gold cones connected by a long link to a penannular ring. The cones are made of tightly coiled, strip-twisted wire. In contrast, the large penannular ear-piece was cast first and then hammered into its present shape.

Under a microscope, the strip-twisted gold wire that forms the three cones of this earring has a right-hand twist, indicated by faint diagonal spiral lines. Gold earrings, each consisting of a round ring and similar cones, were discovered in tomb 2 at the nomadic site of Xigoupan, in Jungar banner, western Inner Mongolia, dated to the late fourth to early third century B.C.[39] A comparison of the Mengdiexuan cones and the Xigoupan cones indicates that both groups were made with strip-twisted gold wire that has a right-hand twist.[40] By comparison, the strip-twisted wire that forms the long connecting link on the Mengdiexuan earring twists in both directions.

The gold cones on this earring compare favorably with their excavated counterparts from Xigoupan. The long, connecting link has no known counterparts, suggesting that the present arrangement may not be reliable.

—ECB

17 Garment Hook
東周/戰國包金獸紋青銅帶鉤

Eastern Zhou, Warring States period, 4th–3rd century B.C.
Bronze with gold foil overlay
L: 9.5 cm W: 5.1 cm D: 1.6 cm
H-055

A fantastic sinuous animal whose body has been twisted into a figure eight forms the main part of this gilded-bronze garment hook. The head of the animal is shown from above, but the body is represented in profile, with only two legs showing. The head of another animal forms the hook. The main body has been gilded but not the neck or the hook. The reverse side displays a round button placed slightly off center.

Mold-joint seams flanking the button on the reverse side indicate that this hook was cast in a multisection mold. The gilding was accomplished by the application of a thin sheet of gold foil over the raised animal design, which was cast integrally with the piece. Microscopic examination reveals areas where bits of the foil have broken off. File marks occur on the sides over the gilding.

Garment hooks adorned with fantastic animals in such conventionalized poses were extremely popular during the second half of the Warring States period. A drawing of a less stylized version of this figure-eight composition demonstrates the intricacies of this pose.[41] A similar example was found at Fengshuiling, Changzi, in Shanxi,[42] and a later version was found in a pre-Han level at Erligang, Henan.[43]

—ECB

18 Garment Hook

東周/戰國包金雙獸面紋青銅帶鉤

Eastern Zhou, Warring States period, 4th–3rd century B.C.
Bronze with gold foil overlay
L: 19.1 cm W: 3.2 cm D: 3.2 cm
H-048

This long thin garment hook has two animal heads separated by three longitudinal bands which are fluted and concave. The two animal heads each have raised, almond-shaped, slanting eyes, but differently shaped ears. The ears on the bottom head are slightly pointed, while those on the upper head are more rounded. The hook is not gilded and appears to project from the mouth of one of the animal heads. The button on the reverse side is positioned two-thirds down the body from the hook end.

Although no mold-joint seams are visible, this hook was probably cast in the same way as was the hook in catalogue number 17. The gilding was achieved by the application of gold foil over the cast decoration.

Garment hooks similar to this example have been found at several pre-Han sites in central China, such as Shaogou, near Luoyang,[44] and Erligang,[45] both in Henan province. An ungilded version was found at a Zhao-state site in Handan, Hebei province.[46] The Zhao hook clearly shows that the two animal heads were intended to be different, with slightly different ears and facial features, like the two animal masks on the Mengdiexuan hook.

—ECB

19 Garment Hook
東周/戰國包金豹紋青銅帶鉤

Eastern Zhou, Warring States period, 3rd century B.C.
Bronze with gold foil overlay
L: 7.0 cm W: 3.2 cm D: 1.9 cm
H-026

A leopard whose body has been shaped into a figure eight occupies the main body of this gilded-bronze garment hook. The head of another animal forms the hook itself. The leopard's head is shown full face and its body in profile, with only two legs showing. Its eyes are represented by circular bosses within a slanting, almond-shaped outline. The ears are each described by a raised, curved line that ends in a small, inward spiral. The leopard's fur is indicated by a myriad of tiny intaglio dots. The back displays a circular button in the center. The design of this garment hook is similar to but more stylized than that of catalogue number 17.

This garment hook was made of heavy, solid, cast bronze, which was gilded with an overlay of gold foil. The back of the hook was gilded over a silver foil layer, which shows through the worn gilding here and there. The front was chased after it was gilded to add details, such as the dots that suggest a leopard's fur. The surface is also marked by small green patches of corrosion.

—ECB

20 Belt Hook
東周/戰國錯金銀動物紋鐵帶鉤

Eastern Zhou, Warring States period, 3rd century B.C.
Iron with gold overlay and silver-strand inlay
L: 17.1 cm W: 3.8 cm
H-058

This cast-iron belt hook has been overlaid with gold foil and inlaid with silver strands in an overall curvilinear design. Tiny stylized animal figures, including a crouching dog, inhabit the decoration. The lute-shaped belt hook is triplanar in cross section, a type that became popular during the late fourth and third centuries B.C.[47] The reverse side of the hook is undecorated and displays a circular button. Due to exposure to air and dampness, the iron is badly corroded, making it difficult to distinguish some of the details.

The decoration of this belt hook is highly sophisticated. Gold foil was applied, in one piece, to the surface of the hook, and then certain sections were cut away with a chisel. The resulting gold lattice was further embellished with silver-strand inlay. This particular overlay technique, in which sections are cut away, developed in the Central Plains during the third century B.C. to imitate metallic inlay.[48]

An almost identical version of the Mengdiexuan hook is in the collection of Paul Singer.[49] The only difference between the two objects appears to be the addition of many more small animals amid the curvilinear decoration on the Singer hook.   —ECB

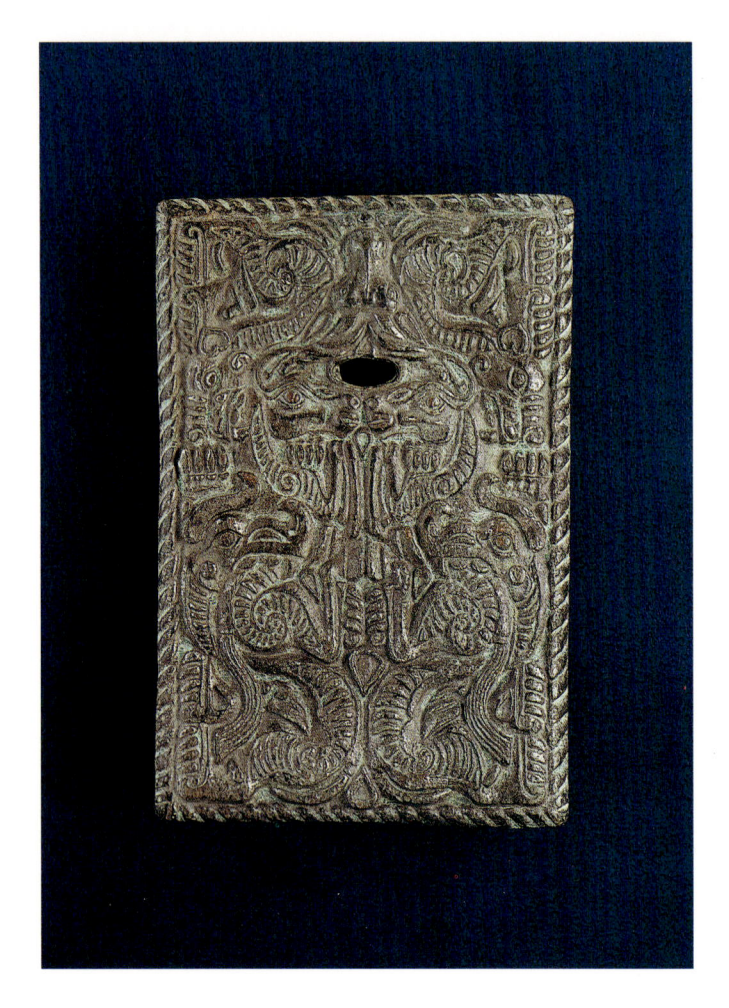

21 Belt Buckle Plaque
東周/戰國鍍錫獸紋青銅飾牌

Eastern Zhou, Warring States period, 3rd century B.C.
Tinned bronze
L: 10.9 cm W: 7.3 cm
BP-012

This plaque displays an extremely sophisticated and complex animal-combat design. Two recumbent horses, each attacked by a wolf and a tiger, are superimposed on the flattened body of a takin.[50] The horses, wolves, and tigers are all shown in profile. Additionally, the hindquarters of the tigers and wolves are twisted 180 degrees. By contrast, the takin is seen from above, with its four feet in profile. Its two front hooves can be seen under the bellies of the two tigers, and its rear hooves under the bellies of the wolves. All the animals are marked with striated enclosures which follow and accentuate the contours of their bodies. An oval opening near one end of the plaque and a longitudinal rounded loop with a square cross section on the reverse at the other end are part of the attachment system. Small bits of cloth remain on the reverse side of the plaque.

Shiny white patches here and there suggest that the front surface of the plaque was originally tinned, a surface enrichment employed during the Warring States period to enhance belt ornaments. A raised woven pattern on the back of the plaque indicates that the plaque was cast by the lost-wax-and-lost-textile process, a variation of the indirect lost-wax process developed in north China during the late Warring States period. The attachment loop appears to have been cast integrally with the plaque.

A buckle consisting of two almost identical gold plaques, each with the same complex animal-combat motif and a woven pattern on its reverse side, was recently discovered in tomb 30 at Xinzhuangtou, near Yixian, in Hebei province.[51] Xiadu served as the southern capital of the state of Yan from 311 until 222 B.C., when it was destroyed by Qin in its final drive to unite China. Excavations at Xiadu have revealed workshop areas for manufacturing silver and gold ornaments, bronze mirrors, and all sorts of commodities for a diverse market including northern pastoral as well as Chinese clientele.

The close relationship between the excavated gold plaques and the plaque shown here suggests that the Mengdiexuan example originally had a matching plaque, and that both were cast at Xiadu specifically for nomadic taste. The striated patterns marking the animals' pelts are stylistically related to the ubiquitous designs carved on artifacts made of wood and bone and imitated in felt and leather appliqués found at ancient burial sites throughout southern Siberia.[52]

—ECB

22 Circular Plaque

東周/戰國鎏金狼噬駱駝紋圓形銀飾牌

Eastern Zhou, Warring States period, 3rd century B.C.
Gilded silver
D: 9.5 cm
Published: Jessica Rawson and Emma C. Bunker,
Ancient Chinese and Ordos Bronzes, p. 300, fig. 6
GI-028

An arrangement of three identical animal-combat motifs, represented within a herringbone frame, reinforces the circular character of this gilded-silver plaque. The combatants are Bactrian camels and wolves. The camels are shown in profile, kneeling. Each camel bites the preceding camel on the back, between the humps. The wolves are also represented in profile, but only their necks and heads are shown, each with a long muzzle sinking its fangs into the nearest camel's neck. The camels' bodies and the wolves' necks are distinguished by the same striated enclosures that mark the bodies on the tinned-bronze belt plaque in catalogue number 21. Animal combat was an obvious power theme among the northern pastoral tribes. Plaques displaying such a theme presumably reflected the status and similar power of their owner.

This round plaque was cast by the lost-wax process from silver that, judging from its color, appears to have been alloyed with copper. The zoomorphic design has been cleverly mercury-amalgam gilded to highlight the camels' humps. The background has also been gilded to make the camel figures stand out more clearly. After the gilding process, the lines of the design were redefined by chasing.

In the center of the back of the plaque is a heavy curved loop that was cast integrally with the piece. A series of Chinese characters beside the loop were engraved into the surface after the piece was cast. These characters give the weight of the piece in *liang* and *zhu*, the weight system used by the state of Yan during the late Warring States period. The weight given is equivalent to 163 grams;[53] the actual weight of the piece is 165 grams.

A round gold plaque that carries the same triple animal-combat design was recently excavated from tomb 30 at Xinzhuangtou, near Yixian, in Hebei province.[54] The excavated example also carries reference to its weight in Chinese script on its reverse side.

The zoomorphic subject matter and the striated enclosures marking the animals' bodies relate this silver plaque to the tinned-bronze belt plaque in the Mengdiexuan collection (cat. no. 21) and ultimately to the workshops at Xiadu, which appear to have made luxury items for nomadic consumption. The presence of inscriptions denoting weight on many of these pieces is evidence of Sino-nomadic commercial transactions. The inscriptions also suggest that the nomads may have been functionally literate and capable of reading Chinese, although they had no written language of their own. The use of scales is implied by the emphasis on weight. The earliest known Chinese weighing apparatus dates to the Warring States period.[55]

—ECB

23 Belt Hook
東周/戰國鎏金銀嵌松石獸首鶚紋青銅帶鉤

Eastern Zhou, Warring States period, 3rd century B.C.
Gilded and silvered bronze inlaid with turquoise
L: 21.6 cm   W: 2.2 cm   D: 2.5 cm
H-015

This openwork bronze belt hook is embellished with gilding, silvering, and inlaid turquoise. The hook is formed in the shape of a fantastic feline head. Just below the hook is another fantastic animal head, and at the opposite end of the piece is a third head, with long ears. In the center of the belt hook is an owl-headed creature with elongated ears, clutching some turquoise inlay with its front claws. The reverse of the belt hook displays simple gold- and silver-colored geometric designs. A slightly convex button is centered on the back.

The piece was cast by the lost-wax process. The inlay channels for the turquoise were integrally cast with the piece. Various parts of the decoration were either mercury-amalgam gilded or silvered.

Two more elaborate examples of this type of hook are in the collection of the Freer Gallery of Art, in Washington, D.C.[56] Another belt hook of this type was excavated from the Qin or Western Han site of Shuoxian, in Shanxi,[57] and similar examples were found at Jincun, in Henan.[58]

—ECB

24 Belt Hook
東周/戰國鎏金包銀嵌松石青銅帶鉤

Eastern Zhou, Warring States period, 3rd century B.C.
Gilded bronze with silver overlay and turquoise inlay
L: 14.3 cm W: 1.3 cm D: 2.5 cm
Published: Jessica Rawson and Emma C. Bunker,
Ancient Chinese and Ordos Bronzes, no. 133
H-022

The body of this bronze belt hook is overlaid with silver foil. Both the animal-headed hook and the convex button on the back are mercury-amalgam gilded. An inlaid turquoise decoration of arrow-shaped projections and straight connecting lines runs the length of the belt hook.

The inlay channels for the turquoise were cast integrally with the belt hook. In contrast, the silver is overlaid on both the front and the back. File marks can be detected on the bronze where the silver is missing.

Related belt hooks have been associated with the famous Zhou site at Jincun, near Luoyang, in Henan.[59]

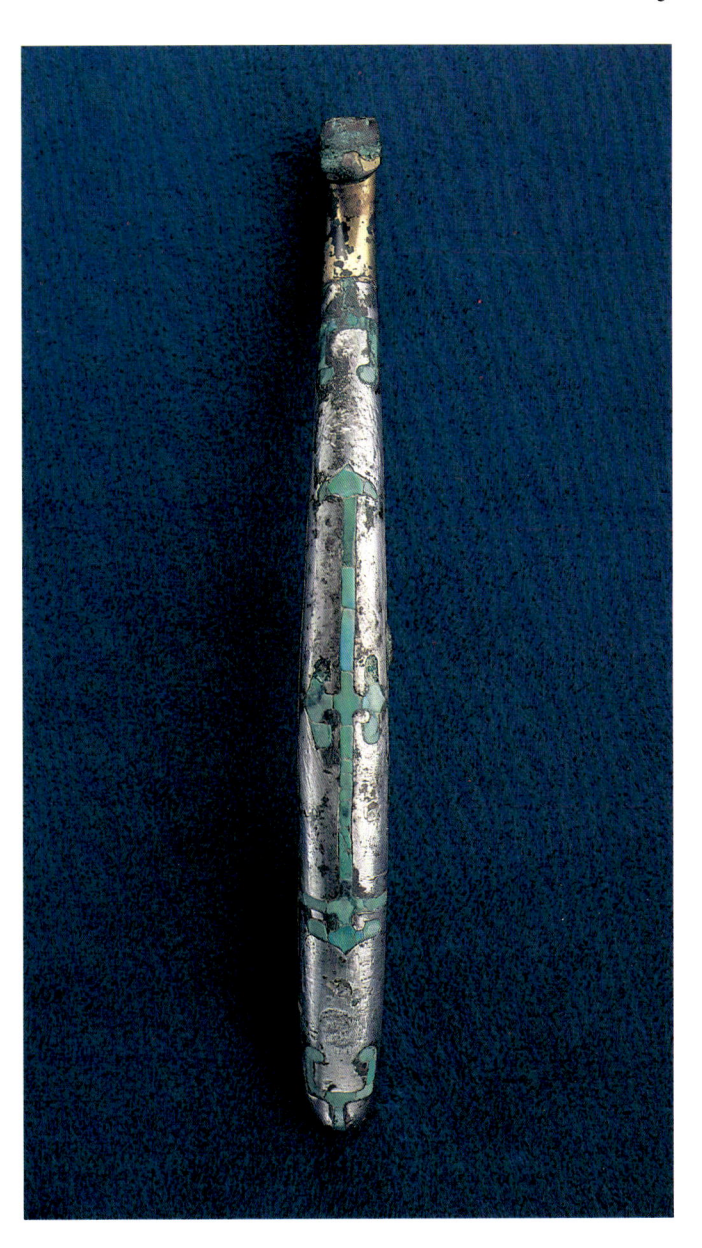

—ECB

104　EARLY PERIOD

25 Belt Hook
東周/戰國錯金銀嵌寶石龍紋青銅帶鉤

Eastern Zhou, Warring States period, 3rd century B.C.
Bronze inlaid with gold, silver, turquoise, lapis lazuli, and glass
L: 21.3 cm W: 1.3 cm D: 5.1 cm
Published: Jessica Rawson and Emma C. Bunker,
Ancient Chinese and Ordos Bronzes, no. 131
H-003

This bronze belt hook is lavishly embellished with gold, silver, glass, turquoise, and lapis lazuli. The body of the hook is covered with tiny scales represented by turquoise inlays set in cells formed by hammered gold strips that were set on their edges and attached to the bronze surface with some unidentified organic substance. Three delicately drawn elongated dragons seen from above are inlaid in gold amid the turquoise scales. Their bodies are outlined with a silver beading, and their ears, claws, and bodies are marked in silver. The neck and head of the hook are separated from the body by a gold band enhanced with beading. The borders of the hook are also marked by beading. Two sinuous *qi* dragons seen from above on the neck of the hook are overlaid with gold foil. The wings and backs of the dragons are inlaid with lapis lazuli which has become degraded with age and is difficult to recognize. The lapis lazuli on the back is inlaid with a tear-shaped turquoise stone. Below the two dragons is an owl head. One owl's eye and one dragon's eye of glass still remain. The cross section of the hook's body is D-shaped. The back of the hook is covered with a silver sheet and has a small, round button with a slightly convex top.

An almost identical garment hook was published as coming from Jincun, the late Zhou capital near Luoyang, in Henan.[60] Two belt hooks in the Freer Gallery of Art stylistically related to the Mengdiexuan hook have also tentatively been given a Jincun provenance.[61] Further evidence for a Central Plains manufacture of such hooks is demonstrated by the similarity between the dragons on this hook and those represented on mirrors associated with the vicinity of Luoyang.[62]

The second-century B.C. tomb of the second king of Nanyue at Xianggang, in Guangzhou, yielded a garment hook that displays the same type of tiny turquoise inlaid scales on the body and the same gold-relief *qi* dragons on the neck seen on the Mengdiexuan hook.[63] The first king of Nanyue was a native of Zhengding county, Hebei, and fled south to the Guangzhou area after the fall of the Qin dynasty in 207 B.C. It is possible that such belt hooks were royal treasures taken south at that time. This discovery suggests a third-century B.C. date rather than the fourth-century B.C. date usually given to hooks of this type.   —ECB

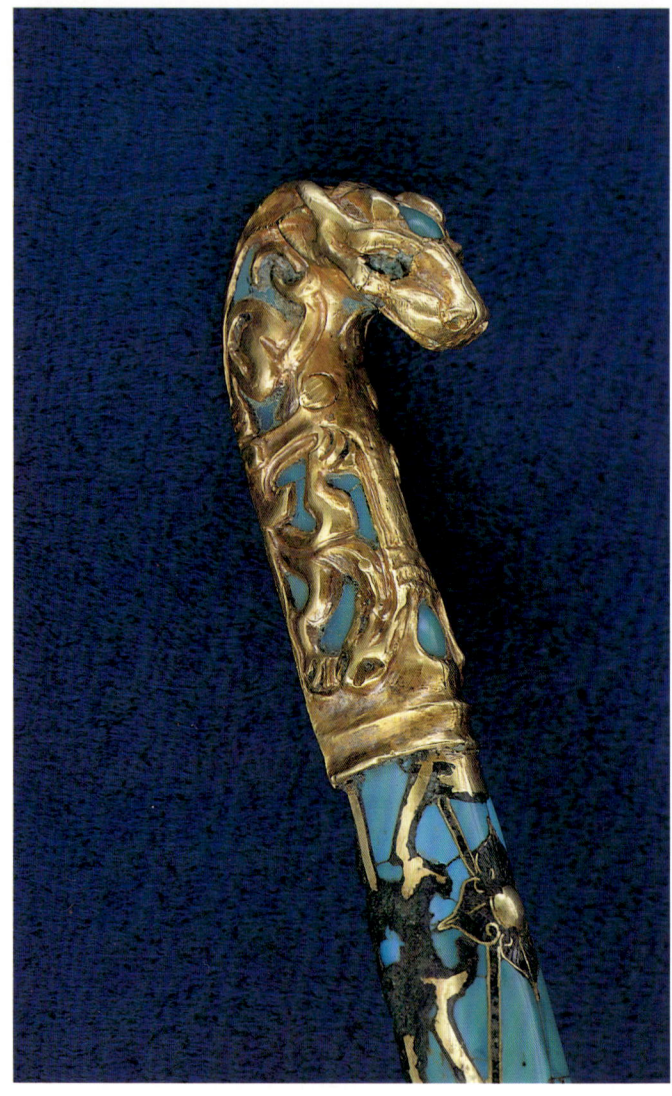

26 Belt Hook
東周/戰國錯金銀嵌松石野豬紋青銅帶鉤

Eastern Zhou, Warring States period, 3rd century B.C.
Bronze, silver, gold, and turquoise
L: 20.1 cm W: 1.2 cm
H-067

An intricate overall lozenge design with interior volutes inlaid in gold on a turquoise ground embellishes the body of this long, elegant belt hook. Two quatrefoils flanking a large round turquoise bisect the lozenge design longitudinally. The turquoise ground consists of innumerable irregular shapes cut and set in cells formed by hammered gold bands laid on their edges and glued, with some kind of resinous adhesive, to the base metal. Two realistically portrayed racing wild boars represented in gold and turquoise are set in the sides of the hook. The inlay material for the boars appears to be an amalgam of ground turquoise and some organic material mixed into a paste. Tiny silver dots inlaid in the amalgam suggest the texture of the boars' bristles.

The body of the belt hook is D-shaped in cross section. The silver sheet that presumably covered the back is now missing. Only a squared stump in the middle of the back remains where the button would have been placed, suggesting that the button was cast separately and then attached. An animal head forms the head of the hook. The neck is not inlaid but overlaid with gold in an openwork design of two sinuous dragons shown in relief on a turquoise-inlaid ground along the sides.

The production of this type of belt hook was extremely labor intensive. A designer, a bronze caster, a lapidary expert, a gold-sheet cutter, and an adhesive maker would all have been needed to create such a masterpiece.

A very similar hook was published as coming from Jincun, near Luoyang, in Henan.[64] Instead of the racing wild boars seen on the Mengdiexuan hook, the Jincun hook depicts several realistically portrayed fantastic beasts along the sides. A hook with the same type of decoration was also found among the riches of the second king of Nanyue's tomb at Xianggang, Guangzhou,[65] and a similar type of hook with very realistic animals represented in stone paste is in the Erickson collection at the Metropolitan Museum of Art in New York.[66] Two other hooks related stylistically to this group were recently offered for sale in London.[67] —ECB

108 EARLY PERIOD

27 Belt Hook
西漢錯金銀變形龍獸紋青銅帶鉤

Western Han period, 3rd century B.C.
Bronze inlaid with silver and gold
L: 22.9 cm W: 1.9 cm D: 3.2 cm
H-060

Curvilinear zoomorphic designs inlaid in silver and gold embellish the surface of this long, elegant belt hook which is circular in cross section. A feline head with pointy ears in relief, eyes with pupils inlaid in gold, and silver-inlaid whiskers forms the head of the hook. The back is inlaid with ten silver chevrons, five pointing upward and five pointing downward. A large round button placed at the middle of the hook's back is inlaid with silver in the shape of a quatrefoil and filled with silver-inlaid dots for texture. The butt end is decorated with two concentric circles in strand inlay.

The body of the hook is divided into four registers which are decorated with silver inlay accented with gold. The top register below the hook is decorated with an abstract lozenge pattern inlaid in silver with gold-inlaid dots. The second and fourth registers each display an S-shaped dragon in profile with a wolflike head and two heavy legs with soft wolflike paws. The head, which is turned 180 degrees, has heart-shaped ears, an upward-curled upper lip, and a shorter lower jaw. In contrast, the third register contains an S-shaped birdlike creature, with its head and one wing lying along a side border. Some repaired damage in this area makes the bird figure hard to read.

The silver inlay is set in channels with deep edges. The channels may have been cast integrally with the piece and the edges then given greater depth with an engraving tool.

Long slim belt hooks inlaid in silver with similar zoomorphic-derived designs have been discovered in Henan, but their designs are far more stylized than that of the hook under discussion. One was excavated from tomb 650 in Luoyang,[68] and another is said to have come from burials at Jincun, near Luoyang.[69] Several related examples can be found in the Freer Gallery of Art,[70] and in collections in Stockholm.[71] The fluidity with which the zoomorphic motifs are represented on the Mengdiexuan hook is related ultimately to painting. Similar mythological creatures abound on late Warring States and Western Han painted lacquerware.[72] The symbolism of these zoomorphic designs is no longer understood, but they must have figured prominently in ancient Chinese society as indicators of status and rank.   —ECB

28 Belt Buckle Plaque
秦鎏金鷹獸野山羊相搏紋青銅飾牌

Qin period, 3rd century B.C.
Gilded bronze
L: 11.0 cm H: 7.5 cm
Published: Jessica Rawson and Emma C. Bunker,
Ancient Chinese and Ordos Bronzes, no. 217
GI-022

A fallen ibex under attack from a fantastic carnivore, who in turn is being bitten in the neck by an equally fantastic eagle with almond-shaped eyes, adorns this plaque. The carnivore's crestlike mane and tail each terminate in a stylized raptor head. This iconography has been associated with Indo-European-speaking nomadic tribes of mounted archers who arrived on the northwest borders of dynastic China in the fourth century B.C., displaced by Alexander the Great's Central Asian campaigns.[73]

The plaque was cast by the indirect lost-wax process using a wax model that had first been formed in an open mold and then cast. The edges of the openwork design are slightly raised on the back of the plaque, indicating that they were pushed through on the wax model from the front and then trimmed with a knife. The design was chased before it was heavily mercury-amalgam gilded. The gilding is very pure gold, as indicated by its rich color. There is evidence of burnishing under the tail and head of the carnivore.

This plaque was originally one of a pair of mirror-image matching plaques that together constituted one complete belt buckle. An ungilded plaque with the same animal-combat motif was found in a Qin-period tomb excavated at Zaomiao, Tongchuan, in Shaanxi province.[74] A complete buckle consisting of both plaques was found in grave 7 at Derestui, near Lake Baikal, in Russia.[75] Such plaques were common belt ornaments among the nomadic tribes that inhabited the northern fringes of China during the Eastern Zhou, Qin, and Western Han periods. It has been suggested that they served not only as clan and rank symbols, but also to illustrate mythological beliefs that governed the lives of the mounted warrior-herdsmen who wore them.[76] The fact that some plaques are mercury-amalgam gilded suggests that Chinese craftsmen were involved in their production, since there is no evidence that the pastoral tribes knew how to mercury-amalgam gild at this early date. Such gilded plaques were made either at some Chinese metalworking center or by itinerant Chinese craftsmen in nomadic employ. —ECB

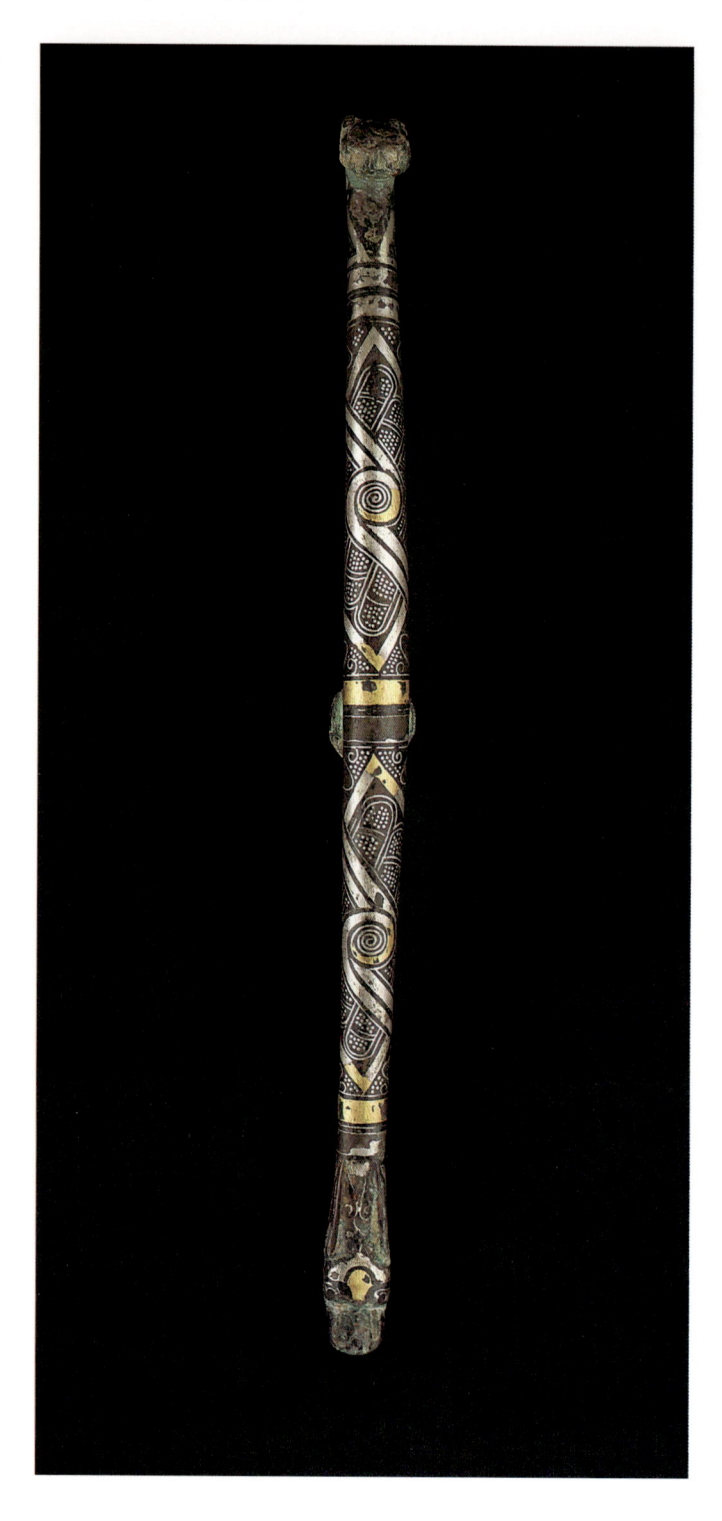

29 Belt Hook 西漢錯金銀變形鳥紋青銅帶鈎

Western Han period, 3rd–2nd century B.C.
Bronze inlaid with silver and gold
L: 17.1 cm W: 1.0 cm D: 2.2 cm
H-037

Silver and gold inlaid designs enhance this long belt hook. The front of the piece is divided into two main sections decorated with bird-derived, curvilinear, abstract patterns with featherlike projections and inlaid dots. An animal head forms the hook itself. Another animal head adorns the end of the piece. The back of the hook has four inlaid silver bands, a round convex button, and a very graceful heart and spiral design at the bottom.

The decoration was achieved by sheet and strand inlay in rather shallow channels. The round inlaid dots were intended to imitate the visual effect of granulation. A similar belt hook with animal heads at both ends was discovered at Jincun, in Henan province.[77] —ECB

30 Belt Hook 西漢錯銀變形獸紋青銅帶鉤

Western Han period, 3rd–2nd century B.C.
Bronze inlaid with silver
L: 10.5 cm W: 1.9 cm D: 1.6 cm
Ex. Collection: Lord Cunliffe, London
H-038

This belt hook is inlaid with strand silver in a complex abstract design of spirals and curvilinear forms. A few recognizable animal motifs hint at the design's zoomorphic ancestry. The hook terminates in an animal head with long pointed ears. A convex button cast integrally with the hook projects from the back for attachment purposes. Inlaid in silver within a silver circle on the button is a variation of the character for *gu,* meaning ancient, in seal form.[78]

The inlay was accomplished with many thin strands of silver placed side by side and worked into the channels in the bronze. After the inlay process was completed, the inlay was ground flush with the bronze surface. In some areas, the silver strands are so tightly compacted that they look like sheets. Only in a few areas can the separate strands be identified under the microscope. Strand inlay was the standard form of inlay from the sixth century B.C. until the Han period. The surface appears to have an enhanced bronze patina that may not have developed naturally.

The inlay decoration on the Mengdiexuan hook is stylistically related to designs found on late Eastern Zhou–period artifacts, such as those that embellish the superb bronze ox excavated at Shou county, Anhui province.[79] Similar inlaid designs in silver occur on a *hu* excavated from the Western Han tombs at Mancheng, in Hebei province.[80] These similarities suggest a third- to second-century B.C. date for the Mengdiexuan hook.

—ECB

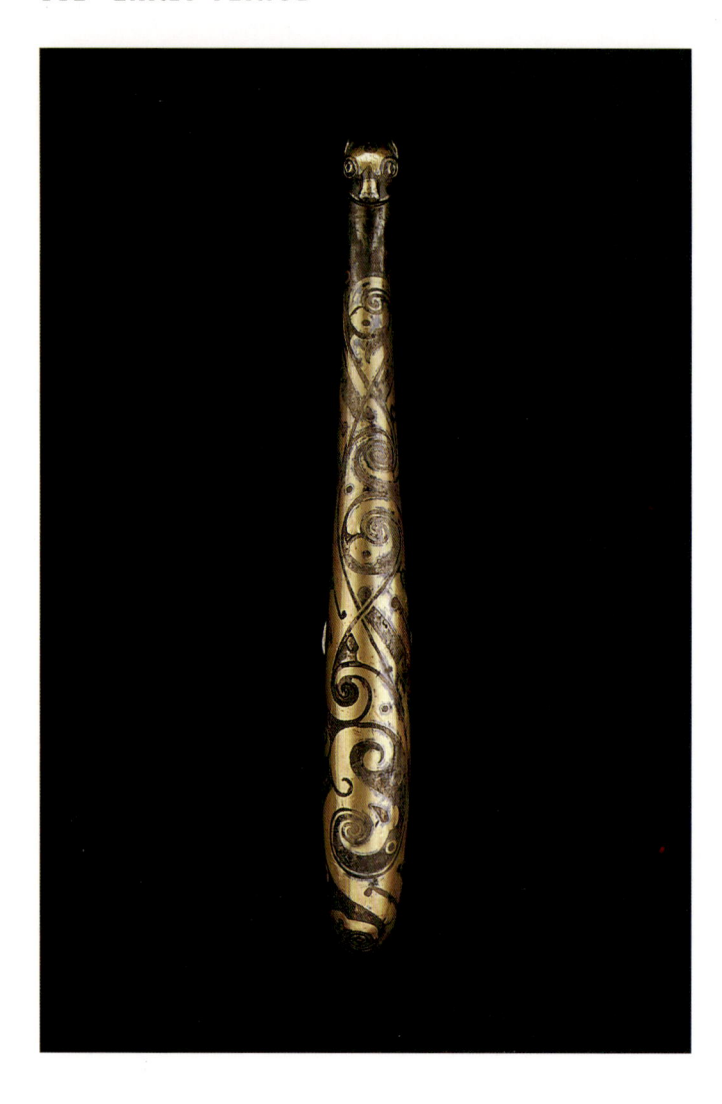

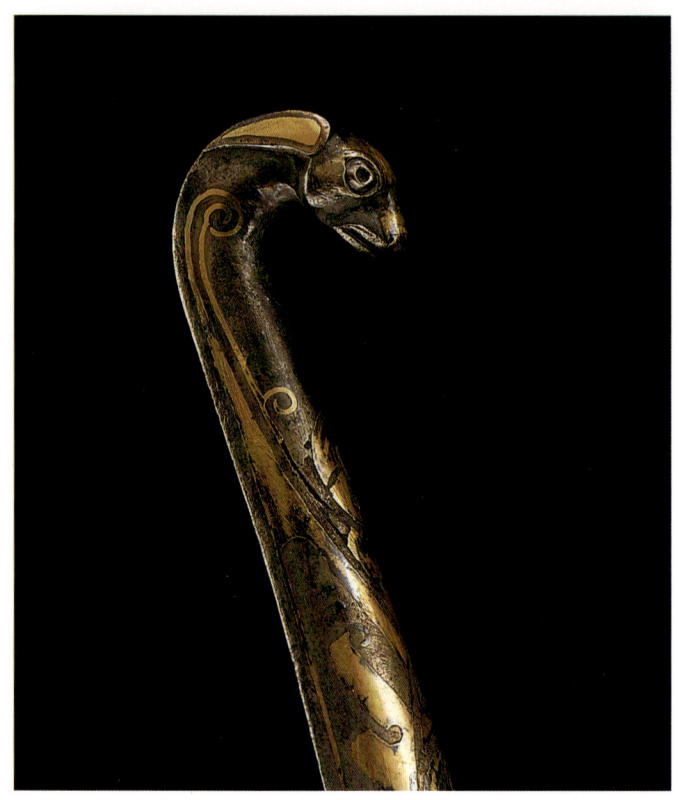

31 Belt Hook 西漢錯金鳥首蛇紋青銅帶鉤

Western Han period, 3rd–2nd century B.C.
Bronze inlaid with gold
L: 12.1 cm W: 1.3 cm D: 2.5 cm
H-033

This bronze garment hook terminates in a long-eared animal head and is adorned with a design of three intertwined serpentine creatures with stylized bird heads inlaid in thin gold foil. Feathered wings occur in the decoration, suggesting further avian associations. The reverse is undecorated and displays a round convex button. The bronze itself appears to be a copper alloy with high tin and high lead content, which gives it a silvery appearance and considerable weight.

The quality of the casting is excellent; the animal-headed hook is very crisp, with pronounced intaglio eyes. The decoration is achieved by inlaying gold foil into channels with slightly slanting inner sides and deep edges below the channel floor. This is typical of the inlay work associated with Jincun, where hooks with similar shapes and inlaid designs have been discovered.[81]   —ECB

32 Belt Buckle Plaque
西漢鎏金犛牛紋青銅飾牌

Western Han period, 2nd century B.C.
Gilded bronze
L: 11.0 cm H: 5.5 cm
Published: Jessica Rawson and Emma C. Bunker,
Ancient Chinese and Ordos Bronzes, no. 222
GI-023

This gilt-bronze belt plaque carries an openwork design of two opposed oxen within a rectangular frame. The oxen are shown with their bodies in profile, with all four legs and their heads full face. The frame consists of a series of sunken rectangles, each one bisected by a raised longitudinal line. Vestigial tear-shaped inlay cells indicate the oxens' hairy bodies. This plaque was originally one of an identical pair which together constituted one belt buckle.

This plaque was cast by the indirect lost-wax process, as was the plaque in catalogue number 30. The gilding is quite thick but much paler than that on catalogue number 30, suggesting that the gold alloy contained as much as 5 percent or more silver.

A pair of identical plaques was excavated at Xichagou, Xifeng, in Liaoning province, from a nomadic cemetery dated to the Western Han period.[82] Numerous other examples have been collected from sites throughout southern Siberia.[83] Both areas are known to have been under the control of the Xiongnu, a nomadic group that united all the other eastern Eurasian steppe tribes into a mighty confederacy which rivalled the Han on the other side of the Great Wall.[84] —ECB

33 & 34 Two Bronze Ornaments
西漢嵌孔雀石瑪瑙青銅飾牌兩件

Western Han period, 2nd–1st century B.C.
Bronze inlaid with malachite and agate
33: H: 6.6 cm W: 10.2 cm
34: D: 9.4 cm
BP-006 and BP-010

These two bronze plaques were used to adorn clothing of the tribes who inhabited the Lake Dian area of Kunming, in present-day Yunnan, during the Western Han period. The saucer-shaped ornament has a red agate set in its center, surrounded by two concentric bands of pierced malachite disks. The rectangular piece is also inlaid with tiny, pierced, malachite disks and has an openwork border based on connected spiral forms. The malachite disks are attached with some brown-colored fixative, possibly lacquer.[85]

The back of the round plaque displays a heavy horizontal hook which is placed off center. This hook is supported by a strut. A space was formed between the strut and the hook through which a piece of fabric or leather could have been threaded to secure the plaque's attachment. The rectangular plaque has the same kind of hook on its back. Such hooks are peculiar to artifacts belonging to the Dian culture, which flourished in the Kunming area of Yunnan during the first millennium B.C. Both pieces were cast with sunken areas to accommodate the malachite inlay. The absence of mold marks on the disk suggests that this piece was cast by the lost-wax process, but the flashing around the edges of the openwork design of the rectangular plaque suggests that it was cast in a two-piece mold.

Similar ornaments have been excavated from the Dian cemetery at Shizhaishan, in Jinning, near Kunming, Yunnan.[86] Some similar ornaments are quite ornate, with small animal and human figures adorning their rims; others are simply enriched by colored-stone inlays.

Circular ornaments are often shown at the waist or on the chest of bronze figures excavated at the Shizhaishan cemetery.[87] It has been suggested that such ornaments served as protective amulets for the wearer. As late as the Qing dynasty, minority tribes of the Southwest valued precious stones as amulets to ward off evil influences and to protect their bodies in battle.   —ECB

35 Plaque 西漢熊首雙羊紋金飾牌

Western Han period, 2nd–1st century B.C.
Gold
H: 4.4 cm W: 4.3 cm
GI-041

Two ram's heads in profile and a bear mask at top center are shown on this spade-shaped plaque. Finely chased lines alternate with smooth ridges delineating the rams' horns. Similar chasing defines the rams' features, with detailing around the muzzles and eyes. The bear-faced creature stares directly out, its features also highlighted by chasing. A pair of holes perforates the thinly hammered gold at the top, bottom, and on both sides, indicating that the plaque was likely sewn onto a piece of fabric or otherwise attached to a support.

Similar plaques have been found in the extremely rich tomb of the second Nanyue king from the Western Han. Excavated in 1983, it is one of the most important finds from Guangzhou and included eight plaques represented by the two shown at left.[88] The tomb was also rich in jade, including a jade suit with belt hooks and seals indicating the status and rank of its owner. —JMW

Two of the eight plaques from a Western Han–period tomb in Guangzhou. (Drawing after *Xi Han Nanyue wangmu,* vol. 2, pl. 18, no. 1.)

36 Mirror 西漢漆繪幾何紋青銅鏡

Western Han dynasty, 206 B.C.–A.D. 9
Bronze and lacquer
D: 8.1 cm
M-123

This mirror with a double-fluted knob is coated on its back with a layer of black and red lacquer. A double-lined crisscross pattern with the knob at its center is drawn in reddish lacquer to divide the black center square into four compartments, each being further divided diagonally into halves. The resulting pattern is a fascinating combination of squares and lozenges created by the interlacing of the black and red colors. On each corner of the large black square is a symmetrical, hooklike motif drawn in red, echoing the small red square within it.

Lacquer-painted mirrors are extremely rare. The lacquer coating here has distorted in many places due to humidity, but there has been no flaking.

A lacquer-painted mirror found in a Warring States tomb in a Chu cemetery at Baoshan, Jingmen, Hubei, has a similar thin, flat profile.[89]

—CPF

36a. Box for lacquered bronze mirror (M-123.a–.b).
西漢漆繪木鏡盒

37 Belt Hook 西漢鎏金翼龍紋青銅帶鈎

Western Han dynasty, 206 B.C.–A.D. 9
Gilded bronze
L: 12.4 cm W: 3.5 cm
H-031

This gilt-bronze hook was cast in the shape of a winged, horned dragon, depicted from above, that curls across the front of the belt hook, grasping a snake in its claws and jaws. The head of the hook is a well-articulated dragon head. The gilding is thinly applied across the front of the hook, while the back appears to be covered with a silvery-colored gold alloy. The button is small and gilded across the top.

The robust form of the dragon and the deep modelling evident in the entire hook is typical of sculpture in bronze and other materials, such as jade, of the late Warring States period and Western Han dynasty. A Western Han tomb near Luoyang yielded a bronze hook with a similar design of a curled animal.[90]   —JMW

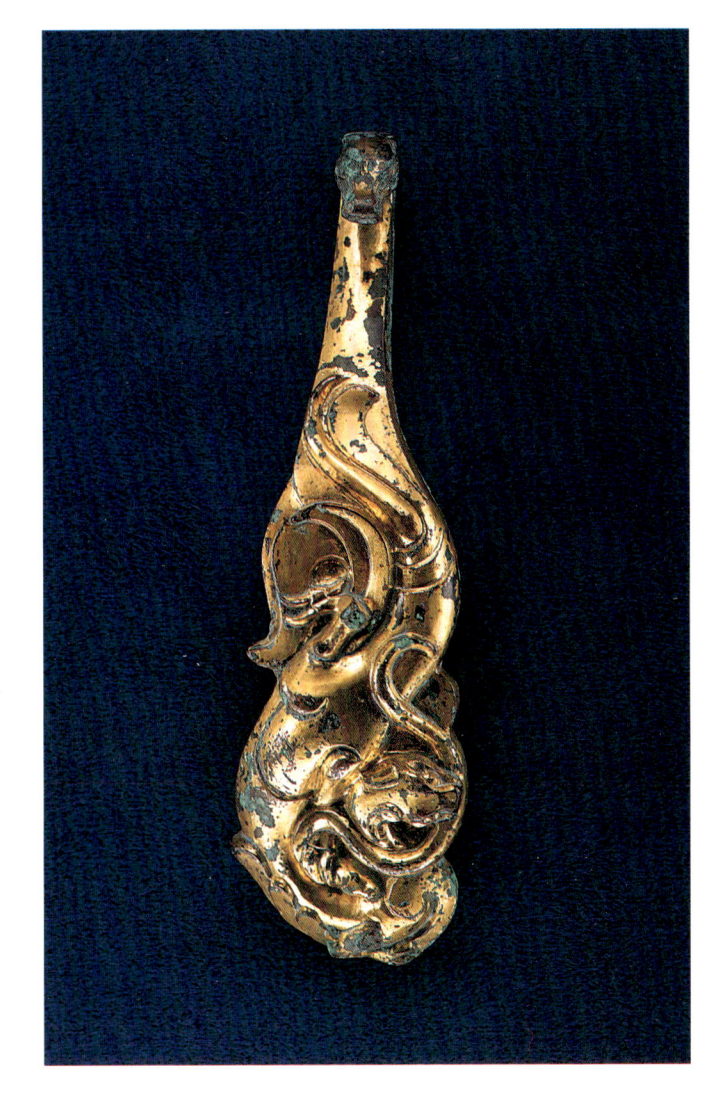

38 Belt Hook

西漢鎏金錯銀嵌寶石神獸紋青銅帶鉤

Western Han dynasty, 206 B.C.–A.D. 9
Bronze, silver, gilt, glass, turquoise, agate, and serpentine
L: 13.0 cm W: 1.1 cm
H-019

This elaborately decorated hook was cast in bronze and inlaid with silver strands and gemstones, besides being partially gilded. The head of the hook resembles a dragon; it has well-defined features and lozenge-shaped ears that may have been inlaid with stones. There is some residue of silver inlay on the head. The decoration on the face of the hook may be divided into three parts: the silver inlay portion, which is slightly higher than the surrounding gilt section and appears as feathery scrolling; the gilt portion, with its rough texture; and the inlaid stones that have been affixed to round and teardrop-shaped depressions in the bronze.

The body of the hook was cast, probably in a ceramic mold that carried all the small indentations for the stones. The roughened bronze surface that has been gilded was chiselled out of the cold metal. When examined under the microscope, the channels for the silver inlay also prove to have been chiselled.

The back of the hook is elaborately decorated with a pictorial scene created by an inlaid silver wire. The long sinuous dragon with its head pointing to the head of the hook is trailed by a humanlike "spirit" figure on the tail of the dragon. The button back is decorated with a tiger head with wide cheeks and long whiskers. A prowling tiger also appears on the back in the same silver-thread inlay. The imagery is typically Han and is reminiscent of the type of imagery seen on contemporaneous lacquer designs. Fantastic animal imagery appears on lacquer pieces from the tomb of Mawangdui outside Changsha.

The inlaid stones on the front of the belt hook are glass (red and bluish white on the head), turquoise (green), agate (brown), and serpentine (white).[91] The use of these stones to decorate this bronze belt hook reflects the Han-period interest in imported gems. As early as the Western Han, the Chinese were importing gems, glass, and other luxury items from the West and Central Asia.[92] An example of a similar type of bronze inlay can be seen in the bronze censer now in the Freer Gallery of Art, Washington, D.C.[93] An almost identical example was found in Shandong in a Han tomb belonging to the royal family of the state of Lu.[94]

—JMW

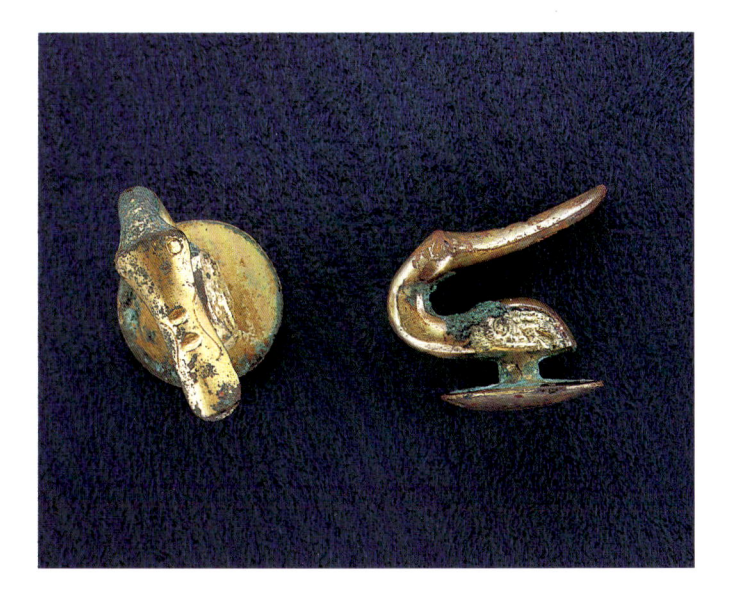

39 Pair of Garment Hooks 戰國或西漢鎏金水禽形青銅帶鉤一對

Warring States period or Western Han, 3rd–2nd century B.C.
Gilded bronze
L: 3.0 cm (along bill) D: 2.0 cm (across button)
H-065.1–.2

These two hooks in the shape of long-billed waterbirds were cast in bronze and then gilded. The heads and bills of the birds turn back over small compact bodies. On the top of the bill are two parallel indentations with scroll lines on either side. Each hook has two round eyes at either side, well back on the head. The sides of the bodies were cast with featherlike designs. The buttons are relatively large and are convex on the back.

From the size of these hooks it would appear that they were used as collar hooks or as accessory hooks, like the much earlier gold hooks seen in catalogue numbers 2, 3, and 4. This type of small hook with convex button first appeared around the beginning of the Warring States period in Shaanxi province and was used throughout the Warring States period.[95] Shanxi has also been a source for small hooks of this type from the Han period onward.[96] A very similar hook was found in a Qin tomb at Gaozhuang, Fengxiang, Shaanxi.[97]   —JMW

40 Garment Hook 漢水禽形青銅帶鉤

Han dynasty, 206 B.C.–A.D. 220
Bronze
L: 4.2 cm W: 1.8 cm
H-027

This small bronze hook was cast in the shape of a long-billed waterbird, perhaps intended to be a cormorant. The bird's head and neck arch back gracefully over the rounded surface of its body. The wings are detailed by two slightly raised areas on the back of the bird's body. The button is wide, plain, and slightly convex. The underside of the bird is roughly filed, but the body, neck, and bill are buffed smooth.

Similar bronze hooks developed out of an earlier waterbird shape during the Western Han period.[98] A cast-silver hook with a similar overall shape is in the collection of the Metropolitan Museum of Art, New York.[99]

—JMW

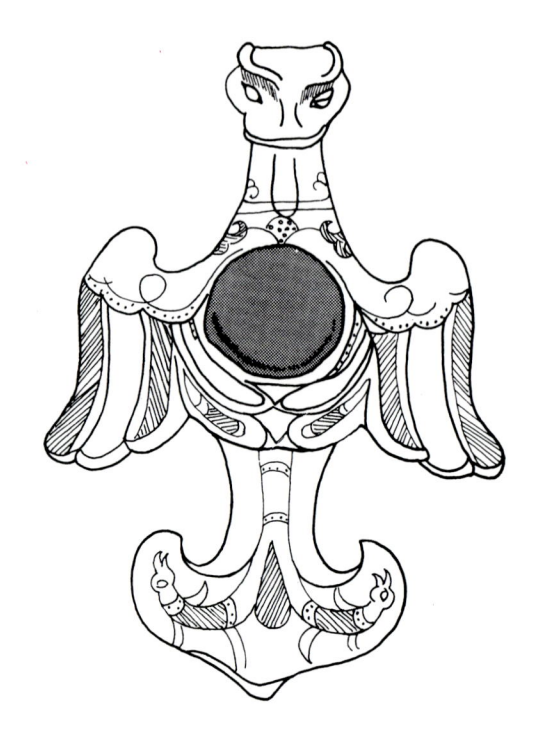

41 Garment Hook
漢鎏金銀嵌玻璃鳥形青銅帶鉤

Han dynasty, 206 B.C.–A.D. 220
Bronze, gilded and silvered, and glass
L: 6.8 cm W: 5.4 cm
H-039

This cast-bronze hook in the shape of a bird with outspread wings is inlaid with a large piece of blue-colored glass. The glass is old, although it appears to have been attached with a modern epoxy. The hook is covered with delicate chased designs across the tail, wings, and neck, underneath a gold-foil application. The designs across the tail of the hook are of fantastic bird-headed creatures. The back of the hook is covered with a gold-foil application over a silver-foil base. The silver shows through across the back.

The overall bird shape was a popular form during the Han period. The size and broad shape of this hook suggest that it may have been used as a hook for a sword or other belt attachment, rather than as a belt hook.[100]

—JMW

42 Garment Hook
漢鎏金龍首鳥形蟬紋青銅帶鉤

Han dynasty, 206 B.C.–A.D. 220
Gilded bronze
L: 10.7 cm W: 5.5 cm
H-050

This gilt-bronze hook consists of three animals combined to form one hook. The overall shape is that of a long-necked, dragon-headed bird tapering into a combination of two animals, a cicada being consumed by a bat that is superimposed onto the bird's body. The hook was cast and then covered with gilding achieved by an amalgam-paste process. The casting is robust, with the details of the animals defined in bold lines. There is none of the subtlety of design that is seen in catalogue number 41.

This overall shape is seen frequently on Han dynasty hooks, although this particular design of one animal devouring another is not very common.[101] The size of the hook and its shape may indicate that it was, similar to catalogue number 40, a secondary hook from which a sword might have hung.[102]   —JMW

43 Mirror 東漢神人神獸畫像青銅鏡

Eastern Han dynasty, 1st–2nd century A.D.
Bronze
D: 13.4 cm
M-081

The base of the large round central knob is encircled by six bands of decoration, with the two pictorial bands divided by geometric patterning. Occupying the four sides of the high-relief zone are four crouching mythical animals, each with a deity on its back. One of the deities is Xiwangmu, Queen Mother of the West; opposite her is Dongwanggong, King Father of the East. Except for the King Father of the East, the deities are attended by a bird on the left and a winged immortal on the right. Enclosing this zone is a band of sawteeth beyond a grooved ring. The mirror is slightly convex and has a black patina.

The border is made up of two decorative bands. The inner one contains three groups of motifs: one consists of divinities in chariots drawn by six dragons preceded by phoenixes with wavy feathers; another shows two *gui*, tortoises, entwined by snakes (a symbol of the north, sometimes called the "dark warrior"),[103] and two dragon-like creatures, the dragon on the left having a rider on its back; the third group consists of five winged immortals, one of which is holding the sun. The outer band is made up of geometrical patterns.

Beliefs during the Eastern Han included the pursuit of immortality, and deities and mythical animals associated with the ascent to Heaven were popular decorative motifs of the period. Dongwanggong and Xiwangmu had many specific attributes and were not abstract deities. The other imagery on this mirror is equally rich in symbolic intent. Mirrors with this theme usually depict deities alternating with animals; the special feature of this mirror is that it shows deities riding on animals' backs.

This type of mirror is known as a *huaxiang*, or pictorial mirror. Such mirrors usually come from southern China, particularly the Shaoxing region of Zhejiang.[104]

—CPF

44 Mirror 東漢連弧柿蒂紋青銅鏡

Eastern Han dynasty, A.D. 25–220
Bronze
D: 14.3 cm
M-082

The high round knob on a circular seat rests on a quatrefoil resembling the calyx of a persimmon with exaggerated cusped and pointed petals. Rising from between these petals are four smaller petals of similar design, set against a field studded unevenly with tiny dots. Enclosing this inner zone is a band of eight semicircular segments parted by eight petals of the same form. Beyond lies a striated ring and immediately next to this is a broad, thick border with no decoration. The reflective side of the mirror is slightly domed. This is a so-called "black mirror." The decoration may refer to a cosmological interpretation of heaven and earth.

A textile pseudomorph is visible on the decorated front of the mirror, suggesting that it was wrapped in fabric during burial.

This type of mirror is often referred to as *sibalianhu*, four-blossom linked arcs. Mirrors of similar design have been unearthed from Xi'an and Luoyang, and this particular piece can probably be dated to between the mid- and late Eastern Han period. Similar mirrors with simple designs have been found in late Eastern Han and post-Han tombs.[105]   —CPF

45 Mirror 東漢長宜子孫鳥獸紋青銅鏡

Eastern Han dynasty, 1st–2nd century A.D.
Bronze
D: 14.6 cm
M-107

From the circular base of the semi-spherical knob projects a quatrefoil decoration inscribed with the four characters *chang yi zi sun,* meaning "may you forever have dutiful sons and grandsons." From between the petals rise scrolling clouds that divide the field into four compartments, each containing a mythical animal. A long-necked dragon is located in the two compartments next to the characters *chang* and *zi;* a bird with a rooster's body, wings stretched, and an elaborate tail like that of a peacock is located next to the character *sun;* a trotting horse with a saddle on its back is located next to the character *yi.* Surrounding these animals is a belt of sixteen arcs, and beyond is a ring of striae. The slightly raised border is flat and plain. The knob is comparatively large and the motifs are rendered in low relief. The mirror can be dated to the late Eastern Han period. —CPF

46 Mirror 東漢四獸紋青銅鏡

Eastern Han dynasty, 1st–2nd century A.D.
Bronze
D: 22.0 cm
M-095

The high round knob surrounded by a floral collar is set upon a square seat with a scooped edge. The reflective surface of the mirror is slightly domed. Four bosses divide the animal zone into four quadrants, occupied respectively by the azure dragon, white tiger, *tianlu* horned deer, and *bixie* chimera. In between this zone and the broad border with running cloud pattern is a narrow striated ring. Usually the four supernatural animals appearing on Han mirrors are the azure dragon, white tiger, scarlet bird, and sombre warrior (tortoise and snake), each representing one of the four directions. The animals used on this particular mirror form a rare combination.

This mirror is comparatively large and exquisitely molded, making the scales of the dragon's body and the fur on the tiger's body clearly visible. This suggests that it can be attributed to the late Eastern Han period. Other mirrors of this type, known as *shoudai,* or animal belt mirrors, flourished during the Han and the third century A.D. A similar mirror is said to have been found in Shaoxing, Zhejiang.[106]

—CPF

Notes

1. *Wenwu*, 1962.4–5, pp. 33–34, fig. 10.
2. Lin Yun, "A Reexamination of the Relationship between Bronzes of the Shang Culture and of the Northern Zone," in K. C. Chang, ed., *Studies in Shang Archaeology*, pp. 237–73, and p. 249, fig. 50:4–5.
3. *Wenwu*, 1972.4, pp. 62–66, figs. 2–3.
4. George W. Weber, Jr. *The Ornaments of the Late Chou Bronzes*, pp. 549–50.
5. Jenny So, verbal communication—ECB.
6. *China Pictorial*, 1987.5, p. 15; *Xi'an—Legacies of Ancient Chinese Civilization*, p. 75, fig. 1; and *Wenwu*, 1993.10, p. 5, fig. 9:1, and pl. 1:1–2.
7. Burton Watson, trans. *Records of the Grand Historian: Qin Dynasty*, rev. ed., pp. 19–20.
8. *Kaogu yu wenwu*, 1991.2, p. 9, fig. 5:7.
9. *Kaogu yu wenwu*, 1981.1, p. 30, fig. 19:20.
10. *Wenwu*, 1993.10, p. 11, fig. 23:1.
11. For a similar hook that still retains its turquoise inlay see Giuseppe Eskenazi, *Early Chinese Art from Tombs and Temples*, p. 58, no. 12.
12. *Kaogu yu wenwu*, 1981.1, p. 30, fig. 19:2 and 10.
13. *The David-Weill Collection: Catalogue of Fine Early Chinese Bronzes, Jades, Sculpture, Ceramics and Silver*, no. 150.
14. *Luoyang Zhongzhoulu*, p. 105, fig. 73:2.
15. Thomas Lawton, *Chinese Art of the Warring States Period*, no. 51.
16. *Xinyang Chumu*, pl. 64:3.
17. J. G. Andersson, "Hunting Magic in the Animal Style," *Bulletin of the Museum of Far Eastern Antiquities* 4 (1932) pp. 304–06.
18. Ibid., pl. 14:3.
19. *Wenbo*, 1989.4, pls. 4:4, 5:1.
20. *Gems of China's Cultural Relics 1992*, no. 112.
21. Jessica Rawson, *Chinese Bronzes: Art and Ritual*, no. 35.
22. *Kaogu*, 1964.3, p. 134, fig. 26:1, and pl. 5:11.
23. *Kaogu yu wenwu*, 1982.6, p. 11, fig. 7:5.
24. For an illustration of the Jin-state garment hook see Keith Wilson, "A Recently Acquired Archaic Sculptural Bronze," *Oriental Art* 38, no. 4, fig. 8.
25. Emma C. Bunker, "Significant changes in iconography and technology among ancient china's northwestern pastoral neighbors from the fourth to the first century B.C.," *Bulletin of the Asia Institute* 6 (1992), pp. 99–100.
26. Bo Gyllensvärd, *Chinese Art from the Collection of H. M. King Gustaf VI Adolf of Sweden*, pl. 28.
27. Nils Palmgren, *Selected Chinese Antiques from the Collection of Gustaf Adolf, Crown Prince of Sweden*, p. 62 and pl. 33.1. Palmgren considers the date still open to question, since the mirror retains traces of gilding which would indicate a date later than the Spring and Autumn period.
28. *Kaogu yu wenwu*, 1986.1, p. 17.
29. *Jiangling Mashan yihao Chumu* (Chu tomb no. 1 at Mashan in Jiangling, Jingzhou Museum), pl. 44.
30. Decorated with the sun, the moon, and interlocking dragons.
31. Without the sun and the moon.
32. Under the entry *Chunguan, Sichang*, Ministry of Spring, Manager of the Royal Banner.
33. See James J. Lally, *Chinese Archaic Bronzes, Sculptures and Works of Art*, no. 32.
34. For a bronze Shang comb see *Kaogu*, 1972.4, p. 29. Copper, gold, silver, and ivory were used from the Sui and Tang periods, see Zhou Xun and Gao Chunming, *Zhongguo lidai funu jiangshi*, p. 74. See also Thomas Lawton, *Chinese Art of the Warring States Period*, pp. 146–47, for similarly shaped combs made of jade, and Sueji Umehara, *Rakuyo kinson kobo shuei*, pl. 80, nos. 1–2, for horseshoe-shaped combs made of jade. For Han examples see Yoshito Harada, *Chinese Dress and Personal Ornaments in the Han and Six Dynasties*, p. 126, fig. 33.
35. *Hunan kaogu jikan*, vol. 4, pp. 79–86, 1987.
36. See *Wenwu*, 1973.9, pl. 9, illus. no. 3 for an example of combs found together with a mirror and other ladies' items. A set of horn combs was found in a Tang dynasty tomb in Jiangsu. See *Wenwu*, 1982.11, pp. 15–24, and p. 22, illus. no. 20. A Song dynasty tomb in Anhui contained another comb set made of horn. See *Kaogu*, 1986.10, p. 920, fig. 7, no. 6.
37. *Hebei sheng chutu wenwu xuanji*, no. 110.
38. Nils Palmgren, *Selected Chinese Antiquities from the Collection of Gustaf Adolf, Crown Prince of Sweden*, pl. 22:8 and p. 28.
39. *Wenwu*, 1980.7, p. 7, fig. 12.
40. For a good photograph of the Xigoupan earrings see Yang Boda, ed., *Zhongguo meishu quanji* 10, pl. 13.
41. Bernhard Karlgren, "Chinese Agraffes in Two Swedish Collections," *Bulletin of the Museum of Far Eastern Antiquities* 38 (1966), pp. 83–159, illus. nos. N 19 and N 23.
42. *Kaogu*, 1964.3, pl. 5:17.
43. *Zhengzhou Erligang*, p. 72, fig. 28:4, and pl. 26:17.
44. *Kaogu xuebao*, 1954.8, fig. 21:11, pl. 7:10.
45. *Zhengzhou Erligang*, p. 72, fig. 28:5, and pl. 26:15.
46. *Kaogu*, 1982.6, p. 603, fig. 12:9.
47. Note the shape of the belt hook worn by the standing male figure holding a lamp from the excavations of the Zhongshan royal tombs at Pingshan, Hebei, *Treasures from the Tombs of Zhong Shan Guo Kings*, no. 41.
48. Robert Dale Jacobsen, *Inlaid Bronzes of Pre-Imperial China: A Classic Tradition and Its Later Revivals*, p. 202.
49. Max Loehr, *Relics of Ancient China from the Collection of Dr. Paul Singer*, p. 159 and pl. 85:a.
50. The takin inhabits parts of northwest China and is a member of the goat-antelope sub-family. See G. H. H. Tate, *Mammals of Eastern Asia*, pp. 325–26.
51. Shi Yongshi, "Xiadu: Beijing's Twin Capital in Warring States Times," *China Reconstructs* (December 1987), pp. 57–59. See also Emma C. Bunker, "Significant changes in iconography and technology," p. 108, fig. 20.
52. S. I. Rudenko, *The Frozen Tombs of Siberia: The Pazyryk Burials of Iron Age Horsemen*, M. W. Thompson, trans.
53. According to a translation of the inscription provided by the owners.
54. Shi Yongshi, "Yanguo de hengzhi," *Zhongguo kaogu xuehui dierci nianhui lunwenji*, pp. 172–75, pl. 8:1–2. See also *Chugoku no kingin garasu*, pl. 6.
55. Joseph Needham, *Science and Civilisation in China*, vol. 4:1, pp. 22–25. A balance with a beam of equal arms supported centrally was known in China by the fourth century B.C.

56. Thomas Lawton, *Chinese Art of the Warring States Period*, pp. 108–09, nos. 57–58.

57. *Wenwu*, 1987.6, p. 6, fig. 17:12.

58. William Charles White, *Tombs of Old Loyang*, pls. 55:134d, 59:145a.d.

59. Sueji Umehara, *Rakuyo kinson kobo shuei*, pl. 69:1–2.

60. William Charles White, *Tombs of Old Loyang*, pl. 56:135. See also Sueji Umehara, *Rakuyo kinson kobo shuei*, pl. 94:1.

61. Thomas Lawton, *Chinese Art of the Warring States Period*, pp. 99–100.

62. James J. Lally, *Chinese Archaic Bronzes, Sculpture and Works of Art*, no. 32.

63. *Xi Han Nanyue wangmu* (Nanyue king's tomb of the Western Han), vol. 2, pl. 96:3.

64. Sueji Umehara, *Rakuyo kinson kobo shuei*, pl. 94:1.

65. *Nanyue king's tomb of the Western Han*, vol. 1, p. 166, fig. 105.

66. Maxwell K. Hearn, *Ancient Chinese Art: The Ernest Erickson Collection in the Metropolitan Museum*, no. 60.

67. Giuseppe Eskenazi, *Inlaid Bronze and Related Material from Pre-Tang China*, no. 41. See also Giuseppe Eskenazi, *Early Chinese Art from Tombs and Temples*, no. 13.

68. *Kaogu xuebao* 8, p. 154, pl. 7:8.

69. William Charles White, *Tombs of Old Loyang*, pl. 55:b.

70. Thomas Lawton, *Chinese Art of the Warring States Period*, pp. 124–25, no. 73.

71. Bernhard Karlgren, "Chinese Agraffes in Two Swedish Collections," pp. 83–159, pls. 1–3.

72. Teng Rensheng, *Lacquer Wares of the Chu Kingdom*, passim.

73. For a discussion of this iconography see Emma C. Bunker, "Significant changes in iconography and technology," pp. 99–112.

74. *Kaogu yu wenwu*, 1986.2, p. 10, fig. 4:17.

75. E. H. Minns, *The Art of the Northern Nomads*, vol. 28, pp. 47–99.

76. Jessica Rawson and Emma C. Bunker, *Ancient Chinese and Ordos Bronzes*, p. 302.

77. Sueji Umehara, *Rakuyo kinson kobo shuei*, pl. 76:3.

78. Sosui Fujiwara, *Shodo rikutai daijiten Fujiwara Sosui hen*, p. 153, seventh column from the right, fourth character. I am very grateful to Terese Bartholomew for help in identifying this character—ECB.

79. *Wenwu*, 1959.4, pp. 1–2.

80. *Mancheng Hanmu fajue baogao*, vol. 2, pl. 18.

81. Sueji Umehara, *Rakuyo kinson kobo shuei*, pl. 94:2.

82. *Wenwu cankao ziliao*, 1957.1, p. 53.

83. M. A. Devlet, *Sibirskie poyasnye azhurnye plastinki*, pp. 38–42.

84. For information on the Xiongnu see Jessica Rawson and Emma C. Bunker, *Ancient Chinese and Ordos Bronzes*, pp. 301–04.

85. For a technical analysis of the malachite in a similar piece see Giuseppe Eskenazi, *Early Chinese Art from Tombs and Temples*, entries 18–20.

86. *Yunnan Jinning Shizhaishan gu mu qun fajue baogao*, vol. 2, p. 72, no. 1. See also *The Chinese Bronzes of Yunnan*, pp. 235–36, figs. 208–09.

87. *The Chinese Bronzes of Yunnan*, nos. 178–79.

88. *Nanyue king's tomb of the Western Han*, vol. 2, pls. 18, no. 1, and 121, no. 4.

89. *Baoshan Chumu* (Chu cemetery at Baoshan), p. 298, fig. 94:4. For two other lacquer-painted bronze mirrors see color pl. 2:4–5.

90. *Kaogu xuebao*, 1963.2, pl. 24, no. 6.

91. The stones were identified by master goldsmith Richard Kimball —JMW.

92. Michele Pirazzoli-t'Serstevens, *The Han Dynasty*, p. 162.

93. Ibid., p. 95.

94. *Wenwu*, 1972.5, p. 65:4.

95. Wang Renxiang, "Daigou gailun" (A general survey of Chinese belt hooks), *Kaogu xuebao*, p. 281, pl. 7.

96. Ibid.

97. *Kaogu yu wenwu*, 1981.1, p. 30, pl. 19, no. 8.

98. Wang Renxiang, "A general survey of Chinese belt hooks," p. 281, pl. 7.

99. Paul Singer, *Early Chinese Gold and Silver*, p. 27, pl. 21.

100. Thomas Lawton, *Chinese Art of the Warring States Period*, pp. 90–91.

101. Nagahiro Toshio, *Taiko no kenkyu*, pl. 31.

102. Thomas Lawton, *Chinese Art of the Warring States Period*, pp. 90–91.

103. Wolfram Eberhard, *A Dictionary of Chinese Symbols: Hidden Symbols in Chinese Life and Thought*, pp. 294–96.

104. Suzanne Cahill, *Chinese Bronze Mirrors*.

105. *Kaogu tong*, 1956.6, no. 67.

106. Anneliese Gutkind Bulling, *The Decoration of Mirrors of the Han Period*, p. 73 and pl. 55.

Middle Period

Six Dynasties period, 265–589

through

Liao Dynasty, 907–1125

47 Plaque 六朝雙龍紋金冠飾牌

Six Dynasties period, 265–589
Gold
H: 4.8 cm W: 4.0 cm
GI-099

This gold headdress plaque with beaten-gold backing has a cutout front panel decorated with beaded granulation. This panel is made from a separate piece of gold, carefully chiselled away to reveal an elaborate design of two confronting dragons. The dragons rise toward two large gold beads which represent the pearls often associated with wisdom. The openwork front panel is attached to the back by a thin strip of gold that is wrapped around the edges. In a remarkably delicate treatment of gold-granulation beading, the bodies and heads of the dragons writhe delicately in a golden space.

The gold-granulation beaded work is very evenly applied, with a slight graduation in the sizes of the beads. The technique, derived from the West, is seen in China as early as the Han dynasty.[1] Other plaques with similar granulation and cutout designs have been excavated in China from northern and northwestern tombs.[2] Two stunning examples of granulation on belt buckles, one from a Western Han site and another from a Western Jin site, demonstrate the popularity of the technique from an early time (see pp. 20–21, figs. 9 and 10).[3]

Later ornaments, particularly earrings, copy the granulation technique used in this piece, looking for the same effect without the meticulous process involved in true granulation. Examples in the Mengdiexuan collection include catalogue numbers 72, 73, and 74, all of which are Liao-period examples of the different ways in which pseudo-granulation came to duplicate the process of granulation.   —JMW

48 Comb 六朝嵌珠玉寶石金梳

Six Dynasties period, 265–589
Gold with inset pearls and stones
H: 4.4 cm W: 5.7 cm
GI-077

With its large plaque of inset translucent jade (nephrite), this beaten-gold hair comb combines many of the finest qualities of the goldsmith and the jeweler. Two small pearls and two green-colored stones are set into the gold of the top and front panels. The panels are decorated with rows of gold granulation surrounding thin wire bands of alternating circles and diamond shapes. These meet at the middle, where a circle is flanked by two almond shapes. The central panel consists of the same repetitive pattern. The row of silver teeth is a modern addition.

The combination of gold and jade, which according to Chinese sensibilities are two of the most precious materials, is rare. Chinese interest in precious jewels was undoubtedly influenced by the West, particularly by the Persian merchants who actively sold jewels in the Tang capital of Changan.[4]   —JMW

49 Earring and Pendant
六朝垂葉形金耳墜

Six Dynasties period, 3rd–6th century
Gold and turquoise
H: 13.5 cm (approx.) W: 4.5 cm (approx.)
GI-098

This gold earring is decorated with small pendants attached to each other by tiny wire loops. The four central pendants each have a basic rectangular shape, with alternating triangular and semicircular forms projecting from the perimeter. Tear-shaped pendants are suspended from the outer sides of each central pendant. Each of these has an empty cell on one side that once must have been inlaid.

A separate element which was acquired with the earring consists of an oblong turquoise bead whose two leaf-shaped pendants are also attached by tiny wire loops. The circular ear-piece has a loose ring with a tiny iron fragment adhering to it.

The pendants were all chisel-cut from thin gold sheets. The cloisons on the leaf-shaped pendants were formed by gold strips set on edge and attached by hard solder. The loops that attach the various elements of the pendant are made of previously prepared figure eight–shaped loops linked together in a complex manner. Such loops are a variation of the loop-in-loop chain.[5] Under microscopic examination, the wire from which these loops are formed appears to be strip-twisted with a right-hand twist.[6] The loop that attaches the overall pendant to the ear-piece is spiral and appears to have been drawn.

The separate, smaller pendant has not been reattached to the earring because the workmanship appears to be different and the proper way to attach it is unclear. The leaf-shaped pendants are of a different shape from those on the earring proper and do not carry cloisons. The band from which the leaf shapes are suspended is decorated with a piece of loop-in-loop chain formed out of strip-twisted wire and attached with hard solder.[7]

There are few excavated pieces with which to compare this earring, which is very difficult to date. A close look at two earrings recently excavated from a Northern Wei tomb in the southern suburbs of Datong in northern Shanxi reveals tiny figure eight–shaped attachment loops, suggesting that such loops were current during the late Six Dynasties period.[8] Earrings with pendants that move appear to have been very popular among the northern pastoral tribes and their descendants who moved into China during the last centuries of the first millennium B.C. and the Six Dynasties period. Further information concerning this earring must await future archaeological discoveries.   —ECB

50 Belt Set 西晉鎏金龍鳳虎紋青銅組帶飾

Western Jin dynasty, 265–316
Gilded bronze
11 pieces
2 rounded end-pieces:
  H: 4.8 cm W: 8.9 cm
  H: 4.8 cm W: 8.6 cm
1 vertical phoenix plaque: H: 11.4 cm W: 3.2 cm
4 phoenix-and-dragon plaques: H: 9.5 cm W: 3.2 cm
4 dragon-and-tiger plaques: H: 9.4 cm W: 5.4 cm
BP-017.1–.11

50a. Gilded bronze belt set (GI–017).
西晉鎏金龍紋青銅組帶飾

50b. Silvered bronze belt set (GI–018).
西晉鎏銀龍紋青銅組帶飾

This elaborately decorated belt set of gilt bronze is made up of eleven pieces which were probably attached to a leather backing. When buckled together the two rounded end-pieces created a design of two confronting dragons, setting the tone for the rest of the designs, which are variations on dragon, tiger, and phoenix motifs. The four pairs of plaques, which have flamelike projections on the top and rounded plaques suspended from the bottom, show a dragon design on top and a fierce tiger design on the lower portion. The four pairs of plaques with lozenge- and heart-shaped pendants are decorated with a phoenix design on top and a winged dragon below. A set of plaques consisting of a five-sided top plaque decorated with a winged dragon on top and a scroll pattern on the lower portion completes the belt set.

The eight pairs of plaques and two end-pieces all have a three-part sandwich construction. This consists of a solid backing plate with a cutout middle plaque carrying the chased design, topped with a rounded rim that is riveted through from front to back. The vertical plaque is a simpler, two-piece construction without the rim. With the eight suspended pairs, the rim extends down to form a tab that wraps through the pierced lower portion. The top portion of the plaques would have made up the belt itself, with the lower portion hanging down.

A smaller and less complete gilt-bronze set from the Mengdiexuan collection (cat. no. 50a) is chased with a dragon design on the end-piece and on two pairs of the round-bottomed plaques. The backing plates are missing, as are the rim attachments. The Mengdiexuan collection also includes an example of the same type of belt in silvered bronze (cat. no. 50b). This nine-piece belt set has a similar construction and a chased design.

A similar set of paired belt plaques was found in a dated Jin tomb in Jiangsu and has been carefully analyzed.[9] This twenty-piece set was found around the body of the tomb occupant.[10] Belts of similar construction have been found in Korea; they resemble the plaques in catalogue number 50a more than the others.[11] It would seem that belt-plaque sets may have first become fashionable during the Jin, and then grew in popularity over the Tang period. The Western Jin belts are earlier, with the Korean belts dated to the Silla period (fifth to seventh century). Belt sets made up of numerous plaques had replaced belt hooks completely by the Western Jin period.   —JMW

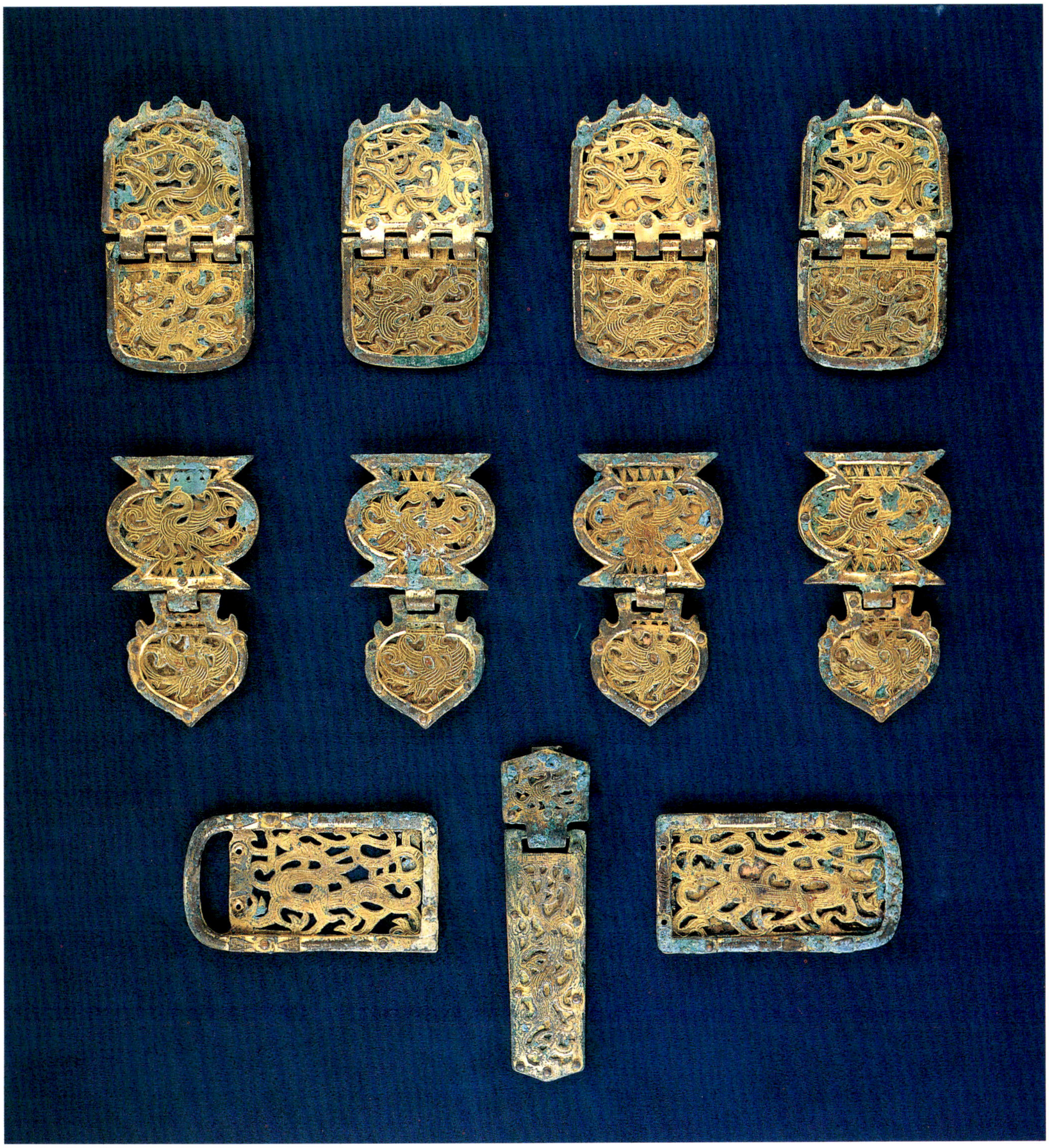

134   MIDDLE PERIOD

51 Belt Set 唐初鎏金狻猊紋銅或青銅組帶飾

Early Tang period, 7th century or earlier
Gilded copper or bronze
12 pieces
1 buckle: H: 4.0 cm W: 7.3 cm
5 disks: D: 2.6 cm
1 long plaque with hinge: H: 3.9 cm W: 7.4 cm
4 rectangular plaques: H: 2.8 cm W: 4.8 cm
1 strap end with pendant hinged plaque: H: 11.2 cm W: 5.0 cm
Published: Jessica Rawson and Emma C. Bunker, *Ancient Chinese and Ordos Bronzes*, no. 146
GI-032.1–.12

These fittings once decorated a leather or cloth belt. The designs on the rectangular plaques each portray two rampant lions with raised S-shaped tails flanking a central boss amid an openwork tendril background. Rampant lions also decorate the strap end, which terminates in a luscious, engorged palmette. The circular plaques repeat the round bosses.

The construction of these belt mounts is quite complex. The frames, the decorated panels, and the backs were all cast separately in piece-molds and then riveted together. This construction continues an earlier tradition associated with some Western Jin belt plaques.[12] It has no relationship with later Tang belt plaques, which resemble in shape and construction those used by the Turkic-speaking tribes of Central Asia, such as those in catalogue number 54.

The lion was not a Far Eastern creature, but was a very popular motif in China during the Six Dynasties, Sui, and Tang periods, due to its importance in Buddhist iconography. Representations of lions abound on bronze mirrors and Buddhist sculpture. Lions were also among the exotic animals kept at the ancient Tang capital of Changan, present-day Xi'an.

The rampant-lion design shown on the Mengdiexuan belt set represents an early attempt to sinicize a foreign motif. Similar rampant lions, with their raised tails forming an S-shape, occur on textiles preserved in the Shosoin repository at Nara, Japan.[13] Such lions are foreign motifs that go back ultimately to Western models found on Sasanian and Byzantine textiles, such as those preserved in medieval treasuries in Europe.[14] The palmette form also descends from Byzantine and late- or post-Sasanian ornament.[15] Textiles played an important role in the transmission of designs throughout the Eurasian and Western worlds.

A belt similar to the Mengdiexuan belt with a floral pattern and a palmette-decorated strap end has been recently excavated from a Tang dynasty site near the Xianyang airport in Shaanxi.[16] Although no belt plaques with rampant lions of this type have been excavated scientifically, there are examples in several collections around the world. A similar set of mounts in the British Rail Pension Fund sale was erroneously described as harness ornaments.[17] There is no evidence that such ornaments were ever used on horses, particularly in view of the fragility of the hinges. The decorations on the British Rail mounts of carnivores amid cloud scrolls are completely sinicized and typically Tang. Another set including a belt buckle, a strap end, and five plaques decorated with *qilin* was recently offered for sale in London.[18] Other related examples are in collections in Japan.[19] Two similar rectangular plaques with rampant lions are in the collections of the estate of Arthur M. Sackler.[20] The function of the pierced oval plaque originally associated with this Mengdiexuan belt set is unclear.[21] It has been suggested that this plaque reinforced the leather around the hole used for the buckle tongue, but this use has not been confirmed archaeologically.

—ECB

136 MIDDLE PERIOD

52 Belt Set 唐鎏金鸚鵡紋青銅組帶飾

Tang dynasty, 618–906
Gilded bronze
14 pieces
12 square plaques: H: 3.2 cm W: 3.5 cm
2 end-plaques: H: 3.2 cm W: 7.0 cm
BP-007.1–.14

This large belt set was cast in bronze in high relief and then gilded. The two end-plaques are decorated with two parrots, one turned back toward the other, amid a design of grape vines. The smaller, square plaques are of similar design, with one bird per plaque. Of these single-parrot designs, six face left and six face right, making a balanced and harmonious design. The design is remarkable for its crisp detail, from the parrot's feathers to the evenly punch-marked background. All of the plaques have a high rim around the front edge, and all are backed with plain flat pieces of bronze which are attached by plain posts, four on the smaller plaques, five on the end-plaques.

Though parrots were once plentiful in the heartland of China, around the Shaanxi and Gansu border areas, they were intensively collected and eventually became extinct. Later, they were reintroduced to the north from southern China, and still later from India. They were used as tribute and were considered very exotic. There is an example of a parrot from India being given as a gift in 720; the donor was rewarded with a "brocaded caftan and a girdle of gilded leather" by the Tang ruler Xuan Zong.[22]

Belts with high raised-relief patterns from the early Song period have been excavated from northern tombs.[23] Some later belts from the Yuan period have been found in central Chinese locations; they tend to have even higher raised relief and more elaborate designs.[24]

—JMW

53 Belt Set 唐鎏金雙鳥鴨紋青銅組帶飾

Tang dynasty, 618–906
Gilded bronze
17 pieces
15 square plaques: H: 2.7 cm W: 3.0 cm
1 belt end: H: 2.8 cm W: 4.4 cm
1 belt buckle: H: 4.0 cm W: 6.5 cm
GI-042.1–.17

Each element of this seventeen-piece gilt-bronze belt set was cast with a design of paired birds in high relief. The square plaques are decorated with paired ducks facing each other over a rectangular cutout, and leaf motifs surround their edges. The buckle and end-piece are decorated with paired birds, probably falcons since they have slightly hooked beaks, large talons, and pointed wings. They are covered by a canopy of bell-shaped flowers. The details of decoration, including the elaborately pseudo-punched background and details describing the birds' bodies, were all cast in bronze before the piece was gilded.

Each of the square plaques is backed with a plain bronze covering attached to the face by four posts. A few of the plaques still contain remnants of the original leather belt. Although it seems likely that the rectangular openings on the plaques served as points where attachments to the main belt could be made, it appears (at least in the case where the original belt remains) that the leather ran tightly between the plaques and left no place for anything to be looped onto the belt. It is possible that the leather beneath some of the plaques may have been cut away, making the holes more functional. It was a court regulation in the early part of the Tang period for this type of belt to have seven points from which objects could be suspended.[25]

The buckle and end-piece also show remnants of the original leather. In addition, the buckle carries a textile pseudomorph on its bronze backing. The actual tab and buckle appear to be made of iron and are attached to the gilt-bronze buckle plaque.

The imagery on this belt set, with its paired ducks and falcons, speaks of the Tang-period interest in exotics and birds. The ducks are symbols of marital fidelity, while the falcons represent the exotic imports of this period. Birds of all kinds were kept in Tang China, some for food, some to inspire the imagination.[26] Falcons were used as hunters beginning in the Han period, and during the Tang the art of falconry was well developed and enjoyed imperial patronage.[27]

—JMW

56 Mirror 唐明逾滿月神禽神獸青銅鏡

Tang dynasty, 618–906
Bronze
D: 24.0 cm
M-111

The design across the back of this mirror is divided into seven distinct bands. The surface of the mirror varies considerably, making sharp delineations between patterns. The round knob rests on a base in the form of lotus petals. The inner zone is decorated in high relief with eight quadrupeds, each of a different appearance and posture. Beyond are two rings of sawteeth enclosed by a band of lengthy inscriptions. The forty characters form a poem of ten lines, with four characters to each line. The poem praises the beauty of bronze mirrors:

> Bright as the full moon;
> Smooth and lustrous as jade and pearl.
> Behind the mother-of-pearl inlay fly
>   beautiful birds;
> In front of the mirror-stand phoenixes dance.
> When hung on the wall, it looks like a real
>   caltrop;
> When put into the water, it looks like
>   a peaceful lotus.
> Vividly, it reflects all forms and movements;
> Fairly, it reflects the beautiful countenances
>   of ladies.
> It can purify the spirit and reflect all objects;
> It shall be passed down from generation to
>   generation.[34]

The outer zone is decorated with running animals and flying birds in a very lively manner. The border is taken up by a band of sawteeth and tendril scrolls. The decorative motifs and inscriptions suggest that this mirror should be dated to the early Tang. Mirrors with similar inscriptions are recorded in the books *Jinshisuo*, Compendium of metals and stones; *Xiaotanluan baojingying*, Catalogue of a group of beautifully molded precious mirrors; *Shanzhai jijinlu*, Catalogue of metals by Shanzhai; and *Xiaojiao jingge quanwen*, Complete text of the classics with brief collations.   —CPF

57 Mirror 唐狻猊葡萄青銅鏡

Tang dynasty, 618–906
Bronze
D: 12.5 cm
M-089

This round mirror with fully decorated back has a high exterior rim separate from the central design of five cavorting lions that move counterclockwise around a large knob. The exterior rim is embellished in high relief in which a continuous pattern of bunches of grapes is linked by vines interspersed with pairs of running foxes and pairs of perched and flying long-tailed birds. The interior section, dominated by a large knob decorated on either side with a scroll pattern, has a raised pattern of five lions. One is seen from above, crouching and moving forward; the next is seen in profile with head turned back; the following one is seen in partial profile and from above as he attempts to scratch his right ear with his right hind paw; the fourth is also seen in partial profile; the fifth is seen in complete profile. —JMW

58 Mirror 唐鴛鴦鸚鵡青銅菱花鏡

Tang dynasty, 618–906
Bronze
D: 22.0 cm
M-106

Surrounding the round knob in the main decorative field are four groups of heart-shaped motifs enclosed in entwined branches, with a lotus capping each apex and another lotus at the base. On the seats perch four birds: two mandarin ducks alternate with two parrots, each displaying a different posture. While two stand still with heads turned or raised, the other two, with wings outstretched, are either lowering their heads or ready to fly. Where two motifs meet, a floral design grows. The barbed border in the shape of an eight-petal caltrop blossom is slightly raised. Each petal is decorated with floral sprigs and cloud heads. This mirror is comparatively large in size and the motifs, though elaborate, are neatly arranged and well balanced.

The large knob in the center shows some green patination as well as some evidence of a textile pseudomorph. The back of the mirror has been tinned. Its front is heavily encrusted with a green-and-rust colored patination that shows remains of a textile pseudomorph. —CPF

The reflective surface of this mirror is heavily encrusted with patina and textile pseudomorph.

59 Mirror 唐魚獸海磯青銅鏡

Tang dynasty, 618–906
Bronze
D: 15.6 cm
M-090

The irregularly shaped central boss of this mirror is surrounded by four fantastic mountain formations interspersed with cloud, water, animal, and fish designs. The fish resemble *makara,* the Buddhist-inspired curved fish that came to be known in China as *zhiwen.* The two other animals are probably representations of the mythical unicorn of China, the *jilin.*

This mirror's emphasis on landscape demonstrates the Tang interest in depicting the natural world. The "cell" organization of the landscape pattern is similar to the methods of landscape painting seen in contemporaneous painting at Dunhuang and in other Tang-period painting.

Mirrors of similar design can be found in a private Osaka collection.[35] Another mirror that has a very similar design is in the Imperial Treasure of the Shosoin in Japan.[36]

—JMW

60 Mirror 宋雙鳳青銅方鏡

Song dynasty, 960–1279
Bronze
L: 11.6 cm W: 11.6 cm
M-083

This square mirror has a flat rim that angles into a surface decorated with incised and raised linear designs. The bridge-shaped knob rests on a base within two concentric circles inside a band of overlapping petals. The main decorative zone is circular and depicts two gracefully flying phoenixes. They have long-feathered wings and tendril-like tails that flutter in the air. The four corners of the mirror are also ornamented, three with a leafy tendril and the fourth inscribed with six characters reading *Jianzhou Huang Xiaoba zhu,* meaning molded by Huang Xiaoba of Jianzhou. Jianzhou was located in the present-day Jilin province, and Huang Xiaoba was the name of either the mirror-maker or an establishment selling mirrors.

During the Song and Yuan dynasties, paired dragons and phoenixes were popular motifs for mirror backs. This mirror is unusual because the main decorative area within the overall square shape is circular. The circular area with phoenixes represents the sky, while the square ground with leafy tendrils symbolizes the earth. This echoes the traditional idea of "Heaven is round and the Earth is square."
—CPF

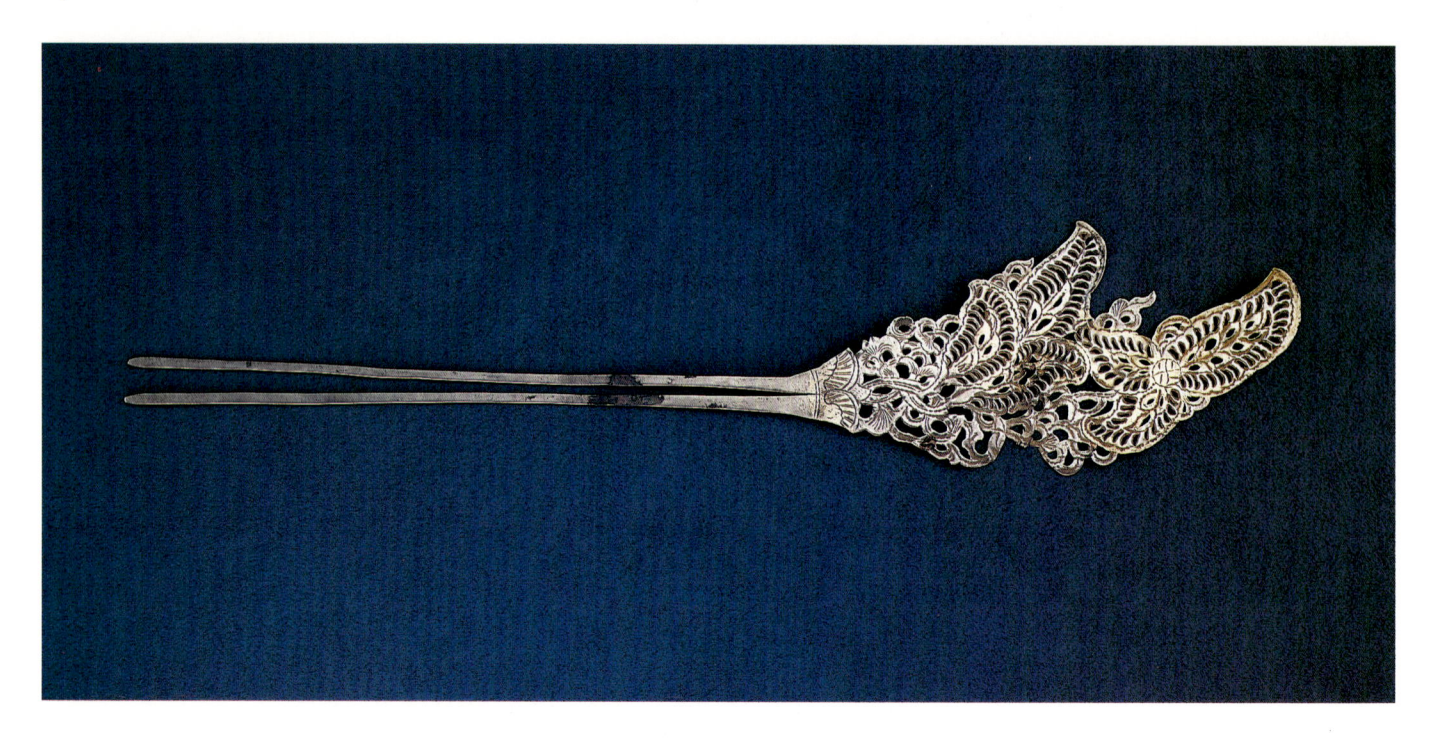

61 Hairpin 唐鎏金透雕花卉紋銀髮簪

Tang dynasty, 618–906
Gilded silver
H: 7.3 cm L: 33.0 cm
GI-084

This very large, two-tined, hammered-silver hairpin features cutout designs of floral motifs. Partially gilded, the head of the pin has been chased and polished on only one side. In addition to the repoussé, the pin has been chased with a blunt tool intended to displace only the silver into a rhythmic pattern around the cutout leaf pattern, giving the decorated portion greater depth and interest. The two prongs are hammered flat from the same sheet of silver. A similar pair of hairpins has been excavated along with other Tang silver objects from Zhejiang.[37] —JMW

62 Pair of Hairpins
唐鎏金透雕飛天及仙童法輪銀髮簪一對

Tang dynasty, 618–906
Gilded silver
Apsaras: H: 6.0 cm L: 19.1 cm
Boy: H: 5.7 cm L: 25.7 cm
GI-040.1–.2

This pair of silver hairpins is fully decorated with cut-out designs, chasing, and repoussé. The back of each pin is left unchased and unshined. Both pins are decorated with symbols typically associated with Buddhism. The top, single-tined hairpin is made of silver with gilding, and depicts an *apsaras* riding atop a fully opened lotus petal. The chased decoration begins at the top of the tine, where a lotus bud opens into a flowing design of intertwined leaves and flowers. The *apsaras* is shown in three-quarter frontal view. Her hands are raised as if in offering, and she holds a lotus bud. Her lower torso is wrapped in a gilt skirt; the upper torso is left undraped except for flowing scarves wrapped around both arms and the body.

The larger, two-tined hairpin is decorated with a lotus design similarly executed by chasing and repoussé. Atop this pin is a naked boy playing with a ball (symbol of the Buddhist "wheel of life"). He is positioned in three-quarter rear view and is clothed only in a flowing, ribbonlike decoration that drapes around his shoulder.

—JMW

63 Hairpin 唐鎏金龍魚紋銀髮簪

Tang dynasty, 618–906
Gilded silver
H: 5.7 cm   L: 25.9 cm
GI-076

A number of metalworking techniques are employed in this large, silver, single-tined hairpin. The initial shape has been established by smithy work, with both repoussé and chasing techniques used to create the design and fine detail. The design depicts a dragon-fish atop a lotus leaf. The fish's fins and the lotus flower are lightly gilded. The fish carries a silver jewel in its open mouth.

The design shows the influence of Buddhism on Tang-period central Chinese design, as both the lotus and the fish are symbols of Buddhism. The design became increasingly popular as an image for items of personal adornment and can be seen in its most mature form in Ming-period earrings from the Mengdiexuan collection (cat. no. 71a). A hairpin with a similar design was excavated near Xi'an, Shaanxi, where the ancient Tang capital of Changan was located.[38]   —JMW

64 Hair Ornament 唐鎏金雙鳳紋銀髮飾

Tang dynasty, 618–906
Gilded silver
H: 7.6 cm W: 13.3 cm
GI-033

Two confronted phoenixes in flight are depicted on this hair ornament of repoussé silver. The birds hold in their beaks branches of the floral growth that surrounds them. The bodies of the birds and the branches have been chased to create patterns of feathers on the birds and veins on the leaves. The back is unpolished and exposed, although the plaque may have originally been attached to a cloth backing.

Excavated examples of Tang-period hair ornaments have been unearthed in Shaanxi.[39] Designs of two confronted birds holding floral elements in their beaks are found on Tang silver boxes.[40]   —JMW

65 Hair Ornaments
唐鎏金牡丹菊花紋銀髮飾兩件

Tang dynasty, 618–906
Gilded silver
a: H: 4.1 cm W: 9.8 cm
b: H: 7.3 cm W: 14.9 cm
GI-072.a–.b

Designs of peony and chrysanthemum flowers adorn this pair of gilded-silver hair ornaments. Both ornaments are of repoussé work with cutout portions to add clarity and dimension. Details of leaves and petals have been chased into the metal. The surface is partially gilded, highlighting parts of the design. Neither ornament has a backing, although it seems likely that each was attached to some kind of strengthening and attachable backing material such as cloth.

The two flowers represented here are symbols of the seasons spring (peony) and fall (chrysanthemum). Ladies' hair ornaments frequently were made in the shape of flowers denoting the seasons or aspects of beauty.

Tang dynasty tombs in Shaanxi have yielded similar ornaments in gilded silver.[41] This kind of openwork is also found on Five Dynasties ornaments.[42]   —JMW

66 Hairpin 唐纏枝葡萄鳥獸紋銀髮簪

Tang dynasty, 618–906
Silver
H: 3.2 cm   L: 30.5 cm
GI-063

This long, flat, hammered-silver hairpin has fine repoussé and chased work along the top half. The decoration consists of intertwining vine scrolls occasionally breaking out from the edge of the pin. Within this pattern are birds, including a phoenix and a mandarin duck, with a scratching lion between them. The background is filled with small ring-stamp designs. The reverse side is plain and unbacked.

The designs resemble the "lion-and-grapevine" patterns found on Tang-period mirrors, and the western influence evident in those objects is probably at play here as well. The use of silver in the making of hairpins appears during the Han period and is continued through the Qing period.[43]   —JMW

67 Hair Comb 唐雙飛天紋銀梳

Tang dynasty, 618–906
Silver
H: 12.4 cm W: 15.2 cm
GI-068

Some teeth remain on this large, round, repoussé and chased silver comb. The central panel consists of a highly symmetrical, raised pair of flying *apsaras* with feathered, birdlike lower bodies. Thin tendrils wrap gently around the heads and across the backs of the two female figures, who hold between them a three-leafed floral offering. Below the two, but in the same panel, is a central floral motif flanked by *ruyi*-shaped floating objects. The entire background of the central panel is ring punched.

A well-defined pseudo-granulation border separates the central panel from the repoussé design of fruits and leaves connected by a gracefully intertwined vine. The numerous teeth of the comb are narrow and evenly spaced, cut from the same sheet of silver. The reverse is undecorated.

A similar, though gilded, comb-back with *apsaras* designs is in the Carl Kempe collection.[44] Song tombs have also yielded silver comb-backs with the same rounded appearance.[45] A gilt-silver comb-back with similar pseudo-granulation was found in a Tang tomb in Jiangsu.[46] Another comb, also with pseudo-granulation, ring-punched background, and teeth created from the same sheet, was illustrated in a London sales catalogue in 1990.[47]

—JMW

68 Comb 唐鎏金鍍錫喜鵲紋青銅梳

Tang dynasty, 618–906
Tinned and gilded bronze
H: 10.8 cm W: 13.0 cm
GI-069

This round-backed comb is made from bronze that was tinned and then gilded across the repoussé handle. The design on the upper section consists of three magpies around a central floral motif. The central bird appears to be in flight, while the other two have their legs extended onto ribbonlike tendrils. In the center, a flower radiates flowing branches that make up part of the background. The whole surface of the central panel and the lower horizontal band is punched with small circles interspersed with fanlike intrusions into the band. The central zone of the design is delineated by evenly spaced rows of raised circles. The top outer rim is further elaborated by tufted leaves radiating from the top center.

The teeth of the comb are cut evenly from the same piece of bronze as the upper section. The two end prongs are wider than the rest. The back of the comb is tinned but otherwise undecorated. An old repair is evident on the far left.

Combs in the shape of this one have been excavated from Tang dynasty tombs in Jiangsu and in Northern Song tombs in Jiangxi.[48] This basic shape for combs became popular as early as the Warring States period, but over time the shape became wider and the materials changed from bronze to wood to silver and gold.[49] This shape, so characteristic of the Sui and Tang periods, is often decorated with symbolic floral designs as well as Buddhist motifs.   —JMW

69 Neck Ornament
唐鎏金雙飛鳥雲紋銀項飾

Tang dynasty, 618–906
Gilded silver
H: 16.5 cm W: 15.9 cm
Greatest width: 3.2 cm
GI-078

This ornament consists of a flat, beaten band of thick silver with a chased design and was probably intended to be worn around the neck. The partial circle is finished on both ends with a hooking device. The left end is banded by a tightly wound silver wire. The right end shows evidence of a similar kind of banding, which is now lost. The edge is scalloped, and the band is decorated with a pair of confronted birds in flight. Tendrils of flowers and cloudlike motifs flow out from the birds' tails. The back is undecorated.

It is unusual to see neck ornaments as part of Chinese adornment before the Sui dynasty, and it is assumed that these ornaments came to China from the West.[50] A gold necklace dated to the late Tang period is in the Minneapolis Institute of Arts.[51]

—JMW

70 Pendant Set 唐或較早期金玉寶石組佩飾

Tang period or earlier, 6th–7th century
Gold, jade, lapis lazuli, and turquoise
11 pieces
1 large jade *ruyi*-shaped plaque: H: 3.5 cm W: 6.4 cm
1 small jade *ruyi*-shaped plaque: H: 2.6 cm W: 3.5 cm
2 triangular jade plaques: H: 1.2 cm W: 3.0 cm
3 square jade plaques: H: 2.5 cm W: 2.5 cm
1 flower-shaped jade plaque: D: 2.0 cm
3 gold plaques: H: 2.1 cm W: 2.0 cm
GI-113.1-.11

This pendant set consists of eight jade plaques of various shapes and three gold plaques inset with lapis lazuli and turquoise. The large and small *ruyi*-shaped jade plaques are fitted on all sides by small, gold, flower-shaped ornaments that may have served as hangers. (The fitting at the top of the larger *ruyi* plaque is missing.) These are identical on both sides; in some cases the cloisons of the petals are filled with turquoise. The triangular and flower-shaped plaques are perforated in the center by round holes, while the square plaques are perforated with square openings.

The three gold plaques of flat, hammered gold each have a whimsical creature on the front. Laid out in gold cloisons of flat gold wire turned on edge, the creature's robust body is made of sectioned pieces of carved and detailed lapis lazuli. Flamelike protrusions on the figure's head are filled with light blue turquoise. The creature resembles the kind of mythical animals that appear in early Chinese texts, such as the *Shanhaijing,* and later as guardians at Buddhist monuments. The background for each of the gold plaques is delicately finished, with minute gold granulation adding texture to the surface. Each gold plaque is approximately 0.4 cm deep and is pierced with eight holes for attachment to the rest of the set.

The way that this pendant set would have been arranged is difficult to determine, and the arrangement presented here is only a suggestion. Pendant sets like this one, as well as sets of hair ornaments and earrings, were frequently made of a combination of materials utilizing a variety of manufacturing techniques.[52] Such sets were frequently worn hanging from a girdle and made a pleasant sound when the wearer walked.[53] Examples of how these pendant sets were worn hanging from a girdle can be seen in tomb material, including tomb figures, from Hubei and Henan.[54]

—JMW

MIDDLE PERIOD 157

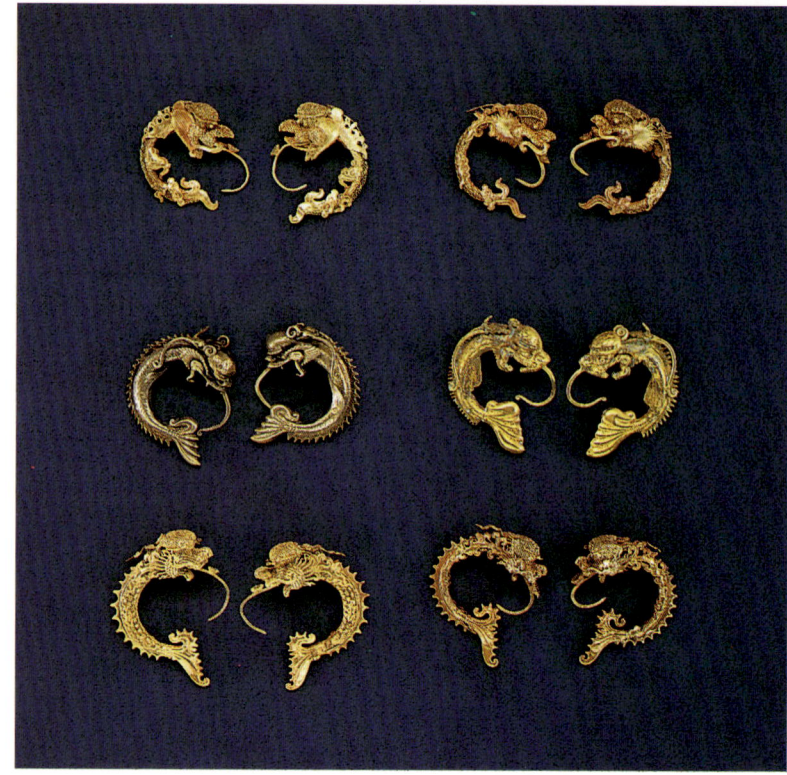

71a. Six pairs of Ming-period dragon-fish earrings (GI-029.1ab–.6ab).
明龍魚紋形耳環六對

71 Earring 遼龍魚紋金耳環

Liao dynasty, 907–1125
Gold
H: 5.7 cm (including hook) W: 5.7 cm (including hook)
GI-044

This hollow gold earring takes the form of a dragon-fish pursuing a pearl. The main body is made of two pieces worked in repoussé in a high relief that dramatically describes the creature's scales and fins. A thin line running vertically down the body shows how the pieces were joined. The head curls up and is crowned by a tuft protruding from its center-back. A gold "pearl" is attached to the animal's mouth by a wire that runs through the pearl and terminates on the reverse side. The pearl also appears to have been made in a two-piece mold, with a horizontal line across the middle portion. A gold wire is attached to the mouth of the dragon-fish and serves as the earring hook. The inside base of the tail is perforated, indicating that some kind of attachment may originally have hung from the tail of the fish.

Being a mythological animal, the dragon takes many different forms. One form, according to the *Qian que lei shu,* by Chen Renxi, is called a *zhiwen,* and its image is carved on the roofs of buildings and beams of bridges. The *zhiwen* is said to have a fondness for water and is depicted as a fish with uplifted tail.[55] It appeared on Liao-period funerary ornaments, particularly earrings, and probably served as a kind of talisman.[56] Paired fish are generally understood to be a Buddhist symbol and, as other Buddhist imagery had found its way into Chinese ornament by this time, it is likely that this very popular image on earrings was the result of Buddhist influence.

The pronunciation of the word *yu,* fish, is similar to that of the word for abundance, making the image of a fish a rebus for wealth. Though this kind of rebus did not develop in China until later,[57] it is possible that this linguistic suggestion may have been intended in six pairs of Ming-period dragon-fish earrings (cat. no. 71a) in the Mengdiexuan collection. These animated dragon-fish were made using a variety of techniques, often combined, including repoussé, chasing, and soldering, as well as filigree, a technique new to the Chinese at this time.

—JMW

72 Earring 遼垂葉形金耳環

Liao dynasty, 907–1125
Gold
H: 4.1 cm W: 2.2 cm
GI-090

This U-shaped earring was hollow cast from a two-piece mold, as evidenced by a thin vertical mold-joint mark along the face and back of its main body. The plain hook extends as a single piece of gold into the main body of the earring. The pendant shape is broken by the protrusion of a hollow knob on the face of the earring and again at the lower edge by a leaf shape. The pseudo-granulation around the edge of the leaf was achieved by laying a thin, rhythmically compressed wire around the edge of the leaf, creating the appearance of a row of beads. This process was likely accomplished in the mold form and the piece cast as a single unit, including the hook.

This same shape is seen in jade examples that are robust in form but which lack the grace of the slender, cast gold. See for example, catalogue number 72a in the Mengdiexuan collection.

A pair of gilt-bronze earrings of similar shape was found in a Liao dynasty woman's tomb near Tianjin.[58] It does not appear that these earrings were graced with the same sort of pseudo-beadwork found on the Mengdiexuan earring. Two gold earrings from a Heilongjiang tomb of the Jin dynasty show a very similar shape, with the leaflike design protruding from the lower area of the U-shape, but they are solid, rather than hollow, and are of much coarser manufacture and finish than the Mengdiexuan pair.[59]

—JMW

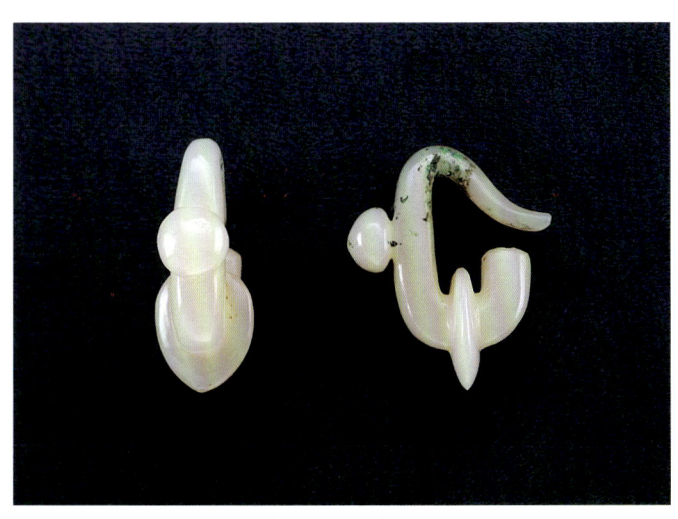

72a. Pair of jade earrings (J-002.a–.b).
遼垂葉形玉耳環一對

73 Pair of Earrings
遼鎏金連珠紋青銅耳環一對

Liao dynasty, 907–1125
Gilded bronze
a: H: 3.8 cm W: 3.5 cm
b: H: 4.0 cm W: 3.3 cm (in profile)
GI-061.a–.b

Pseudo-granulation follows the contours of each of these hollow-cast gilded-bronze earrings. Strings of beaded wire follow the vertical portion of the body continuously, while the horizontal sections are patched in. Both the lower leaflike form and the center front protrusion are part of the whole cast, with the effect being somewhat softer than the result in catalogue number 72. A small pierced hole at the base of each earring indicates that there may have been an additional piece, now lost, hanging from the base. The hook appears to have been cast in the original mold.

This pair of earrings is closely related to the gilt-bronze earrings from a Liao tomb find near Tianjin.[60] These forms are variously referred to as "fish-shaped"[61] or "chestnutlike forms with a leaf pendant."[62]

—JMW

74 Pair of Earrings 遼連珠紋金耳環一對

Liao dynasty, 907–1125
Gold
a: H: 3.2 cm W: 2.9 cm (in profile)
b: H: 3.5 cm W: 2.9 cm (in profile)
GI-081.a–.b

A pseudo-granulation band rims the flat bisecting planes of this pair of U-shaped earrings. The beadlike appearance is formed by one continuous piece of material that was evenly pinched and then applied to the body. The earrings appear to have been cast with the beaded design worked into the original mold. A half-circle scallop pattern is punched onto the surface of only one side, with the interior and top planes left undecorated. At the top, a knob resembling a flower bud protrudes. The hook appears as a part of the horizontal plane of the body, as if it were made of the same continuous piece of material and cast in the original mold.

A very similar pair of earrings was excavated from a Liao-period tomb site.[63] Two objects from the same tomb described in the excavation report as "finger sheaths" (probably fingernail protectors, although it is difficult to determine from a photograph how they would have been used) have identical stamplike patterns and pseudo-beading around the contours.[64] Judging from the workmanship, materials, and overall appearance, they were made by the same craftsman, perhaps as a set.   —JMW

75 Two Pendants 遼纏枝花紋金佩飾兩件

Liao dynasty, 907–1125
Gold
1: H: 3.5 cm W: 2.0 cm
2: H: 5.7 cm W: 1.3 cm
GI-100.1–.2

One of these two hollow gold pendants has a narrow octagonal shape, the other is in the form of a teardrop. Both are surmounted by round flattened knobs. Their decoration consists of a flowing flower-and-tendril design, with a background of stamped circle designs characteristic of Liao metalwork. The decoration appears to have been chased into the face of the objects, each of which were made of two pieces joined together. Both pendants are pierced at the top and horizontally through the slight knob as if at one time they were strung together. Both have a reddish tint to their surface which may be a result of the aging of the gold.

A Liao dynasty tomb in Jianping county, Liaoning province, produced two very similar objects.[65] It is difficult to tell from a photograph if that pair is decorated in the same manner as the ones shown here. A pair of dragon-fish earrings very similar to the single earring in the Mengdiexuan collection (cat. no. 71) was found in the same tomb. In 1972 a Liao stone tomb in Chaoyang county was excavated and similar pendants were discovered, but again it is unclear if they are chased or not.[66] Again, an earring similar to one in the Mengdiexuan collection (cat. no. 74) was found in the same tomb.[67]

—JMW

76 Set of Seven Hairpins
遼花卉形金髮簪一組七件

Liao dynasty, 907–1125
Gold
a: H: 9.8 cm W: 5.1 cm
b: H: 8.3 cm W: 5.1 cm
c: H: 8.3 cm W: 4.4 cm
d: H: 9.5 cm W: 4.4 cm
e: H: 9.2 cm W: 5.7 cm
f: H: 9.2 cm W: 5.7 cm
g: H: 8.9 cm W: 6.0 cm
GI-045.a–.g

This set of seven flower-shaped hairpins was made from fine, thin, hammered and chisel-cut gold sheets. The flower blossoms are formed from an assemblage of cutout and chased sheets of gold, attached to the backing by thin gold wire that makes up a portion of the flower stamen. The leaves are attached to the backing by solder, as is the tapered, beaten-flat pin shaft. The flowers are stylized, resembling prunus and chrysanthemum more than other flowers.[68]
—JMW

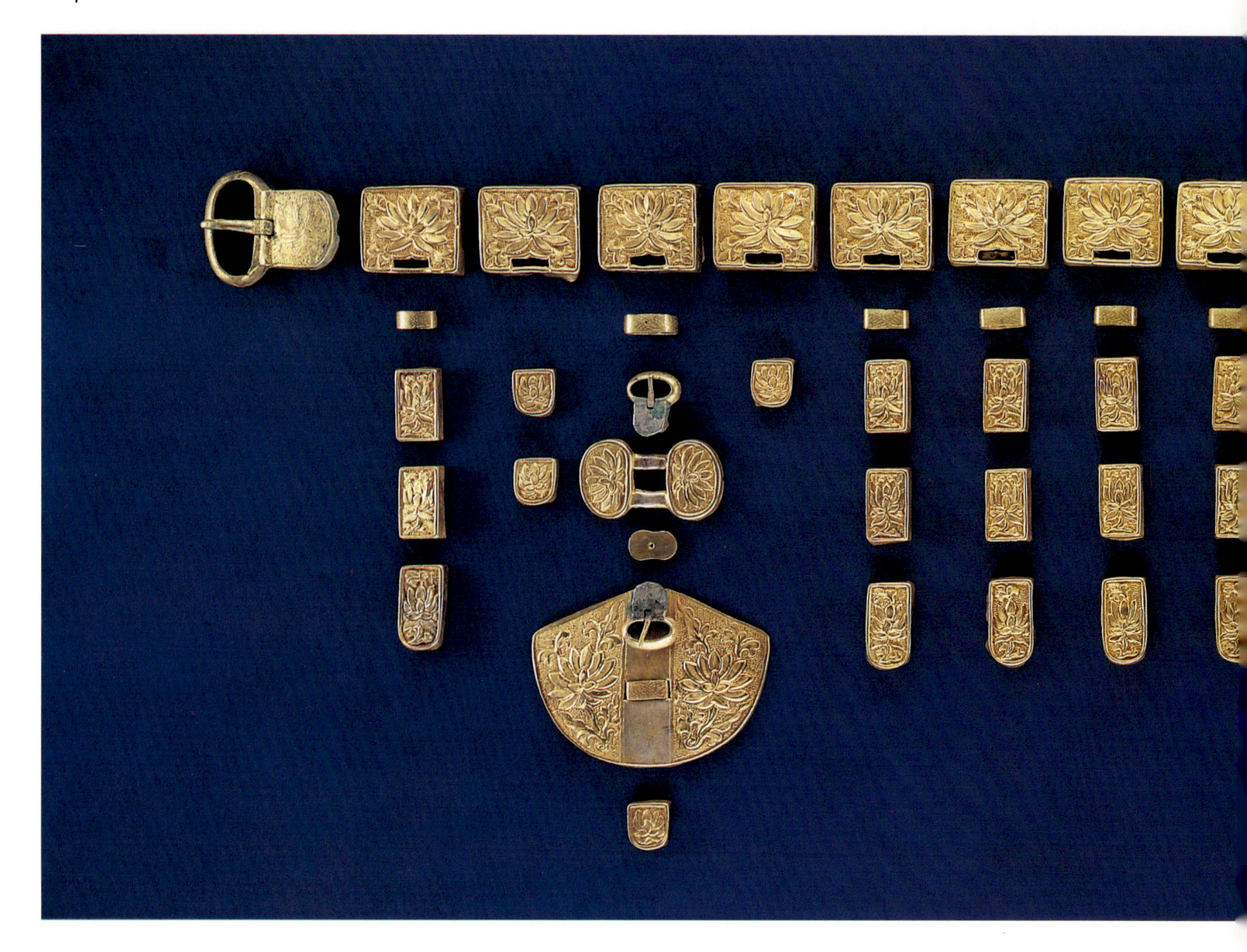

77 Belt Set 遼鎏金牡丹紋銀組帶飾牌

Liao dynasty, 907–1125
Gilded silver and gilded bronze
71 pieces
13 square plaques: H: 3.7 cm W: 4.1 cm
1 large end-plaque: H: 3.8 cm W: 7.0 cm
1 large buckle: H: 4.9 cm W: 6.0 cm
1 small buckle: H: 2.4 cm W: 2.9 cm
8 small U-shaped plaques: H: 1.9 cm W: 1.9 cm
9 large U-shaped plaques: H: 3.8 cm W: 1.9 cm

18 rectangular plaques: H: 2.9 cm W: 1.9 cm
11 loops: 2, H: 1.3 cm W: 2.1 cm
       9, H: 0.6 cm W: 1.9 cm
1 flat kidney-shaped pin: H: 1.3 cm W: 1.9 cm
5 heart-shaped plaques: H: 3.2 cm W: 2.8 cm
1 double-headed plaque: H: 3.2 cm W: 6.0 cm
1 pocket: H: 7.6 cm W: 12.4 cm
1 pocket buckle: H: 2.4 cm W: 2.9 cm
BP-014.1–.71

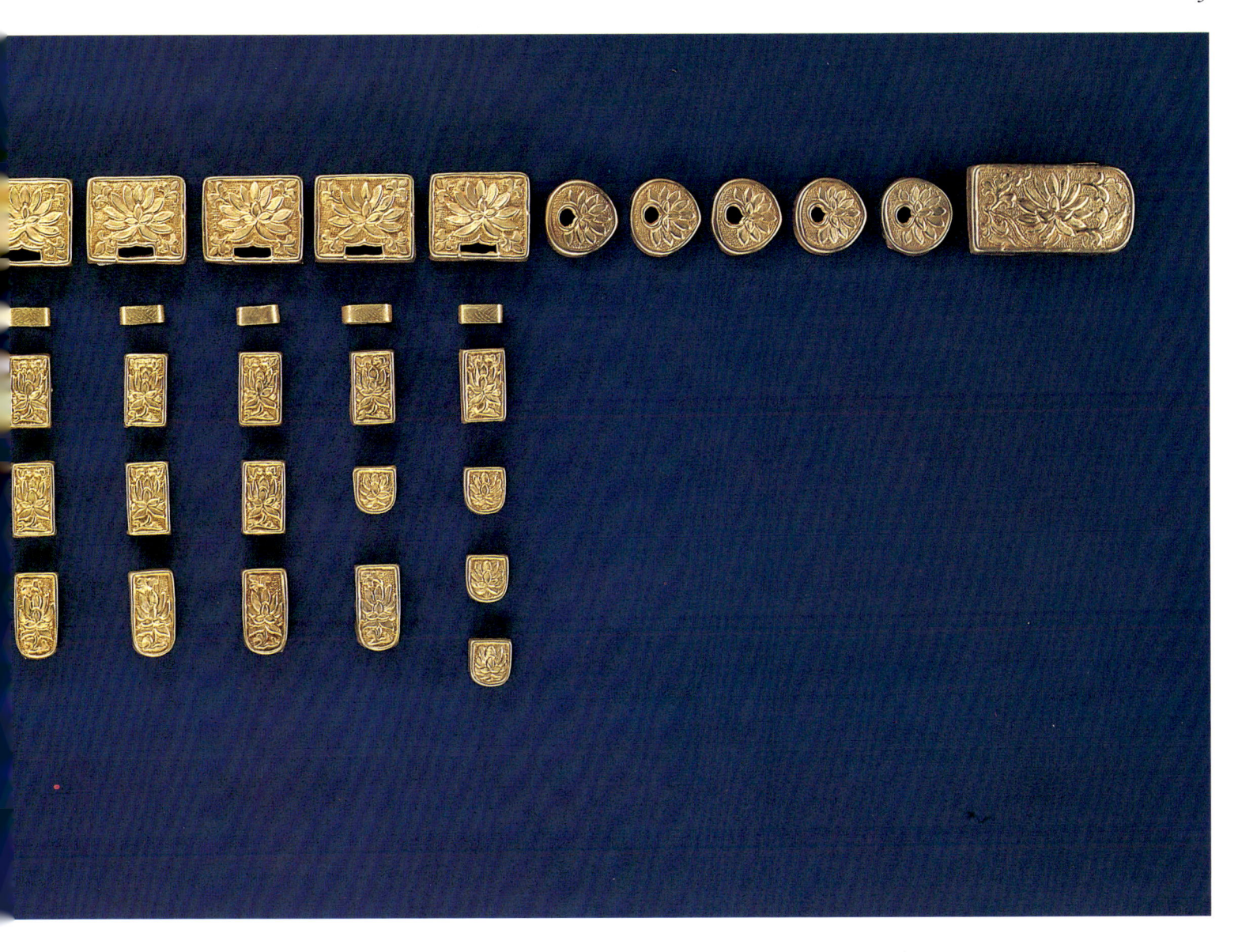

Each plaque is made of gilded silver employing the techniques of repoussé and chasing. The central design is a peony motif with a ring-punched background.

The loops and buckles are bronze with gilding. The design on these elements was chased into the surface prior to gilding and lacks the depth of the repoussé designs on the plaques.

The arrangement of the plaques can be reconstructed, thanks to archaeological evidence.[69] The square plaques served as the main body of the belt, with decorative sashes hanging off the lower portion through the openings at their bases.

The larger square plaques each have four posts that were used as attachment devices for the silver backing plate. The rectangular and U-shaped plaques have two posts each to hold the silver backing onto the face; only a few backings for these plaques remain. The backings on these, unlike those on the square plaques, are of minimal construction, with simple flat tabs holding the front to the belt.

—JMW

78 Belt Set 遼鎏金花卉鳳紋銀組帶飾牌

Liao dynasty, 907–1125
Gilded silver
11 pieces
9 square plaques: H: 3.9 cm W: 4.2 cm
2 tabs: H: 10.6 cm W: 4.7 cm
BP-016.1–.11

Floral and phoenix designs decorate this partial belt set of gilt silver. The thin sheets of silver were worked in repoussé with chasing defining the details of feathers and leaves. The background is filled with circular punch designs typical of Liao metalwork. Each of the plaques is perforated by a horizontal slit at its base. Each vertical tab is perforated at the top by the same type and size of opening. The vertical plaques clearly hung down from the square plaques, but whether or not there were additional vertical plaques is difficult to say.

The phoenix is an image frequently associated with the empress, which raises the question of whether these belts were worn by both men and women. It seems from the evidence found in paintings and from archaeological evidence that women and men both wore leather belts with attached plaques.[70] It is therefore possible that this belt set with a phoenix design belonged to a woman.

—JMW

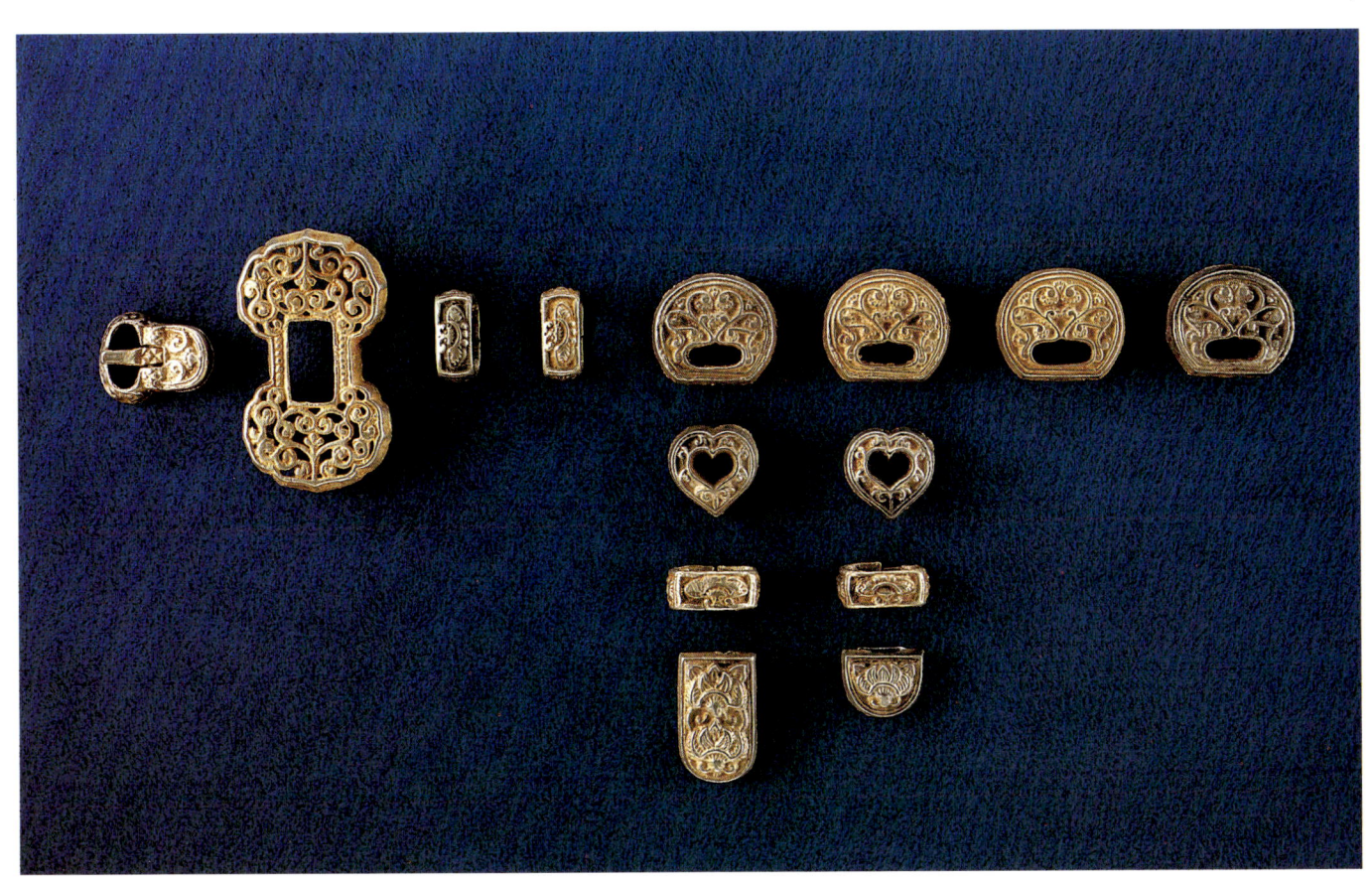

79 Belt Set 遼鎏金蝙蝠花卉紋銀組帶飾

Liao dynasty, 907–1125
Gilded silver
14 pieces
4 loops: H: 0.6 cm W: 1.6 cm
1 buckle: H: 1.9 cm W: 2.4 cm
2 heart-shaped plaques: H: 1.6 cm W: 1.6 cm
4 round pierced plaques: H: 1.9 cm W: 2.4 cm
1 large pierced fitting: H: 4.8 cm W: 2.7 cm
2 belt ends: H: 1.6 cm W: 2.4 cm
             H: 1.6 cm W: 1.3 cm
BP-013.1–.14

This belt set, cast in silver and then gilded, combines a floral design with a flying-bat motif. The floral design on the four rounded plaques, two heart-shaped plaques, and belt buckle consists of a raised linear arabesque pattern. The large fitting was cast and pierced with scroll patterning. The four loops were cast flat, shaped into loops, and then soldered onto the reverse side. All four have a bat design; the larger fitting has two bats.

Remnants of leather are visible in the smaller endpiece and in the buckle. Each of the plaques, but not the buckle, has three posts that would have held the leather and silver backing in place. The exact order of the pieces in this belt is not known, but it is clear that they were held together by a leather belt. —JMW

80 Belt Set 遼鎏金花卉紋銀組帶飾

Liao dynasty, 907–1125
Gilded silver
21 pieces
1 buckle: H: 4.9 cm W: 6.1 cm
4 round plaques: H: 4.0 cm W: 4.7 cm
2 teardrop plaques: H: 3.5 cm W: 3.0 cm
1 large belt end: H: 3.8 cm W: 6.5 cm
4 small tabs: H: 2.1 cm W: 1.8 cm
3 large tabs: H: 3.6 cm W: 1.9 cm
2 small buckles: H: 2.9 cm W: 2.4 cm
2 small rings: H: 0.3 cm W: 2.0 cm
2 horizontal tabs: H: 3.1 cm W: 7.7 cm
BP-015.1–.21

This twenty-one-piece belt set is made of hammered silver repoussé with gilt surfaces depicting a beautiful four-petalled flower motif. The buckles are made of gilt bronze, for strength, with a similar surface pattern but cast rather than repoussé. The floral decoration has been chased to highlight the details of leaves and petals on the flowers. The background is evenly punched with small circular designs that are a hallmark of Liao metalwork. Each plaque has two thin wires soldered to the back of the interior of the plaque. Some of the plaques retain a thin sheet of silver that was used as a backing device to hold the plaque to a leather belt. The two small buckles contain some traces of the original leather backing at their attachment point.

This type of belt has been found in Inner Mongolia in Liao dynasty tombs and is said to have entered China through the influence of Turkic-speaking people.[71] A variety of different configurations, for instance the horizontal plaques on this set, can be noted among these belt sets and may indicate different levels of status or rank.[72] Certainly those found in royal tombs, such as the tomb of Princess Chenguo in Liaoning, help establish an association with high rank.[73]

—JMW

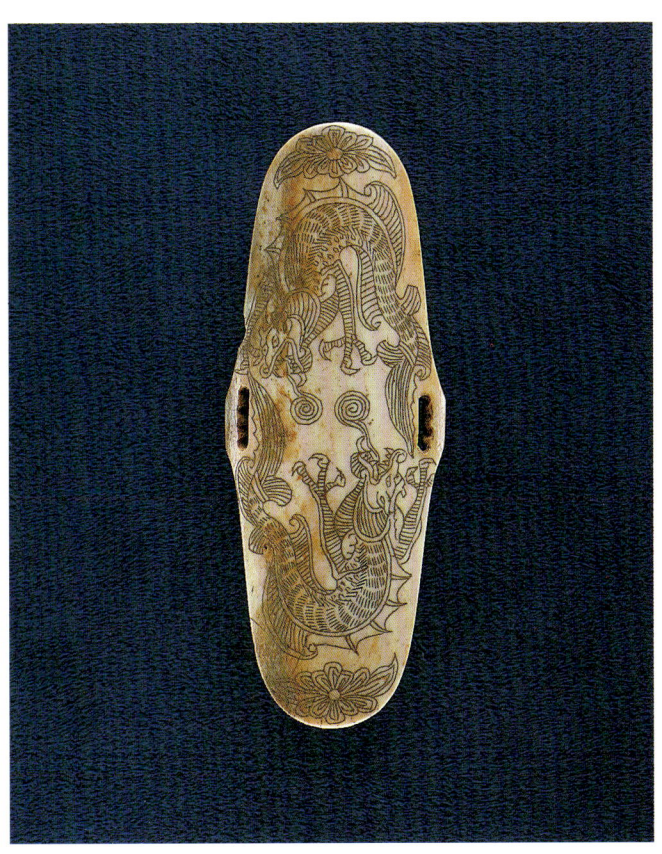

81 Wrist Protector
遼放鷹用瑪瑙腕飾

Liao dynasty, 10th century
Agate
H: 9.2 cm W: 4.4 cm
BP-001

82 Wrist Protector
遼放鷹用雙龍紋骨製腕飾

Liao dynasty, 10th century
Bone
H: 9.5 cm W: 3.8 cm
BP-009

These two wrist protectors of oblong and slightly convex shape are made of natural materials. The agate protector was carved and polished to expose the natural inclusions in the stone and to bring out its inherent beauty. The bone protector is decorated on the top with an etched design of two swirling, three-clawed, fire-breathing, scaly dragons.

Both are pierced on each side at the point of greatest width. The vertical holes appear to have been made by a series of linked drilled holes. A leather or cloth band would have been threaded through these slits and then tied or laced onto a falconer's wrist. The function of such rests was primarily to protect the falconer's wrist from the hawk's talons; the rests may have been covered with leather or another material on which the hawk could land and be carried.[74] There is evidence that the practice of falconry required a number of special ornaments, for both the bird and the falconer.[75] The birds and the practice of hunting with falcons are discussed briefly in catalogue number 53. Falcons appear to have been introduced into China, at least during Tang times, from the north, from both Manchuria and Korea, although hunting birds were also imported from farther west, including Dunhuang and Shaanxi.[76]   —JMW

Notes

1. *Wenwu*, 1981.11, pp. 1–11, illus. nos. 5 and 6 from tomb 2, the Han tomb at Ganchuan in Hanjiang, Jiangsu province.

2. A pierced plaque from a northern Yan grave dated to the early 5th century in Liaoning province shows a similar type of granulation technique, see *Wenwu*, 1973.3, pp. 2–19. A pierced plaque from an early Jin tomb in Dunhuang dated to A.D. 369 is shown in *Kaogu*, 1974.3, pp. 191–99, illus. no. 3. The northern Yan grave piece was found with a sheet of beaten gold that was clearly the original backing for the plaque, but it is pierced in a way that indicates it may have been sewn onto the front plaque. The plaque from Dunhuang, found close to the deceased's head, has no apparent backing. There are several similar plaques in western collections, for example see Bo Gyllensvard, *Chinese Gold and Silver in the Carl Kempe Collection*, pp. 77–78, nos. 17, 18, 20. See also Annette L. Juliano, *Art of the Six Dynasties: Centuries of Change and Innovation*, p. 32, pl. 10. An interesting gilt plaque is illustrated in Yoshito Harada, *Chinese Dress and Personal Ornaments in the Han and Six Dynasties*, p. 117, fig. 30.

3. For a description, see *Gems of China's Cultural Relics 1993*, pls. 113, 114, and p. 311. The Western Han piece comes from Xinjiang and the Western Jin buckle from Hunan.

4. Edward H. Schafer, *The Golden Peaches of Samarkand: A Study of T'ang Exotics*, pp. 222–23.

5. See description of loop-in-loop chains in the section on metalworking in this catalogue, p. 47. A few of these loops may be later additions, as they are not strip-twisted.

6. See description of strip-twisted wire in the metalworking section, p. 46.

7. See glossary for definition of hard solder.

8. *Wenwu*, 1992.9, p. 9, fig. 26. For a good color photograph see *Chugoku no kingin garasu*, no. 17.

9. For a full discussion of the metal content in the belt set see *Kaogu xuebao*, 1959.4, pp. 91–95. The tests, which now appear to have been flawed, indicated that the belt plaques were aluminum; further research has proven this to be inaccurate. See Jan Fontein and Tung Wu, *Unearthing China's Past*, p. 144.

10. The report of the excavation of the site at Yixing can be found in *Kaogu xuebao*, 1957.4, pp. 86–106.

11. See Roger Goepper and Roderick Whitfield, *Treasures from Korea*. Korean belt sets have been seen at a recent auction, see *Korean Works of Art*.

12. For a suggested arrangement of plaques and danglers see *Wenwu*, 1994.1, p. 62.

13. Ryoichi Hayashi, *The Silk Road and the Shoso-in*, pl. 27. See also Cecile Beurdeley, *Sur les routes de la soie*, p. 157, fig. 164. This textile is described as Tang, but its decoration derives totally from western sources, and it may even be an import from the West.

14. Beurdeley, *Sur les routes de la soie*, p. 125, fig. 121, and p. 126, fig. 123.

15. I am most grateful to Dr. Noël Adams of London for her assistance in researching this and the following belt set (cat. no. 54). The stylistic relationship of these belt mounts to certain Byzantine and Sasanian sword and belt fittings of the sixth and seventh centuries A.D. is the subject of a forthcoming study by Dr. Adams—ECB.

16. *Kaogu yu Wenwu*, 1993.6, p. 50, illus 4, no. 3.

17. *British Rail Pension Trust*, no. 33.

18. Sotheby's auction catalogue (London, 8 June 1993), no. 127. This set, originally part of the collection of Eugene Bernat, is now in the collection of S. Bernstein. See S. Bernstein, *Ritual and Belief: Chinese Jade and Related Arts*, vol. 3, no. 28.

19. *Zui Tō no bijutsu*, p. 35, figs. 66–67.

20. Acc. nos. V-3875 and V-3874.

21. Jessica Rawson and Emma C. Bunker, *Ancient Chinese and Ordos Bronzes*, no. 146. Compare with similar oval plaques in another Tang belt set, see *Wenwu yu kaogu lunji*, p. 309, fig. 11.

22. Edward H. Schafer, *The Golden Peaches of Samarkand*, p. 101.

23. *Wenwu*, 1978.11, pp. 11–25, illus. 1, no. 2.

24. For a Yuan-period belt-end found in Jiangsu province and now in the Nanjing Provincial Museum, see Yang Boda, ed., *Zhongguo meishu quanji*, no. 133.

25. Zhou Xun and Gao Chunming, *5000 Years of Chinese Costumes*, p. 93.

26. Edward H. Schafer, *The Golden Peaches of Samarkand*, pp. 92–104.

27. There are legends concerning an earlier form of falconry having been practiced in the seventh-century B.C. state of Chu, although as Edward Schafer points out, "[i]t may even be, then, that the early medieval tradition about the hawking of King Wen rested on a solid foundation, though it would be surprising to find the first Chinese falconers in a region so remote from the steppes, the supposed homeland of the art." Edward H. Schafer, "Falconry in T'ang Times," p. 296.

28. For a treatment of belt mounts in the Tang see *The Silk Road: Treasures of Tang China*.

29. For drawings of stone figures dating from the 6th to 10th centuries A.D. see S. A. Pietneva, ed., *Arkheologiya SSSR*, 1981, pp. 29, 100, 127–28. I am most grateful to Dr. Noël Adams for this reference—ECB.

30. Wang Chong of the Eastern Han, *Shuaixing*, Natural Disposition, in *Lunheng*, Disquisitions.

31. *Kaogu*, 1986.5, color pl. 8, no. 1.

32. Wu Jun (Tang), poem *Guiyuan*, The grievance of a lady.

33. Wang Bo (Tang), *Shang Huangfu Changbo qi*, To Huangfu Changbo.

34. Translated by Brenda Li and Kenneth Chu.

35. Sueji Umehara, *Tokyo taikan*, vol. 2, pls. 68–70.

36. Ryoichi Hayashi, *The Silk Road and the Shoso-in*, p. 177, pl. 206.

37. *Wenwu*, 1982.11, p. 40, illus. no. 12. A better illustration of the same hairpins can be found in *Tangdai jinyin qi*, pl. 266, description p. 189.

38. *Wenbo* 48, no. 3 (1992), p. 29.

39. *Kaogu yu wenwu*, 1982.1, p. 47, illus. no. 5.

40. Zhou Xun and Gao Chunming, *Zhongguo lidai funu jiangshi*, p. 48.

41. *Kaogu yu wenwu*, 1982.1, p. 47, illus. 5, nos. 1–7, and pl. 9, no. 2.

42. *Wenwu*, 1980.8, p. 41, pl. 6, no. 1.

43. Zhou Xun and Gao Chunming, *Zhongguo lidai funu jiangshi*. For a discussion of Han hairpins see p. 55. Illustration of the different types of hairpins and the materials used is on pp. 70–71.

44. Bo Gyllensvard, *Chinese Gold and Silver in the Carl Kempe Collection*, p. 217, no. 142.

45. *Wenwu*, 1980.5, pl. 4, no. 5.

46. *Kaogu*, 1985.2, pl. 5, no. 9.

47. Christian Deydier, *Imperial Gold from Ancient China*, p. 30, no. 7.

48. *Wenwu*, 1986.5, pl. 4, and *Wenwu*, 1980.5, pl. 4, no. 5.

49. For a complete chart of comb shapes and materials see Zhou Xun and Gao Chunming, *Zhongguo lidai funu jiangshi*, pp. 80–81.

50. Hugh Tait, ed., *Jewelry, 7000 Years*, p. 115. It is noted that a necklace was found in a Sui tomb constructed in 608.

51. *The Arts of the T'ang Dynasty*, p. 112, no. 306. Described as a "torque," this necklace is said to be of filigree work.

52. For example, see the headdress and earring set from tomb 4, Xigoupan, Jungar banner, Yikezhao league of Inner Mongolia in Adam T. Kessler, *Empires Beyond the Great Wall: The Heritage of Genghis Khan*, p. 62, fig. 35.

53. Patricia Berger, "China," in *Beauty, Wealth, and Power: Jewels and Ornaments of Asia*, p. 45.

54. Zhou Xun and Gao Chunming, *Zhongguo lidai funu jiangshi*, p. 271.

55. C. A. S. Williams, *Outlines of Chinese Symbolism and Art Motives*, p. 137.

56. *Kaogu*, 1960.2, pl. 3, no. 4. See also *Kaogu*, 1986.10, pp. 922–25, illus. 5, no. 27. For a good color photograph see Zhou Xun and Gao Chunming, *Zhongguo lidai funu jiangshi*, p. 154, no. 188.

57. Rebus expert Terese Tse Bartholomew shared with me her opinion that rebuses generally do not account for symbolism in ornament prior to the Ming period. However, literary references and word puns do make up symbolic imagery in other art forms, including painting, as early as the Song dynasty—JMW.

58. *Beifang wenwu*, 1992.3, pp. 36–41, illus. 4, no. 6. Zhao Wengang, "Tianjinshi Jixian Yingfangcun Liaomu" (The Liao dynasty tomb in Yingfang village, Ji county of Hebei province).

59. *Wenwu*, 1977.4, pp. 27–37, illus. no. 3. "Cong chushi wenwu kau Heilongjiang dichu de Jin dai shehui" (The society of Chin dynasty in Heilungkiang area in the light of archaeological finds). For a good color photograph see Zhou Xun and Gao Chunming, *Zhongguo lidai funu jiangshi*, p. 154, no. 190.

60. *Beifang wenwu*, 1992.3, pp. 36–41, illus. 4, no. 6.

61. Ibid., p. 38.

62. *Wenwu*, 1977.4, p. 30.

63. Xiang Chuansong, "Keshike tengqi erba di Liao mu," *Nei Menggu wenwu kaogu* 3, pp. 80–90; for illustration see pl. 5, no. 3.

64. Ibid., pl. 5, no. 2.

65. *Kaogu*, 1960.2, pp. 15–24, pl. 3, no. 4.

66. *Wenwu*, 1980.12, pp. 17–26, p. 21, illus. 16, nos. 2–4.

67. Ibid., p. 21, no. 5.

68. A set of three similar hairpins was illustrated in Christian Deydier, *Imperial Gold from Ancient China*, pp. 44–45. A similar set of six can be found on pp. 46–47 of the same catalogue.

69. *Wenwu*, 1987.11, pp. 4–24, 29–35.

70. *Exhibition of Cultural Relics from the Tomb of Princess Chenguo of the State of Liao*, n.p. See also Zhou Xun and Gao Chunming, *5000 Years of Chinese Costumes*, pp. 93, 111.

71. Sun Ji, "Lun jinnian Neimenggu chushi de Tujue yu Tujueshi jinyin qi" (The gold and silver wares of Turk and Turk styles unearthed in Inner Mongolia in Recent Years), *Wenwu*, 1993.8, pp. 48–58, in Chinese.

72. Ibid., p. 54.

73. *Exhibition of Cultural Relics from the Tomb of Princess Chenguo of the State of Liao*, n.p.

74. See Edward H. Schafer, "Falconry in T'ang Times," p. 314, "Falconers wear a heavy glove or wristlet to protect their arm from the charp (*sic*) talons of the hawk." Schafer further explains that the Chinese *gou* or wristlet was usually made of leather, and sometimes decorated, a fact he draws from the ninth-century writings of Lu Guimeng.

75. Edward H. Schafer, *The Golden Peaches of Samarkand*, p. 95, ". . . they provided their goshawks with tail bells of jade, gold, and chased metals, and their sparrow hawks with embroidered collars. All their hunting birds were fitted with jesses of leather or green silk or clouded brocade, leashes with jade swivels, gilded perches and carved and painted cages."

76. Ibid., p. 94.

Late Period

Song Dynasty, 960–1279

through

Ming Dynasty, 1368–1644

83 Hairpin 宋鎏金雙鳳花卉紋銀髮簪

Song dynasty, 960–1279
Gilded silver
L: 19.1 cm W: 12.4 cm
GI-079

A pair of flying phoenixes in fine repoussé work tops this large, flat, silver pin with gilding. The bodies, wings, and tails of both birds are elaborately chased, creating different levels of texture. The tails curl in two directions, mingling with an openwork leaf-and-flower pattern. The top is mounted to the tine, with the birds' heads facing down, by means of a securely attached round silver wire. To further secure it, the tine is split at the top and curls across the back of the plaque. The back of the plaque is reinforced with a round stiff wire that has been attached to the plaque at four points with fine silver wire. This method of attachment differs from earlier methods of soldering the tine directly to the decorated portion, and from the equally common technique of creating the top and the tine from the same piece of metal.

The symbolism of the phoenix has a long history in China. An imaginary bird, the phoenix is depicted in a variety of ways and is almost always entirely benevolent. It is an element that is frequently seen on ladies' hair ornaments and is often associated with the empress.[1]

—JMW

84 Hairpins 宋鎏金花果雙鴨紋銀髮簪三件

Song dynasty, 960–1279
Gilded silver
1: H: 15.9 cm W: 2.9 cm
2: H: 14.3 cm W: 3.2 cm
3: H: 14.3 cm W: 2.7 cm
GI-060.1–.3

High repoussé relief with hammered and chased details highlight this trio of silver-gilt hairpins with bird, flower, and fruit designs. The tines are flat; chased-dot floral patterns run down the face of the tines of numbers 1 and 3.

A four-character inscription on the largest pin (number 1) reads *Yin hua yin zao,* meaning Yinhua made this silver pin. The decoration on this pin, shown here in the center, includes a pair of lychee fruits at the top and a six-petalled flower blossom at the base. The head of the pin was probably first worked in repoussé and then chased to produce the details. Six leaves surround the fruit and flower decoration. The tine is attached to a cutout backing which has been soldered to the face. The top of the tine is wrapped over the top of the face and curls back on itself.

The pin at the right was constructed in an identical fashion. The decoration here consists of a pair of melons, with vine and leaf wrapping over and above the central design. Below the melons is a five-petalled blossom. The whole design is encircled by leaves.

The pin on the left is of a slightly different construction, with the tine soldered directly onto the backing. The chased and repoussé decoration is slightly shallower than on the other two pins. The orientation of the central design appears to be reversed, with a pair of ducks, heads toward the tines and beak to beak, resting on a lotus leaf. The tine is undecorated.

This kind of repoussé work, as well as the motifs, is frequently associated with Song and Yuan metalwork, and similar hairpins have been found in diverse areas, including Hunan and Inner Mongolia.[2] There are several similar examples of beaten-silver work in the collection of Paul Singer.[3]

—JMW

85 Set of Hairpins
宋鎏金龍雲紋銀髮簪一組十一件及花形銀髮飾八件

Song dynasty, 960–1279
Gilded silver
19 pieces
Hairpins (two sizes):
1–3: L: 20.3 cm W: 5.1 cm D: 2.5 cm
4–11: L: 23.2 cm W: 5.1 cm D: 1.3 cm
Flowers: D: 1.3 cm
GI-038.1–.19

This large set of hairpins is made up of eight long-tined pins, three shorter-tined pins with slightly different decoration, and eight loose flower-shaped buttons. The top of each of the pins consists of two separate panels attached to each other at two points with gilt-silver wire. These flat, cutout panels are pierced and chased and shaped like clouds. The decoration on the central roundel consists of two dragons with wide gaping mouths entwined in combat. They are winged, with scaly bodies and stiff, flame-shaped manes running down their backs. The central panels are joined to the long vertical panel of punched floral design with three gilt-silver wires. The vertical panel is attached to the flat backing by means of soldering.

The method of construction and basic motifs are identical on the three shorter pins shown here on the far left and the two pins on the far-right side of the arrangement. The dragon design on the smaller pins is slightly softer and the color of the gilding is lighter.

The eight flowers are made up of three separate layers: a broad, eight-petalled, lotus-shaped base, pierced and chased; a six-petalled piece that is chased and slightly cut out to permit the tips to pull up; and a raised, six-petalled flower.

Complete hairpin sets are rare. Such elaborate head decoration is consistent with the crown and hair decorations of the Song court.

—JMW

86 Hairpin 宋鎏金花卉紋銀髮簪

Song dynasty, 960–1279
Gilded silver
H: 15.6 cm W: 24.8 cm D: 3.5 cm (flower)
GI-043

The decoration of this large hairpin consists of nine flowers mounted on a horizontal flat band that ends on either side in an upward spiral. Each flower has two parts: the first is a sixteen-petalled outer flower which is edged by a double border of simulated beading that encircles a six-petalled cutout design; the second is a twenty-four-petalled flower with a large central boss that has been chased to give a textured appearance.

The flowers were probably hammered into a die and then chased. They are attached to the horizontal bar by a flat tab attached to the back of each flower, then further secured with thin round wire that anchors the flowers to the band.

A similar silver hairpin with round flowers was excavated in Zhejiang province.[4] *Mingqi,* or tomb figures, from as early as the Han period are shown wearing this type of hair ornament.[5] —JMW

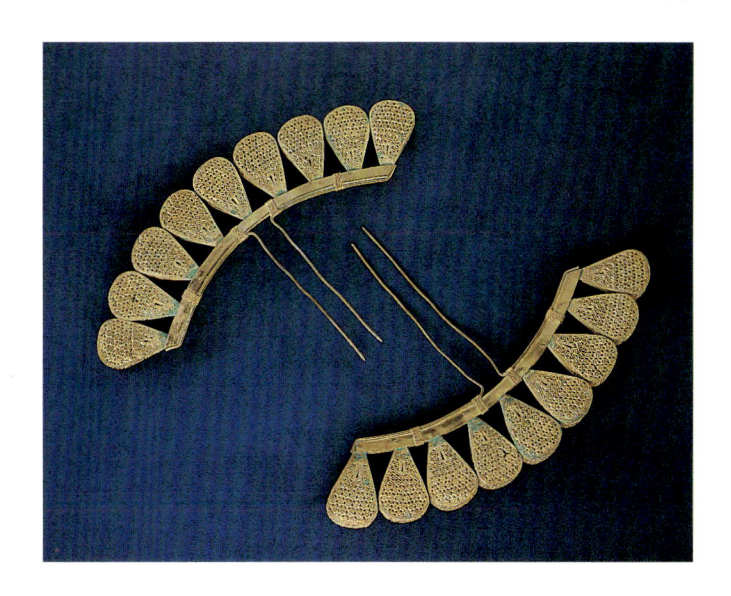

87 Pair of Diadems
宋金銀合金花卉紋橫枝式髮釵一對

Song dynasty, 960–1279
Gold and silver alloy
a: H: 12.7 cm W: 19.7 cm D: 1.3 cm
b: H: 14.6 cm W: 19.7 cm D: 1.3 cm
GI-037.a–.b

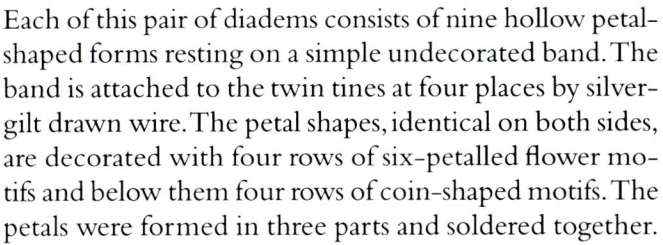

Each of this pair of diadems consists of nine hollow petal-shaped forms resting on a simple undecorated band. The band is attached to the twin tines at four places by silver-gilt drawn wire. The petal shapes, identical on both sides, are decorated with four rows of six-petalled flower motifs and below them four rows of coin-shaped motifs. The petals were formed in three parts and soldered together.

Two similar single diadems, catalogue numbers 88 and 89, although not a pair, have considerably more elaborate bases. These two appear to be of gold and silver alloy, with the intricate openwork having been created by a punch technique. The tines on both of these diadems are of hammered, instead of drawn, wire.

A number of Song dynasty examples of similar construction have been found in Zhejiang province.[6] One, with eight silver petals, is single-tined and inscribed.

—JMW

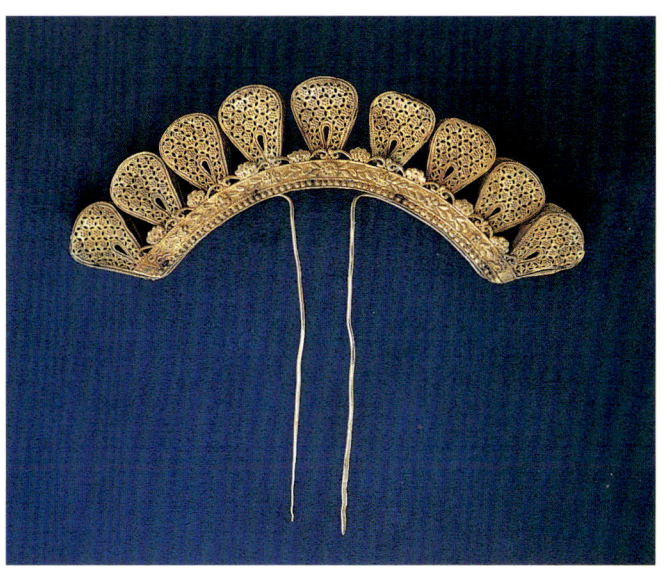

88 Diadem
宋金銀合金花卉紋橫枝式髮釵

Song dynasty, 960–1279
Gold and silver alloy
H: 14.6 cm W: 16.2 cm D: 1.3 cm
GI-053

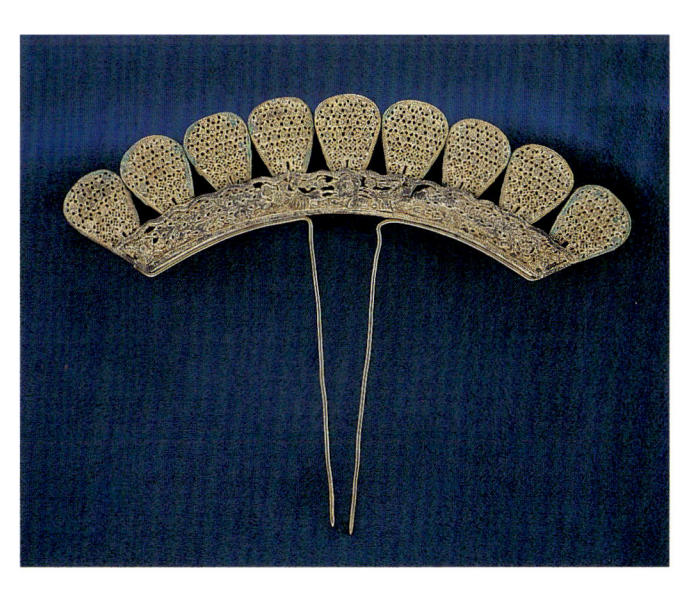

89 Diadem
宋金銀合金花卉紋橫枝式髮釵

Song dynasty, 960–1279
Gold and silver alloy
H: 13.0 cm W: 19.4 cm D: 1.3 cm
GI-085

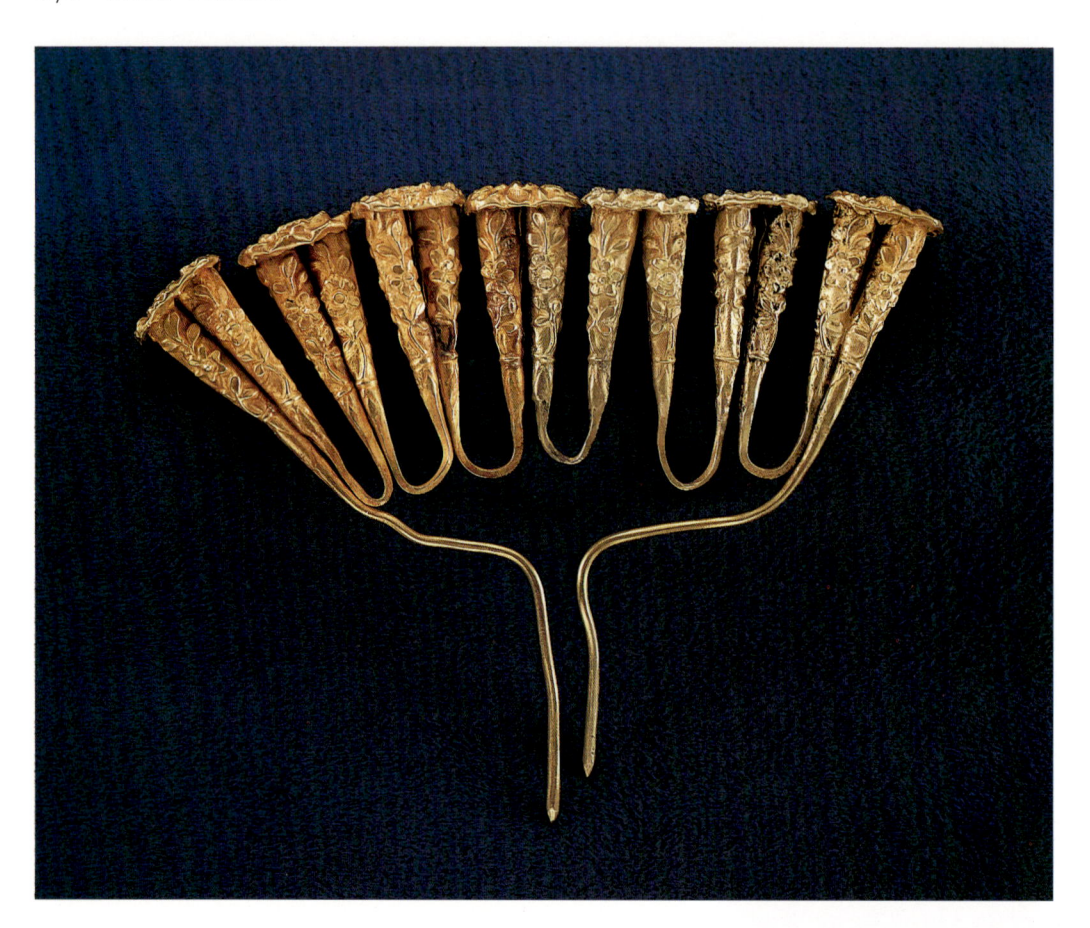

90 Diadem 宋或元花卉紋橫枝式金髮釵

Song or Yuan dynasty, 13th–14th century
Gold
H: 8.9 cm W: 11.4 cm
GI-089

This diadem consists of two tines and seven cone-shaped forms, each capped with thin, repoussé flower designs. Each tine develops into a cone shape, which is attached by the cap and soldering to another cone. This leads down in a U-shape to the next pair of cones. The three U-shaped forms on the right in this illustration are slightly lighter in color than the three on the left, perhaps an intentional design element, but more likely a difference in the gold alloys.

Four different flower designs are worked into the caps. They are flowers of the four seasons: peony (spring), lotus (summer), chrysanthemum (autumn), and plum (winter).[7]

Archaeological evidence points to the development of this type of pin beginning in the Song dynasty and continuing through the Yuan dynasty.[8] Another pin from the Mengdiexuan collection has a slightly different bar-like base (cat. no. 90a).　　　　　　　　　—JMW

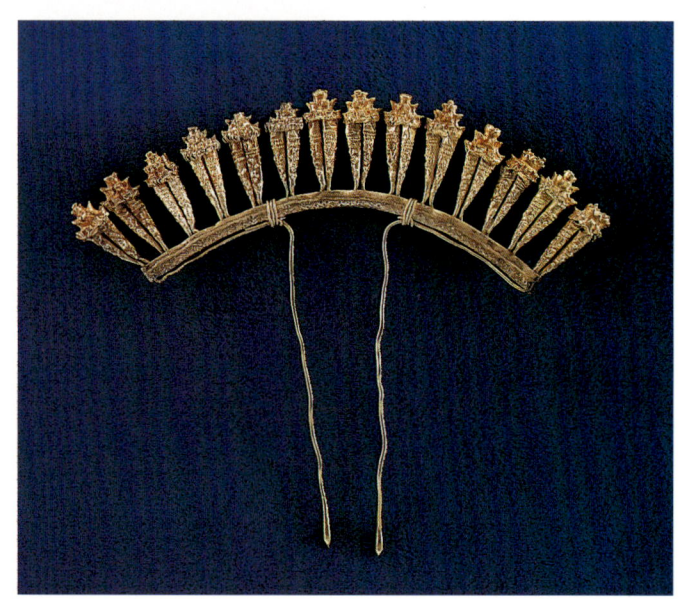

90a. Gold diadem (GI-080).
宋或元花卉紋橫枝式金髮釵

91 Hairpin 宋靈芝紋金髮簪

Song dynasty, 960–1279
Gold
L: 7.0 cm
L: 24.9 cm (with wooden pin, modern addition)
W: 3.3 cm
GI-111

This *lingzhi*-shaped hairpin is made of delicately wrapped and twisted gold wire combined with areas of flat cloisons and open areas. The central floral motif on the head of the hairpin consists of three levels combining flat, leaf-shaped cloisons with granulation around the edges of the design and wire in the central portion. The overall effect is a flowing form that appears quite light. Both sides of the hairpin are identical. It is very likely that the leaf-shaped cloisons were originally filled with stones or enamel.

The *lingzhi* shape is frequently seen as a decorative motif in painting, textiles, and ornaments. The *lingzhi*, or plant of immortality, is a fungus which is frequently pictured in a Daoist context and is associated with immortals. Its appearance is also believed to be a sign of a virtuous ruler.[9]

—JMW

92 Hairpin 宋鳳紋金髮簪

Song dynasty, 960–1279
Gold
L: 15.9 cm H: 3.8 cm (phoenix) W: 4.1 cm (phoenix)
GI-088

An elaborately decorated phoenix tops this flat, single-tined hairpin. The tine is tapered, with incised floral decoration filling approximately one-half of the flat surface from the head of the pin. The phoenix decoration has been applied to the tine by soldering. The mythical bird is constructed from two repoussé pieces that have been soldered together, probably prior to attachment to the tine. A fine vertical solder line can be traced from the base of the phoenix up through the chest and head of the bird. The body has been thoroughly chased, creating a beautiful sculptural surface.

A similar two-tined phoenix hairpin was discovered in an eleventh- to twelfth-century excavation in Shaanxi province in 1974.[10] A single-tined dragon hairpin with the same profile orientation to the top of the pin is in the collection of the Shanghai Museum.[11] Two pairs of phoenix-topped hairpins were found in tombs in Jiangxi and Hubei.[12] Phoenix-headed pins appear to have occurred commonly in pairs and became popular as early as the Six Dynasties period.[13]   —JMW

93 Hairpin 宋西王母乘鳳金髮簪

Song dynasty, 960–1279
Gold
L: 13.3 cm H: 2.5 cm
GI-047

This is a flat-tined hairpin, its top mounted flush with a tine of beaten gold. The head of the pin is set horizontally and depicts a figure, perhaps the Queen Mother of the West, seated on a phoenix and holding a container in her left hand. The head has been decorated using a combination of highly detailed repoussé work and careful chasing to define the delicate features of the figure. The tendrils of the figure's scarves wrap around its back and shoulder. The back of the decoration has been soldered onto the relatively thick front. The tine was soldered onto the backing, forming a double layer.

The Queen Mother of the West was a popular subject in art from the Han period through the Tang period, and later.[14]

—JMW

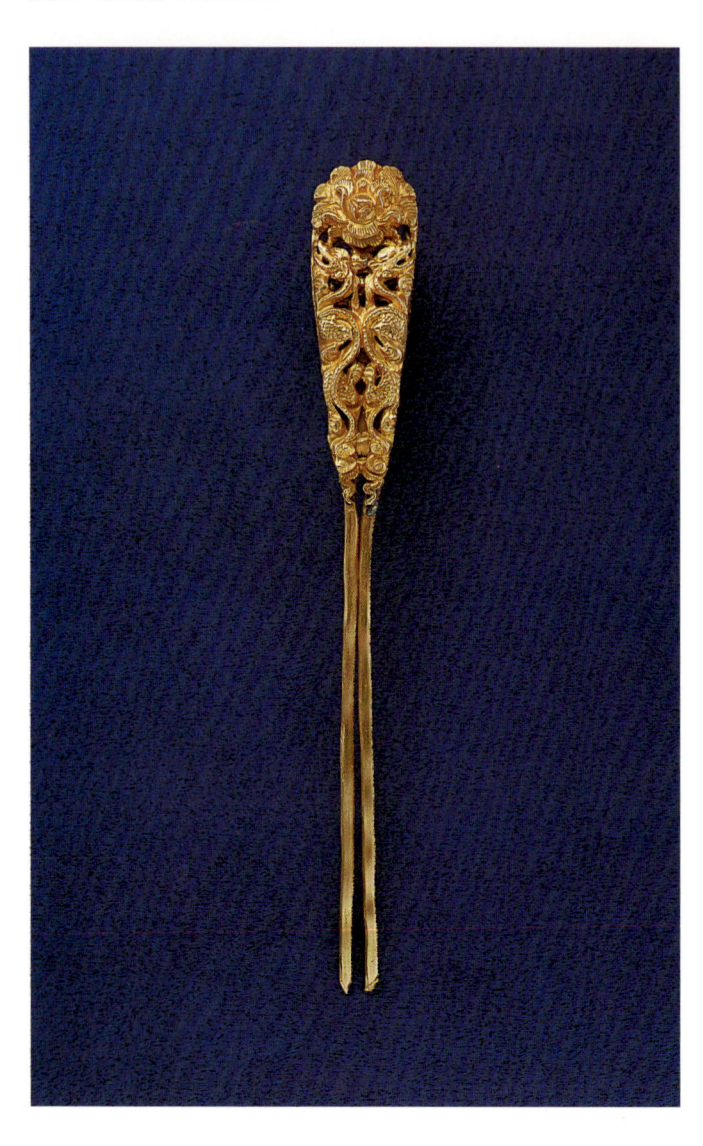

94 Hairpin   宋牡丹蟠龍紋金髮簪

Song dynasty, 960–1279
Gold
H: 15.6 cm W: 2.1 cm
GI-086

Two coiling dragons topped by a peony blossom decorate this two-tined hairpin. The dragons and peony are well modelled and defined by chasing that emphasizes their shapes and contours.

The decorated face of the pin has been worked separately and soldered onto a thin, cutout piece of gold. This piece and the tines appear to have been beaten from the same sheet of gold. The tines are slightly elliptical, with sharp points.

The use of floral motifs in Song design, from jewelry to architectural ornament, is often attributed to the influence of Buddhism in China.[15]   —JMW

95 Two Hairpins 宋花卉紋金髮簪兩件

Song dynasty, 960–1279
Gold
a: H: 15.6 cm W: 1.6 cm
b: H: 20.6 cm W: 1.6 cm
GI-046.a–.b

These gold hairpins with floral designs were made using a repoussé technique, probably begun while the gold sheet was flat. The sheet was then wrapped around a core and additional chasing done. The hairpin was finally soldered shut. The two-tined hairpin is capped with a broad chrysanthemum-shaped flower, also repoussé, with four wire attachments extending onto the pin. The two main portions, made separately and soldered together along the top two inches, have long undecorated tines which appear to be hollow.

The decoration on the top of the two-tined pin is a well-articulated floral motif representing blossoms of the four seasons: peony, chrysanthemum, plum, and magnolia. The symbolism of flowers and their association with feminine beauty is well documented.[16] A similar two-tined pin made of silver was discovered in a Southern Song tomb in Fuzhou, Fujian.[17]

The single-tined hairpin is also decorated with the flowers of the seasons and has been worked in similar repoussé and chasing techniques. A gold cap in the form of a chrysanthemum blossom has been pinched onto the top of the hollow pin. The central band of floral decoration is followed by a band whose geometric design has a flange-and-ring decoration. A single-tined pin discovered in a Southern Song tomb in Jiangxi has been dated to the year 1197.[18]
—JMW

96 Pair of Hairpins   宋花卉紋金髮簪一對

Song dynasty, 960–1279
Gold
H: 19.7 cm D: 1.9 cm
GI-101.1–.2

Repoussé-worked tops and attached caps adorn this pair of double-tined, hollow gold hairpins. The objects were formed using repoussé techniques from a flattened piece of gold that was then rolled on a core and finished with chasing. The two tines of each pin are soldered together at the top.

    A symmetrical floral motif is executed in high relief in identical fashion on both pins. The right tine on each pair shows a peony blossom above leafy patterns and a chrysanthemum blossom on the lower portion. The left tine is decorated with a lotus flower above and a plum blossom below. Each pair is bordered under the lower portion of the floral design with a geometric swirl and double-V pattern. The caps of each pin are in the form of a pair of chrysanthemum blossoms.

    Similar two-tined pins of silver have been excavated from a Southern Song tomb near Fuzhou, in Fujian province.[19] The tomb contained a wooden comb, a perfumer, cosmetic boxes, and bronze mirrors, as well as a rich array of textiles.   —JMW

97 Pair of Hairpins 宋花卉紋金髮簪一對

Song dynasty, 960–1279
Gold
H: 12.7 cm W: 1.3 cm
GI-066.1–.2

On each of these two hollow gold hairpins a six-petalled blossom capped by a three-tiered flower design is surrounded by a six-sided honeycomb pattern. This pattern, repeated over the upper quarter of the pin, is separated at top and bottom by a chased floral or geometric band. The lower portion has a punched floral motif running vertically down the shaft of the pin. The end of the pin is undecorated and tapers to a fine point.

The pins were constructed by repoussé work on a flat thin sheet of gold that was later rolled into a tube. Some areas were punched up from behind to give the background an appearance simulating granulation. The tines are partially soldered. Evidence of a seam as well as inconsistencies in the joining of the pattern show that the pins were cut from a larger sheet. The floral top has been pinched, rather than soldered, onto the top of the pin.
—JMW

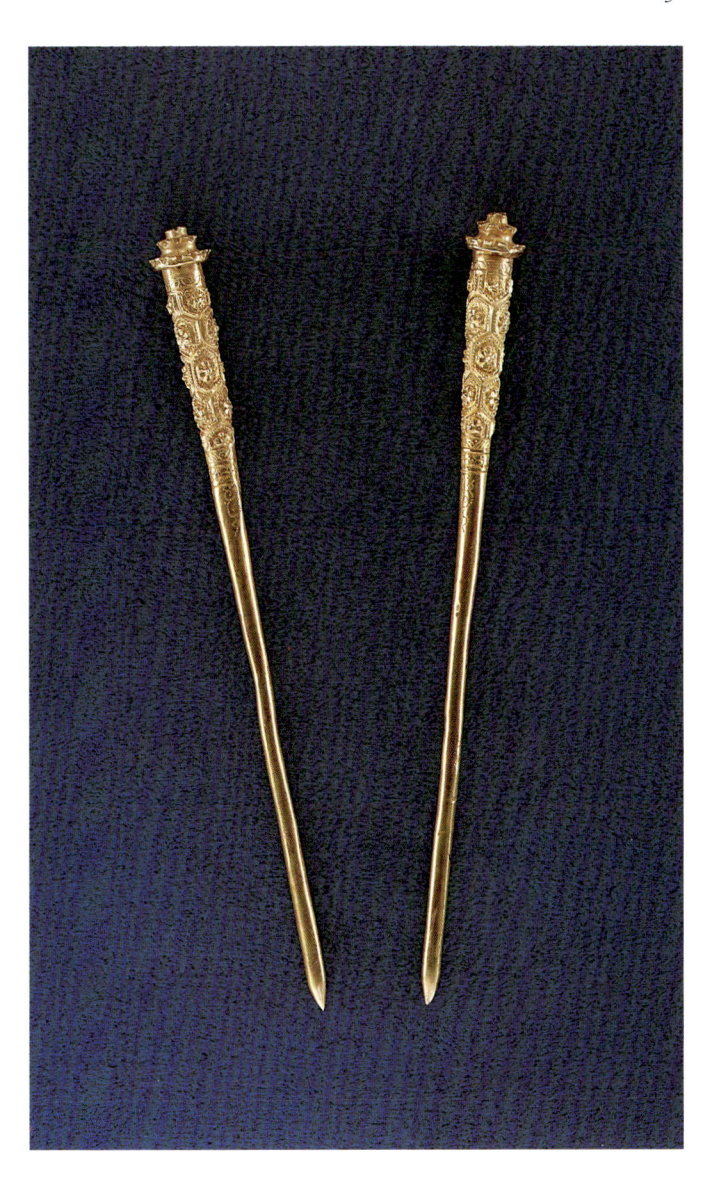

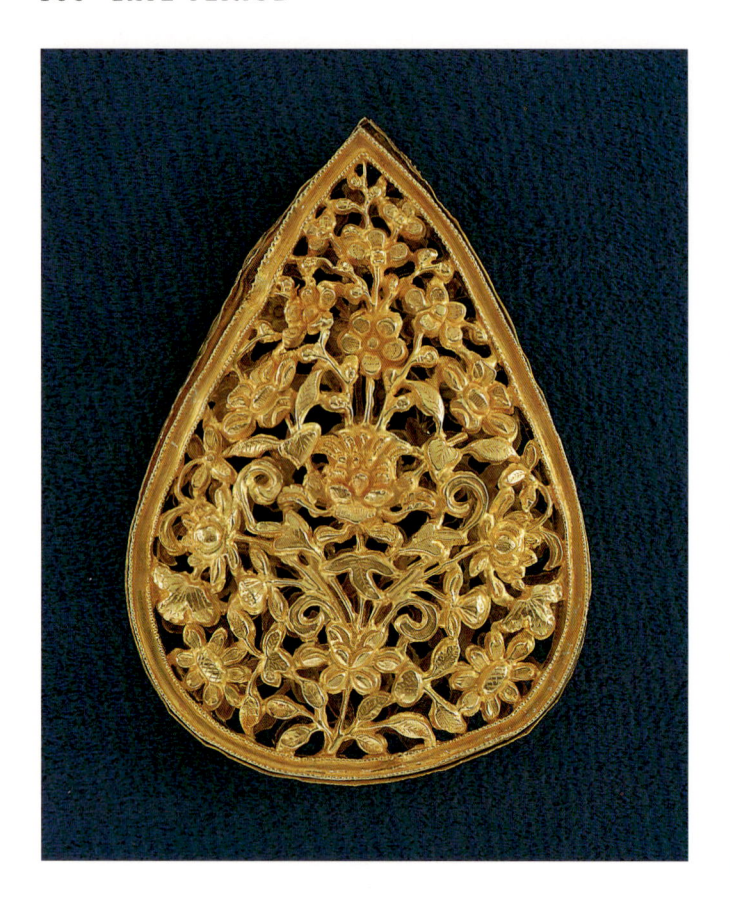

98 Perfume Container
宋四時花卉紋金香囊或霞帔墜子

Song dynasty, 960–1279
Gold
H: 8.9 cm W: 6.4 cm
GI-039

This teardrop-shaped ornament with repoussé, cutout, and chased designs was made in two halves from a sheet of gold. Identical symmetrical floral designs adorn the front and back. The rim of one half fits tightly inside that of the other. An interior rim of solid gold has a pseudo-granulation decoration running around the edge.

The central peony motif is surrounded by chrysanthemum, peony, lotus, and plum-blossom designs. These flowers represent the four seasons, and are frequently associated with women and used as decorative motifs on their dress and ornamentation.

This ornament is a censer that would have been suspended by a hook from a belt or perhaps from a shawl.[20] The censer would have contained fragrant leaves or other scented material to freshen the wearer's clothing. Similar examples have been recovered from Northern and Southern Song tombs. A Nanjing tomb of a woman, excavated in 1980, yielded such an ornament.[21] Another excavation in Anhui revealed a similar object made of gilt silver.[22] Others have been found in Fuzhou, Fujian, and Liaoning.[23]

—JMW

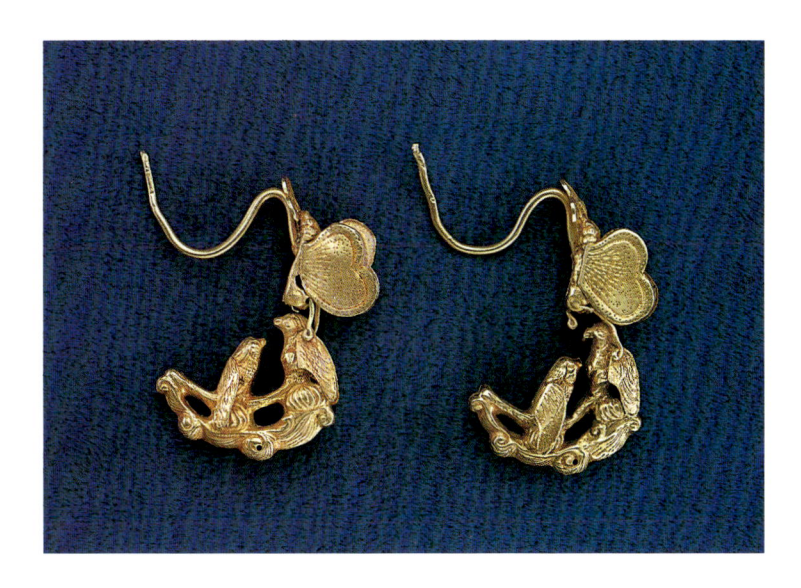

99 Pair of Earrings 宋鳥蝶形金耳環一對

Song dynasty, 960–1279
Gold
a: H: 3.8 cm W: 4.0 cm
b: H: 2.5 cm W: 5.2 cm (including hook)
GI-062.a–.b

A butterfly hovers above a pair of birds on each of this pair of hollow repoussé gold earrings. Join-marks on the main body of the earring take the form of a vertical line running through the birds on front and back. The wings of the birds and butterflies are soldered onto their bodies. The butterfly is attached to the main body of the earring by two wires representing the butterfly's antennae, which are attached to the upper portion of the wing of the top bird. The hook extends from the underside of the butterfly. Both earrings are pierced at the foot of the lower bird, indicating that attachments may have originally hung from the bases.

The lyrical and pictorial qualities of this pair of earrings are in keeping with the light and often whimsical view of nature seen in other Song arts.[24] The butterfly is frequently associated with the Daoist philosopher Zhuang Zi.[25]   —JMW

100 Headdress 宋花卉紋金頭飾

Song dynasty, 960–1279
Gold
H: 9.5 cm W: 14.0 cm
GI-048

This headdress consists of a single sheet of thin hammered gold from which are suspended rows of flowers connected by thin twisted wire. The arched sheet is decorated in three main panels: a top portion decorated with a perforated scroll and plum-blossom pattern; a row of repoussé bosses; and a horizontal row of repoussé flowers from which the rest of the headdress hangs. On the right edge of the band is a small fragment of a solid sheet of gold decorated with a chased floral pattern. The dangling flowers are hammered into four petals, with punched holes on the four opposite corners for the attachment of the twisted wire.

This type of headdress was most likely worn in the hair with the tips of the band pointing upward. The flowers would be draped across the front of the hair and the forehead.[26]

A strikingly similar headdress, described as a crown, was discovered among the grave goods of a woman in a stone-chambered tomb in Henan province dating from the Southern Song.[27]

—JMW

101 Belt Hook 宋錯金銀雙龍紋青銅帶鉤

Song dynasty, 10th–13th century or later
Bronze inlaid with gold and silver
L: 21.3 cm W: 2.9 cm D: 4.1 cm
H-059

This impressive curved belt hook is triplanar in cross section. The body is embellished with a linear design of two intertwined dragons inlaid in gold and silver. The sides of the belt hook are decorated with simple gold and silver lines and geometric forms. The reverse is undecorated except for the slightly convex circular button, which carries a design inlaid in strand silver of five spirals radiating from the inner edges of a circle. The hook terminates in an unidentifiable animal head which has been broken off and awkwardly reattached in recent times.

The inlay process that produced the latticelike designs on this handsome hook is quite complex. The major part of the design was first chisel-cut from a piece of gold foil and then inlaid into very shallow channels which were cut into the bronze after the hook was cast. Inlaid silver dots, spirals, and heart shapes produced by strand inlay lend contrast to the gold. The dark lines in the design represent the bronze of the hook body, which was not inlaid. The resulting surface of the belt hook is rough to the touch, not smooth, indicating that it was not ground down and polished after it was inlaid.

The dragon heads have flaccid, flowery profiles which are indistinct and have none of the robust presence of late Eastern Zhou– and Western Han–period dragons. Instead, the dragons on this hook recall the rather curvilinear decorative creatures that inhabit the surfaces of late archaistic bronzes. A conscious quest for antiquity in order to gain intellectual access to the past resulted in the production of archaistic paraphernalia for the scholar's studio during the Song and later periods.

The intention of later craftsmen was to imitate the visual effect seen on ancient artifacts, such as the superb Mengdiexuan late Warring States iron inlaid hook (cat. no. 20), but the later technique was entirely different. The latticelike decoration of the Warring States pieces was achieved by overlaying the bronze with gold sheet and then cutting sections away. By contrast, the decoration on this hook uses a piece of gold foil with a pre-cut latticelike design, an identifiable archaistic characteristic.[28] This technique is recognizable because the resulting surface is marked by small bubbles that occur where the foil did not lie flat. The fact that the inlay area was not ground down to produce a flush surface is also an archaistic trait.

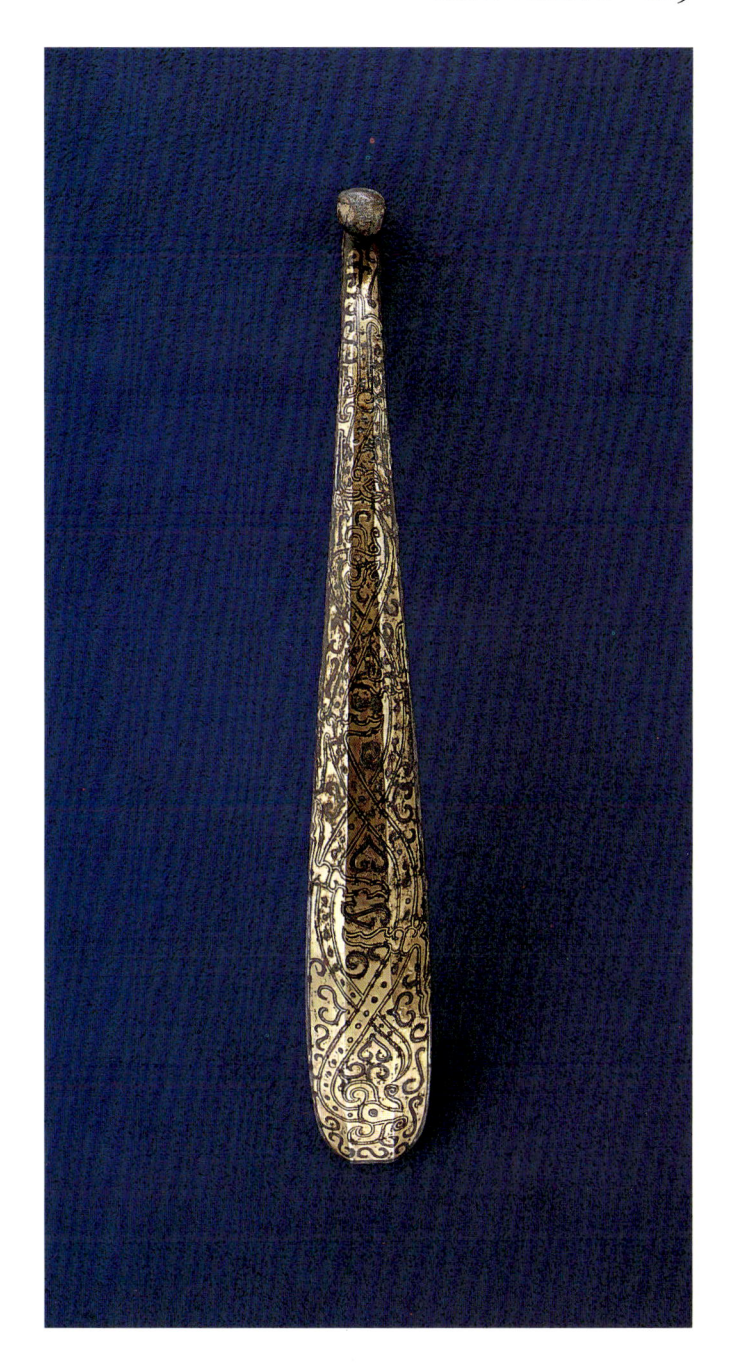

The belt hook itself appears to be ancient, as are the inlay patterns on the sides and the button. The decoration of a bronze belt hook in the Freer Gallery of Art is a similar case. The Freer belt hook is ancient, as are the inlaid designs on the sides and the button. By contrast, the inlay on the front of the Freer piece is later and, seen in an X-ray, does not have deep inlay channels as it would if the inlay were ancient.[29]

—ECB

102 Head Ornament 元雙龍紋金頭飾

Yuan dynasty, 1279–1368
Gold
H: 5.4 cm W: 7.8 cm
GI-095

This four-lobed, two-part head ornament is decorated with a double dragon design. The dragons are shown in high relief circling the surface in a counterclockwise direction. The body of each dragon is well articulated, with the sinuous uncoiling of the body defined by semicircular punched designs covering the surface to imitate a scalelike texture. One foreleg and one hind leg extend onto the interior rim. The other foreleg reaches out in front of the head, appearing to grasp for the tail of the other dragon with its three claws. The head is large relative to the body and is elaborately accented by a large mane, a wide gaping mouth, and bulging eyes.

The top portion of the ornament is a single sheet of gold worked in repoussé and attached to its backing by twenty-seven vertical supports on the exterior of the rim and by eighteen supports on the interior. The vertical supports are extensions of the top element. The back consists of a flat, lobed band with a chased floral motif.

This ornament may have been part of a headdress. Its strong depiction of dragons, typically symbols of the emperor, indicates that it was probably used by a man.

—JMW

103 Pair of Hairpins
元花卉紋金髮簪兩件

Yuan dynasty, 1279–1368
Gold
1: H: 15.9 cm W: 4.8 cm
2: H: 14.0 cm W: 4.8 cm
GI-056.1–.2

These two round-headed hairpins with single flat tines of gold were probably cast as gold button ingots and then hammered out in one piece from tine to head. The heads are exquisitely worked in bold repoussé, with touches of chasing to highlight details of the leaves and flowers. The tine on the longer pin shows signs of having been folded over as it was worked.

A similar lady's hairpin was found among a cache of silver and gold discovered in Inner Mongolia.[30] Another similar pin, made of silver, said to be from Hunan, is now in an American collection.[31] Flowers are a favorite theme of the ornament of the time and represent a significant trend that began in the Tang period.[32]   —JMW

104 Two Hairpins
元雙龍及雙鳥紋金髮簪各一件

Yuan dynasty, 1279–1368
Gold
Dragon: H: 14.0 cm W: 1.9 cm
Birds: H: 14.9 cm W: 2.5 cm
GI-094.1–.2

One of these hairpins is decorated with a pair of dragons, the other with a pair of birds. Both hairpins are of hammered gold repoussé in high relief with a cutout background. The pin with the two dragons is topped by a peony blossom. The three-clawed dragons, back to back, coil toward the blossom. A fan-shaped leaf cuts across the lower part of the tail as it changes from high relief into a chased ring-punch pattern on each flattened tine.[33]

The pin with birds and a peony blossom is worked in much the same way, although its single tine is not a continuous part of the upper decorated portion but has been attached to the repoussé work by pressure at the back center, then clipped to the top. The tine is incised with a graceful floral pattern of lotus leaf, peony, and plum blossom. The pair of birds, standing on twisted branches and surrounded by lotus leaves and lotus pods, dominates the high-relief head of the pin. The female bird coyly remains behind the large peony blossom in the upper right of the design. Similar examples are known in silver.[34]   —JMW

105 Two Hairpins 元花卉龍紋金髮簪兩件

Yuan dynasty, 1279–1368
Gold
1: H: 14.6 cm W: 1.1 cm
2: H: 13.7 cm W: 1.3 cm
GI-093.1–.2

Flower and dragon motifs dominate this pair of gold hairpins. The dragons' bodies are defined by twisted gold, with the scales of the dragons worked in a combination of chasing and punching. The longer pin shows the dragons coiling up the pin, with heads facing away from each other. The top of the pin is crowned with a peony. The reverse side is formed by the back of the dragon as it coils around the pin, but as it reaches the top of the pin the decoration becomes floral, with tooled, etched work leading to two half-flowers. There is a six-character inscription incised on the lower front portion of the twin prongs. It reads *huang xu qing jin zao,* meaning Huang Xuqing made this of red gold.

The shorter pin has a very similar design: two dragons coiling around a pin topped with a peony. On the reverse of the pin, the two dragon bodies end in another set of heads, so this pin has four dragon heads. The top reverse is also crowned with a floral motif. The dragons' bodies are more crudely defined, with simpler chasing, but are created by a fantastic twisted-gold design.

Twisted gilt hairpins of this two-tined type have been found in Inner Mongolia and appear to belong to a type that originated in the north and was brought to the south during the Yuan dynasty.[35]

—JMW

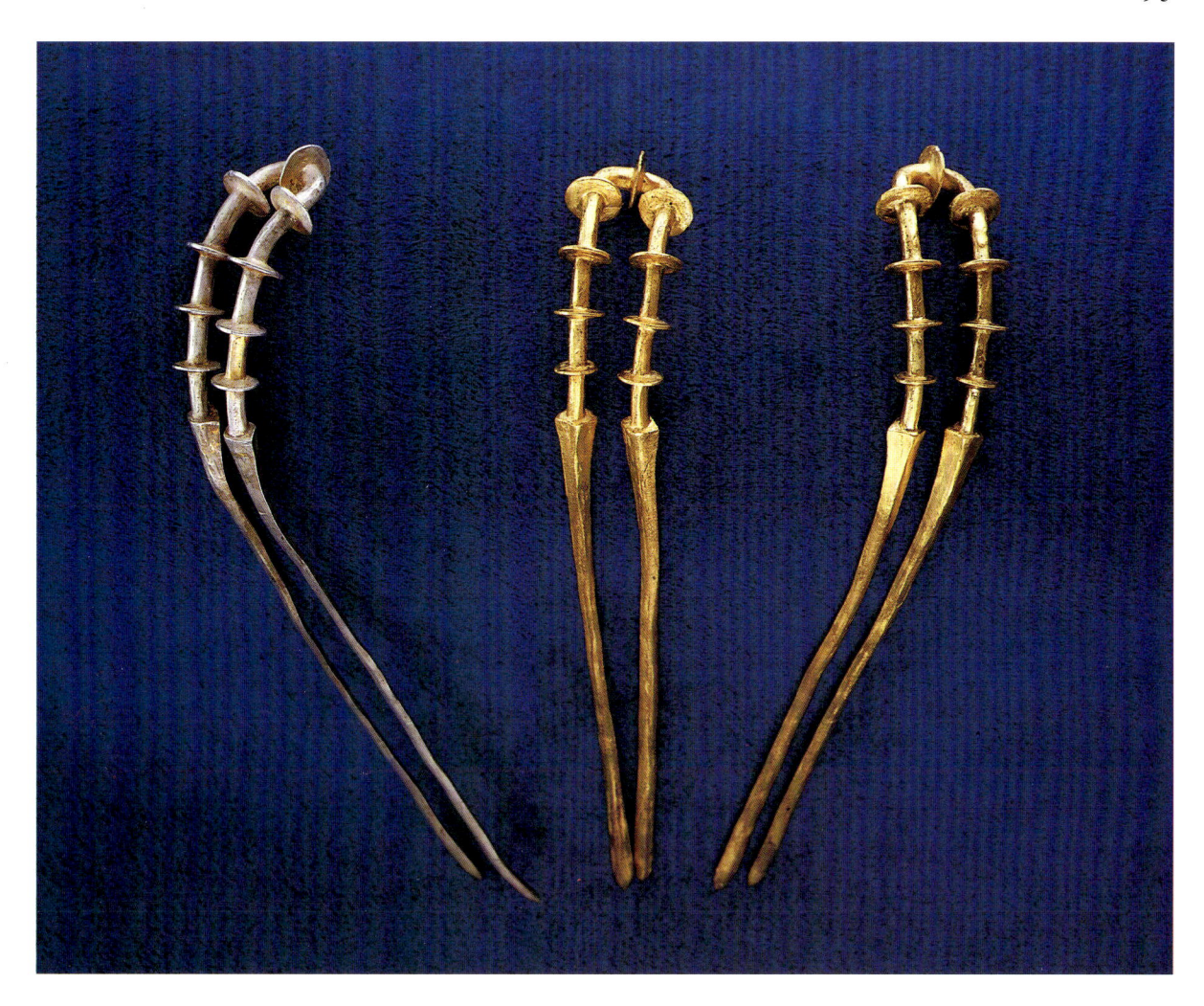

106 Three Hairpins
元環節紋鎏金銀及金髮簪三件

Yuan dynasty, 1279–1362 (1 only)
Modern period (2 and 3)
Gold and silver with some gilding
1: H: 13.7 cm W: 1.9 cm D: 3.2 cm
2: H: 13.3 cm W: 1.9 cm D: 3.2 cm
3: H: 13.0 cm W: 1.7 cm D: 3.2 cm
GI-059.1–.3

In this trio of nearly identical double-tined hairpins, simple disk shapes crown the top of each pin with four more on either side, for a total of nine disks per pin. The body of each pin has been rounded above the disks, while below the disks the tine is wedge shaped, gradually narrowing to a point.

The two gold pins appear to have been cast from a mold based on the silver pin. The gold pins show signs of having been heavily filed, while the original silver pin is left unfiled. Marks on the upper portion of the silver pin suggest that it was used as the basis for a latex mold, which would then have been used for the casting of the gold pins.[36] The silver pin appears to have lost some gilding in this process, although traces do remain on the underside of the pin.

A similar group of double-tined hairpins was discovered at Sanjiacun, in Inner Mongolia, in 1984.[37] Another find in a Yuan dynasty grave in Suzhou, Jiangsu province, proves this type of hairpin was not limited to the far north, even though it may have originated with northern peoples.[38]

—JMW

107 Three Hairpins 明雙鳳紋金髮簪三件

Ming dynasty, 1368–1644
Gold
1: H: 9.4 cm W: 7.0 cm
2: H: 7.0 cm W: 6.4 cm
3: H: 8.7 cm W: 7.6 cm
GI-054.1–.3

Paired phoenix designs are the prominent elements of this group of hairpins. The two smaller pins show two phoenixes in flight, one pursuing the other. The larger pin shows one phoenix above the other, their beaks together. The background of the raised repoussé design consists of scroll and floral motifs. On the larger pin the openwork is created by repoussé, with fine bands branching out in places to the flowers and parts of the birds. The raised portions of the two smaller pins appear to have been beaten out of individual sheets, with the background appearing regular and punched.

Each of the three consists of a rounded sheet, with cutout, repoussé, and chased designs, which has been attached to a flat gold sheet by thin gold wires. The two smaller pin fronts are held on with four twisted threads, while the larger pin's backing is held on with three wires that have been brought to the front and attached like clips. All three have straight, flat, gold tines. The two smaller tines are attached flush with the back, while the larger pin is attached by a flat, floral-shaped attachment that has been bent to lie perpendicular to the backing.

The backings are plain, except for worked edges that appear as a punched design on the front panels.

The larger pin has an inscription on the tine, *yi liang san qian wu fen,* designating the weight of the pin.

Pins of this size and workmanship may be assigned to royalty and have been found in princely Ming tombs around Nanjing.[39]

—JMW

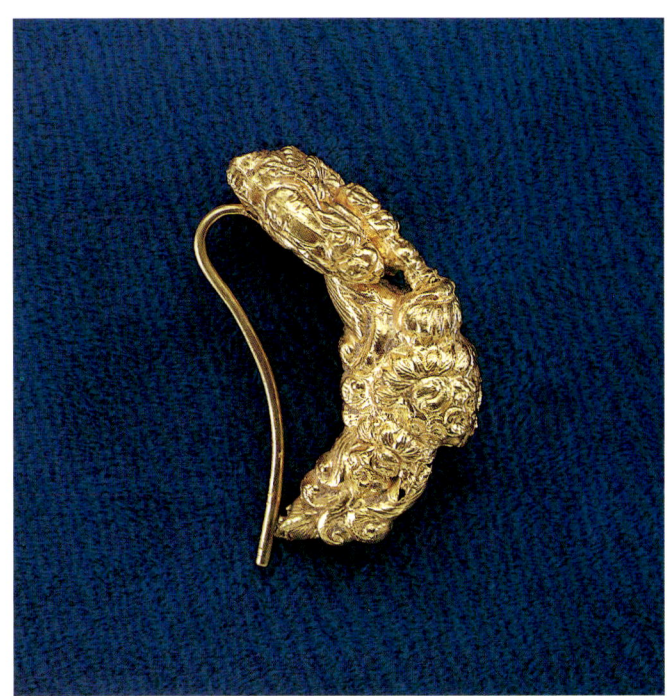

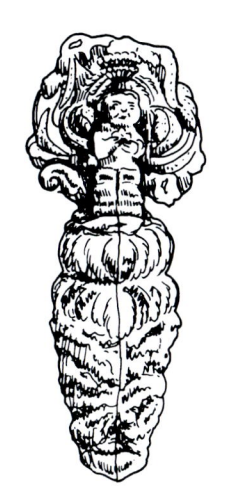

108 Earring with Flowers and Figure
明花卉人物金耳環

Ming dynasty, 1368–1644
Gold
H: 5.1 cm W: 3.5 cm (in profile)
GI-091

Repoussé designs of flowers encircle a small figure on the front of this large, hollow, gold-foil earring. The single earring consists of three main units: a lower bulbous body with floral decoration which acts as a dais for the separate standing human figure; the figure itself; and a top section which acts as a canopy to the figure. The hook runs through the top portion and is then attached to the top of the lower section. Each unit has been modelled in two parts. Seam lines can be seen along the outside edge of the top unit and figural unit, and similar lines are discernible along the face of the lower unit.

The flowing floral designs of this exquisite piece point to a Ming origin. The design of a human figure, possibly with offering in hand, has precedents in two other earrings from the Yuan and Ming.[40] Both of these examples take the form of a carved jade bead depicting a figure which has been set in a gold-wire wrapping. The figure on the Mengdiexuan earring is shown standing on a lotus dais and is therefore probably a Buddhist image.

—JMW

109 Gourd-Shaped Earrings
明葫蘆形金耳環三對

Ming dynasty, 1368–1644
Gold with pearls
1ab: H: 3.5 cm W: 3.8 cm
2ab: H: 2.5 cm W: 3.2 cm
3ab: H: 3.5 cm W: 1.6 cm
GI-083.1ab–.3ab

Three pairs of gourd-shaped gold earrings make up this group. The top and bottom pair (numbers 1 and 3) are hollow cast, and the middle pair (number 2) is made of filigree gold with inset pearls that were probably added later. Excavated examples of similar earrings have been found in Ming tombs in Nanjing and in Sichuan province.[41] The wide distribution of this type of earring indicates its popularity. Because of the gourd's durability and association with immortality, its shape was often worn as a charm for longevity.[42] —JMW

110 Belt Ornament 明如意龍紋金帶飾

Ming dynasty, 1368–1644
Gold
H: 8.6 cm W: 3.2 cm D: 0.8 cm
GI-096

A swirling dragon design with a *ruyi* pattern in the background decorates this hollow-cast gold belt ornament. The ornament was probably part of a larger belt set, now lost. The design of a scaly dragon with five claws and a flowing mane depicts a mythical animal of tremendous vitality. A flat rim surrounds the whole design. The back is a flat piece of gold with a rough hole torn in it.

The dragon was a symbol of many things, including by this time the emperor himself. The quality of the casting suggests that the owner of this object was of high status. —JMW

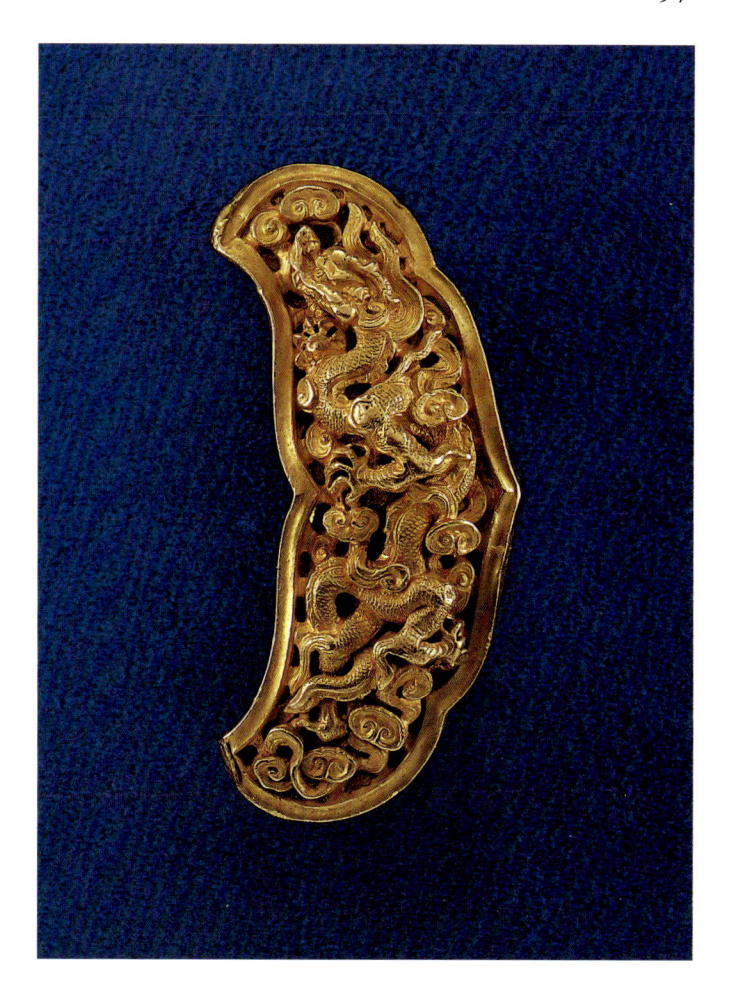

111 Belt Set 明鎏金牡丹鳳紋銀組帶飾

Ming dynasty, 1368–1644
Silver with traces of gilding
18 pieces
2 tab ends: H: 4.0 cm W: 7.2 cm
6 teardrop-shaped plaques: H: 4.0 cm W: 4.7 cm
6 large horizontal plaques: H: 3.8 cm W: 6.4 cm
4 small rectangular plaques: H: 4.0 cm W: 2.8 cm
BP-011.1–.18

A die or form was probably used for the initial construction of this large repoussé and chased silver belt set. It is decorated with phoenixes and peonies in panels surrounded by an edging of pseudo-granulation. The background has been left plain. The repoussé relief is high, but the silver itself is thin and the depth of each plaque is minimal. There are no posts attached to the back of the plaques; the small pairs of holes that can be seen on each plaque probably served as attachment points for the plaques to their cloth or leather backing.

This silver belt set is typical of the type worn by the Ming court. The Ming, in an attempt to reinstate Chinese customs following the foreign Yuan rule, established clothing rules and regulations that reflected much earlier traditions. Certain types of belts and the material they were made of became a part of formal court wear; for example, a silver belt designated an official of the fifth, sixth, or seventh rank.[43]

—JMW

112 Belt Set 明牡丹鳳紋銀組帶飾

Ming dynasty, 1368–1644
Silver
18 pieces
6 teardrop-shaped plaques: H: 6.3 cm W: 6.1 cm
7 large rectangular plaques: H: 6.4 cm W: 8.0 cm
3 small rectangular plaques: H: 6.4 cm W: 2.9 cm
1 belt end: H: 6.4 cm W: 10.9 cm
1 attachment end: H: 6.3 cm W: 9.6 cm
BP-018.1–.18

This very elaborate belt set is made of silver with a repoussé and chased design of phoenixes and peonies. The decoration on the large plaques consists of paired birds encircling a large blossom surrounded by four additional blossoms. The phoenix-and-flower designs are in high relief against a plain background. The central motifs are surrounded by a line of pseudo-granulation. Thin backings are attached to some of the plaques by a thin silver wire that has been soldered directly onto the back of the plaque.

The elaborate and sophisticated design of this belt set, as well as its extremely well-executed technique, permits a glimpse into the high level of workmanship achieved during the Ming period. A Ming-period tomb in Liaoning province yielded gilt-bronze belts of a similar type.[44]

Paintings of Ming court life frequently depict figures of high status, including the emperor, wearing this type of belt set.[45] The type of materials employed in the belt set would determine the rank and status of the wearer (see cat. no. 111).   —JMW

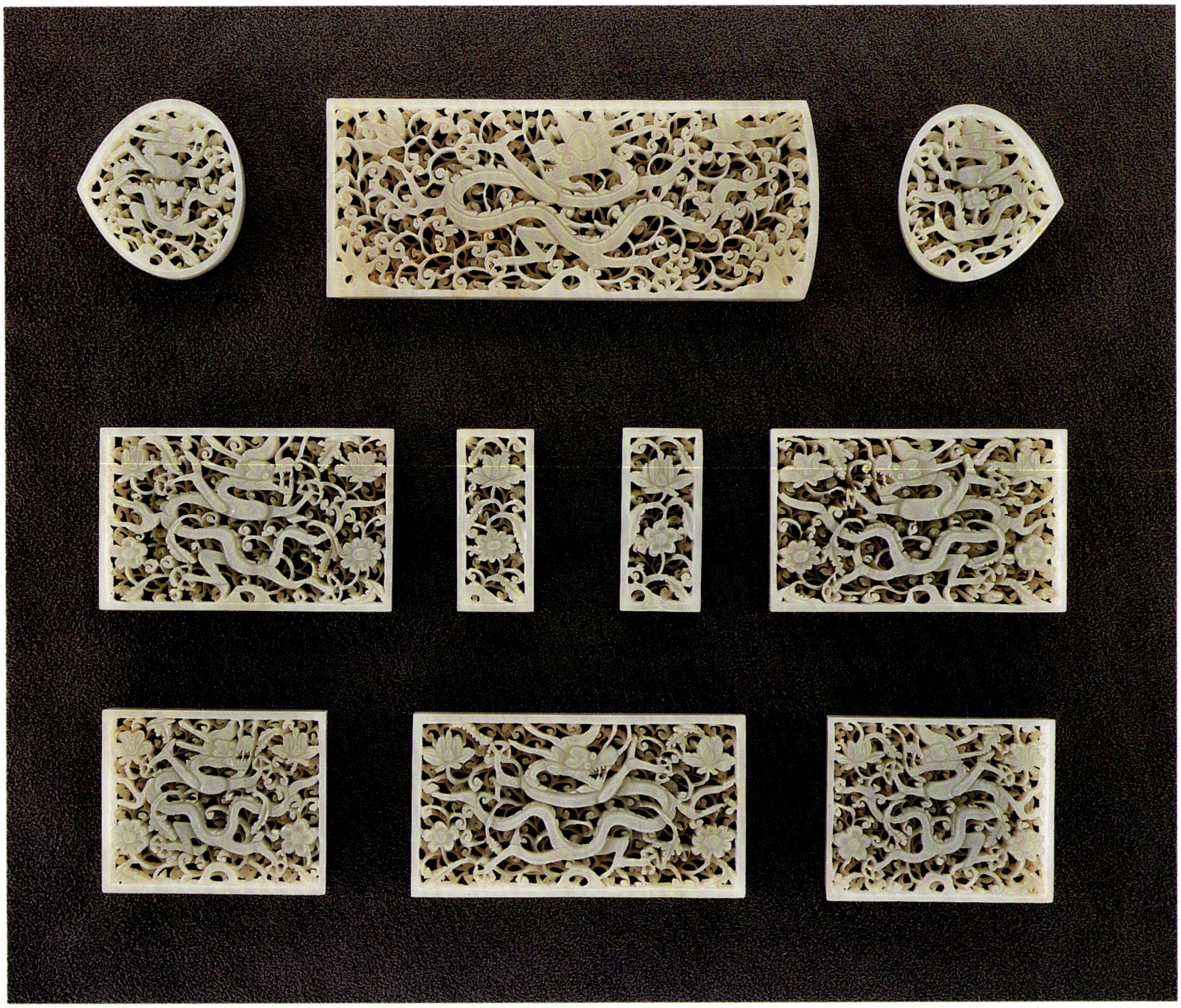

113 Belt Set 明龍紋及四時花卉玉雕組帶飾

Ming dynasty, 1368–1644
Jade
10 pieces
1 end-plaque: H: 5.1 cm W: 13.2 cm
3 large rectangular plaques: H: 2.2 cm W: 7.8 cm
2 small rectangular plaques: H: 2.2 cm W: 7.8 cm
2 small vertical plaques: H: 2.2 cm W: 2.1 cm
2 heart-shaped plaques: H: 2.2 cm W: 4.4 cm
BP-002.1–.10

Dragons floating on a floral background form the central motif on this set of ten jade (nephrite) belt plaques. The principal designs are carved into the surface of the jade, while the background is abraded more severely, giving an effective impression of depth. In addition, the reverse of each dragon's body is abraded, increasing the translucency of the plaques. Tool marks indicating the use of a round drill appear in the abraded areas.

Each of the larger plaques has four pairs of holes which could have been used to attach them to a belt. The small vertical plaques have two pairs of holes, while the heart-shaped plaques have one pair. A belt of leather or silk may have been used as a backing for this belt set, which would have been worn loosely draped over a robe.

The large end-plaque is decorated with a raised and intricately carved dragon. A bat can be seen in the top left corner of the end-plaque, and a bird is carved into the top right corner. The large and small rectangular plaques are decorated with flowers of the four seasons—peony, plum, chrysanthemum, and lily—one in each corner, surrounding the central dragon design. The two small vertical plaques are decorated with two of the flowers: on the left, lily and plum; and on the right, peony and chrysanthemum. Each of the heart-shaped plaques is decorated with a swirling dragon and only one flower: lily on the left-hand plaque and plum on the right-hand plaque. Flowers represent the four seasons but are also symbols of feminine beauty.

There are several other known sets of elaborately decorated jade belts. In the collection of the National Palace Museum in Taipei there is a set of twenty pieces carved in jade with a dragon motif that is dated to the Ming dynasty.[46]

—JMW

Notes

1. C. A. S. Williams, *Outlines of Chinese Symbolism and Art Motives*, pp. 323–26.

2. *Hunan kaogu jikan*, vol. 4, 1987, pp. 68–72, p. 72, illus. 10:1. For similar style of workmanship and floral motifs in the Yuan dynasty see the cache from Inner Mongolia illustrated in *Nei Menggu wenwu kaogu*, 1991.1, pp. 89–100, especially p. 91, illus. 6, nos. 2–3, and p. 96, illus. 11, no. 1.

3. Paul Singer, *Early Chinese Gold and Silver*, p. 63. A–C have been worked in a cutout fashion, but D is quite close to the Mengdiexuan example.

4. *Wenwu*, 1984.5, pl. 6, no. 7.

5. For a pottery figure from a Han dynasty tomb in Chengdu, Sichuan, with a similar headdress see Zhou Xun and Gao Chunming, *Zhongguo lidai funu jiangshi*, p. 86, pl. 100.

6. *Wenwu*, 1984.5, pl. 5, no. 2. The number of petals on the excavated pin is eight. Two smaller examples on the same page, nos. 5 and 6, are of similar construction.

7. C. A. S. Williams, *Outlines of Chinese Symbolism and Art Motives*, p. 192.

8. See an example of Song-period work from Zhejiang Province in *Wenwu*, 1984.5, p. 85, illus. nos. 9 and 11, and a Yuan-period example in *Hunan kaogu jikan*, vol. 2, 1984, p. 118.

9. C. A. S. Williams, *Outlines of Chinese Symbolism and Art Motives*, pp. 328–29.

10. Yang Boda, ed., *Zhongguo meishu quanji* 10, text p. 37, illus. p. 65, no. 130–31. But see also *Wenwu*, 1974.8, pp. 73–75, illus. no. 2.

11. Zhou Xun and Gao Chunming, *Zhongguo lidai funu jiangshi*, p. 63, no. 69.

12. Ibid., p. 64, nos. 70–71.

13. Ibid., p. 55. Here described as the Nanbei dynastic period, 420–581.

14. Michael Loewe, *Ways to Paradise: The Chinese Quest for Immortality*, pp. 86–155.

15. Cheng Te-k'un, *Jade Flowers and Floral Patterns in Chinese Decorative Art*, p. 74.

16. For references to flowers and their symbolism see C. A. S. Williams, *Outlines of Chinese Symbolism and Art Motives*, pp. 320–21.

17. *Wenwu*, 1977.7, p. 10, no. 29.

18. *Kaogu*, 1988.4, p. 330, illus. 1, no. 1.

19. *Wenwu*, 1977.7, p. 10, illus. no. 29. See also Christian Deydier, *Imperial Gold from Ancient China*, part 1, pp. 38–41, nos. 10–12.

20. Sun Ji, "Xiapei zhuizi," *Wenwu tiandi*, 1994.1, pp. 22–24.

21. *Wenwu*, 1982.3, pl. 3, no. 1. A better photograph can be found in Yang Boda, ed., *Zhongguo meishu quanji* 10, p. 41, pls. 86–87.

22. *Kaogu*, 1986.10, pl. 8, no. 7.

23. *Wenwu*, 1977.7, pl. 3, no. 4, also gilt silver from a Southern Song tomb in Fuzhou, Fujian. *Wenwu*, 1992.7, p. 11, illus. no. 20.

24. See examples in painting from the same period in James Cahill, *Chinese Painting*.

25. The story of the butterfly is told in chapter 2 of the *Zhuang Zi*. "Once upon a time, Chuang Chou [Chuang Tzu] dreamed that he was a butterfly, a butterfly fluttering about, enjoying itself. It did not know it was Chuang Chou. Suddenly he awoke with a start and he was Chuang Chou again. But he did not know whether he was Chuang Chou who had dreamed that he was a butterfly, or whether he was a butterfly dreaming that he was Chuang Chou." From Wm. Theodore de Bary, *Sources of Chinese Tradition*, p. 75.

26. See Zhou Xun and Gao Chunming, *Zhongguo lidai funu jiangshi*, p. 88. Illus. no. 108 shows a woman with a very elaborate headdress; the top front portion is not dissimilar to the headdress illustrated here.

27. *Kaogu*, 1988.1, pp. 63–65, pl. 9. Another, said to be Liao, is illustrated in Christian Deydier, *Imperial Gold from Ancient China*, part 1, pp. 56–57, no. 22.

28. Robert Dale Jacobsen, *Inlaid Bronzes of Pre-Imperial China*, p. 104.

29. W. Thomas Chase, *Chinese Belt-Hooks in the Freer Gallery of Art*, pl. 55, acc. no. 48.26.

30. *Nei Menggu wenwu kaogu*, 1991.1, p. 98, illus. 14, nos. 4–5.

31. Paul Singer, *Early Chinese Gold and Silver*, p. 63, no. 88d.

32. For a discussion of the motifs see Cheng Te-k'un, *Jade Flowers and Floral Patterns in Chinese Decorative Art*, pp. 74–78.

33. For a Song or later example see Bo Gyllensvard, *Chinese Gold and Silver from the Carl Kempe Collection*, p. 122, no. 63.

34. For an example in silver see Paul Singer, *Early Chinese Gold and Silver*, p. 63, no. 88, a–b.

35. *Nei Menggu wenwu kaogu*, 1991.1, p. 94. Illus. 9, no. 4 is from a cache at Sanjiacun. Another from Taijihecun is illustrated in the same article, p. 96, illus. 11, no. 4.

36. Richard Kimball, master goldsmith, observed that the gold pins were heavily worked, and this led him to investigate the silver pin for traces of mold casting. Kimball also observed that the gold pins carry traces of the shape of the silver pin but are distorted versions of that original. I am very grateful to Mr. Kimball for pointing out this condition as well as for his assistance in determining the materials and methods of construction of many other objects in the exhibition—JMW.

37. *Nei Menggu wenwu kaogu*, 1991.1, pp. 9, 94, 100.

38. Zhou Xun and Gao Chunming, *Zhongguo lidai funu jiangshi*, p. 71, illus. no. 3.

39. *Wenwu*, 1993.2, pp. 63–76, p. 67, illus. no. 12.

40. For the Yuan example from Shaanxi, Xi'an, see Zhou Xun and Gao Chunming, *Zhongguo lidai funu jiangshi*, pp. 151–55, with line drawing 5.9 on p. 152 and a color photograph of the Ming example from Jiangsu on p. 155, no. 198. *Wenwu cankao ziliao*, 1978.2, pp. 137–41, illus. nos. 2, 3, and 5.

41. *Wenwu*, 1982.2. For the Nanjing find see pp. 28–32, pl. 4, no. 3. For the Sichuan find see pp. 34–38, pl. 5, no. 8. Another gourd-shaped earring was found in Yunnan, see *Wenwu*, 1983.2, pp. 81–83, illus. 9, no. 1.

42. C. A. S. Williams, *Outlines of Chinese Symbolism and Art Motives*, p. 217.

43. Zhou Xun and Gao Chunming, *5000 Years of Chinese Costumes*, p. 146.

44. *Wenwu*, 1978.11, p. 17.

45. Chinese portraiture is one source for paintings depicting real people in their formal court dress. See Richard Vinograd, *Boundaries of the Self: Chinese Portraits, 1600–1900*. See page 3 for an anonymous portrait of a Ming official wearing a sectioned belt. Another source comprises paintings of scholars, sometimes identifiable, other times not, within a landscape setting. For example see Barry Till and Paula Swart, *Arts of the Middle Kingdom: China*, pl. 85, description p. 108. A painting by the Ming artist Wang Sheng, "Travelers Resting Near a Stream," shows a group of scholar-officials wearing sectioned belt plaques.

46. *The National Palace Museum Monthly of Chinese Art*, no. 104, pp. 4–21.

Emma C. Bunker

Select Glossary

Establishing a common terminology for the materials and techniques related to the study of ancient Chinese metals is a project which has only recently been undertaken. For their research and assistance in this regard, sincere thanks are due to a number of people, particularly Professor Han Rubin, Ms. Li Xiuhui, and Mr. Mei Jianjun of the Institute of Historical Metallurgy at the University of Science and Technology Beijing, and Ms. Wang Dongning of Lehigh University Graduate School. I am especially grateful to Dr. Tsun Ko for his invaluable guidance and suggestions. Explanations in the following works were helpful in establishing definitions for the terms: Ann Gunter and Paul Jett, *Ancient Iranian Metalwork in the Arthur M. Sackler Gallery and the Freer Gallery of Art* (1992); Herbert Hoffman and Patricia Davidson, *Greek Gold: Jewelry from the Age of Alexander* (1966); *Jewellery Through the Ages* (British Museum Publications, 1976); Jack Ogden, *Jewellery of the Ancient World* (1976), and *Ancient Jewellery* (1992); David Scott, *Metallography and Microstructure of Ancient and Historic Metals* (1991); and Hugh Tait, ed., *Seven Thousand Years of Jewellery* (1986), and *Jewelry, 7,000 Years* (1991). Thanks also to Page Shaver for providing some of the more uncommon Chinese characters with the TwinBridge 3.2 Chinese language word processor. Where applicable, simplified characters are shown in parentheses.

Alloy   *héjīn* 合金
A mixture of two or more metals.

Amalgam   *gǒngjí* 汞齊 (汞齐)
An alloy of mercury with other metals. (The character 齊, *jí*, is the ancient and modern term for "alloy" and should not be confused with 劑, *jì*, which indicates a medical preparation.)

Beading   *chuànzhūzhuàng yuánshì* 串珠狀緣飾 (串珠状缘饰)
An arrangement of solid gold grains to form a border.

Beaded wire   *zhūzhuàng jīnshǔsī* 珠狀金屬絲 (珠状金属丝)
Wire that has been indented to resemble beading.

Brazing   *qiānhàn* 釺焊 or *yìnghàn* 硬焊
Joining metals together with a brazing alloy with a melting point above 450 degrees centigrade.

Burnish   *cāliàng* 擦亮
To polish a metal surface.

Carbon-14 dating   *tànshísì niándài cèdìng* 碳十四年代測定 (碳十四年代测定)
Scientific method to determine the age of carbon-bearing material by making use of the half-life of the radioactive isotope of carbon absorbed from air under living conditions.

Casting   *zhùzào* 鑄造 (铸造)
The process of pouring metal into a mold.

Casting-on   *zhùjiē* 鑄接 (铸接)
The process of pouring metal into a joint.

Chasing   *loùkè* 鏤刻 (镂刻) or *sàlou* 鈒鏤
Displacement of metal to produce indented lines on the front to define details.

Cloison   *qiàsī* 掐絲 (掐丝)
A cell formed of thin strips of metal applied to a metal base.

Cloisonné   *jǐngtàilán* 景泰藍 (景泰蓝)
A design made up of a network of cloisons filled with enamel, glass, or other material.

Crimping   *yǎohé* 咬合
A mechanical join between two pieces of metal achieved by compressing the metal into a fold.

Cupellation   *huīchuīfǎ* 灰吹法
A process used in the extraction of precious metals from their lead alloy by oxidation of lead on a porous vessel.

Diffusion bonding   *kuòsàn jiēhé* 擴散接合 (扩散接合)
Joining two metals by heating them together without a bonding agent.

Drawing　*bāsī* 拔絲 (拔丝)
The act of pulling a metal wire through a die to reduce the cross section.

Engraving　*diāokè* 雕刻
Cutting a design on a metal surface.

Filigree　*jīnsī zhuāngshì* 金絲裝飾 (金丝装饰)
A decorative openwork pattern made of wires.

Forge　*duànzào* 鍛造 (锻造) or *rèduàn* 熱鍛 (热锻)
Shaping metal by heating it to a high temperature and hammering.

Foundry　*zhùzào zuòfāng* 鑄造作坊 (铸造作坊)
A casting establishment.

Foundry work　*zhùjiàn* 鑄件 (铸件)
Objects shaped by casting.

Gilding (mechanical)　*bāojīn* 包金
Applying a thin sheet of gold to another metal without mercury.

Gold foil　*jīnbó* 金箔
Any gold sheet thinner than 0.0015 mm or 0.006 in.

Granulation　*hànjīnzhū wénshì* 焊金珠紋飾 (焊金珠纹饰)
Small spherical grains of gold attached to a gold object.

Hammering　*chúidǎ* 錘打 (锤打) or *lěngduàn* 冷鍛 (冷锻)
Shaping metal at room temperature.

Hard solder　*yìnghàn* 硬焊
Gold or silver alloy used to join precious metals together.

Inlay　*xiāngqiàn* 鑲嵌
Material such as gemstones, glass, etc., inserted into prepared grooves or depressions in an object's surface.

Lost wax　*shīlàfǎ* 失蠟法 (失蜡法)
Casting from a wax model.

Lost wax and lost textile　*shīzhī shīlàfǎ* 失織失蠟法 (失织失蜡法)
Casting from a wax model supported by a piece of textile.

Mercury-amalgam gilding　*gǒngjí liūjīn* 汞齊鎏金 (汞齐鎏金)
A mixture of mercury and gold applied to a metal surface followed by baking and burnishing to form a gold surface film.

Mercury-amalgam silvering　*gǒngjí liūyín* 汞齊鎏銀 (汞齐鎏银)
A mixture of mercury and silver applied to a metal surface followed by baking and burnishing to form a silver surface film.

Mercury-amalgam tinning　*gǒngjí liūxī* 汞齊鎏錫 (汞齐鎏锡)
A mixture of mercury and tin applied to a metal surface to form a tin-rich surface film.

Metalsmithing　*jīnshǔ jiāgōng* 金屬加工 (金属加工)
Working metal directly by hammering.

Metal wire　*jīnshǔsī* 金屬絲 (金属丝)
Metal wire that has been strip-twisted or drawn.

Microscope　*xiǎnwēijìng* 顯微鏡 (显微镜)
An optical instrument for enlarging or magnifying images of minute objects.

Punch　*chōngtóu* 沖頭 (冲头)
A chasing tool with a rounded end.

Punch　*chōngyā* 沖壓 (冲压)
A chasing technique used to produce an indented repeated design.

Repoussé　*chúichōng tūwénshì* 錘沖凸紋飾 (锤冲凸纹饰)
A design produced by working sheet metal from behind to raise a pattern.

Riveting　*mǎojiē* 鉚接 (铆接)
Joining of metal sheets by small metal pegs.

Scanning electron microscopy (SEM)　*sǎomiáo diànzǐ xiǎnwēishù* 掃描電子顯微術 (扫描电子显微术)
Examination of surface structure by scanning with a focused electron beam to produce a raster image.

Section mold　*fànkuài* 範塊 (范块) or *zhùfàn* 鑄範 (铸范)
A casting mold made of two or more fitted pieces.

GLOSSARY

Sheet metal *jīnshǔ bóbǎn* 金屬薄板 (金属薄板)
Thin sheet of metal either hammered or cast.

Silver foil *yínbó* 銀箔 (银箔)
Any silver sheet thinner than 0.0015 mm or 0.006 in.

Silvering (mechanical) *bāoyín* 包銀 (包银)
Applying a thin sheet of silver to a metal surface without mercury.

Soft soldering *ruǎnhàn* 軟焊 (软焊)
A joining technique using lead-tin alloys; not used for precious metals.

Solder *hànxī* 焊錫 (焊锡)
An alloy which has a melting point below 450 degrees centigrade for joining two metal pieces.

Strand inlay *biānsī xiāngqiàn* 編絲鑲嵌 (编丝镶嵌)
Thin strands of metal placed side by side in prepared or cast channels.

Tinning *dùxī* 鍍錫 (镀锡)
Tinning with hot molten tin without the use of mercury.

Weld *rèduànjiē* 熱鍛接 (热锻接)
To join two metals by heating without the use of solder.

Wrought *jiāgōng biànxíng* 加工變形 (加工变形)
The process of hammering or deforming a metal, as opposed to casting. (Compare to the character for *shu*, in *shutie*, wrought iron.)

X-ray fluorescence spectrometry (XRF)
Aìkèsī shèxiàn yíngguāng guāngpǔ fēnxī
愛克斯射線熒光光譜分析 (爱克斯射线荧光光谱分析)
Determination of composition by measuring the intensity of the characteristic radiation of elements excited by X-rays.

Metals and Materials

Agate *mǎnǎo* 瑪瑙 (玛瑙)

Brass *huángtóng* 黃銅 (黄铜)

Bronze *qīngtóng* 青銅 (青铜)

Carnelian *hóng yùsuǐ* 紅玉髓 (红玉髓)

Copper *tóng* 銅 (铜) or *hóngtóng* 紅銅 (红铜)

Electrum *huángyín* 黃銀 (黄银)
  or *jīnyínshí* 金銀石 (金银石)

Glass *bōli* 玻璃

Gold *jīn* 金

Iron *tiě* 鐵 (铁)

Jade *yù* 玉

Lapis lazuli *qīngjīnshí* 青金石

Lead *qiān* 鉛 (铅)

Malachite *kǒngquèshí* 孔雀石

Mercury *gǒng* 汞

Pearl *zhēnzhū* 珍珠

Silver *yín* 銀 (银)

Tin *xī* 錫 (锡)

Turquoise *lǜsōngshí* 綠松石 (绿松石)

Zinc *xīn* 鋅 (锌)

Bibliography

Allan, Sarah. *The Shape of the Turtle: Myth, Art and Cosmos in Early China.* Albany: State University of New York Press, 1991.

Andersson, J. Gunnar. "Hunting Magic in the Animal Style." *Bulletin of the Museum of Far Eastern Antiquities* 4 (1932), pp. 221–321.

———. "The Goldsmith of Ancient China." *Bulletin of the Museum of Far Eastern Antiquities* 7 (1935), pp. 1–38.

Art Treasures of Dunhuang. Compiled by Dunhuang Institute for Cultural Relics. Hong Kong: Joint Publishing Co., 1981.

The Arts of the T'ang Dynasty: A loan exhibition organized by the Los Angeles County Museum of Art from collections in America, the Orient and Europe. Introduction by Henry Trubner. Los Angeles: Los Angeles County Museum of Art, 1957.

Bagley, Robert. *Shang Ritual Bronzes in the Arthur M. Sackler Collections.* Washington, D.C., and Cambridge, Mass.: Harvard University Press, 1987.

———. "Shang Ritual Bronzes: Casting Technique and Vessel Design." *Archives of Asian Art* 43 (1990), pp. 6–20.

———. "An Early Bronze Age Tomb in Jiangxi Province." *Orientations* 24, no. 7 (July 1993), pp. 20–36.

Banpo Site: A well preserved site of a Neolithic village. Xi'an, Shaanxi: Banpo Museum, 1987.

Baoshan Chumu (Chu cemetery at Baoshan). Beijing: Cultural Relics Publishing House, 1991.

Barnard, Noel. *Bronze Casting and Bronze Alloys in Ancient China.* Canberra: Australian National University and Monumenta Serica, 1961.

———. *"Casting-On"—A Characteristic Method of Joining Employed in Ancient China.* Paper presented at the international conference La Cività Cinese Antica, Venice, 1985. Pre-print no. 13. Canberra, June 1985.

———. *Bronze Vessels with Copper Inlaid Decor and Pseudo-Copper Inlay of Ch'un-Ch'iu and Chan-Kuo Times.* Part two, pre-print no. 16. Canberra, August 1987, pp. 102–34.

———. *The Entry of Cire-Perdue Investment Casting, and Certain other Metallurgical Techniques (Mainly Metalworking) into South China and Their Progress Northwards.* Pre-print no. 15. Canberra, 1987.

———. "Thoughts on the Emergence of Metallurgy in Pre-Shang and Early Shang China, and a Technical Appraisal of Relevant Bronze Artifacts of the Time." *Bulletin of the Metals Museum* 19 (1993), pp. 3–48.

Barnard, Noel, and Cheung Kwong-yue. *Studies in Chinese Archaeology, 1980–1982.* Hong Kong: Wen-hsueh-she, 1983.

Barnard, Noel, and Sato Tamotsu. *Metallurgical Remains of Ancient China.* Tokyo: Nichiosha, 1975.

Beauty, Wealth and Power: Jewels and Ornaments of Asia. San Francisco: Asian Art Museum of San Francisco, 1992.

Bernstein, S. *Ritual and Belief: Chinese Jade and Related Arts,* vol. 3. San Francisco, 1994.

Beurdeley, Cecile. *Sur les routes de la soie.* Fribourg: Seuil, 1985.

Brill, Robert H., and John H. Martin. *Scientific Research in Early Chinese Glass.* Proceedings of the Archaeometry of Glass, Sessions of the 1984 International Symposium on Glass, Beijing, 7 September 1984, with supplementary papers. Corning, N.Y.: Corning Museum of Glass, 1991.

British Rail Pension Trust. Sotheby's auction catalogue, London, 12 December 1989.

Bulling, Anneliese Gutkind. *The Decoration of Mirrors of the Han Period.* Ascona: Artibus Asiae Publishers, 1960.

———. "The Dating of Chinese Bronze Mirrors." *Archives of Asian Art* 25 (1971–72), pp. 36–57.

Bunker, Emma C. "Lost Wax and Lost Textile." In Robert Maddin, ed., *The Beginning of the Use of Metals and Alloys.* Cambridge, Mass.: Massachusetts Institute of Technology Press, 1988, pp. 222–27.

———. "Gold Belt Plaques in the Siberian Treasure of Peter the Great: Dates, Origins and Iconography." In Gary Seaman, ed., *The Nomads Trilogy 3, Foundations of Empire: Archaeology and Art of the Eurasian Steppes.* Los Angeles: Ethnographics Press, Center for Visual Anthropology, University of Southern California, 1989, pp. 201–22.

———. "Ancient Ordos Bronzes with Tin-Enriched Surfaces." *Orientations* 21, no. 1 (January 1990), pp. 78–80.

———. "Sino-Nomadic Art: Eastern Zhou, Qin and Han Artifacts Made for Nomadic Taste." *International Colloquium on Chinese Art History.* Proceedings, part 2. Taipei: National Palace Museum, 1991, pp. 569–90.

———. "The Chinese Artifacts Among the Pazyryk Finds." *Source: Notes in the History of Art* 10, no. 4 (Summer 1991), pp. 20–24.

———. "Significant changes in iconography and technology among ancient China's northwestern pastoral neighbors from the fourth to the first century B.C." *Bulletin of the Asia Institute* 6 (1992), pp. 99–115.

———. "Gold in the Ancient Chinese World: A Cultural Puzzle." *Artibus Asiae* 53, no. 1/2 (1993), pp. 27–50.

———. "A New Dilemma: Recent Technical Studies and Related Forgeries." *Orientations* 25, no. 3 (March 1994), p. 90.

Cahill, James. *Chinese Painting.* Geneva: Editions d'art Albert Skira, 1960.

Cahill, Suzanne. *Chinese Bronze Mirrors.* Gallery guide. Washington, D. C.: Freer Gallery of Art, 1983.

Catalogue of the Exhibition of Qing Dynasty Costume Accessories. Taipei: National Palace Museum, 1986.

Chandra, Rai Govind. *Indo-Greek Jewellery.* New Delhi: Abhinav Publications, 1979.

Chang, K. C. *Early Chinese Civilization: Anthropological Perspectives.* Cambridge, Mass.: Harvard University Press, Harvard-Yenching Institute Monograph Series, vol. 23, 1980.

———. *Shang Civilization.* New Haven: Yale University Press, 1980.

———. *The Archaeology of Ancient China.* 4th ed. New Haven: Yale University Press, 1986.

———, ed. *Studies in Shang Archaeology: Selected Papers from the International Conference on Shang Civilization.* New Haven: Yale University Press, 1986.

Changsha Mawangdui yihao Hanmu. 2 vols. Beijing: Wenwu, 1973.

Chase, W. Thomas. *Chinese Belt-Hooks in the Freer Gallery of Art.* Master's thesis, Graduate School of Arts and Sciences of New York University, 1967.

———. "Bronze Casting in China: A Short Technical History." Draft form, May 1981.

———. "Bronze Casting in China: A Short Technical History." In George Kuwayama, ed., *The Great Bronze Age of China: A Symposium.* Los Angeles: Los Angeles County Museum of Art, 1981, pp. 100–23.

———. *Ancient Chinese Bronze Art: Casting the Precious Sacral Vessel.* New York: China Institute of America, 1991.

Chase, W. Thomas, and Ursula Franklin. "Early Chinese Black Mirrors and Pattern-Etched Weapons." *Ars Orientalis* 22 (1979), pp. 215–58.

Cheng Te-K'un. *Jade Flowers and Floral Patterns in Chinese Decorative Art.* Hong Kong: Chinese University of Hong Kong, 1979.

Chugoku no kingin garasu. Osaka: NHK Osaka Hosokyoku, 1992.

Clark, Grahame. *Symbols of Excellence.* Cambridge: Cambridge University Press, 1986.

Creel, Herrlee G. *The Origins of Statecraft in China.* Chicago: University of Chicago Press, 1970.

The David-Weill Collection: Catalogue of Fine Early Chinese Bronzes, Jades, Sculpture, Ceramics and Silver. Sotheby's auction catalogue, London, 29 February 1972.

de Bary, Wm. Theodore. *Sources of Chinese Tradition.* New York: Columbia University Press, 1960.

Devlet, M. A. *Sibirskie poyasnye azhurnye plastinki.* Moscow, 1980.

Deydier, Christian. *Chinese Bronzes.* Trans. Janet Seligman. New York: Rizzoli, 1980.

———. *Chinese Gold, Silver and Gilt Bronze up to the Tang Dynasty.* London, 1985.

———. *Imperial Gold from Ancient China.* London, 1990.

———. *Imperial Gold from Ancient China,* part 2. London, 1991.

Eberhard, Wolfram. *A Dictionary of Chinese Symbols: Hidden Symbols in Chinese Life and Thought.* Trans. G. L. Campbell. London: Routledge, 1986.

Ebrey, Patricia Buckley, and Peter N. Gregory, eds. *Religion and Society in T'ang and Sung China.* Honolulu: University of Hawaii Press, 1993.

Eliade, Mircea. *The Forge and the Crucible: The Origins and Structures of Alchemy.* Chicago: University of Chicago Press, 1962.

Eskenazi, Giuseppe. *Chinese and Korean Art from the Collections of Dr. Franco Vannotti, Hans Popper and others.* London, 1989.

———. *Inlaid Bronze and Related Material from Pre-Tang China.* London, 1991.

———. *Early Chinese Art from Tombs and Temples.* London, 1993.

Exhibition of Cultural Relics from the Tomb of Princess Chenguo of the State of Liao. Inner Mongolia Cultural Relic Archaeology Institute and Shaanxi History Museum, n.d.

Farag, Mahmoud M. "Metallurgy in Ancient Egypt." *Bulletin of the Metals Museum* 6 (1981), pp. 15–30.

Fontein, Jan, and Tung Wu. *Unearthing China's Past.* Boston: Museum of Fine Arts, 1973.

Fujiwara, Sosui. *Shodo rekutai daijiten Fujiwara Sosui hen.* Tokyo: Sanseido, 1961.

Gale, Esson M. *Discourses on Salt and Iron.* Translated from the Chinese of Huan K'an. Leiden: E. J. Brill, 1931.

Gems of China's Cultural Relics 1992. Beijing: Cultural Relics Publishing House, 1992.

Gems of China's Cultural Relics 1993. Beijing: Cultural Relics Publishing House, 1993.

Gimbutas, Marija. *Bronze Age Cultures in Central and Eastern Europe.* Paris: Mouton and Company, 1965.

Goepper, Roger, and Roderick Whitfield. *Treasures from Korea.* London: The British Museum, 1984.

Golas, Peter J. "History of Mining Technology in China." Working draft for Joseph Needham, ed., *Science and Civilisation in China.* Cambridge: Cambridge University Press, forthcoming.

Gunter, Ann C., and Paul Jett. *Ancient Iranian Metalwork in the Arthur M. Sackler Gallery and the Freer Gallery of Art.* Washington, D.C.: Smithsonian Institution, 1992.

Gyllensvard, Bo. *Chinese Gold and Silver in the Carl Kempe Collection.* Stockholm, 1953.

———. *Chinese Art from the Collection of H. M. King Gustaf VI Adolf of Sweden.* Tokyo: Asahi Shimbun, 1971.

———. *Chinese Gold, Silver and Porcelain: The Kempe Collection.* New York: The Asia Society, Inc., 1979.

Han Rubin. "Recent Archaeometallurgical Achievements at the University of Science and Technology Beijing." A paper delivered at the international conference Chinese Archaeology Enters the Twenty-First Century, marking the opening of the Arthur M. Sackler Archaeological Museum at Peking University, 29 May 1993.

Han Rubin and Emma C. Bunker. "Biaomian fuxi de Eerduosi gingtong shipin de yanjiu" (The study of ancient Ordos bronzes with tin-enriched surfaces in China). *Wenwu,* 1993.9, pp. 80–96.

Harada, Yoshito. *Chinese Dress and Personal Ornaments in the Han and Six Dynasties.* Tokyo: The Toyo Bunko Ronso, Series A, vol. 23, 1967.

Hartman-Goldsmith, Joan. *Chinese Jade.* Hong Kong: Oxford University Press, 1986.

Hawkes, David. *Ch'u Tz'u, The Songs of the South.* Oxford: Clarendon Press, 1959.

Hayashi, Ryoichi. *The Silk Road and the Shoso-in.* Tokyo: Weatherhill/Heibonsha, The Heibonsha Survey of Japanese Art, vol. 6, 1975.

Hearn, Maxwell K. "The Terracotta Army of the First Emperor of Qin (221–206 B.C.)." In Wen Fong, ed., *The Great Bronze Age of China.* New York: Metropolitan Museum of Art and Alfred A. Knopf, 1980.

———. *Ancient Chinese Art: The Ernest Erickson Collection in the Metropolitan Museum.* New York: Metropolitan Museum of Art, 1987.

Hebei Sheng chutu wenwu xuanji. Beijing: Cultural Relics Publishing House, 1980.

Ho, Ping-ti. *The Cradle of the East.* Hong Kong: The Chinese University of Hong Kong, 1975.

Hoffman, Herbert, and Patricia Davidson. *Greek Gold: Jewelry from the Age of Alexander.* Boston: Museum of Fine Arts, 1966.

Hsia Nai. "The Classification, Nomenclature, and Usage of Shang Dynasty Jades." In K. C. Chang, *Studies in Shang Archaeology.* New Haven: Yale University Press, 1986.

Hsu, Cho-yun, and Katheryn M. Linduff, *Western Chou Civilization.* New Haven: Yale University Press, 1988.

Hui Xian fajue baogao. Beijing: Kexue chubanshe, 1956.

Hunt, L. B. "The Long History of Lost Wax Casting over Five Thousand Years of Art and Craftsmanship." *Gold Bulletin* 13, no. 2 (April 1980), pp. 63–79.

Important Ancient Chinese Bronzes, Ceramics, and Works of Art. Sotheby's auction catalogue. London, 19 June 1984.

Jacobsen, Robert Dale. *Inlaid Bronzes of Pre-Imperial China: A Classic Tradition and Its Later Revivals.* Ph.D. dissertation. University Microfilms International, no. 8429460, Ann Arbor, 1984.

Jett, Paul. "A Study of the Gilding of Chinese Buddhist Bronzes." In Susan La Niece and Paul Craddock, eds., *Metal Plating and Patination: Cultural, Technical and Historical Developments.* Oxford: Butterworth and Heinemann, 1993, pp. 193–200.

Jettmar, Karl. "The Altai Before the Turks." *Bulletin of the Museum of Far Eastern Antiquities* 23 (1951), pp. 135–223.

———. *The Art of the Steppes.* New York: Crown Publishers, 1967.

Jewellery Through the Ages. London: British Museum Publications, 1976.

Jiangling Mashan yihao chumu (Chu tomb no. 1 at Mashan in Jiangling, Jingzhou Museum). Beijing: Cultural Relics Publishing House, 1985.

Juliano, Annette L. *Art of the Six Dynasties: Centuries of Change and Innovation.* New York: China House Gallery, 1975.

Kao Mayching, ed. *Chinese Ivories from the Kwan Collection.* Hong Kong: Art Gallery, The Chinese University of Hong Kong, 1990.

Karlbeck, Orvar. "Notes on the Fabrication of Some Early Chinese Mirror Molds." *Archives of Asian Art* 18 (1964), pp. 48–54.

Karlgren, Bernhard. "Early Chinese Mirror Inscriptions." *Bulletin of the Museum of Far Eastern Antiquities* 6 (1934), pp. 9–79.

———. "Huai and Han." *Bulletin of the Museum of Far Eastern Antiquities* 13 (1941), pp. 1–25.

———. "Glosses on the Kuo Feng Odes." *Bulletin of the Museum of Far Eastern Antiquities* 14 (1942), pp. 71–247.

———. "Chinese Agraffes in Two Swedish Collections." *Bulletin of the Museum of Far Eastern Antiquities* 38 (1966), pp. 83–159.

Keightley, David N. "Early Civilization in China: Reflections on How It Became Chinese." In Paul S. Ropp, ed., *Heritage of China.* Berkeley: University of California Press, 1990.

Kelley, Clarence W. *Chinese Gold and Silver from the Tang Dynasty (A.D. 618–907) in American Collections.* Dayton, Ohio: Dayton Art Institute, 1984.

Kerr, Rose. *Later Chinese Bronzes.* London: Victoria and Albert Museum, 1990.

Kessler, Adam T. *Empires Beyond the Great Wall: The Heritage of Genghis Khan.* Los Angeles: Natural History Museum Foundation, 1994.

Keyser, Barbara W. "Decor Replication in Two Late Chou Bronze *Chien.*" *Ars Orientalis* 11 (1979), pp. 127–62.

Keverne, Roger, ed. *Jade.* Hong Kong: Anness Publishing Limited and Van Nostrand Reinhold, 1991.

Korean Works of Art. Christie's auction catalogue. New York, 26 October 1992.

Kuwayama, George, ed. *The Great Bronze Age of China: A Symposium.* Los Angeles: Los Angeles County Museum of Art, 1981.

———, ed. *Ancient Mortuary Traditions of China: Papers on Chinese Ceramic Funerary Sculptures.* Los Angeles: Far Eastern Art Council, Los Angeles County Museum of Art, 1991.

Lally, James J. *Chinese Archaic Bronzes, Sculpture and Works of Art.* New York, 1992.

La Niece, Susan, and Paul Craddock, eds. *Metal Plating and Patination: Cultural, Technical and Historical Developments.* Oxford: Butterworth and Heinemann, 1993.

Laufer, Berthold. *Jade: A Study in Chinese Archaeology and Religion.* New York: Dover Publications, Inc., 1974. [An unabridged republication of the 1912 edition.]

Lawton, Thomas. *Chinese Art of the Warring States Period: Change and Continuity, 480–222 B.C.* Washington, D.C.: Freer Gallery of Art, Smithsonian Institution, 1982.

———, ed. *New Perspectives on Chu Culture During the Eastern Zhou.* Princeton: Princeton University Press, 1991.

Legge, James. *The Chinese Classics,* vol. 3, *The Shoo King,* original published 1893–95, reprinted from last editions, Shanghai: Oxford University Press, 1935.

———. *The Chinese Classics,* vol. 4, *The She King,* original published 1893–95, reprinted from last editions, Shanghai: Oxford University Press, 1935.

Li Jinghua. "Metallurgical Archaeology Over the Past Forty Years in Henan Province, China." *Bulletin of the Metals Museum* 20 (1993.11), pp. 19–35.

Li Xueqin. *Eastern Zhou and Qin Civilizations.* Trans. K. C. Chang. New Haven: Yale University Press, 1985.

———. "Chu Bronzes and Chu Culture." In Thomas Lawton, ed., *New Perspectives on Chu Culture During the Eastern Zhou Period.* Princeton: Princeton University Press, 1991, pp. 1–22.

Li Zehou. *The Path of Beauty: A Study of Chinese Aesthetics.* Trans. Gong Lizeng. Beijing: Morning Glory Publishers, 1988.

Liang Shangchun. *Yanku cangjing* 4 (1941–42), suppl.

Lim, Lucy, ed. *Stories from China's Past: Han Dynasty Pictorial Tomb Reliefs and Archaeological Objects from Sichuan Province, People's Republic of China.* San Francisco: The Chinese Culture Center of San Francisco, 1987.

Lin Yun. "A Reexamination of the Relationship between Bronzes of the Shang Culture and of the Northern Zone." In K. C. Chang, ed., *Studies in Shang Archaeology.* New Haven: Yale University Press, 1986, pp. 237–73.

Linduff, Katheryn. "Here Today and Gone Tomorrow: The Emergence and Demise of Bronze Producing Cultures Outside the Central Plains." *Bulletin of the Institute of History and Philology.* Taipei: Academia Sinica, 1994 (forthcoming).

Lins, P. A., and W. A. Oddy. "The Origins of Mercury Gilding." *Journal of Archaeological Science* 2 (1975), pp. 365–73.

Loehr, Max. *Relics of Ancient China from the Collection of Dr. Paul Singer.* New York: The Asia Society, Inc., 1965.

Loewe, Michael. *Ways to Paradise, The Chinese Quest for Immortality.* London: George Allen & Unwin, 1979.

Lu Shizong, Lu Benshan, Hua Jueming, and Zhou Weijian. "Antiker Kupfererzbergbau von Tongling bei Ruichang (Provinz Jiangxi)." *Der Anschnitt* 45, H. 2–3 (1993), pp. 50–62.

Luan Bing'ao. *Zenyang jianding gu yuqi.* Beijing, 1984.

Luoyang Zhongzhoulu. Beijing: Kexue chubanshe, 1959.

Ma Chengyuan. *Ancient Chinese Bronzes.* Hsio-yen Shih, ed. Trans. Tang Bowen. Hong Kong: Oxford University Press, 1986.

Ma Yue et al., eds. *Xi'an—Legacies of Ancient Chinese Civilization.* Beijing: Morning Glory Publishers, 1992.

Maddin, Robert, ed. *The Beginning of the Use of Metals and Alloys.* Cambridge, Mass.: Massachusetts Institute of Technology Press, 1988.

Major, John S. *Heaven and Earth in Early Han Thought: Chapters Three, Four, and Five of the Huainanzi.* Albany: State University of New York Press, 1993.

Mancheng Hanmu fajue baogao. 2 vols. Beijing: Cultural Relics Publishing House, 1980.

Meeks, Nigel D. "Tin-rich Surfaces on Bronze: Some Experimental and Archaeological Considerations." *Archaeometry* 28.2 (August 1986), pp. 133–63.

———. "Patination phenomena on Roman and Chinese high-tin bronze mirrors and other artifacts" and "Surface characterization of tinned bronze, high-tin bronze, tinned iron and arsenical bronze." In Susan La Niece and Paul Craddock, eds., *Metal Plating and Patination: Cultural, Technical and Historical Developments.* Oxford: Butterworth and Heinemann, 1993, pp. 63–84, 248–75.

Minns, E. H. *The Art of the Northern Nomads.* Proceedings of the British Academy, vol. 28. London, 1942, pp. 47–99.

Nagahiro Toshio. *Taiko no kenkyu.* Kyoto: Tohōbunka Kenkyusho, 1943.

Needham, Joseph. *Science and Civilisation in China,* vol. 2. Cambridge: Cambridge University Press, 1956.

———. *Science and Civilisation in China,* vol. 3. Cambridge: Cambridge University Press, 1959.

———. *Science and Civilisation in China,* vol. 4. Cambridge: Cambridge University Press, 1962.

———. *Science and Civilisation in China,* vol. 5. Cambridge: Cambridge University Press, 1974.

Oddy, Andrew. "Gilding Through the Ages." *Gold Bulletin* 14.2 (April 1981), pp. 75–79.

O'Donoghue, Diane M. "Reflection and Reception: The Origins of the Mirror in Bronze Age China." *Bulletin of the Museum of Far Eastern Antiquities* 62 (1990), pp. 5–183.

Ogden, Jack. *Jewellery of the Ancient World.* London: Trefoil Books, 1976.

———. "Classical Gold Wire: Some Aspects of its Manufacture and Use." *Jewellery Studies* 5 (1991), pp. 95–105.

———. *Ancient Jewellery.* London and Berkeley: British Museum Press and the University of California Press, 1992.

Pak, Young-sook. "The Origins of Silla Metalwork." *Orientations* 19, no. 9 (September 1988), pp. 44–53.

Palmgren, Nils. *Selected Chinese Antiquities from the Collection of Gustaf Adolf, Crown Prince of Sweden.* Stockholm: Generalstabens Litografiska Anstalts, 1948.

Pietneva, S. A., ed. "The Eurasian Steppes in the Middle Ages." In *Arkheologiya SSSR.* Moscow, 1981.

Pirazzoli-t'Serstevens, Michele. *The Han Dynasty.* Trans. Janet Seligman. New York: Rizzoli International, 1982.

Prakash, B. "Metallurgy in India through Ages." *Bulletin of the Metals Museum* 8 (1983), pp. 23–36.

Rawson, Jessica, foreword. *The Chinese Bronzes of Yunnan.* London: Sidgwick and Jackson, Limited, 1983.

———. *Chinese Ornament, the Lotus and the Dragon.* New York: Holmes and Meier Publishers, 1984.

———. *Chinese Bronzes: Art and Ritual.* London: British Museum Publications, 1987.

———. *The Bella and P. P. Chiu Collection of Ancient Chinese Bronzes.* Hong Kong, 1988.

———. *Western Zhou Ritual Bronzes from the Arthur M. Sackler Collections.* Cambridge, Mass.: Harvard University Press, 1990.

———, ed. *The British Museum Book of Chinese Art.* London: British Museum Publications, 1992.

Rawson, Jessica, and Emma C. Bunker. *Ancient Chinese and Ordos Bronzes.* Hong Kong: The Oriental Ceramic Society of Hong Kong, 1990.

Ropp, Paul S., ed. *Heritage of China.* Berkeley: University of California Press, 1990.

Rudenko, S. I. *The Frozen Tombs of Siberia: The Pazyryk Burials of Iron Age Horsemen.* Trans. M. W. Thompson. Berkeley: University of California Press, 1970.

Schafer, Edward H. "Falconry in T'ang Times." *T'oung Pao Archives.* London: E. J. Brill, 1958.

———. *The Golden Peaches of Samarkand: A Study of T'ang Exotics.* Berkeley: University of California Press, 1963.

Scott, David A. *Metallography and Microstructure of Ancient and Historic Metals.* Los Angeles: The Getty Conservation Institute, The J. Paul Getty Museum, 1991.

Seligman, C. G. "Far Eastern Glass: Some Western Origins." *Bulletin of the Museum of Far Eastern Antiquities* 10 (1938), pp. 1–64, and pls. 1–16.

Shi Yongshi. "Yanguo de hengzhi." In *Zhongguo kaogu xuehui dierci nianhui lunwenji*. Beijing: Wenwu, 1980, pp. 172–75.

———. "Xiadu: Beijing's Twin Capital in Warring States Times." *China Reconstructs* (December 1987), pp. 57–59.

Shi Yongshi and Wang Sufang. "Yan wenhua jian lun" (The concise edition of Yan culture). Paper presented at the International Academic Conference of Archaeological Cultures of the Northern Chinese Ancient Nations. Hohhot, Inner Mongolia, 1992.

The Silk Road: Treasures of Tang China. Singapore: Landmark Books PTE Ltd., 1991.

Singer, Paul. *Early Chinese Gold and Silver.* New York: China House Gallery, 1971.

Sivin, Nathan. *Chinese Alchemy: Preliminary Studies.* Cambridge, Mass.: Harvard University Press, 1968.

———. "Research on the History of Chinese Alchemy." In Z. R. W. M. von Martels, *Proceedings of the International Conference on the History of Alchemy at the University of Groningen*. Leiden: E. J. Brill, 1990, pp. 3–20.

Smith, Cyril Stanley. "Art, Technology, and Science: Notes on their Historical Interaction." *Technology and Culture* 11, no. 4 (October 1970), pp. 493–549.

So, Jenny. *Chinese Neolithic Jades.* Washington, D.C.: Smithsonian Institution, 1993.

Sun Ji. "Lun jinnian Neimenggu chushi de Tujue yu Tujueshi jinyin qi" (The gold and silver wares of Turk and Turk styles unearthed in Inner Mongolia in recent years). *Wenwu,* 1993.8, pp. 48–58.

———. "Xian Qin, Han, Jin, yaodai yong jinyin daigou" (The gold and silver belt buckles of the pre-Qin period, the Han dynasty, and Jin dynasty). *Wenwu*, (1994.1), pp. 50–64.

———. "Xiapei zhuizi." *Wenwu tiandi,* 1994.1, pp. 22–24.

Sun Shuyun, Ma Zhaogeng, Jin Lianji, Han Rubin, and T. Ko. "The Formation of Black Patina on Bronze Mirrors." In *Proceedings of the Archaeometry Conference.* Los Angeles, 1992.

Sung Ying-hsing. *T'ien-Kung K'ai-Wu*. Trans. E-Tu Zen Sun and Shiou-Chuan Sun. University Park: Pennsylvania State University Press, 1966.

Swann, Peter. *Art of China, Korea and Japan.* New York: Frederick A. Praeger, 1963.

Tait, Hugh, ed. *Seven Thousand Years of Jewellery.* London: British Museum Publications, 1986.

———, ed. *Jewelry, 7,000 Years: An International History and Illustrated Survey from the Collection of the British Museum.* 2nd ed. New York: Harry N. Abrams, 1991.

Tangdai jinyin qi. Beijing: Wenwu Press, 1985.

Tate, G. H. H. *Mammals of Eastern Asia.* New York: The Macmillan Company, 1947.

Teng Rensheng. *Lacquer Wares of the Chu Kingdom.* Hong Kong: Woods Publishing Company, 1992.

Thorp, Robert L. *Son of Heaven: Imperial Arts of China.* Seattle: Sons of Heaven Press, 1988.

———. "Mountain Tombs and Jade Burial Suits: Preparations for Eternity in the Western Han." In George Kuwayama, ed., *Ancient Mortuary Traditions of China*. Los Angeles: Far Eastern Art Council, Los Angeles County Museum of Art, 1991, pp. 26–39.

Tian Guangjin and Guo Suxin, eds. *E'erduosi shi qingtong qi*. Beijing: Cultural Relics Publishing House, 1986.

Till, Barry, and Paula Swart. *Arts of the Middle Kingdom: China.* Victoria: Art Gallery of Greater Victoria, 1986.

Tong Enzheng. "Zhongguo gudai qingtong qi zhong xi yuan liao de laiyuan." In *Zhongguo xinan mingzu kaogu lunwenji*. Beijing: Wenwu Press, 1990, pp. 224–39.

Treasures from the Tombs of Zhong Shan Guo Kings. Tokyo: Tokyo National Museum, 1981.

Tylecote, R. F. *A History of Metallurgy.* London: The Institute of Materials, 1992.

Uberti, Maria Luisa. "Glass." In Sabatino Moscati, ed., *The Phoenicians.* New York: Abbeville Press, 1988, pp. 474–90.

Umehara, Sueji. *Rakuyo kinson kobo shuei.* Kyoto: Kobayashi shashin seihanjo shuppanbu, 1937.

United States Central Intelligence Agency. *Communist China.* Map folio, October 1967.

The Valuable Cultural and Historic Sites of Liaoning Province. Liaoning Artistic Publishing House, n.d.

Vinograd, Richard. *Boundaries of the Self: Chinese Portraits, 1600–1900.* Cambridge: Cambridge University Press, 1992.

Wagner, Donald B. *Iron and Steel in Ancient China.* Leiden: E. J. Brill, 1993.

Wang Renxiang. "Daigou gailun" (A general survey of Chinese belt hooks). *Kaogu xuebao,* 1985.3, pp. 267–312.

Wang Zhongshu. *Han Civilization.* Trans. K. C. Chang. New Haven: Yale University Press, 1982.

Watson, Burton, trans. *Records of the Grand Historian: Han Dynasty I and Han Dynasty II.* 2 vols. New York: Columbia University Press, 1961.

———. *The Columbia Book of Chinese Poetry: From Early Times to the Thirteenth Century.* New York: Columbia University Press, 1984.

———. *Records of the Grand Historian: Han Dynasty I and Han Dynasty II.* 2 vols., rev. ed., and *Qin Dynasty,* vol. 3. New York: Columbia University Press, 1993.

Watson, Ernest. *The Principal Articles of Chinese Commerce.* Published by the order of the Inspector General of Customs, Shanghai, 1930.

Watson, William, ed. "Pottery and Metalwork in T'ang China: Their Chronology and External Relations." *Colloquies on Art and Archaeology in Asia* 1. London: University of London Percival David Foundation of Chinese Art, 1970.

———. "Technique in Bronze and Precious Metals." In Giuseppe Eskenazi, *Chinese and Korean Art from the Collections of Dr. Franco Vannotti, Hans Popper and Others.* London, 1989, pp. 7–20.

Weber, George W., Jr. *The Ornaments of the Late Chou Bronzes.* New Brunswick, N.J.: Rutgers University Press, 1973.

Wen Fong, ed. *The Great Bronze Age of China.* New York: Metropolitan Museum of Art and Alfred A. Knopf, 1980.

Wen Guang. "A Geoarchaeological Study of Ancient Chinese Jade." A paper delivered at the international conference Chinese Archaeology Enters the Twenty-First Century, marking the opening of the Arthur M. Sackler Museum of Art and Archaeology at Beijing Daxue, 29 May 1993.

Wenwu yu kaogu lunji / Treatises on Archaeology and Cultural [sic]. Beijing: Editorial Department of the Cultural Relics Publishing House, 1987. [In Chinese and English.]

White, William Charles. *Tombs of Old Loyang.* Shanghai: Kelly and Walsh, 1934.

Whitehouse, Ruth. *The Macmillan Dictionary of Archaeology.* London: Macmillan, 1983.

Whitfield, Roderick, ed. "The Problem of Meaning in Early Chinese Ritual Bronzes." *Colloquies on Art and Archaeology in Asia* 15. London: University of London Percival David Foundation of Chinese Art, 1990.

Williams, C. A. S. *Outlines of Chinese Symbolism and Art Motives.* 3rd rev. ed. New York: Dover Publications, Inc., 1976.

Wilson, Keith. "A Recently Acquired Archaic Sculptural Bronze." *Oriental Art* 38, no. 4.

Xi Han Nanyue wangmu (Nanyue king's tomb of the Western Han). 2 vols. The CPAM of Guangzhou, the Institute of Archaeology, CASS and the Museum of Guangdong Province. Beijing: Cultural Relics Publishing House, 1991.

Xiasi Xichuan Chun Qiu Chumu (Chu tombs of the Spring-Autumn period at Xiasi, Xichuan). Beijing: Cultural Relics Publishing House, 1991.

Xinyang Chumu. Beijing: Cultural Relics Publishing House, 1986.

Xiong, Victor Cunrui, and Ellen Johnston Laing. "Foreign Jewelry in Ancient China." *Bulletin of the Asia Institute* 5 (1991), pp. 163–73.

Yang Boda, ed. *Zhongguo meishu quanji* 10. Beijing: Cultural Relics Publishing House, 1987.

Yunnan Jinning Shizhaishan gumuqun fajue baogao. 2 vols. Beijing: Cultural Relics Publishing House, 1959.

Zeng Hou yi mu wenwu yishu / Artistic Style of Cultural Relics from the Tomb of Zenghouyi. Hubei Provincial Museum, Hubei Fine Arts Publishing House, 1991. [In Chinese and English.]

Zhang Anzhi. *A History of Chinese Painting*. Beijing: Foreign Languages Press, 1992.

Zhao Wengang. "Tianjinshi Jixian Yingfangcun Liaomu" (The Liao dynasty tomb in Yingfang village, Ji county of Hebei province). *Beifang wenwu*, 1992.3, pp. 36–41.

Zhengzhou Erligang. Beijing: Kexue chubanshe, 1959.

Zhou Baoquan, Hu Youyan, and Lu Benshan. "Ancient Copper Mining and Smelting at Tonglushan Daye." In Robert Maddin, ed., *The Beginning of the Use of Metals and Alloys*. Cambridge, Mass.: Massachusetts Institute of Technology Press, 1988, pp. 125–29.

Zhou Xipao. *Zhongguo gudai fushi shi*. Taipei: Nantian Book Co., 1983.

Zhou Xun and Gao Chunming. *Zhongguo lidai funu jiangshi*. Taipei: Nantian Book Co., 1988.

———. *5000 Years of Chinese Costumes*. Hong Kong: Commercial Press, 1988.

Zhu Shoukang. "Ancient Metallurgy of Non-Ferrous Metals in China." *Bulletin of the Metals Museum* 11 (October 1988), pp. 1–13.

Zhu Shoukang and He Tangkun. "Studies of Ancient Chinese Mirrors and other Bronze Artifacts." In Susan La Niece and Paul Craddock, eds., *Metal Plating and Patination: Cultural, Technical and Historical Developments*. Oxford: Butterworth and Heinemann, 1993, pp. 50–62.

Zui Tō no bijutsu. Osaka: Osaka Municipal Museum, 1976.

Periodicals:

Archaeology

Archaeometry

Archives of Asian Art

Archives of Chinese Art

Ars Orientalis

Artibus Asiae

Beifang wenwu

Bulletin of the Asia Institute

Bulletin of the Metals Museum

Bulletin of the Museum of Far Eastern Antiquities

China Pictorial

China Reconstructs, *now* China Today

China Today

Der Anschnitt

Early China

Gold Bulletin

Hunan kaogu jikan

Kaogu

Kaogu tong

Kaogu xuebao

Kaogu yu wenwu

National Palace Museum Monthly of Chinese Art

Nei Menggu wenwu kaogu

Oriental Art

Orientations

Qinghai ribao

Technology and Culture

Wenbo

Wenwu

Wenwu cankao ziliao

Wenwu tiandi